THE WORKS

.

THE WORKS

The Industrial Architecture of the United States

BETSY HUNTER BRADLEY

New York | Oxford

Oxford University Press

1999

Oxford University Press

Oxford   New York
Athens   Auckland   Bangkok   Bogotá   Buenos Aires   Calcutta
Cape Town   Chennai   Dar es Salaam   Delhi   Florence   Hong Kong   Istanbul
Karachi   Kuala Lumpur   Madrid   Melbourne   Mexico City   Mumbai
Nairobi   Paris   São Paulo   Singapore   Taipei   Tokyo   Toronto   Warsaw

and associated companies in
Berlin   Ibadan

Library of Congress Cataloging-in-Publication Data
Bradley, Betsy H.
The works : the industrial architecture of the United States
by Besty Hunter Bradley.
p.   cm.
Includes bibliographical references and index.
ISBN 0-19-509000-4
1. Architecture, Industrial—United States.   I. Title.
NA6402.B73   1998
725'.4'0973—DC21   97-48871

9   8   7   6   5   4   3   2   1
Printed in the United States of America
on acid-free paper

FOR TOM, ANNE, AND BEN

PREFACE

My work as an architectural historian and historic preservationist has long included industrial buildings. Even though this type of structure seemed as interesting, if not more so, than others, factories have seldom been studied by architectural historians. So a project presented itself: a survey of American industrial architecture.

This work has a broad scope; it encompasses many sorts of manufacturing industries without concentrating on any one. Because a small number of building types were utilized by a wide range of operations, it is possible to collectively examine manufacturing works. Even as assembly processes and products were continually modernized, the program of industrial buildings changed little. Moreover, the requirements of a foundry or pattern storehouse remained essentially the same no matter where the structure was located. Consequently, a national context provides a valid framework for inquiry and comparison.

Although architecture is the subject matter, the reader will find barely a trace of conventional formal artistic analysis and the categorization of buildings by style that dominates architectural studies. Industrial architecture demands a different type of analysis. My research was guided by the assumption that every aspect of the factory, from its form and structure to its loading platform, was related to the manufacturing process and that it served industry as a tool of production. It soon became evident that an understanding of industrial architecture had to be grounded not only in these functional factors but also in an appreciation for the aesthetic ideals of engineers and their emphasis on efficiency and processes. After all, the mechanic, or engineer, was involved in most factory building projects. The proprietor of the works—the client who determined when and what to build—usually had technical knowledge and experience comparable to that of an engineer. And an engineer, either as owner or manager of the works or as a consultant, most often designed the works.

The few historians who have taken a serious look at industrial architecture have identified themes that I have also found to be important. For instance, William Pierson's early study of eighteenth-century industrial architecture noted an interrelationship between the factory and the powering of the machinery it housed. According to Pierson, the architectural requirements of the factory were to provide adequate space for machines and bring them into the most efficient relationship with the source of power. He identified three outstanding technological innovations—the steam engine, the use of metal in millwork, and the utilization of iron as a structural material—that governed factory design during the nineteenth century.[1] I will draw our attention to a second technical triumvirate—electric drive, the powered crane, and the steel frame—that revolutionized manufacturing and industrial architecture for the next century. James Marston Fitch assigned great significance to the American factory as a source of new standards in building practice. He asserts that more has been asked of the factory than of any other building type and that as a structure, it has performed well. My evidence supports Fitch's contention that factories have often led the way in the use of innovative building technology.[2]

AN OVERVIEW OF THE WORKS

Part I introduces the manufacturing works and its components. Perceptions of the works during the nineteenth century frame a context in which to understand industrial buildings; indeed, I focus on the work of building designers *as they intended it*. Historic images of manufacturing works and factories provide a sense of how these buildings appeared in the American landscape when they were new and regarded as modern and vital resources of an industrial nation. I rely on the written record left by engineers, architects, and technical journalists, as well as trade literature. At this point in the survey, I draw the reader's attention to the variety of occupations that were responsible for both the technical and aesthetic components of buildings and manufacturing works: manufacturers, builders, industry specialists, mill engineers, consulting engineers, and architects.

I present and describe the variations of the three main types of buildings that comprise the works—one-story production sheds, multistory industrial lofts, and powerhouses. The evolution of the layout of the works, the conceptualization of manufacturing space, and the role of materials handling are examined through recommendations that accompanied engineers' model plans and other works admired for their design. This evidence supports my contention that despite the posturing of architects and engineers who turned their attention to the factory design problem during the late nineteenth century, conceptually these professions brought little new to the project. All those who planned industrial buildings and manufacturing works strived toward the same goal: factories that incorporated the most modern production methods, held the appropriate machinery and equipment, were large enough and laid out in a rational manner, and could easily be expanded. A tradition of excellence in designing for industry responded to changes in technology, the demands of competition, and the cost of rebuilding as American industry developed. Consequently, there is little reason to be attentive to the claims of specialists in industrial engineering and design who asserted that factory buildings had not advanced in proportion to the progress made in the modernization of manufacturing techniques.

The extensive midsection of the book presents the industrial building as the *engineered factory*. My use of this term and the phrase *the master machine* is based on the technological integration of machinery and the structure that housed it, not on rationalized planning and management.[3] The term *engineered factory* refers to the factors that governed the design of factories and acknowledges the project to be an engineering problem. I find two versions of the master machine: the industrial loft linked to the machinery it housed through millwork and the steel-framed production shed and its electric-powered crane and equipment.

This portion of *The Works* identifies functional components of industrial buildings and reviews their development over time. The engineering of the factory was dominated by the type of power used to drive machinery and the manner in which it was distributed throughout the works. We must understand the different set of circumstances that prevailed in both factory design and operation during the age of millwork and the era of electric drive.

The study describes requirements for strength, span, and the containment of fire, as well as the manner in which these engineering problems were met through the use of various building materials—wood, stone, brick, iron and steel, and reinforced concrete. The degree to which the engineered factory was tailored to function is evident in the differences in two similar types of buildings that served as models throughout industry— the urban store and loft and the textile mill. Other engineering solutions are evident in the innovations made by the Berlin Iron Bridge Co. and other "bridge shops" in the design of iron and steel-framed production sheds. In this context I explore the particular ways that walls and roofs of factories were designed to maximize light and ventilation through window walls filled with steel sash, monitor roofs, and other distinctive elements of industrial architecture.

These chapters discuss change and progress in various aspects of the industrial building design problem. Factories did improve over time in order to provide a setting for profitable manufacturing. As Tom Peters asserts, the belief in progress manifested itself in building during the nineteenth century. This type of progress in industry includes the ideas that science and technology should be used to improve building materials and the engineering of structures and that the engineer could better control the production sequence and costs of manufacturing through the design of factories.[4] The improvements in industrial buildings related in these pages are part of a normal design process. Not until the emergence of the controlled conditions plant—based on the complete artificial control of light and ventilation—was there a dramatic shift in design intentions.

Part III addresses the aesthetic component of industrial architecture, a topic that is as subjective today as it was to the engineers and architects working during the period of study. Here I argue for an appreciation of the work of engineers whom I obviously consider to have produced industrial architecture, not merely facilities. Indeed, the dominant role of engineers in both aesthetic and technical matters requires a rejection of the traditional deference to architects in the evaluation of industrial building design. In order to recognize an engineering aesthetic, we must understand the contrasting aesthetic ideals of engineers and architects—the engineer's allegiance to a functional beauty and interest in process over product, and the architect's devotion to formal art. These views, particularly when applied to the appropriate appearance of factory buildings, provide a framework for considering the aesthetic aspect of American industrial architecture.

The final chapter presents an analysis of how an engineering-based aesthetic was translated into practice. I identify several design principles and take a close look at three ways they were translated into practice. As engineers worked with brick to interpret the American round-arched style, they developed an appropriate aesthetic for industrial buildings. The collective angst of architects over the "architectural problem of concrete" represented their rationalized approach to utilitarian building design and, in particular, reinforced concrete industrial lofts. The present-day notion of the existence of an American industrial modernism is explored, specifically through the design of one-story production sheds and the work of a noted practitioner, Albert Kahn. I contextualize and analyze Kahn's industrial architecture and examine his design vocabulary.

At the end of the study I provide a glossary of industrial architectural terms, as well as extensive documentation. As architectural historians expect, the date of construction, the designer of a building, and location have been supplied. The designer's identity as an engineer or architect is indicated when possible.

ACKNOWLEDGMENTS

U nder the broiling sun of the West Indies, I became aware that factory buildings were intriguing combinations of building construction and industrial
technology. The exploration of ruins of sugar mills and boiling houses on
the island of St. Croix, in the good company of Tom Bradley, Betsy Rezende,
William Chapman, and William Cissel, gave way to wanderings through
other industrial areas. Ned Kauffman and Michael Kwartler provided an
introduction to the Gowanus Canal area of Brooklyn in a preservation planning class at Columbia University.

Marjorie Pearson, director of the research department at the New York
City Landmarks Preservation Commission, not only indulged my interest
in industrial buildings through the assignment of projects and hours spent
in the library but also patiently instructed me in the craft of writing architectural history. My other colleagues at the commission, including Sarah
Bradford Landau, Elisa Urbanelli, Charles Savage, David Breiner, Gale Harris,
Jay Schockley, Margaret Pickart, and Donald Plotts, provided thoughtful
reflection and guided my thinking on many topics.

Though architectural critics and historians have largely absented themselves from the study of industrial architecture and focused their attention
elsewhere, I have learned much from the work of several scholars. I am especially indebted to William Pierson, Theodore Sande, and Richard Candee for
their work on textile mills as well as to Carl Condit, Ada Louise Huxtable

and Reyner Banham. Alan Holgate and Tom C. Peters provide insight into the work of engineers. The dissertations of Duncan Hay, Betsy Bahr, Lindy Biggs, Amy Slayton, Mark Brown, and Sara Wermiel, which examine various aspects of industrial architecture, are indicative of the recent interest in this topic.

This book is the richer, and I am the wiser, because of the psychological, intellectual, and financial support that I received from the Hagley Museum and Library. Its holdings in published material, trade literature, archives, and photographs made a library research project on this topic rewarding. The interest of Glenn Porter, Philip Scranton, and Roger Horowitz in my work has been much appreciated. Carol Lockman oversaw arrangements for my research trips and made them more enjoyable in many ways. Susan Hengel, Lynne Joshi, and others facilitated my use of the library collection. Jon Williams and Barbara Hall made the pictorial collections available, and Michael Nash and Marjorie McNinch did the same with the archival collections.

The science and technology department of the New York Public Library was a valued resource made accessible by the staff of the old 43rd Street Annex. The Avery Architectural and Fine Arts Library and Science and Engineering Division of the University Libraries at Columbia University, as well as the United Engineering Center Library, were other repositories I often visited. The Cleveland Public Library, with its impressive holdings in engineering and technology, became a prime resource. Mary Beth Betts made the Cass Gilbert collection at the New-York Historical Society available to me. Jim Roan made accessible the collection of trade literature at the Museum of American History of The Smithsonian Institution.

During the last stages of this project I was fortunate to be working with the faculty of the history department at Case Western Reserve University. Carroll Pursell and Miriam Levin helped me reflect on this topic in reference to the history of technology. Mark Brown, by chairing a session on industrial architecture at an Annual Society of Architectural Historians meeting, helped to bring this project about. My thanks also to William Littman and Sara Wermiel, with whom I shared time at Hagley and discussions on factories. I am indebted to Margaret Pickart, Vince Leskosky, Rob Bobel, and Michelle Hardman for reading and commenting on my manuscript. Ellyn Goldkind provided both architectural drawings and enthusiasm for the project. I must also thank Joyce Berry, Jessica Ryan, and their colleagues at Oxford University Press for their interest in my book project. No amount of thanks recognizes the support of my husband during this project, the assistance of my daughter in libraries, or the challenge of hearing from my son, "Aren't you done with your book yet?"

Shaker Heights, Ohio   B. H. B.
October 1998

CONTENTS

It is the dream of every manufacturer to have the best planned and best equipped plant for doing his special work. Whatever his neighbor has, he wants something a little better, and the manufacturer who builds last always has the advantage of his competitors in this respect. . . . The designing and building of modern manufacturing plants has therefore become a science, comparatively new in this country, but at the same time of great importance.

THE BERLIN IRON BRIDGE COMPANY, C. 1892

THE NOTION OF THE WORKS I

The planning of these workshops is remarkable, and every detail seems to have been considered. . . . One feels that some brain of superior intelligence, backed by a long technical experience, has thought out every possible detail.

PAUL DE ROUSIERS, 1892, DESCRIBING
THE PULLMAN PALACE CAR WORKS

Factory buildings and manufacturing works appear throughout the American cultural landscape. The buildings of industry stand in small towns near streams that provided waterpower, along filled-in canals and forgotten turnpike arteries, near sources of raw materials, and alongside commercial ports. They dominate sections of large cities and extend along rail corridors in industrial areas. Each factory is an essay in pragmatism and functional beauty derived from the attempt to perfectly adapt means to an end. Yet, oddly enough, we know little about these structures in which the prosperity of our nation was generated and the laborers of industry spent their workdays. It is the intent of this book to explain what these manufacturing facilities are and why they look the way they do.

In their varied forms, American industrial works comprised a number of buildings engineered specifically for manufacturing yet adaptable enough to house various types of industrial operations (fig. 1.1). The factory building and manufacturing works provided a setting for industrial work by creating a space and identity for each aspect of the operation and, to varying degrees, addressed the comfort and health of their occupants through the control of heat, light, and ventilation. The industrial building also provided a stable foundation for machinery and a rigid framework for power transmission and materials handling. Moreover, the manufacturing works was the physical embodiment of the proprietor's well-thought-out plan for the layout and routing of the manufacturing process.

FIGURE 1.1 During the 1830s, the Newark Foundry of O. Meeker & Co. was housed in a number of small buildings that were engineered to accommodate the operation. A chimney rose through the roof of the foundry building, and shutters near the ridge could be opened to dissipate heat. A multistory loft building, positioned to take advantage of changes in grade, was fitted with an exterior hoist.

This study covers the 100 years prior to 1940 for several reasons. During that time, industrial building design evolved toward a single ideal—the exploitation of natural light and ventilation in structures with maximum span and strength. The period also coincides with the development and expansion of American manufacturing industries and the construction of numerous factory buildings. This growth in American industry gave impetus to the engineering of factory buildings as their numbers increased. Industrial building design matured as American industry passed through several periods of growth, consolidation, recession, and modernization. During the 1930s, experiments were made with the forms that would characterize the next era of industrial architecture, *controlled conditions plants*. The new model was based on the utilization of artificial lighting, air-conditioning, and forced air circulation to optimize working conditions in structures with few openings. The new type of factory became common during the defense industry buildup just before World War II and brought to a close the era of factory design that sought to optimize natural conditions.

COMING TO TERMS: AN UNFAMILIAR AND OBSOLETE TERMINOLOGY

The term "works" itself may be made to include plants for producing on a large scale every article made for the use of man or beast.

ENGINEERING MAGAZINE, 1904

My investigation of industrial architecture immediately encountered a problem with terminology that ranged from an appropriate name for a building to a term that denoted a complex of such structures. Industrial buildings, historically, have been referred to by names based on the manufacturing processes they housed rather than on architectural criteria. This historical terminology is difficult to adopt because it includes specialized terms familiar only to engineers and architects as well as too generic and interchangeable terms used by the general public.

The terms used most often for industrial buildings have been *manufactory* and *factory*, *workshop* and *shop*, and *mill*, while *the works* and *plant* have referred to the manufacturing complex. Like much early American industrial technology, these terms have British origins. In the Americanization of the language, the terms were often combined with specific modifiers, resulting in the compound nouns like *tinware manufactory*, *boiler erecting shop*, and *dye house*. More definitive names like *brewery*, *pottery*, and *foundry* were used as well.

American gazetteers and other nineteenth-century publications tended to use *manufactory*, *factory*, *shop*, and *establishment* interchangeably to describe industrial operations. Actually, long phrases like "establishment for the manufacture of . . ." were typical. During the first decades of textile production in the United States, it was not uncommon for operations to be referred to as *cotton* or *woolen manufactories*, though by the mid–nineteenth century, the term *textile mill* had come into dominant use. Terminology was sometimes particular to a specific industry. For instance, the facilities owned by railroads for the repair of rolling stock were invariably *car shops*, though independent railroad car manufacturers operated *car works*.[1]

Textile production was one of the few industries housed in a standard type of building, the textile mill, which had distinctive architectural characteristics, such as form, size, and even building materials. In other fields, there was no definitive correlation between building name and form. A machine shop was as likely to occupy a floor in a multistory building as a one-story structure. Late-twentieth-century usage, which relies almost exclusively on *factory*, provides no useful alternatives; from an architectural analysis, there is no factory building type per se.[2]

The Works, The Plant

By the term "iron works" we do not mean the furnaces where ore is converted into pig iron, nor the rolling mills . . . but those establishments erected for the purpose of manufacturing iron into boats, buildings, engines, machinery and tools.

SCIENTIFIC AMERICAN, 1860

The works predominated among the terms used for manufacturing facilities in technical and commercial literature during the 1800s and remained in common use well into the following century. A collective term for a group of buildings, *the works* also implied the presence of a certain scale, permanence, and technical competence (fig. 1.2). When Silsby, Race & Holly, machinists and iron founders in Seneca Falls, New York, erected a new facility in 1852, it was presented as their "Island Works," not just as a new foundry.[3]

The works was a term of British origin that initially referred to civil engineering projects, such as fortifications, and later to docks and bridges. *The works* was used in Great Britain to refer to processing operations like gasworks, printworks, and brickworks, and also for the engineering works of heavy industry. Americans adopted the terms *gasworks* (as they began to replicate British gas-making operations) and *brickworks*, but not *engineering works* to any great extent. They soon applied *the works* to compound facilities, such as ironworks that consisted of a furnace, forge, rolling mill, and shops, and to mechanized operations, like machine works. Indeed, Americans considered nearly all types of manufacturing operations *the works*, and in only the textile industry, housed in mills, was the term rarely used. The terms *factory*, *shop*, and *mill*, however, were also used to refer to a complete industrial facility, as well as to individual buildings. Toward the end of the nineteenth century, *plant* began to replace *the works* as the term for a manufacturing facility. *Plant* referred to the permanent grounds, buildings, machines, and tools required to carry on a business, such as a mine or a railroad. During the 1880s Americans began using *plant* to mean buildings and equipment. For example, Worcester Steel erected a "new and complete plant" in 1884. The American Nail and Machine Co. (St. Louis) advertised a "valuable plant for sale" in 1890 that included a foundry and nail and

FIGURE 1.2 The Hayden, Gere & Co. in Haydensville, Massachusetts, made brass items and plumbers' goods in a works erected in 1874. The works comprised a large three-story industrial loft, a one-story production shed that housed the brass foundry, and a stately office building.

machine shops with machinery, engine, boiler, and tools. Some types of facilities were nearly always referred to as *plants*, such as printing plants. Around the turn of the century *the works* and *plant* were used interchangeably. *Plant* then acquired a connotation of a modernized facility and was the term favored by industrial engineers, who eventually added the distinctions *special-purpose plant* and *universal space plant*.[4]

The Manufactory, The Factory

Factory. Abbreviated from manufactory, a building in which manufacturing is carried on.

A DICTIONARY OF ARCHITECTURE AND BUILDING, 1902

Factory, the universal twentieth-century term for all industrial buildings, is an abbreviation of *manufactory*. Etymologically, a manufactory was an operation quite different from the mechanized factory, one in which a group of workers performed manual tasks in a subdivided routine without many machines. But the term most often meant an operation in which machinery was essential. Andrew Ure, a British political economist, stated in 1835 that manufacturing was the making of products with machinery and with little or no aid of the human hand. In a factory, *operatives* tended with skill a system of productive machines continuously propelled by a central power. Ure included cotton, flax, silk, and woolen mills and some engineering works in this definition, but not ironworks or foundries. He did concede that others considered the term factory to refer to all extensive establishments where a number of people cooperated in a complex processing operation, such as ironworks, soapworks, and breweries. Nearly all subsequent definitions of *factory* have been similarly based on a type of operation, not the structure that houses it.[5]

Americans used the terms *manufactory* and *factory* throughout the nineteenth century (fig. 1.3). Noah Webster's dictionary of 1839 noted that factory was a contraction of *manufactory* and defined manufacturing as the act of reducing raw materials into a form suitable for use—by hand, by machinery, or by art. Around the turn of the twentieth century, *factory* came into more general use and was favored by architects and engineers. The 1914 New York State law for factory regulation, representative of statutes passed by many states, defined a factory as any place where goods or products were manufactured or repaired, cleaned, or sorted. Mills, workshops, and manufacturing businesses, as well as all buildings, sheds, and structures used in connection with such operations (except powerhouses, barns, and storage houses) were considered factories in New York. A *model factory* was one that had high standards of industrial efficiency and emphasized labor-management relations. It usually provided employee welfare programs and often offered medical, recreational, and educational facilities. Today, *factory* is used to refer to a single building, or to an entire facility

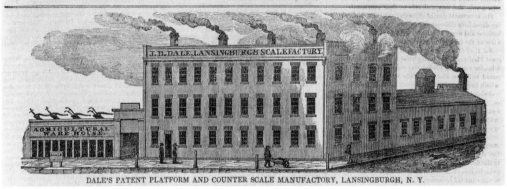

MECHANIC'S ADVOCATE.

A WEEKLY PAPER, DEVOTED TO THE INTERESTS OF THE MECHANIC, AND THE ELEVATION OF LABOR.

JOHN TANNER,]   Late Publisher of the Mechanic's Mirror,   [EDITOR AND PROPRIETOR.

VOLUME I.—NUMBER 13.   ALBANY, THURSDAY, FEB. 25, 1847.   TERMS—$1 PER ANNUM.

DALE'S PATENT PLATFORM AND COUNTER SCALE MANUFACTORY, LANSINGBURGH, N. Y.

FIGURE 1.3 During the 1840s, the Dale Scale Factory in Lansingburgh, New York, was a works that comprised several special-purpose buildings.

consisting of a number of structures, where manufacturing takes place. In this survey, I use it as a synonym for industrial building, a general term that does not connote any specific architectural form or characteristics.[6]

HISTORIC PERCEPTIONS OF THE WORKS

Factory sections have this in common with other purely individual and utilitarian things, they can be interesting beyond any intention of those who plan them.

THEODORE DREISER, A HOOSIER HOLIDAY

Although manufacturing works became an important addition to the built environment during the nineteenth century, they are not well documented in the texts of the period. Reporting on American industrial works by the general press focused on the sublime aspects of industry and often included explanations of production processes. Authors of such pieces conveyed a sense of astonishment at the complexity of machinery and the immense scale of operations. As these articles celebrated the progressive and dramatic aspects of industry, they suggested that the works was a distinct and fascinating aspect of the American landscape.[7]

Technical literature of the mid–nineteenth century tended to focus on the design and operation of new machines and production methods rather than on the buildings that housed them. After all, it was relatively easy to remain well versed in matters of building, in comparison to the rapid changes in other types of technology. Architectural pattern books, the most prevalent type of architectural publication of the period, did not address industrial buildings either. Like ladies' fashion magazines, they presented the latest architectural styling. Since industrial buildings generally did not reflect current architectural modes, they were not included in style manuals. As the general press presented more information on American industry and the technical press matured, manufacturing works were presented in conventionalized verbal descriptions and pictorial images.

A deeper regard for the individual industrial concern, its works, and its history coincided with the centennial celebration of 1876. The displays of American manufactured items in the Machinery Hall at the Centennial Exposition and an upsurge in interest in American history led to efforts to document the country's industrial heritage. In addition to the biographical anthologies published by many communities during the 1870s, in which manufacturers and their operations were featured, publications appeared devoted solely to American industrialists. Flattering accounts of large firms appeared in volumes like *Industrial America* and invariably emphasized the achievements of the founder, the large number of machines in use at each establishment, the immense size of the works, and the most innovative or best-selling products of the firm. This attentiveness to industrial history continued, and during the early twentieth century, monographs on many prominent manufacturing operations appeared.[8]

Field Trips to the Works

When we reached the location of the works, we were struck with the artistic beauty and substantial appearance of the brick buildings, as well as the admirable foresight displayed in the selection of the site. . . . In closing, we will say that no master mechanic should visit this city without calling at the office and works of this company.

MANUFACTURER AND BUILDER, 1874

Industrialists' and engineers' knowledge of up-to-date industrial building design and works layout practices could most easily be expanded by visiting other works. Buildings were inspected, and even measured, during such visits. This tradition of firsthand inquiry, which dates from the earliest years of the textile industry, substituted for and later supplemented published information about industrial buildings and the works.

The industrial field trip seems to have originated as a form of industrial espionage when Americans contrived to visit British operations because the exportation of machines and plans and the immigration of mechanics were prohibited. Historian Richard Candee recounts an expedition, undertaken by an employee of the Dover Manufacturing Company (Dover, New Hampshire). After he examined nearby American bleaching and printing operations in 1826, the chemist traveled to England to observe printing methods and specifically to study building construction, the size and lighting of

FIGURE 1.4 This view of the New-York Steam Engine Co. (Passaic, New Jersey), accompanied a description of the facility that noted the dimensions, materials, and the fireproof qualities of the structures.

spaces, and details of the equipment and its arrangement. In fact, the use of existing facilities as models for new buildings was standard in the textile industry, and Candee also documents how the facilities at Waltham, and then Lowell, were copied. That practice accounts for increasingly uniform textile mills with nearly identical forms and organization.[9]

Buildings comparable to the Lowell Mills—standards that were widely replicated in the textile industry—are less well known for other industries. The manner in which the Whitin Machine Works (1847; Whitinsville, Connecticut) mirrors the form of the machine shop of the Mason Machine Works, even to the castellated stair towers (1845; see fig. 3.6), suggests that manufacturers did not hesitate to copy other structures. Certainly, both trained engineers and manufacturers surveyed existing facilities devoted to similar purposes as they prepared plans for new works. Around 1847, when making plans for the machine shop of the Essex Company in Lawrence, Massachusetts, engineer Charles Bigelow traveled throughout New England and as far south as Paterson, New Jersey, to visit machine shops. A memoranda of this trip recorded two factors that made a strong impression: inadequate lighting and ventilation of shops and the prevalent use of cranes and hoisting apparatus to facilitate shop work.[10]

Investigative field trips continued to be an important source of information on new developments in works design even as published technical information on the subject became available. A journalist recommended that the first steps taken by a firm, after deciding to build a new facility, should be visiting the best nearby operations and searching technical literature to determine the best system to adopt. During the late 1880s, the senior engineering students of the Lehigh University made a trip through New England to visit several prominent firms considered to have well-designed works, including Brown & Sharpe (see fig. 7.6) and the American Watch Co. (see fig. 9.2). In 1893, George Gifford, a civil engineer, shop superintendent, and master mechanic of the King Bridge Co. (Cleveland), spent a week visiting shops in different parts of the country, noting designs of buildings, arrangements of machinery, and methods of handling work, before designing the firm's new riveting shop. Around the turn of the century, the Weston Electrical Instrument Co. hired mechanical and engineering experts to visit the most notable manufacturing establishments in the country to study physical conditions while another team explored labor issues.[11]

Armchair Visits to the Works

The manufacturing works was heralded as the physical setting of industry by the technical and engineering press that emerged during the last third of the nineteenth century. Matter-of-fact in tone yet still always complimentary, descriptions of industrial works presented the type of information that was important to the industrialist and engineer. Though "visit to the works" articles had occasionally appeared before, during the 1870s they became a standard type of report, an illustrated profile of an establishment. These profiles emphasized the machines in use and the products made and usually provided a general description of the works; occasionally, they recounted in detail particularly well designed buildings. They served as an armchair version of a visit to the works.

As the format of these reports became standardized, certain phrases became prevalent. "Built in the most substantial manner" appeared in an 1842 description of the Buffalo Steam Engine Works and almost all subsequent reports of that type. An 1866 account in *Scientific American* of the Albany Locomotive Works of the New York Central Railroad noted the fireproof qualities and immense proportions of the new buildings. The company's various shops were situated in the most convenient manner, and the buildings and workshops were spacious and adequately ventilated and lighted. These phrases appeared repeatedly in a *Scientific American* series titled "Industries in America," inaugurated in 1879 to provide "a concise and intelligent description of the leading industries of this continent." The series, which ran for about five years, profiled nearly one hundred American firms.[12]

"Visits to the works" reports became formulaic in other ways as well. They generally included the acreage covered by the works, transportation connections, and the dimensions and number of stories of major buildings and continued to note attributes such as fireproof construction. The author often strayed into hyperbole when describing the size of the works or buildings within an industry or geographical area: An appropriate statistic, such as the number of square feet or processes involved, or a geographic frame of reference, could always be found. Nevertheless, information on the type and number of buildings indicated production capabilities and the amount of capital invested in the works. Barring the devastation of a fire, or problems with power supply or machinery repairs, this intelligence facilitated the evaluation of capacity claims.[13]

Descriptions of works implied that the highest-quality work or service was available from the best-equipped and -managed firms. The inclusion of certain adjectives, though they were admittedly clichés, emphasized the attributes of the works that were most valued. Nearly always, the facilities were "commodious" and "substantial." "Commodious" works were well adapted to their purpose and provided convenient working space. "Substantial" buildings were strong and solid enough to house machinery in motion with a minimum of vibration and oscillation. The terms *systematic* and *orderly* and the phrase *with economy* denoted an efficient layout of the works; the "industrial economy" noted in these reports was later known as "production efficiency." The language used to describe the 1870s reconstruction program of the Roger's locomotive works in Paterson, New Jersey (see fig. 3.9), was of the era before efficiency was the byword: The remodeling resulted in a facility that was planned with economy in time, labor, and space and designed for the comfort and convenience of workers. Even after the adjectives *commodious*, *substantial*, and *orderly* were replaced with *functional*, and *efficient*, the positive attributes of industrial buildings remained the same.[14]

When the construction of industrial buildings passed from large-scale building projects that could be erected with common engineering knowledge to specialized construction, another form of technical report appeared. These new articles, often prepared by the project engineer, presented design intentions and explanations of why materials and construction methods were chosen, as well as the factors that influenced the layout of the works. This type of technical reporting expanded, around the turn of the twentieth century, to book-length treatises on the new iron- and steel-framed production sheds: for instance, Henry Grattan Tyrrell's *Mill Building Construction* (1901).

Views of the Works

Note the names of the buildings, as given by the owners, and imagine the routing of work through the shops.

ENGINEERING MAGAZINE, 1916

Verbal descriptions in "visits to the works" articles, local histories, and anthologies on industrial works were often accompanied by "views of the works," drawings of the entire facility made from a bird's-eye perspective. These images also appeared in commercial directories, catalogues, and advertisements and on company stationery. The detail with which the buildings were represented suggests that the views, made with the aid of photography, were intended both to convey technical information and to present the establishment in a positive light. A comparison of two images—a typical view of the works and a photograph—of the Tanner & Delaney Engine Co. facility bears out this assertion (figs. 1.5 and 1.6). It seems likely that the maps and drawings used by fire insurance companies helped to establish a tradition of detailed and realistic representation of the works.[15]

Many views were complete, even to the inclusion of powerhouses and such auxiliary buildings as storage sheds and buildings were often identified by name (see figs. 1.4, 1.5, 2.2, 2.6, and 3.9). These labels allowed manufacturers and engineers to evaluate how the works was laid out and follow the routing of processes. They could project the capacity of portions of the operation from the size of buildings and from such details as the number of forge chimneys rising above the blacksmith shop. The canals and railroads that were always present in these views were reminders of the methods of shipping available.

Views of the works also conveyed some less obvious information and cultural meaning through artistic conventions. The respectability and prosperity of the establishment were implied by the depiction of well-dressed visitors. The necessary and functional reservoir that provided water for

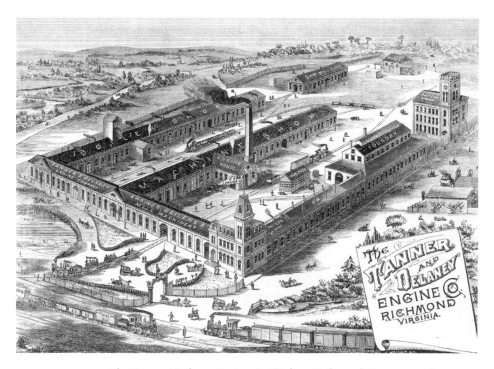

FIGURE 1.5 The Tanner & Delaney Engine Co. Works in Richmond, Virginia, used this bird's-eye view in 1883 to promote its new facility. The careful labeling of the buildings allowed viewers to imagine the route of the work. Liberties were taken with the depiction of formal gardens near the entrance to the works.

FIGURE 1.6 An historic photograph of the Tanner & Delaney Works demonstrates how the 1883 drawing of the facility (fig. 1.5), like views prepared for other companies, was made from a photograph and was a realistic representation of the property.

fire-fighting was often transformed into an ornamental pond in a parklike setting, thereby signifying the owners' concern for the workers' environment and the firm's standing in the community. The inclusion of adjacent dwellings in the view suggested that the operation could depend on a stable and healthy workforce accommodated in company housing. Copious smoke (an aspect of industry that was not yet reviled) pouring from chimneys documented a busy, and therefore successful, enterprise.

WHO'S WHO IN THE DESIGN OF THE WORKS

Rolling Mills, blast furnaces, iron works of all descriptions erected upon the most improved plans, steam or water power; drawings, plans, estimates for buildings, furnaces, machinery.

ADVERTISEMENT OF S. B. MERKEL, 1846

Building a well-designed factory was no easy matter during the 1870s, according to J. W. Carpenter, an architect who worked as a "constructional engineer." The manufacturer often built, on the spur of the moment, a structure with four walls, a floor, and a roof in which window openings were placed at random or in military order. It was not until after he began to regard this first building as unsuccessful that the industrialist looked for a proper model to copy. But often he had to furnish his own better scheme. When a factory owner worked out plans for a new facility with a builder, the end result was not any better. If an architect was engaged to provide plans, the factory building might have harmoniously arranged windows and a costly, fancy roof like that of a school or college but would not be superior in functional ways. After all this effort, the manufacturer was likely to have spent considerable money and acquired a structure with shaking walls and a roof ready for a tumble. This scenario supported Carpenter's argument that architects were "unqualified and too fantastic in elaborations" to serve manufacturers.[16]

Architect Harvey Wiley Corbett related a differing view of the history of factory design and his profession's role in it. The "mechanical man" (factory superintendent) could improve the factory beyond a shack but was limited by a too intimate knowledge of his special work. If an engineer was called in, he might make improvements. But working with a limited point of view as a "practical man," the engineer found it hard to go beyond the purely mechanical aspects of the problem and was little interested in human factors, according to Corbett. When an architect replaced the engineer, some thought he only added frills, but in fact he brought a "comprehensive sense of arrangement" to the problem. Corbett admitted that prior to World War I, to be known as the architect of a factory nearly resulted in professional ostracism. But by around 1920, an architect could design a factory and no longer want to keep it a secret. Yet, some architects still hesitated to frankly confront the economic and financial limitations that guided industrial building projects and lacked any interest in the architectural possibilities of the factory building.[17]

Carpenter's and Corbett's views of factory design candidly depicted the relative strengths of architects and engineers; they also revealed long-held prejudices and cannot be considered accurate descriptions of building practice. Industrial buildings were commonly designed as collaborations between various combinations of industrialists, carpenters and builders, mill engineers, civil and mechanical engineers, consulting or industrial engineers, and architects. A readiness to experiment and adopt new ideas rather than be governed by rigid traditions has predominated in these projects. Historian Tom Peters attributes this design approach to associative thinking that synthesizes various ideas, translates information, and often crosses the borders of disciplines and technical practices. It seems that few designers hesitated to devise an improved truss or ventilating roof form, or yet another method of fireproof floor construction, or to patent a new form of building material. Even adverse conditions, like periods of recession and war, stimulated the inventiveness of architects and engineers and resulted in methods of rapid and economical construction.[18]

From Common Building Practice to Specialized Engineering

As the mechanization, automation, and rationalization of the manufacturing process proceeded during the nineteenth century, corresponding changes took place in the design and construction of industrial buildings. Factory building design blended common engineering or building know-how, an empirical approach, with engineering based on rationalized, technological cal thought and strategic planning. In the course of the nineteenth century, engineering and mathematics contributed to, and then ultimately replaced, the empirical design of engineering structures, including factory buildings.

Common engineering knowledge, a term suggested by historian John Stilgoe, refers to information regarding the customary methods of American building practice; this knowledge included the design and construction of a few common types of industrial structures. Gristmills, sawmills, and blacksmith shops were necessary components of American communities. The need for mills and forges caused many American settlers to make it their business to know how to construct and operate them. The builders of small village mills and blacksmith shops could then draw on these prototypes as they provided larger industrial buildings (see fig. 1.1).[19]

In addition to common engineering know-how and pattern books, American builders also drew upon a vernacular, or nonverbal, practice of building design. A knowledge of past precedents and the employment of a limited number of design elements characterizes vernacular design, according to historian Thomas Hubka. Another influence of the vernacular approach to industrial building design was the tendency to use flexible and informal plans. The type of incremental additions made to dwellings and farm structures also appear in the accretionary form of factories and industrial complexes.[20]

Part-time builders, carpenters, masons, and building contractors were undoubtedly responsible for the design and construction of many factory buildings, even though their roles are not well documented. But concurrent with the development of any manufacturing industry, expertise was sought in the design of structures that would best house the operations. The need for an experienced specialist to oversee construction was recognized by some would-be Pennsylvania industrialists. The Harrisburg Car Manufacturing Company was founded by a group of local businessmen in 1853, but none of the partners had the technological experience to develop and manage the operation. The investors hired William T. Hildrup, who was trained as a carpenter and experienced in car manufacturing and therefore able to supervise the construction of the entire works and then manage it. After a fire in April 1872 destroyed most of the facility, Hildrup was reported to have sketched out plans during the evening and initiated rebuilding the next morning.[21]

Several groups of engineers and industries had influential roles in the development of industrial architecture, and their work was visited and made known through technical journals. Well-trained engineers in the nation's military services oversaw the development of arsenals, armories, and navy yards that included industrial buildings of the same type used in manufacturing industries. The extensive building programs of large railroads afforded engineers the opportunity to improve the design of the industrial structures that housed the lines' railroad shops. These facilities, where locomotives and rolling stock were serviced and sometimes manufactured, served as model works during the heyday of railroad development. For example, the North Carolina Railroad shops, begun in 1855 in a location known first as Company Shops and later as Burlington, established a new scale for industrial works in that state. This complex of shops—seven substantial brick buildings—was the largest facility erected in North Carolina during the antebellum period. Although the scale of the undertaking initially invited accusations of extravagance, the shops were soon considered a "fruitful nursery for mechanical genius" in the state.[22]

There was yet another source for factory designs. Machinery manufacturers provided plans for industrial buildings as a means of promoting the sale of their products. During the 1840s, the prominent Mattewan Company, the Hudson Valley machine shop of Charles E. Leonard, furnished drawings and plans of factories "with all necessary machinery." Machine shops that produced textile machinery also offered advice on mill construction and plans to prospective customers. The Saco-Lowell Shops provided nonstandardized plans at a nominal rate that was deductible from the cost of machinery if an order was placed. By 1885, the competing Whitin Machine Works was also furnishing plans.[23]

The Manufacturer as Designer

Mr. Fisk determined that the new shops should be light, airy, symmetrical in plan and perfect in convenience—in short, the model manufactory of the city. Accordingly, he devoted himself to elaborating a systematic method of utilizing to the best advantage the sixteen-acre plot devoted to the Wason Car-Works.

NATIONAL CAR BUILDER, 1873

In many cases, local builders were directed in their work by the owners or managers of manufacturing operations. Most of the men who started and managed manufacturing operations not only possessed enough technical expertise and common engineering knowledge to determine what type of facility was needed but also understood how to supervise a major construction project. Engineers like George Corliss and William Mason designed and oversaw the erection of their works during the mid–nineteenth century. Catholine Lambert, a silk mill proprietor in Paterson, New Jersey, around 1861, apparently did the same. A new mill, built in 1878, was described as "constructed after a design of and under the personal supervision of Lambert himself."[24]

Industrialists remained involved in works design and construction as long as they had primarily technical, rather than financial or administrative, interests and training. Even after industrial engineers had taken over the design of production lines and works layouts, hands-on executives like Harvey Firestone were involved in plant design and production layout. Company lore depicts Firestone working with string and a scale model of a new plant to study production and materials flow. H. P. Strickland, president and general manager of the Vulcan Iron Works, took on the task of designing and supervising the construction of a new plant (c. 1911; Seattle). A. J. Pitkin, the company's vice president, provided cross sections for the main shops of the American Locomotive Co. (c. 1902; Schenectady, New York). In that case, building specifications were prepared by the company's chief engineer and detailed drawings by the steel contractor.[25]

Owners' willingness to take on the role of engineer and building designer came under attack by the engineers, just as engineers' work, in turn, was later criticized by architects. J. W. Carpenter found fault with the industrialist who thought he knew everything about building. Yet he admitted that the manufacturer generally was a reasonable client, willing to pay for what he wanted—good, substantial, well-arranged shops. Harold V. Coes, one of the new industrial engineers, derisively described a manufacturer's marking the four corners of a proposed structure with his cane and saying "Build me a five-story building in this space for $10,000" without giving thought to equipment layouts or other factors. But surely Coes underestimated the experience that led to the formulation of such simple directions.[26]

Mill Engineers

Lockwood, Greene & Co., Mill Engineers—Carefully prepared plans, specifications, and estimates furnished, for the construction, equipment and organization of new mills and the revision and improvement of old.

LOCKWOOD, GREENE & CO. LETTERHEAD, 1880S

The occupation of "textile mill engineer" developed soon after the initiation of the textile manufacturing industry in the United States. Mill engineering included the work of the millwright (the technician responsible for setting up and operating the machinery, water wheels, and shafting used to drive the machines) and the textile machinery designer. Mill engineers also designed mill buildings and oversaw their construction.

Mill engineers became agents of the transfer of technical knowledge as the textile industry expanded in New England and then to other areas of the country. Before it was common to do so, David Whitman established a consulting business, and as he traveled throughout New England advising various mill owners, he became known as a "mill doctor." Mill engineer Charles Tillinghast James earned a reputation as an ardent advocate of the conversion of textile mills to steam power and played a role in the transfer of New England textile manufacturing technology to the South and West as he traveled and lectured. His message—that steam-powered cotton mills offered small, economically stagnant communities a means of prospering—was one that a group of businessmen in Harrisburg, Pennsylvania, wanted to hear. They engaged James to supervise the construction of a mill there (1850–1851) that replicated its New England counterparts.[27]

During the nineteenth century, the occupation of mill engineer was professionalized, just as other fields of engineering were. Formal training in engineering became more common, and many mill engineers established consulting practices. David Dyer, who had practical experience as a mill engineer in Fall River, Massachusetts, taught himself mechanical and civil engineering and designed numerous cotton mills. He has been credited with helping to make the flat textile mill roof, used on his Mechanics Mill (1868; fig. 1.7), standard practice. The roster of mill engineers recommended by the Whitin Machine Works during the 1870s included Amos D. Lockwood, William A. Thompson, D. M. Thompson, and Shedd & Sawyer (all of whom had practices in the Northeast) and John Rhodes Brown, John Hill, and W. B. Smith Whaley (who worked primarily in the South). A new breed of college-trained consulting mill engineers included Charles T. Main and his partner Francis W. Dean, as well as C. J. H. Woodbury and John Ripley Freeman, who were recruited by Edward Atkinson to professionalize the Fire Insurance Mutuals' advocacy of slow-burning mill construction. Many of these engineers, like Frank P. Sheldon, considered research necessary to provide superior engineering services. Sheldon included short treatises on the testing of various types of roofing materials, heat transmission through different types of sash, and the evaluation of daylight versus sunlight in sawtooth roof construction in his firm's promotional pamphlet, *A Half Century of Achievement*.[28]

Formal training enabled mill engineers to offer their services to various types of industries. They continued to determine the kind and amount of steam and electric power needed and the layout of machinery as they designed all sorts of factories. Leslie P. Langworthy advertised in 1902 to provide plans for woolen mills, bleacheries, dye houses, printworks, machine

FIGURE 1.7
The Mechanics Mill in Fall River, Massachusetts, designed by mill engineer David Dyer in 1868, was among the first textile mills to have flat roofs.

FIGURE 1.8 The commissions of the engineering firm Lockwood, Greene & Co. expanded from textile mills to facilities for many types of industries, including this plant for the Seth Thomas Clock Co.

shops, jewelers' shops, and "all kinds of industrial buildings." Charles T. Main's firm furnished plans for the buildings of Yale & Towne, the Gillette Safety Razor Co., and a Baltimore facility of the American Sugar Refining Co., even though much of the firm's work was for the textile industry.[29]

The engineering firm Lockwood, Greene & Co. evolved from one of the most prominent textile mill engineering firms to an engineering company considered to be an authority on building for industry. Amos D. Lockwood established a consulting practice in 1871 and soon designed the Piedmont Manufacturing Co. mill (in Greenville, later Piedmont, South Carolina), which was considered a model mill for the southern textile industry. Lockwood was a transitional figure who worked with both technicians trained in the field and college-educated mill engineers like Stephen Greene, who became a partner in the firm in 1882. Greene, who earned a civil engineering degree from Brown University in 1873, designed Columbia Cotton Mills (Columbia, South Carolina), America's first electrically driven textile mill, in 1892–1893.

The scope of the work of Lockwood, Greene & Co. expanded as they employed engineers who were specialists in civil and mechanical engineering. Like other consulting mill engineering firms, Lockwood, Greene supplied all architectural and engineering services needed by an owner to set up and equip a complete plant. Though it did not act as the builder or contractor, the firm supervised construction and installation work. Lockwood,

Greene developed an expertise in reinforced concrete design and established an architectural department in 1918 to improve the appearance of industrial plants (fig. 1.8). The firm provided numerous factory and machine shop designs, made surveys for power development, and earned an international reputation with early projects in Cuba and Japan. Lockwood, Greene & Co. continues this work today.

Consulting Engineers and Design-Build Firms

Why not devote your own energies to regular duties and throw the cares for Industrial Betterment, of an existing or new plant, on those who make the subject a life study?
RAEDER & WOOD, ARCHITECTS AND ENGINEERS, 1906

Around the turn of the century, industrial engineering emerged as a distinct subfield of engineering. Frederick W. Taylor was a founder of this specialization, which injected the engineer's rational approach to problem solving into factory management. Many industrial engineers focused their attention on detailed planning, management issues, and time-motion studies instead of the physical setting. Others worked as mill engineers had in the past, planning new facilities, but in the role of consulting engineer.[30]

Many consulting industrial engineers began their careers working for large manufacturing operations. William P. Sargent, for instance, became familiar with several manufacturing operations when he held positions as superintendent of construction, assistant to the engineer in charge of construction, and designing engineer with several firms, including the Niles Tool Works. Hugh M. Wharton worked as production superintendent before he became works engineer for the Westinghouse Electric and Manufacturing Co. works. He established a practice as a consulting engineer around 1914 to plan industrial plants and was responsible for the Remington Arms Union Metallic Cartridge Co. works (1915–1916; Bridgeport, Connecticut).[31]

During the last years of the nineteenth century, engineers began to establish firms that designed and built industrial buildings. John W. Ferguson solicited for work as a "Builder and General Contractor" in an 1897 issue of the *American Silk Journal* based on his experience in textile mill construction. By the time the John W. Ferguson Co. advertised in a 1911 issue of *Harper's Weekly*, it had evolved into a design-build operation specializing in industrial plants of many types. The Arnold Company provided "Complete Industrial Plants from Conception to Operation" and was active throughout the Midwest, from Louisiana to Michigan. By 1909 the James C. Stewart & Co. construction company of St. Louis could boast of an extensive list of clients in the Midwest and the Middle Atlantic region. In 1901 the firm demonstrated American construction efficiency when it was hired to build the Westinghouse Electric Co.'s plant at Manchester, England. The firm completed nine large buildings in ten months, after British contractors had projected a construction schedule of five years.[32]

The firm of Frank D. Chase, an architectural engineer, provided complete industrial engineering services—location selection, site layout, plant design, construction supervision, and equipment installation—as did many of his competitors (see figs. 2.19, 10.16). The firm, headquartered in New York City, specialized in the design of foundries. The Ballinger Co. (established in 1878 and before 1920 known as Ballinger & Perrot) popularized several important advances in industrial design, such as the "Daylight Building," which offered increased window area, and the "Super-Span" trussed saw-tooth roof (see chapters 7 and 8, fig. 7.8). By the 1920s it had become an organization of architects, engineers, appraisers, economists, and business counselors, with offices in Philadelphia and New York.[33]

The Turner Construction Company was established in New York in 1902 by two young college-trained engineers, Henry C. Turner and DeForest H. Dixon, to design and build reinforced concrete structures. The firm's expertise in this work soon led to steady commissions from several large industrial firms and the long-term project of erecting the Bush Terminal in Brooklyn (see figs. 1.9 and 3.19). Among Turner's best-known projects was the rapid construction of the Brooklyn Army Supply Base (1914; Cass Gilbert, architect; see fig. 10.10). Through the establishment of branch offices, the firm gained a national clientele and, later, a worldwide sphere of operations that the company continues to enjoy.[34]

Other firms also developed specialized niches in the industry. The Aberthaw Construction Co., organized in 1894 by a group of young engineers who had recently graduated from MIT, also concentrated on reinforced concrete construction. Stone & Webster was established by two young electrical engineers, Charles A. Stone and Edwin S. Webster. The company's work (fig. 1.10) included power plants and numerous factories.[35]

A Cleveland firm, The Austin Co., was responsible for industrial buildings that ranged from standardized designs offered in catalogs to innovative designs that incorporated welded steel frames (see figs. 7.3, 8.13, 10.1). For a time the firm's Curtiss Aeroplane and Motor Corp. Building (1918; Buffalo, New York) was the largest factory building in the world. The Austin Co. designed the Simonds Saw & Steel Co. plant (1929–1931; Fitchburg, Massachusetts; fig. 7.9), considered to be the first windowless structure with "controlled conditions." In order to survive the depression, The Austin Co. began to promote a distinctive modern appearance for its industrial buildings during the 1930s.[36] (See chapters 7 and 10 for more on The Austin Co.)

Industrial Architects

There is hardly a business of any importance that is not in large measure dependent for its success upon its buildings—that is to say, upon problems of design and plans in construction the solution of which is the one great object for which an architect receives his training.

ARCHITECT GEORGE C. NIMMONS, 1918

FIGURE 1.9 The Turner Construction Co. presented a series of "Turner Cities," such as this one, comprising the projects undertaken by the company from 1911 to 1915.

FIGURE 1.10 Stone & Webster included this view of the Manhattan Rubber Manufacturing Co. plant in Passaic, New Jersey, in an 1918 promotional pamphlet.

The involvement of architects in industrial building design throughout the nineteenth century was limited. Sometimes a commission from a manufacturer for a residence or public building led to a subsequent one for a factory building, as with Captain Edward Lamb's work for the Whitin Machine Shop (Whitinsville, Connecticut). After providing the firm's proprietor with plans for a house, Lamb was entrusted to oversee the construction of an addition to the works.[37]

Around 1900 several architects began to be recognized as specialists in the design of industrial buildings. The *American Architect* noted in 1911 that no longer than a decade earlier, less than 10 percent of manufacturing buildings were designed by architects. But the balance had shifted, and few industrial buildings were erected without the involvement of an architect. This change was attributed to evidence that the highest grades of goods were manufactured where the health and comfort of employees were given attention in architect-designed buildings.[38]

Some architects, including Solon S. Beman in Chicago, Willis Polk in California, and Cass Gilbert in New York City, added industrial building design to busy practices. Other firms, like Prack & Perrine, architects and engineers headquartered in Pittsburgh, and William Higginson in New York City, concentrated on industrial work. A 1929 list of industrial architects included the firms of George Nimmons, Carr & Wright, Alfred S. Alschuler, and S. Scott Joy in Chicago; Albert Kahn in Detroit; Monks & Johnson in Boston; and Lockwood, Greene & Co., Frank S. Parker, Buchman & Kahn, and Russell G. Cory in New York City.[39]

Large architectural firms that focused on industrial building design, like that of Albert Kahn Associates, had extensive office operations and a staff that included many specialists. The organization of Kahn's office has been likened to the assembly-line automobile operation of Henry Ford. A distinct division of labor existed among architectural designers, specification writers, and engineers who concentrated on structural and mechanical work. During the 1930s, the firm's technical division encompassed architectural, structural, and mechanical design; a structural department with specialists in reinforced concrete and steel-framed methods; and experts in the mechanical operations of sanitation, heating, and air-conditioning, as well as electrical and process engineering. Designing through teamwork, as historian Grant Hildebrand puts it, led to a "formulated approach" to design based on standardized plans, column spacings, and story height.[40]

Manufacturing works were familiar sights in the American environment, and descriptions of them emphasized their suitability for the task at hand. A large cast of specialists was involved in their design; engineers held the leading role. The next step in understanding the works is to examine their architectural components.

O nly three main types of industrial buildings comprised the works. The functional divisions of the works that gave structures their common names—the foundry and the machine shop, for example—were all housed either in one-story production sheds or in multistory industrial lofts. Production sheds served as machine, forge, and erecting shops as well as foundries. Lofts might house the entire works or be adapted for use as office buildings or pattern storehouses. The works powerhouse was the third major building type in the works. Testing departments, laboratories, storehouses and other functions were housed in buildings so diverse that generalizations about their architectural character are difficult to develop.

HOUSING MANUFACTURING PROCESSES

Before examining various types of industrial buildings, we must consider some common practices and general characteristics of manufacturing operations. First of all, manufacturing has not always taken place in buildings erected for that purpose. Indeed, the small operations characteristic of the early and mid–nineteenth century were housed in a variety of spaces. Blacksmith shops, barns, and sheds were converted to manufacturing use, as were older dwellings, commercial buildings, and even schools and churches. The manner in which a small residence could be converted to a workshop was demonstrated by a saddler's shop and warehouse offered for sale in 1804. A two-story frame dwelling accommodated the workbenches of saddle makers. The cellar was put to use as a trunk- and harness-making workshop, and materials were stored in the attic. An adjacent fireproof (presumably brick) structure was a storehouse for the operation.[1]

These buildings adapted for, and even those erected for, industrial use (other than textile factories) were often only slightly larger than gristmills, residences, and institutional buildings and were built of the same materials—wood, brick, or stone. The "start-up" quarters of successful industries sometimes became icons of industrial history, the setting for founding myths that demonstrated how far the firm had progressed from its humble origins. Beginning around the time of the nation's centennial in 1876, a firm's first building was often featured in a small vignette accompanying a general view of the works (see figs. 2.2 and 3.1). H. J. Heinz took this celebration of industrial heritage a step further when he relocated "The House Where We Began" (the former family residence) to an honored place at the North Side plant he erected in Pittsburgh during the 1890s.[2]

The importance of a good location and the adaptability of industrial lofts and production sheds to different kinds of manufacturing operations led to their use by several operations. For instance, the three-story brick loft acquired by the Mansfield Machine Works (Mansfield, Ohio) had been built to house a manufacturer of agricultural machines and was later converted for the production of railroad cars. The Walter A. Wood Harvester Co., manufacturers of agricultural machinery in Hoosick Falls, New York, occupied a succession of facilities. After setting up shop in 1853 in an old foundry, the firm purchased a cotton factory and then a foundry formerly used by a competitor. It did not erect its own works until 1870, when a second major fire forced the issue.[3]

Buildings designed and erected as factories had to reflect the fact that manufacturing involved both workers and machines, the presence of which placed different demands on structures. The factory operative was supervised, and therefore housed, by the trade or task he performed; hence, carpenters made wooden patterns for foundry operations in the pattern shop, and blacksmiths worked side by side in their own shop. The organization of the Bartlett, Robbins & Co. ironworks (Baltimore, Maryland) "into departments in a business-like way with a separate foreman and force for each room" characterized many operations. As the scale of manufacturing increased during the late nineteenth century, the layout of manufacturing space was determined in part by the largest area that could be effectively supervised by a single foreman.[4]

The use of machinery generated a different set of requirements. Sturdy framing was needed to resist the vibration and oscillation that accompanied the operation of equipment ranging from power looms to drop hammers. The positioning of machinery was affected by the location of millwork that distributed power to machinery. The size and shape of factory buildings was, in turn, determined by the limitations of mechanical power distribution systems.

The need for daylight in work areas occupied by men and machines was another dominant factor. In the long, relatively narrow manufacturing spaces of the nineteenth century, workbenches lined exterior walls or were placed perpendicular to them, next to windows (fig. 2.1). Workers sat or stood at these benches, usually facing windows, to perform the operations that required the best lighting—precision work and color matching. Farther from the source of light, operators worked at rows of belt-driven machines or assembled parts at workbenches. The center bay of a factory building (typically divided by two rows of columns into three bays), where the lighting conditions were poorest, was used for the storage of parts and products and as a transportation corridor.

During the mid–nineteenth century, two distinct conceptualizations for factory building design emerged. Architectural historian Mark Brown traces the presence of both types in the Bessemer steel industry. Alexander Holley developed a function-driven approach to steel mill layout and design that relied on a compact arrangement of cupolas, a hot-metal delivery system, casting pits, and crane service in buildings that supported and served as an extension of the machinery. In the Vulcan Iron Works (1876; St. Louis) and other projects, Holley illustrated how an industrial building performed as the *master machine* in a *special-purpose plant*. John Fritz, on the other hand,

FIGURE 2.1 The "action room" of the Mason & Hamlin Organ Co., manufacturer of reed organs in Cambridgeport, Massachusetts, suggests how the interior space of industrial loft buildings was utilized. Workbenches were placed near windows for the direct daylighting of close handwork. Interior columns defined a narrow center aisle that was used as a transportation and storage corridor.

used an autonomous approach to design and demonstrated the effectiveness of an undifferentiated shed. His large structures for the Bethlehem Iron Co. Works (1873; Bethlehem, Pennsylvania) provided room for both the orderly progression of production functions and the dispersal of heat. Fritz's model evolved into the *universal space plant*.[5]

The even larger production sheds soon erected to house steel mills, as well as the operations of other industries, actually represented a blend of the two approaches. The immense steel-framed mill buildings of the Pennsylvania Steel Company's Sparrow's Point Works (1887–1891; Frederick W. Wood, engineer; near Baltimore) demonstrated this new conceptualization of manufacturing space. The structures both supported the cranes necessary for the modernized, automated, and mobile casting process, as a master machine, and provided the space needed for a large-scale, decentralized operation.

As the changes in iron and steel mill design suggest, new types of machinery affected factory design. In many industries, the most common chain of events seems to have been that as new machinery or continuous process operations were adopted, they were initially accommodated in existing facilities. Perhaps major investment in new equipment limited the manufacturer's ability to immediately alter existing buildings or initiate new construction. At some critical point, however, it became necessary to redesign and expand facilities. Historian Judith McGaw relates how architectural change followed technical advances in the American paper industry. As paper mills were mechanized, mill owners erected larger buildings with plans that provided more ground-story space to house machinery. An increased concern for loss due to fire led to the use of masonry rather than wood in building construction and the adoption of fire detection and suppression measures. In order to realize the economies in production made possible by new equipment, gaslight and steam heating systems were installed so that the machines could be used for longer periods.[6]

The mechanization of the match industry suggests how advances in production methods were accompanied by periodic updating of the manufacturing works: By regularly modernizing its works, O. C. Barber transformed his family's firm into a corporate giant, the Diamond Match Co. During the 1860s, the production of stick matches was a partially automated process that involved both machine- and handwork. Barber made use of twenty-five machines to cut splints, make paper boxes, and process matches in an operation that was housed in the converted buildings of a wool carding plant. In the early 1870s Barber purchased a splint-making machine for the unheard-of amount of $32,000, converted from water to steam power, and erected a "modern" works in East Akron, Ohio. In 1877 an improved continuous process machine was installed in the works; two years later Barber was the first manufacturer in Akron to equip his factory with electric lights and institute a night shift. Continuous, automatic match-making machines were installed in existing facilities in Akron (where the workforce then was reduced by fifty) and Wilmington, Delaware, during the early 1880s. By the early 1890s, the consolidated Diamond Match Co. could no longer afford to operate the Akron plant or its machinery, even though it had been the model facility of the firm only ten years earlier. A standardized plan for a "technologically superior plant" was used for two new facilities: one in Oswego, New York, and one in Barberton, Ohio (that replaced the Akron plant). These cycles of technological advancement and construction of new works were sustained by consolidation within the industry and corporate investment.[7]

THE INDUSTRIAL LOFT

Mill. A building in which any mechanical trade or manufacture is carried on, more especially one with a number of employees and a good deal of machinery; in this sense, frequently a very large building, with a vast number of windows, so arranged as to throw daylight over all parts of each story, with all uniformity practicable.

A DICTIONARY OF ARCHITECTURE AND BUILDING, 1902

Mill has become an overused and rather indefinite term in industrial architecture. During the decades flanking the turn of the nineteenth century, mill served as a generic term for various types of operations and their buildings. Extrapolated from the grinding machinery it housed, the term was combined with prefixes that indicated the end product of a grinding process (flour mill, spice mill) or the material worked (steel mill), as well as products (textile mill, paper mill) or even the source of power (steam mill).[8]

The term also had a strong association with textile manufacturing. The millwright was a technician responsible for assembling and operating machinery and the water wheels and shafting used to drive it. The mill engineer expanded and professionalized this role. *Mill* also acquired meanings associated with building types and construction methods in the industry. During the course of the nineteenth century the image of a mill as a multistory building erected to house textile manufacturing operations replaced that of the mill as a small structure at the side of a stream in which flour was processed. The textile mill was a building type carefully adapted to the machinery it housed. The slow-burning wood-framed construction advocated by fire insurance companies for textile mills became known as "mill construction" (described in chapter 5).

Considered in the context of industrial architecture, however, the textile mill was a specialized multistory industrial building. A similar type of structure known as the "store and loft" was developed to serve urban commercial, storage, and manufacturing uses. The waterfront blocks of American port cities were built up with four- or five-story brick store and loft buildings during the mid–nineteenth century. These structures were modeled after the tall, narrow warehouse buildings that dominated European port waterfronts. They spanned the widths of standard 20- or 25-foot-wide lots and covered most of their depth. Store and loft buildings often housed a variety

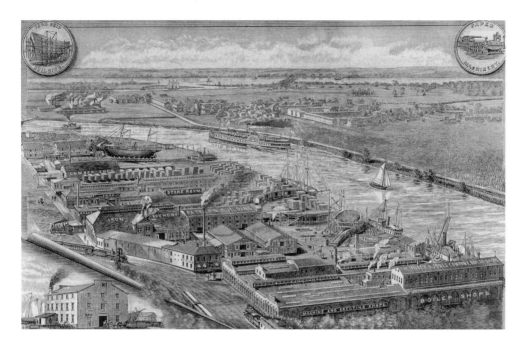

FIGURE 2.2 The single loft building that initially comprised the operation of Pusey & Jones in 1849 was featured in a later view of the works of the shipbuilding firm in Wilmington, Delaware. The versatile loft was adapted to house the joiner shop, mold loft, and pattern building in this works.

of activities: The ground story might be used as a tavern and the lofts rented to various storage and workshop operations. Perhaps a ship chandlery or trading company would occupy the entire building. At the street level, large windows and door openings were framed by granite piers and beams; later the ground stories had iron-framed storefronts.[9]

The term loft came into use during this same time to describe crudely finished, unpartitioned, and often unheated upper-story spaces devoted to such work as canvas stitching in a sail loft. The term *loft* was revived during the late nineteenth century to refer to multistory manufacturing buildings erected in urban areas to house several commercial or industrial tenants. The term *industrial loft*, rather than *mill*, best denotes a general building type, the multistory industrial building (fig. 2.2). Within this category, both the urban store and loft and the textile mill became standards that were replicated widely.[10] (Chapter 5 describes the differences in the construction of these types of structures.)

The Industrial Loft Building Program

The buildings cover a square in the heart of the business portion of Cincinnati, have a frontage of 360 feet, a depth of 100 feet, [are] all of brick [and] four stories high, and give employment to nearly 400 workmen, and 150 in the foundry near by.

THE EGAN COMPANY, 1890

The industrial loft was developed as a building that provided two or more stories of lofts, in which vertical circulation and service areas were grouped so as to intrude into the work space as little as possible. Even as the height, size, and methods of construction of industrial lofts changed, the building program remained little altered (fig. 2.3).

Industrial lofts were built in a variety of materials, though during much of the nineteenth century they were most often structures with an interior wood frame and stone or brick exterior walls. They might also be wood-framed and sheathed with wood siding or shingles. Later, iron- and steel-framed industrial lofts were enclosed with masonry walls, though probably reinforced concrete construction was more often utilized for this type of factory building (fig. 2.4). (Materials of construction are more fully discussed in chapter 6.)

Practical matters of manufacturing and commerce were much in evidence in the detailing of the exteriors of industrial loft buildings. A regular pattern of windows predominated though it could change at the top story, where the total area of window openings was often increased and skylights or roof monitors could provide additional lighting and ventilation. Use-related exterior features included raised loading platforms (sometimes sheltered with awnings), loading bays with vehicular access doors on the street, and hoistways. Fire escapes and towers housing stairs, power transmission belts, and utilities sometimes projected from facades to keep floor areas unobstructed and limit the spread of fire. From flat roofs rose water tanks, perhaps enclosed in towers, and elevator bulkheads.

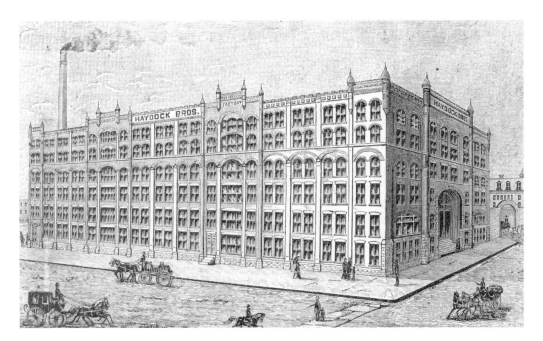

FIGURE 2.3 A carriage factory erected in 1888 by the Haydock Brothers in St. Louis was an extensive six-story industrial loft building. The proprietors spared no expense in having its street facades detailed in the American round-arched style.

FIGURE 2.4 During the 1930s, loft buildings from two eras were utilized at the White Dental Works on Staten Island. Interior lighting conditions were the major difference between the brick structure (on the left) and the later reinforced concrete one.

Since industrial lofts were especially suited to house light manufacturing and finishing operations, the need for good lighting for these types of work influenced their dimensions. When this demand was particularly important, lofts were 30 to 40 feet in width. If a loft's width was pushed to 60 feet, it needed to have relatively high ceilings of 13 to 14 feet. A ceiling height of 15 or 16 feet was recommended for spaces where many employees worked and exceptionally good light was needed; that height also permitted the insertion of a mezzanine floor. Higher ceilings and taller windows made wider structures feasible, but they also increased construction costs. A loft building's length was determined by the size of the operation, the limitations of mechanical power distribution, and the extent of the area that could be effectively supervised. By the mid–nineteenth century, industrial lofts several hundred feet in length were in use, and lofts gradually became even longer as the efficiency of millwork increased. After electric drive was adopted, loft buildings comprised one or more 300-foot-long units.[11]

Materials handling systems were critical to the efficiency of operations housed in industrial lofts. In fact, conveyors and chutes, along with hoists and elevators, helped keep lofts viable alternatives to one-story buildings. Mechanical conveyors could be inserted and rearranged relatively easily in wood-floored structures; a disadvantage of reinforced concrete floors proved to be the difficulty of creating openings for materials handling equipment and millwork shafting. The first elevators in industrial loft buildings were mechanized platform hoists operated by steam engines and millwork (fig. 2.5). Powered platform elevators provided equal access to all levels of a loft

FIGURE 2.5
Platform hoists,
or elevators, made
the upper floors
of industrial loft
buildings suitable
for a variety of
functions. Mill-
work brought
power from the
steam engine to
the hoisting gear.

building and thereby maximized the potential usefulness of upper floors. The size and capacity of elevators operated by hydraulic power and electricity increased, and eventually they accommodated railroad cars and motor trucks. The development of the elevator-served industrial loft culminated in combination freight terminal, warehouse, and manufacturing structures in which elevators functioned as "vertical streets" to enable tenants to receive and ship by rail or truck from each floor.[12]

During the early twentieth century, industrial engineers emphasized the proper design and construction of a general type of loft building (a universal space plant), one planned to meet general requirements rather than to address the particular needs of any one business. Consulting engineer Hugh Wharton recommended that industrial lofts be erected 50 to 60 feet wide, with their interior columns spaced so as to define a narrow center bay that could be used strictly as a passageway. If they were limited to four stories, these lofts did not require passenger elevators and could be erected of mill construction or reinforced concrete at a reasonable cost. Industrial lofts erected in cities were standardized to provide commercial and industrial space at an economical cost. Some urban lofts were designed for specific industries, like printing, where heavy floor loads and vibration made extreme demands on the structure and where maximum daylighting was needed. Because tenants preferred to have their operation on a single level, industrial lofts became much larger during the early twentieth century. Steel-framed and reinforced concrete were used to construct lofts with as many as ten stories, and a footprint of 100 feet by 100 or 200 feet, and eventually to structures that occupied entire city blocks.[13]

Industrial Lofts as the Works

During the early and mid–nineteenth century, a manufacturing works was often housed in a single loft building of modest scale, even if the product was a large one. The Harlan & Hollingsworth Co., for example, began manufacturing railroad cars in Wilmington, Delaware, during the 1830s in rented quarters: a three-story brick building (45 feet by 65 feet) and an adjoining shed (fig. 2.6). Iron was forged into car trucks in the basement of the structure, while the wood superstructures of the cars were built on upper floors. Cars were finished in a small space on the second floor and then lowered by tackle through large trap doors in the floor; on the first story they received running gear and were painted. This facility sufficed until 1841, when a two-story, 60-foot by 100-foot brick loft was erected. In the new building, a small area on the second floor was "fenced off" for the office, and the upholstery and trimming shops were also partitioned from the main work space. The workbenches of carpenters stood under the windows of the remainder of the second floor, where cars were constructed. As before, the cars were lowered through hoistways to the finishing department, which shared the ground floor with a machine shop. A blacksmith shop, a boiler shop, and a new office were soon added to the works.[14]

Industrial lofts were erected to house large machine shops during the first half of the nineteenth century; they easily accommodated relatively small, light machines, facilitated the efficient mechanical transfer of power through millwork, and provided good lighting. When the shop occupied more than one story, the machinery was separated by size and by weight, and hence by function. Standard practice was to use the ground floor for the heavy machinery—planers, drills, bolt- and gear-cutters—and for the manipulation of large and heavy materials and parts with cranes. Lighter machines for milling, cutting, and grinding, and often the brass-working equipment as well, were located in the upper stories. It was recommended that every machine of any size have its own lifting tackle, perhaps a pair of pulley blocks, so that work would not be delayed by a wait for materials handling equipment.[15]

There was no set way to situate manufacturing operations in industrial loft buildings, though there were some common practices. At a wheelwright and coach-making shop in Chester County, Pennsylvania (1847), a wood shop was located in the basement, and painting, drying, trimming, and harness rooms were situated on the second story, where lighting was good. The blacksmith shop was usually located in the basement when a manufacturing operation was housed in a loft structure. A model plan for a small carriage shop suggested that a forge be placed in each corner of the basement blacksmith shop. The larger blacksmith shop of Brewster & Co., carriage makers (New York City), was located in the basement of a five-story loft; the flues of the thirty forges extended to the roofline inside the building's brick piers. During the early 1870s, the works of Otis Brothers & Co., manufacturers of hoisting machinery and elevators (Yonkers, New York),

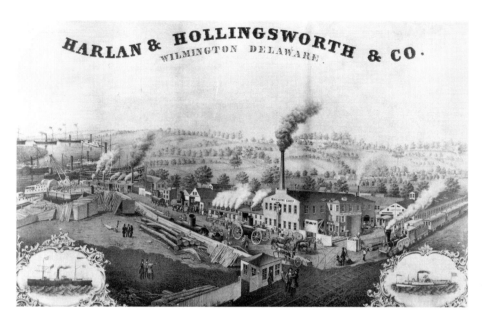

HARLAN & HOLLINGSWORTH & CO.
WILMINGTON DELAWARE

FIGURE 2.6 The building erected in 1841 to house the entire railroad car manufacturing operation of Harlan & Hollingsworth Co. in Wilmington, Delaware, is labeled "machine shop" in this c. 1860 view. Additions made to the works during its first twenty years of operation included a blacksmith shop (with a row of chimneys) and a joined boiler shop and planing mill near the "car shop."

was a three-story, 100-foot-square brick loft. The boiler, steam engine, and blacksmith shop were in the basement. As was the case in many operations, the heaviest work was done on the first floor, which was filled with planers, drills, and lathes. The upper floors were used for smaller and lighter work, and patterns were stored on the third story. Large operations required a series of loft buildings that were placed in various configurations, as described in chapter 3.[16]

Office and Administration Buildings

The offices are in the corner building. . . . This is of red brick; the roof is covered with red Ohio tile, with cresting of the same material. . . . There is a large fire-proof vault, lavatory, and private office. The second story has a large drafting room, with north and east light.

THE DEAN BROTHERS STEAM PUMP WORKS, 1882

The office of the works was housed in either a freestanding structure or a portion of a main loft building. During the mid–nineteenth century, the works office was generally a quite small two-story structure of masonry or wood construction. General offices were accommodated on the ground story of these buildings. The upper level, well lighted and isolated from the dust and vibration of the machine and forge shops, was invariably the firm's

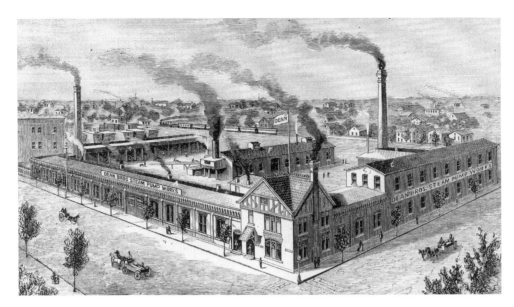

FIGURE 2.7 The two-story office of the Dean Bros. Steam Pump Works in Indianapolis anchored the corner of the street fronts of the works.

drafting room. The office was placed in a central location or near the main gate to facilitate supervision of the works and the yard. Sometimes the office had a slightly remote location, perhaps across the street, so that clerical and design work and valuable records could be separated from noise and the threat of fire. (Offices are labeled in views of the works in figs. 2.6 and 3.9; see also figs. 2.7, 3.7, 3.13, and 6.7.)

The works office was more likely to have *architectural effect* and to be designed by an architect than the other buildings in the works; it often had the quality of a centerpiece. Occasionally the office was the owner's former dwelling, now incorporated into an expanded works. The office of the Wason Car Manufacturing Co., railway car builders (1872–1873; George C. Fisk, proprietor and designer; Springfield, Massachusetts; fig. 2.8), a two-story structure with a porch across the facade, seems likely to have served as both the industrialist's home and his office.[17]

The appearance of the office of the Draper Co. (1860; Hopedale, Massachusetts) suggested that it was designed by an architect. The pressed brick structure featured a projecting portico and a hipped roof and was described as being of the Venetian style (this term was used for what is now known as the "American round-arched style"; see chapter 10). The brick and sandstone office building of the Burden Iron Company (1881; Troy, New York), in the unusual form of a one-story Greek cross, also had considerable architectural effect. Like other office buildings, though, it had an attic drafting room lighted by large skylights and a cupola at the peak of the roof.[18]

Around the turn of the century, the works office became a larger administration building that provided more space for business and executive offices and for the engineers who designed products and oversaw their

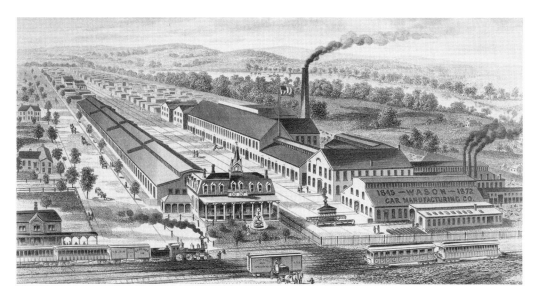

FIGURE 2.8 The office building of the Wason Car Manufacturing Co., a railroad car building works in Springfield, Massachusetts, may have also been the owner's residence. Behind the office stood the paint shop; across the yard structures were placed in accordance with the progression of work.

production. Administration buildings might be placed so as to shield from the public's view the production sheds behind it; they continued to have an architectural character that was more high-style and ornamental than that of the rest of the works.

Pattern Storehouses

An isolated brick building with iron doors constitutes the repository of the patterns, the aggregate value of which, it need hardly be stated, will be very great.

THE WILCOX, TREADWAY & CO. WORKS, 1880

Wood and metal patterns were used in metal casting and other molding operations (such as clay wares) and also served as models for various types of products. Sets of master templates either supplemented or substituted for shop drawings as the design record. The fabrication and storage of these materials were important components of the works, and specialized buildings were erected for their safe-keeping. The pattern department of the E. & T. Fairbanks Scale Co. (St. Johnsbury, Vermont) illustrates the importance of this function. During the 1880s it was a two-story building crowded with models for castings and patterns of the previous forty years of work. Large-scale patterns were kept on the lower story. An upper level was also filled with patterns, on shelves and in trunks, for the hundreds of models the firm produced.[19] (Pattern storage buildings are labeled in the views of the works, figs. 1.5 and 2.2.)

Descriptions of pattern storehouses often emphasized their fireproof quality and their ability to safeguard their contents. The fireproof "pattern safe" of the Excelsior Stove Works (c. 1850; St. Louis) was a detached, three-story brick structure with a door and roof of heavy iron and no windows; light was admitted through sliding iron shutters in the roof. During the 1880s, a large, fireproof pattern storehouse for the Niles Tool Works (Hamilton, Ohio) was erected across the street on a site that was isolated from the rest of the works. It was a production shed with no windows in its side walls and flush skylights in the roof; fire walls divided it into three compartments. A two-story pattern building erected for the B. F. Sturtevant Co.'s works (1903; Hyde Park, Massachusetts) also was divided in half by fire walls that enclosed stairs and elevators. One portion of the structure was devoted to the flask- and pattern-making operations. The other half, used for pattern storage, was fitted with intermediate, mezzanine-like floors filled with shelving. The first story, which had a concrete floor and was served by industrial rail, accommodated the heaviest cast-iron patterns.[20]

THE PRODUCTION SHED

Lofty multi-storied buildings are impressive, but manufacturers should consider the advantages of getting down to earth.

IRON TRADE REVIEW, 1915

The term *mill*, so strongly associated with textile mills, historically referred to another type of building as well. During the last decades of the nineteenth century, some one-story structures became known as "iron mill buildings" or "steel mill buildings." The "mill" portion of these names seems to have been derived from the similar buildings that traditionally had housed iron rolling mills. But as used around the turn of the century, the terms referred to materials of construction. A distinctive form became associated with the building type because frames of iron and steel permitted large, unobstructed spaces and the use of electric-powered cranes.[21]

One-story industrial buildings have also often been called shops. The term shop had traditionally described a facility in which wares were both made and displayed for sale. In the United States, *shop* and *workshop* remain associated with industrial, rather than sales-oriented, facilities (as the term often implies in Great Britain), although both activities took place in independent blacksmith shops. The shops of an industrial works, like machine shops, were functional divisions of the manufacturing process that might be housed in a freestanding structure or in a portion of a larger building.

The confusion inherent in using the terms *mill building*, with various modifiers, or *shop* for one-story structures prompts the adoption of the term *production shed*, as architectural historian Reyner Banham suggests.[22] The shed is perhaps the simplest architectural form, but the production shed was engineered for manufacturing purposes through the careful design of its framing, walls, and roof (fig. 2.9). One-story production sheds were rectangular, often of considerable width (if roof lighting was used), and of any length demanded by the operation, allowed by effective supervision, and permitted by the site. They were engineered to span wide bays and enclose spaces of considerable height, and they often possessed the strength and stability to support overhead traveling cranes. Just as the elevator was the essential materials handling method in industrial lofts, cranes were indispensable components of production sheds.

Production sheds were built of various materials, though structures with an interior frame of wood, iron, or steel and exterior walls of brick were the most common. In these structures, the strength and stability of the load-bearing walls were evident in pilaster wall construction and relatively small window openings. After 1880, exterior walls were often engineered curtain walls and sheathed with a variety of materials (as described in detail in chapter 7). Roofs, usually incorporated means for lighting and ventilation, often had a distinctive—even sculptural—form that revealed the use of the structure (see figs. 3.6 and 3.9).

Initially, the standard configuration of a production shed was a central crane-served bay flanked by lower *lean-tos* that might have mezzanine galleries. The sheds were endlessly varied, and it was not unusual for them to have galleries on one side only. During the last decades of the nineteenth

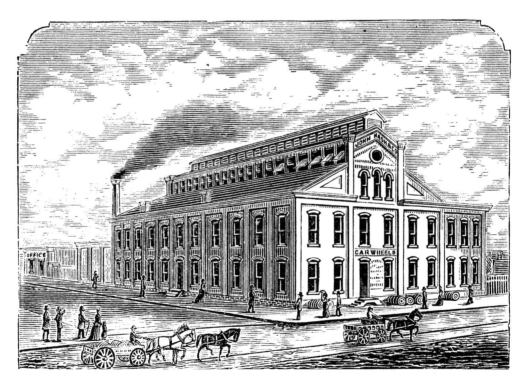

FIGURE 2.9 The structure that housed much of the railroad car wheel foundry of John Nash & Co. in Cincinnati during the mid-1870s was a brick production shed. A double roof monitor lighted and ventilated the interior.

century, the production shed often became a series of bays of various dimensions, some served by cranes. (See chapter 4 for a review of how cranes and electric drive transformed the production shed.)

Foundries

We can only say that the foundry building is handsomely and substantially built, well-lighted, and is fire-proof, and modern in every respect.

THE FRITZ FOUNDRY AND MACHINE WORKS, 1880

The foundry was one of the most common components of manufacturing works of many kinds and was built in a wide range of sizes (fig. 2.10). Though it had the reputation of being dark, oppressive with heat and dust, and poorly ventilated, the production shed housing the foundry was sometimes the only building in a works to have turrets or a roof monitor for improved lighting and ventilation. The chimneys that stood near metal-heating cupolas were signature features of foundries.[23] (Foundries are labeled in the views of the works, figs. 1.4, 1.5, 2.2, and 3.9; see also fig. 7.6.)

The mid-nineteenth-century foundry was a freestanding structure that was situated as far as possible from other buildings in the works because of the heat and smoke it generated. Foundries needed yard room close at hand for the storage of raw materials, flasks, and castings. The works foundry housed a series of activities for making molds, heating iron, pouring molten iron, and processing castings. It was engineered to provide an enclosed casting floor, to facilitate the transport of the molten iron to the molds and of the castings out of the structure, and to exhaust the heat and smoke generated by the casting process through ventilating roofs.

Casting iron began with the preparation of patterns and flasks. Wood patterns were used to make initial castings in metal; after being cleaned and filed to the exact shape desired, these metal castings became working patterns. Sand took the impression of these patterns in flasks, as the containers that received the molten metal were called. Much of the manual work in the foundry was the preparation of flasks and cores (shapes in the form of desired voids that were made of sand and a binder and baked in ovens to give them sufficient strength). This work took place at the perimeter of the main casting floor or nearby in side wings. A portion of the floor was often a casting pit with a deep base of sand or loam (a mixture of sand and clay), so that large molds could be buried below floor level in casting pits.

The actual molding, or casting, took place once during a work shift, often during the midafternoon. While flasks were prepared, the heating, or charging, of the cupola (the furnace used for the heating of pig and scrap iron) was under way. The casting proper was done by workers who carried ladles of molten metal to the flasks. Some operations used ladles that were moved by cranes to fill large castings alongside smaller, hand-carried ones. The

FIGURE 2.10 The foundry of the Niles Tool Works in Hamilton, Ohio, was divided into four molding floors that were equipped with various types of cranes and served by industrial rail. The foundry was constructed with a combination of timber framing, trussed roofs, and brick walls with large arched openings.

foundry crane that commanded the casting floor was sometimes the only crane in the works. Large rotating wood jib cranes gave way to overhead traveling cranes during the late nineteenth century. The foundry also housed several types of finishing operations. Separate areas, often in side wings, were used for the cleaning, or fettling, of castings, and large foundries also had pickling vats and annealing ovens. Trussed roofs often provided the clear floor space required in a foundry. Walls were built to withstand the forces transmitted to them from the action of cranes. Roof monitors, as well as numerous windows and the tall height of the casting floor, helped to disperse heat and smoke upward, away from the work area. Industrial rail often extended through the foundry to transport equipment and materials and to remove castings to the machine shop.[24]

Foundries as large as 100 feet in width and length were common by the mid–nineteenth century, though many were much smaller. For example, the foundry of the Covington Locomotive Works (c. 1853; Cincinnati) was a massive stone structure, 100 feet square, with a "fireproof roof"; it was described as "airy" and well-lighted. The foundry used by the Metropolitan Iron Works of Julius Johnson & Co. (New York City) during the 1870s was a square building, 90 feet on each side, with hoists and cranes for handling pieces that weighed up to 20 tons.[25]

Between 1880 and 1900 the foundry was transformed into a better-lighted structure with a central craneway. As will be recounted in chapter 7, foundries were among the first industrial buildings to be erected with exterior walls filled with window sash. Cupolas were positioned just outside the building (with tapping spouts extending through the wall) to free a central crane-served bay to serve as the molding and casting floor. At the end of the nineteenth century, foundries increasingly contained mechanized systems for charging the cupola and transporting sand, castings, and molds. Many foundries, though, combined traditional, crane-assisted casting with integrated molding, pouring, and cooling operations.[26]

During the early twentieth century, manufacturers experimented with placing foundries on the top floors of loft structures. This location, suggested by a top-down flow of production, also kept the heat and gases produced in casting away from other operations. The works of the Lunkenheimer Co. (c. 1910; Cincinnati) consisted of a five-story reinforced concrete loft building with the foundry on the top floor under a sawtooth roof. When the Highland Park works of the Ford Motor Co. was expanded in 1914, foundries were placed on the top floor of six-story loft buildings.[27]

Blacksmith or Forge Shops

The blacksmith-shop of the car department is a model structure of the kind. . . . Eight stacks with four fires each are located in a line on each side of the building, at such a distance from the side-walls and from each other as to afford ample space for the movement of workmen and handling of material, as well as for a wide central passage-way.

THE NEW YORK CENTRAL AND HUDSON RIVER
RAILROAD CAR SHOPS, 1872

Blacksmith, or forge, shops, where iron was heated in a forge and beaten, or hammered, into desired shapes, were also found in many manufacturing works. The forge shop was typically a production shed with a roof monitor for light and ventilation. It was distinguished from other shop buildings by the number of small chimneys (often of sheet metal) that rose through the roof near the eaves and marked the location of the forges within. Sometimes a brick chimney, which drew a draft on the forges through an underground manifold, stood beside the structure. The forge shop was located close to the erecting shop, because of the related nature of the work, or near the foundry. (Blacksmith shops, with rows of chimneys near the eaves, are visible in figs. 1.4, 2.6, and 3.9.)

Blacksmith shops varied in size and in the arrangement of forges and their flues during the mid–nineteenth century. The shop of the Rock Island Arsenal (1871–1873; Thomas Rodman, Daniel W. Flagler, engineers; Rock Island, Illinois), was considered a particularly advanced design (figs. 2.11 and 2.12). In addition to a monitor roof, it had an experimental single chimney stack fed by underground flues, rather than a series of chimneys piercing the roof. A row of forges stood in one half of the structure. Belt-driven machinery was positioned near the windows on the other side. The contemporary blacksmith shop of the Poole & Hunt works (Baltimore) was a structure 53 feet wide and 153 feet long. It housed twenty-two forges and a furnace for heating large plates. The forging department in the main building of the Paterson Iron Co. (Paterson, New Jersey) during the early 1870s suggests how these shops became more like machine shops. Forging was undertaken with vertical steam-powered hammers; each one was operated by a separate engine and served by a crane that moved large pieces between the hammers and furnaces, where pieces were heated. Industrial rail extended the length of the forge shop and connected it with the steel and blacksmith shops.[28]

The twentieth-century forge shop reflected changes in building design seen in other types of production sheds. Engineers recommended that the forge shop have a clear height under roof trusses of at least 14 feet and that the side walls have 6-foot-tall bands of continuous window sash. By that time, the rows of small forge stacks had mostly been replaced by chimneys that could serve several forges, especially if they were down-draft units equipped with exhaust fans.[29]

FIGURE 2.11 A production shed with walls of local limestone at the Rock Island Arsenal in Rock Island, Illinois, housed a blacksmith shop. A row of windows was inserted into the frieze to provide additional light for the shop floor, which was also lighted and ventilated by roof monitors. (See fig. 2.12 for an interior view.)

FIGURE 2.12 A 1904 view of the blacksmith shop of the Rock Island Arsenal, pictured in fig. 2.11, indicates how forges and machinery might be arranged in such shops. A jib crane, at the far end of the structure, and the hand trucks, in the foreground, comprised the materials handling system.

Machine Shops

This [machine shop] is of brick, two stories high, well lighted, and provided with every improved appliance for handling work rapidly and cheaply.

THE METROPOLITAN IRON WORKS, 1881

In the works, the machine shop could be a portion of a loft structure, an entire loft, or a one-story production shed (fig. 2.13). When possible, it was a separate building or a space partitioned off from other functions, to limit the presence of dust. Machine shops were engineered primarily for strength and resistance to vibration. They provided floor space for machinery and supported millwork that transferred power to this equipment. When the shop housed small machines, interior columns did not hinder the arrangement of the equipment. On the other hand, large machines required bay configurations tailored to their dimensions or space covered by trussed roofs and therefore unobstructed by columns. The machine shop was often located near the works engine and boiler house for the efficient transfer of power and was also close to the erecting and forge shops. (Machine shops are labeled in figs. 1.4, 1.5, 2.2, and 3.9.)

In heavy manufacturing, or when the machinery itself was large and heavy enough, the machine shop was a one-story structure rather than a

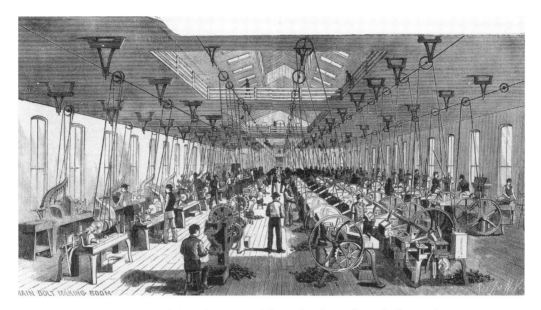

FIGURE 2.13 The main bolt-making room of the works of Russell, Burdsall & Ward in Port Chester, New York, was a machine shop powered by millwork. A trussed roof eliminated columns that would have interfered with the tight arrangement of machinery on the second story of the main works building. A roof monitor and sky-lights admitted daylight to the shop.

FIGURE 2.14 One of the machine shops erected at the Midvale Steel Co. works, Ordnance Machine Shop No. 4 (c. 1905; Philadelphia), was characteristic of shops equipped with electric drive and electric-powered overhead crane service. Numerous windows and skylights and a roof monitor helped to bring daylight to the shop floor.

loft building. By the mid-1850s the Providence Forge and Nut Co. had erected a production shed to house its machines and huge presses. The machine shop erected by the S. W. Putnam Machine Co. (1866; Fitchburg, Massachusetts) had an open plan and interrelated machine and assembly shop spaces. The quite large one-story brick structure had a central spine (48 feet wide and 625 feet long) with a center row of iron columns that supported the main millwork shaft. Extending from this long, unpartitioned machine shop space were seven wings, each of which housed a setting-up department that corresponded to the adjacent section of the machine shop. Small offices for the superintendents of the various departments projected as wings on the opposite side of the central machine shop.[30]

The machine shop and erecting shop were often combined after electric drive was introduced. The condition that had kept them separate—the need to position machines to be served by millwork—was no longer a governing factor. Electric drive also permitted the use of wider machine shops, since roof lighting was more effective when there was no millwork obstructing the overhead area (fig. 2.14).

Erecting Shops

The next section is the main erecting shop. It is 50 feet wide and 32 feet high under the trusses. It is fitted with pits, and foundations suitable for the erection of heavy machinery. Two overhead power traveling cranes, each of 25 tons capacity, span this section, thus equipping it for the handling of the heaviest work. It is also traversed its entire length by a railroad track, which enables us to load heavy machines on cars direct by means of the traveling cranes.

THE NILES TOOL WORKS, 1891

Erecting shops for the final assembly of goods varied according to the size and type of items being manufactured. In general, benches near windows were used for the assembly of small items. Before the use of actual interchangeable parts, this work involved *fitting up*, which workers made pieces fit together. During the mid–nineteenth century, even large products, like agricultural implements and carriages, were erected on the upper floors of loft buildings; this type of work was eventually moved to one-story production sheds.

Two erecting shops (figs. 2.15 and 2.16) in the works of the Holly Manufacturing Co. (established 1859; Lockport, New York) demonstrate how the space required for machine assembly was determined not only by the size and weight of the products but also by traveling cranes. In the older erecting shop, the top story of a loft building, machinery located along one side of the space was served by hoists attached to the lower chords of roof trusses. Pumping engines were erected on the other side, and a single jib crane commanded one end of the shop. Soon after the Holly Co. began producing larger equipment, an erecting shop with overhead crane service was built.

The new shop was a standard wood-framed production shed. Its central bay, commanded by two traveling cranes, was flanked by galleries where small machines were operated by millwork. The adoption of (hand- or steam-powered) traveling cranes went hand in hand with such long, relatively narrow spaces, which were unobstructed by columns and millwork and high enough to permit large objects to be lifted above others of the same scale.[31]

In heavy industry, erecting shops were relatively large spaces kept as free as possible of columns and millwork. They were framed to support a trussed roof and cranes. The height needed for crane operation and the assembly of large items might be equal to a two- or three-story space; however, tiers of windows that replicated the fenestration of a loft structure meant that the height of the open space within was not always evident from the exterior. Jib and overhead traveling cranes lifted pieces into position, supported them as they were attached, and moved completed items out of the shop. Grates formed of I-beams were placed across pits in the floor so that the undersides of large and heavy items were accessible during assembly. Machinery and equipment that facilitated the erecting process was positioned at the perimeter of the space or in side bays or galleries. The erecting shop of an architectural iron manufacturing works, for example, was designed so that a 15-foot-wide gallery, used for bench and vice work, was suspended from the roof trusses on all sides of the space.[32]

The boiler shop was an erecting shop dedicated to the riveting of large steam boilers (fig. 2.17; see also figs. 1.5 and 2.2): "Right merry is the music produced [there], a little loud perhaps, and a continual repetition of the same

FIGURE 2.15 The old erecting shop of the Holly Manufacturing Co. in Lockport, New York, where water pumping engines were assembled, was characteristic of mid–nineteenth century facilities. A jib crane and hoists served a line of machinery positioned under a single line of shafting.

FIGURE 2.16   An erecting shop with a central bay served by traveling cranes was
added to the Holly Manufacturing Co. works during the mid-1880s for the assembly
of larger pumping equipment.

FIGURE 2.17   In 1875 the boiler shop of Lane & Bodley in Cincinnati was a large,
unobstructed space with steam-powered hammers and other equipment set against
one wall. The forge for heating rivets is at the right foreground.

strain."[33] Boiler shops required unobstructed space and large doorways onto the yard through which heavy, bulky boilers could be moved. They were located so that power could be used to drive punches, shears, and rolling equipment.

THE WORKS POWERHOUSE

The modern steam engine has arrived . . . at a comparative perfection of design which has a beauty of its own to the educated eye, and the house built to receive it should be designed and constructed in the same spirit.

CASSIER'S MAGAZINE, 1908

The freestanding engine house, or powerhouse, later known as the "industrial power plant," was a common feature in the works. Even in urban areas where central station power was available, manufacturers often chose to operate their own electric power plants, just as they had relied on their own steam engines. In fact, works power plants produced nearly half of the nation's electric power before World War I. As the steam turbines that ran the generators wore out, many manufacturing companies began to purchase power from a central station rather than replace their equipment. Nevertheless, many industrial power plants remained in use throughout the 1930s.[34]

A major factor in locating and designing structures that housed steam engines to power the works was the threat of steam boiler explosions. For this reason, boilers and engines were housed in freestanding structures that, whenever possible, were separated from other buildings. As engineer Charles Wilcox explained in 1860, "Experience has shown that in explosions the large buildings suffer comparatively little if the boilers are somewhat removed from them."[35] Though it made sense to isolate volatile steam boilers, an explosion nearly always caused the deaths of workers in the vicinity and damage to nearby buildings. The prevention of boiler explosions through careful maintenance and inspection programs became the engineering solution to the problem. To this end, boiler houses and engine rooms had large windows to provide good natural lighting that enabled operators to keep the equipment clean and to constantly inspect it. This isolation of the structure, separation of boilers and engines, and fenestration carried over into the design of electric power plants.

Powerhouses

The requirements and configuration of steam engine houses, or powerhouses, changed little over the years. They were constructed of noncombustible materials, usually stone or brick, and later reinforced concrete. Powerhouses were two-part facilities with separate rooms for boilers and

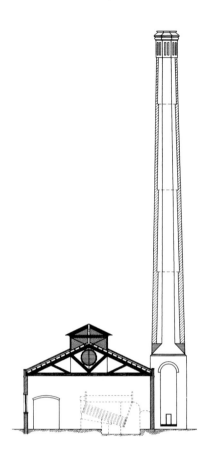

FIGURE 2.18 The firm Babcock & Wilcox, manufacturers of boilers, provided this plan for a boiler house and chimney to the W. C. Hamilton & Sons paper mills in Philadelphia.

engines, and perhaps a third area for coal storage. This division of space kept the coal dust produced by the stoking of boiler fires away from the machinery and gauges in the engine room. Each area was spanned with trussed roofs to eliminate interior columns. The size of the structure was governed by the number of boilers and engines it was to house and the space needed for stoking the boilers, maintaining the equipment, and replacing boiler tubes.

A boiler house erected for the W. C. Hamilton & Sons paper mills (c. 1882; plans provided by Babcock & Wilcox; Philadelphia) was characteristic of late-nineteenth-century structures (fig. 2.18). The one-story building, 111 feet long and 50 feet wide, had a monitor roof. Eight boilers installed in four batteries were set in a single row close to one wall; at their rear, a flue connected them to the chimney that stood adjacent to the building.[36]

Similar steam-electric power plants, which housed steam boilers and electric generators, were engineered for efficiency in operation and maintenance. Fireproof construction was a matter of necessity. The boiler and generator rooms, of similar size and side by side in plan, were separated by brick fire walls. Large exterior doors and overhead traveling cranes facilitated the handling of large pieces of equipment. Expansive windows with operable sash were recommended, as were skylights or monitors (see fig. 5.3). In some large powerhouses, coal bunkers were positioned above the boilers,

FIGURE 2.19 The powerhouse designed by industrial engineer Frank D. Chase and erected in 1919 for the Saginaw Products Co. division of General Motors Co. in Saginaw, Michigan, had the characteristic two-part form of such structures. In the taller portion were the boilers and the apparatus that delivered crushed coal to the boilers. The lower wing housed generators, air compressors, and other equipment. Brick of contrasting color spelled the firm's name out on the radial brick chimneys.

and conveyor systems both delivered coal and removed ashes. This arrangement made the boiler house taller than the adjacent engine room (fig. 2.19). The tower of the coal storage and transfer plant that served these overhead bunkers stood nearby.

The interior spaces of power plants had special features. The engine room was finished in a first-class manner befitting its importance. The work of the crew that operated the power plant, after all, was essential to the smooth running of the works. To leave no doubt, the dials of the master switchboard might be set into white Italian marble. White enamel brick on the walls reflected daylight and thereby maximized lighting conditions in a room where the visual inspection of equipment was an important safety factor. Such interior finishes also suggested a high standard of cleanliness and efficiency.

Chimneys

From an architectural standpoint, there is nothing unlovely in the cylindrical rise of a chimney, towering 100 to 200 feet above the plant. Indeed, the stately shaft of a concrete or masonry chimney visible from afar is a monument to power development.

POWER PLANT ENGINEERING, 1953

The industrial power plant chimney produced a draft that facilitated the combustion of coal (which heated water in boilers to produce steam) and carried off gases that resulted from combustion. The first consideration largely dictated the chimney's height, since the intensity of a draft depended on the difference in weight of the column of air within it and the surrounding atmosphere, not on the diameter of the shaft. The height of a works chimney was also influenced by the type of coal burned and generally ranged from 75 to 150 feet. Engineering criteria favored a cylindrical chimney to a square one because a rounded structure was less exposed to wind pressure. Also, a cylindrical interior flue offered less resistance to gases than a square one and had no corners that could fill with eddy currents. Octagonal chimneys offered only a little more exposure to wind than round ones and took less material to construct than square ones.[37]

Chimneys built of brick were most common in manufacturing works throughout the nineteenth century. It was customary to divide the inner flue wall of fire brick into sections, each of uniform thickness that was less than the section below it, in order to fit it within the tapering outer walls of common brick (see fig. 2.18). Around 1900 radial brick chimneys began to appear in the United States. The European firms of Alphons Custodis and H. R. Heinicke established American branches and provided both design expertise and the new material. Radial bricks, made from a refractory clay, had curved faces 4 inches by 6 inches; their angled ends were part of the radius of the chimney's circular plan (fig. 2.20). Because of the larger sizes of the units, a chimney of radial brick incorporated less mortar and was stronger and less expensive to construct than a chimney of standard brick. The material introduced a sleek, uniform surface for the tapered form of the radial brick chimneys. By using two contrasting shades of brick to create vertical lettering, firms often built their name into the chimney (see figs. 2.19 and 10.11).[38]

A short chimney, particularly a self-supporting one made of sheet metal, was considered a stack. Iron stacks were in common use by the 1870s in areas where sheet-metal-working shops could provide them as an inexpensive alternative to brick chimneys. After the turn of the century, they were considered common in Pennsylvania and the Midwest. An iron or steel stack was more efficient than a brick chimney because there was less air infiltration through the walls of the structure and because it took up less space than its brick counterpart. A number of small steel stacks, held in position by guy ropes, could be used instead of one tall brick chimney as a cost-saving measure. The guy wires, though, betrayed the weakness of metal stacks, and the short life of the "made-while-you-wait" steel chimney was an argument against its use.

Reinforced concrete was a third alternative for chimney construction. Ernest Ransome introduced the idea in 1898 with a 150-foot-high chimney of this material erected at the Pacific Coast Borax Co. (Bayonne, New Jersey). Though reinforced concrete chimneys could have thinner walls than brick ones, they were even more expensive to construct due to the cost of

FIGURE 2.20 Masons and company officials inspected the first courses laid in the construction of a radial brick chimney at the Ferracute Iron Works, Bridgeport, New Jersey, in 1916.

the formwork. Another disadvantage of this type of chimney was that concrete was not as impervious to weathering as the highest-quality brick.

Industrial architecture is definitely a mixture of standardization and variety. Industrial lofts and production sheds were customized with functional features to house the divisions of the works. These buildings and their auxiliary structures were combined in various configurations in manufacturing works. The next chapter describes the most common ways of arranging them.

LAYOUTS OF THE WORKS

3

The efficiency of an industrial plant is *not primarily dependent upon the buildings* [Sargent's italics], but mainly upon personnel, equipment, facilities for handling materials and products, and the arrangement of space. Buildings proper only affect efficiency, if they do or do not provide good light, good air, sufficient headroom and reasonable degree of comfort for workmen.

ENGINEER WILLIAM P. SARGENT, 1908

From the mid–nineteenth to the mid–twentieth centuries, manufacturing works usually consisted of a number of buildings—production sheds, loft structures, and powerhouses—and systems that varied considerably in their layout and placement. During this time, the best locations for manufacturing works changed, as did preferred means of transportation. The physical layout was influenced by the flow of production operations, power generation and distribution, and materials handling methods. There were other considerations as well. Dirty and noisy operations had to be kept isolated and women were often segregated from the main workforce. The works also had to include measures for fire prevention and suppression.

Industrial works, in addition to housing manufacturing processes, also incorporated auxiliary functions. Materials handling equipment facilitated the receipt of raw material and fuel and the shipment of finished products. The means for generation of power and its transfer to machinery, typically boilers and a steam engine in the works powerhouse and a system of millwork, were necessary components of the works. The storage of raw materials and finished products took place in yard areas, storehouses for specific types of materials like lumber and iron, and adjunct spaces in manufacturing areas, such as basements and lean-tos. The manufacturing works included space for the design of products and, in many cases, their testing, as well as offices for the management of the operation and marketing of goods. Many works included carpenter's shops where crates for shipping were produced and perhaps, later, paper box–making operations.

Several common solutions for organizing manufacturing space emerged during the mid–nineteenth century. Plans generally were for compact arrangements that represented a compromise between the need to limit distances over which power was distributed and the desire to separate structures and allow for light and ventilation. For most industries, a functional organization of operations by material to be processed or by type of machine used dictated the layout and the size and type of buildings. The large number of individual buildings that comprised a works reflected to its considerable vertical integration, the processing of raw materials and the fabricating of most components. Nearly all operations that used metal in their products cast their own parts in iron and brass foundries and forged other pieces in their blacksmith shops. Lumber yards and drying kilns were included as well in order to control the quality of wood components. Some firms also produced or modified the machines that were used in their shops.

As conditions changed, particularly as operations expanded significantly in scale because of corporate mergers and vertical integration, works layouts were revised to control costs of production. Advances in technology, building construction, and management practices also changed the configuration of works. Most important, at the end of the nineteenth century, the adoption of electric drive freed the arrangement of works from the domination of power distribution considerations, and the efficient arrangement of production became the primary factor in works layouts. The constant search for effective plans for manufacturing works reflects the dynamic nature of modern manufacturing and the need to generate maximum profits from capital investments. Amid this change was continuity and commonality: All plans addressed problems common to manufacturing works and the need for effective materials handling.

THE LOCATION OF MANUFACTURING WORKS

The most essential consideration in choosing a location is that there shall be a sufficient stream of water, not only to prevent the necessity of closing the works in summer, but also that the plant may be increased in proportion to its success.

E. I. DU PONT, C. 1801

The real estate maxim "location, location, location" pertained as much to the economic viability of an industrial works as to other types of development. Location affected the first cost of the works, the continuing expenses of transportation for raw materials and finished products, and the availability of labor. It also governed expansion plans.

The factors that influenced the locating of manufacturing works by no means remained constant during the nineteenth century. Earlier, the need for "a waterpower," a point of marked descent in a stream where it was easiest to capture and harness the flow of water for power generation, was the determining factor. Manufacturing was dispersed along rivers in the northeastern states in rural areas and small villages. In some towns water-power was more thoroughly exploited through the construction of canals. In Lowell and Lawrence, Massachusetts, and Paterson, New Jersey, such waterways became lined with numerous industrial operations.

The need for an ample supply of fresh water dictated the location of industries like textile printing and dyeing works, paper mills, tanneries, and black powder works. In contrast, manufacturing operations that processed agricultural products and mined raw materials, such as clay, were located near the sources of materials or near inexpensive transportation.

Many early industries were located near transportation canals to take advantage of shipping by water and the link that canals provided to markets (fig. 3.1). Cities and towns that were ports and trading centers were considered good locations for manufacturing because of marketing and transportation opportunities. Consequently, waterfront areas became congested manufacturing zones where facilities were used by a succession of firms. An available labor force also recommended urban locations, even though more rural settings provided economies in land purchase and labor costs based on a lower cost of living.[1]

The presence of industry prompted the development of additional manufacturing operations. A wool or cotton factory was often the catalyst for the

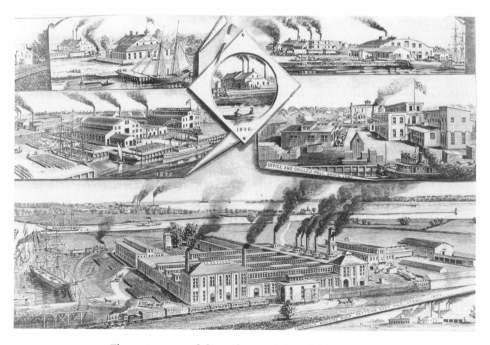

FIGURE 3.1 These views record the evolution of the Lobdell Car Wheel Co. works on the Christiana River in Wilmington, Delaware, as it was redeveloped and reoriented to a rail line during the nineteenth century. The buildings that comprised the works in 1836, depicted in the center cameo, are visible in the later views.

growth of a village where similar establishments or complementary operations gravitated. Textile machinery shops established as adjuncts to large textile factories later often diversified their production and became independent operations. Textile mills were located in mining districts to provide employment for miners' wives. Industries tended to concentrate in cities and regions, like the brass industry in central Connecticut and the silk mills in Paterson, New Jersey, in order to take advantage of skilled labor forces.

As railroads flourished and replaced canals as the main transportation system for industry, manufacturing works were erected along rail lines. Industrial corridors radiating outward from city centers became prime sites for manufacturing works during the mid- and late nineteenth century. Large tracts along rail lines permitted works to be laid out with more yard area and room for expansion. The extension of passenger trolley lines expanded the areas of industrial development by providing transportation for workers. Rail transport also prompted the development of manufacturing districts, later known as "industrial parks."

The Works and the Company Town

To one who, with a thoughtful mind, observes how constantly new villages are created in these eastern states, by the application of associated capital to all sorts of manufacturing industry, it can not but occur that the men who own and control the capital by which these villages are called into existence, are the depositaries of a power which affects, widely and permanently, the welfare of their fellow men.

THE NEW ENGLANDER MAGAZINE, 1849

Among the variables that determined a good location for a manufacturing works, one of those the industrialist could most easily manipulate was the availability of a labor force and adequate housing for workers. If an otherwise good site near a waterpower or natural resources, such as a clay bed, was too far from a village, then housing for future employees, or perhaps even a mill village or company town, was included in the works construction project (fig. 3.2). Because employees walked to work, company housing was erected close to the works. The manufacturer often had little choice in the matter, and it was even considered a "moral duty" for the industrialist to supply appropriate housing. After all, workers had no capital to build homes, let alone churches and schools.[2]

Architectural historian John Garner has identified several types of industry-related communities established during the nineteenth and early twentieth centuries. Small villages that were often poorly planned and short-lived grew up around manufacturing operations to provide housing for mill hands. The company town, on the other hand, was developed, administered, and owned, in total, by a manufacturing firm. Model company towns included landscaping, community facilities, good houses, and programs for maintenance. Corporate towns might originally have been

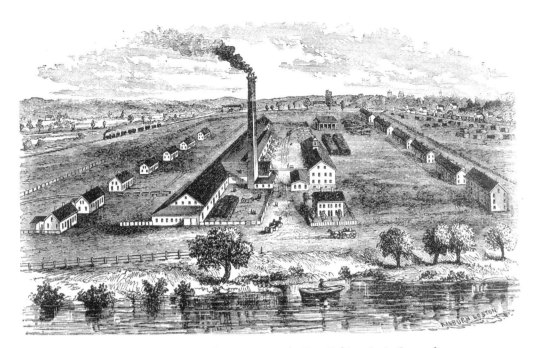

FIGURE 3.2 Boardinghouses and tenements at the Page Belting Co. in Concord, New Hampshire, lined the perimeter of the works property.

planned by a single firm, but they expanded to become large, multienterprise communities, like Lowell, Lawrence, and Holyoke in Massachusetts and Manchester in New Hampshire. In a quasi-company town, where an industry dominated but did not entirely control the community, there was a combination of private homes and businesses and company-built housing, churches, and schools.[3]

During the second half of the nineteenth century the development of a company town often represented a choice on behalf of the industrialist, rather than a necessity, and was associated with the reform movement aimed at improving housing and controlling labor problems in urban manufacturing centers. The provision of company-owned housing was acknowledged more openly as a management tool, even as "profitable paternalism." Besides allowing one to exact more control over the operation, developing a company town offered the privilege of place making and the opportunity to get one's name on the map. In 1880 William Steinway, who embraced this philosophy, began to relocate his New York City piano works from Manhattan to an unsettled area of Queens that became known as Steinway. In this manner, the capitalist "[had] it in his power to fix a high standard of community life . . . and create an atmosphere that is an intangible but very material resource."[4]

Another impetus for industrial community development was articulated by O. C. Barber, head of the Diamond Match Co., who considered it "easier, cheaper and more scientific to build a new town than to modernize an old one." In 1891 Barber established a manufacturing town—Barberton,

Ohio—that would be dependent on industries in which he invested. Adjacent to Akron, the town was laid out with residential areas surrounding a central lake and industrial sites at the perimeter.[5]

GENERAL CHARACTERISTICS OF THE WORKS

The manufacturing plant is the physical instrument through which all the efforts of an industrial enterprise capital, organization, and labor must be applied; and so, in practically every industry, the physical plant must have a very great influence on operating results.

ENGINEER WILLARD CASE, 1922

Every manufacturing works in the United States had a distinctive configuration of facilities that reflected its location, power generation and distribution, and type of product. Not until larger corporations began building standardized plants around the turn of the century did this individuality disappear. Despite such variation, manufacturing works shared many attributes. First and foremost, they were physically dominated by foundries, machine shops, and erecting shops, each of which constituted a fourth to a third of the production space of most works.[6]

The layout of a manufacturing works often demonstrated a concern for a public "facade" for the operation. When the works included a loft building, that structure was often placed along the street frontage, where it shielded the yard area and buildings, including the foundry, from public view. The works office, if not located in the main loft building, was a highly visible freestanding structure on the street. The street front of the works often featured a prominent gate that served as the main entrance for both workers and visitors, provided security, and often physically embodied a sense of strength and authority.

The works gate also gave access to the yard, an outdoor staging and storage area that occupied a central or side location and extended between buildings. The works yard might have offered access to a rail spur, pier, or canal dock. It was often edged with narrow storage sheds for coal, lumber, and raw materials.

Large manufacturing works were interlaced with utility systems commonly combined and placed in underground tunnels. Water and sewer pipes, sprinkler system piping, and, later, compressed air and electric wires were run in tunnels that both protected the lines and made them accessible for repairs. The use of similar tunnels for materials handling seems to have been unusual, though the Providence Tool Co. reportedly had an "underground railroad" to transport materials between distant parts of its works during the mid–nineteenth century. Systems of pipes and pumps moved liquids through processing operations and, later, transported materials like paint and varnish from storage to production areas.[7]

Materials Handling in the Works

Layouts for industrial works incorporated systems for materials handling to facilitate receiving raw materials, moving them throughout the facility, and shipping finished goods. Transporting work-in-progress within processing areas was also a major function of materials handling.

By the time that manufacturing began to flourish during the early nineteenth century, a number of fundamental materials handling concepts and devices had been developed. Oliver Evans exhibited the efficiency of three basic types of mechanical conveyors—the belt, screw, and bucket—in his "automatic" flour mill during the 1780s. He also demonstrated how practical it was to mechanically transfer materials to work stations. By the 1840s, rationalized manufacturing layouts were based on the concept of forward, one-directional movement of materials. Cranes and industrial rail had also been introduced.[8]

The mainstays of materials handling devices during the nineteenth century were simple devices. Hoists were used to position work at machines and move materials vertically. When hung from trollies (small "trucks" with two or four wheels), they served as trams for moving materials horizontally after they were raised. Trams ran on rails of I-beams suspended from the underside of the floor above or the roof's lower truss chords. They provided localized transverse movement, in the direction parallel to the roof trusses, and often worked in conjunction with industrial rail running the length of the shop. An extensive tramrail system installed during the early 1880s throughout the Brush Electric Co. works (Cleveland; fig. 3.3) consisted of 1,500 feet of track equipped with switches and turntables. The assertion that in the Walter A. Wood Mowing and Reaping Machine Co. (Hoosick Falls, New York), five men with just a trolley were able to do the work of forty men, conveying, distributing, and hoisting materials in the foundries and various shops indicates what a difference this simple equipment made.[9]

For the horizontal movement of materials, hand and platform trucks were the devices used to transport small loads. Views of manufacturing spaces with center aisles full of small trucks suggest that these containers provided temporary storage adjacent to work stations as well as transportation. The workforce required to move these trucks was staggering and could account for up to 40 percent of a payroll.[10]

From the earliest years of railroad operation, spur tracks connected industrial works with local rail lines. In small works, one or two "stub end turn outs" sufficed. For larger plants, a loop track connection was essential. A heavy manufacturing plant could not be considered well equipped unless it was served by a system of narrow-gauge industrial rail. At the Wason Car Manufacturing Co. (1872–1873; George C. Fisk, proprietor and designer; Springfield, Massachusetts; see fig. 2.8), the rail incorporated a transfertable, and the works and lumber yard were "seamed" at regular intervals with ninety lateral lines.[11] Track, often a combination of standard and

FIGURE 3.3 The overhead tramrail system installed in the works of the Brush Electric Co. in Cleveland during the 1880s extended throughout the buildings and the yard and incorporated turntables and switches.

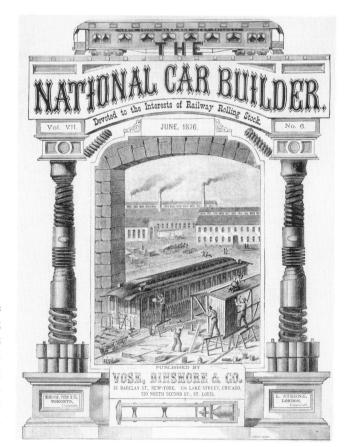

FIGURE 3.4 The covers of the *National Car Builder* during the early 1870s left no doubt that industrial rail was an integral part of railroad car manufacturing works. Even before cars were set on their wheel carriages, they were erected over rail lines and moved through the works on "trucks."

FIGURE 3.5 Column-type jib cranes were incorporated into the structure of erecting shops and foundries. Platform trucks pulled along industrial rail were a common means of materials handling.

narrow-gauge rail, traversed and connected buildings within a large works and often passed through buildings (fig. 3.4). Men pushed cars of ordinary tonnage on industrial rail, while wire-rope hoists and small steam locomotives were used to move larger loads (see figs. 3.5, 4.4, and 6.11).[12]

American manufacturers had a reputation for developing labor-saving and special purpose devices, and this predilection extended to cranes. Indeed, the layouts of many works were developed with the use of cranes in mind, particularly jib cranes. These pivoting cranes consisted of a central mast from which an arm extending laterally and commanded all the space beneath the rotating arm. Jib cranes positioned in works yards were known as "derricks," and those incorporated into a structure were "column cranes" (fig. 3.5). Power, either steam or hydraulic, was applied to jib cranes by the late 1870s, and within a few years electric motors were powering cranes with strong wrought-iron frames. Overhead traveling cranes were used occasionally in American industrial works during the mid– to late nineteenth century. Because this type of crane was more widely utilized after the adoption of electric drive and steel framing, it is described in chapter 4.[13]

A Long Tradition of Works Planning

Mr. Burden has provided ample space in his shops and they were the neatest, and best arranged, that we have seen. The materials are brought in at the upper part of the buildings and descend throughout their passage.

ENGINEER CHARLES BIGELOW, 1846

Nineteenth-century industrialists made conscious and sophisticated choices concerning the layout of their works in response to competition in the marketplace and technological advances. In so doing, they initiated the careful planning that industrial engineers suggested originated in their work around the turn of the century. Since the configuration of the works had a direct effect on the cost of goods production, the goal in works layout was constant, even as the solutions varied over time.

That thoughtful planning of the works was an essential aspect of the operation of a manufacturing concern is illustrated by the prospectus penned in 1800 by E. I. du Pont, "Location and Constructions Necessary for Manufacture of Gunpowder." The plan, informed by what du Pont remembered from his work and study in France, was for the family's American operation in Delaware. The ideal location for a gunpowder works was near a city that offered transportation, labor, and an adequate water supply. Its size must allow for future expansion, though du Pont was aware that efficiency could be hindered in a works that was too spread out. The proposed powder works had a functional, sequential layout that isolated certain functions—in this case, the more dangerous ones.[14]

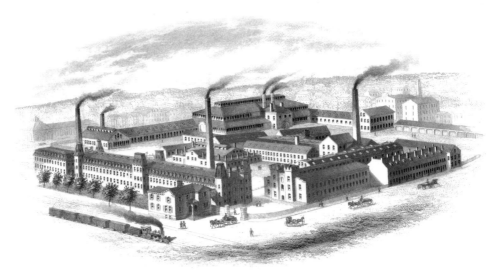

FIGURE 3.6 The Mason Machine Works in Taunton, Massachusetts, was a noted manufacturing works of the antebellum period. This view, from the mid-1870s, depicts the works after they were enlarged in 1852 with an expanded foundry, forging facilities, and erecting shops in preparation for the production of locomotives.

The Mason Machine Works (1845; William Mason, owner and designer; Taunton, Massachusetts; fig. 3.6), a facility that was influential throughout New England, indicates how the works layout developed during the antebellum period. The choice of a location adjacent to a railroad, rather than a waterfront, reveals a shift in the importance of transportation systems. The works consisted of facilities specifically designed for machine manufacturing; functional divisions of the operation were housed in separate buildings yet integrated into a compact arrangement. The size of the structures was impressive: Two- and three-story machine shops were over 300 feet long, and the freestanding blacksmith shop and foundry were each 100 feet long.[15]

TRADITIONAL MULTISHOP PLANS

The most important matter to be guarded against in making plans for a new mill, is that of intricate and original designs, seemingly presenting great advantages on paper, and apparently quite correct to an architect or builder, but really quite wrong to a foreman or manager after a building is completed.

ENGINEER J. RICHARDS, 1885

The various layouts examined in the following sections make it clear that there was not "one best way" to lay out the works. There were many configurations of suboperations that facilitated the flow of production. And we must remember that no matter how ideal a layout might be considered initially, the constant changes that characterized manufacturing—improvements in production technique, the availability of more mechanized equipment, and changes in the product line—could easily render it less effective.

Linear Layouts

When an operation expanded beyond the confines of a single building, it was usually through the construction of another structure attached to the original one. The first addition was often a blacksmith or machine shop. When more structures were added, and if the line of shops turned a corner, the linear layout assumed an L, and perhaps eventually a U, form. Such compact arrangements facilitated the distribution of power and efficient materials handling.

Linear layouts worked well for small to midsized operations established during the early and mid–nineteenth century. The New York City shops of the West Point Foundry, where locomotives were assembled during the 1830s and 1840s (from parts cast at the main foundry north of the city), had such a configuration. The millwright shop, blacksmith shop, works steam engine, machine shop (with a second-story pattern shop), and office building were aligned along the street frontage; the works yard extended to

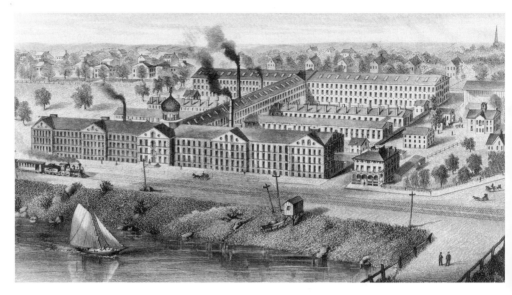

FIGURE 3.7 When it was rebuilt after an 1864 fire, the H-shaped plan of the industrial loft that housed the Colt Armory and Machine Shops was expanded with additional one-story wings. The small homes of night watchmen stood near the street between these wings. The office, across the street, was connected to the main structure by a second-story bridge.

the rear. During the 1840s, the Stanley Bolt Factory (New Britain, Connecticut) consisted of three connected structures in a telescoping linear configuration that was common. Textile mill complexes often had a linear arrangement that followed the course of a river or canal.[16]

A linear plan also worked well for larger operations when buildings were placed in production sequence. This was the case at the Wason Car Manufacturing Co. works (1872–1873; George C. Fisk, proprietor and designer; Springfield, Massachusetts; see fig. 2.8). The foundry was positioned close to the rail spur; machine and forge shops were next in line. The passenger-car erecting shop and its auxiliary shops, along with the works powerhouse, were last in the row. A paint shop and a freestanding office building were placed on the opposite side of a central transfer table.[17]

Large industrial lofts often had complex linear plans. The narrow width of manufacturing space led to the "alphabet layouts" that began with I, L, and U plans and continued with more elaborate E and H forms. The well-known Colt Armory (1855, rebuilt 1864; Hartford, Connecticut; fig. 3.7) was of this type. The four-story loft structure consisted of wings 80 feet wide and 500 feet long. Its H shape provided more floor area than a hollow square plan, was equally well lighted, and shortened travel distances.[18]

Constricted Urban Sites and Accretionary Works

Manufacturing works on urban sites often became densely developed over time through accretion. Operations on large parcels or even entire blocks

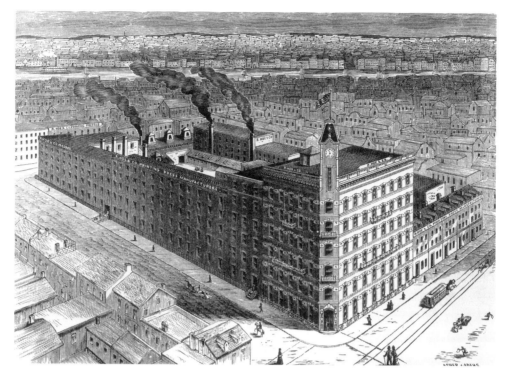

FIGURE 3.8 By the 1870s, R. Hoe & Co., a manufacturer of printing machinery in New York City, had expanded its works to enclose an entire block and had erected a prominent six-story loft building with a corner tower.

could become quite crowded as buildings were erected in the works yard. The advantages of the urban site for transportation and a source of labor, however, outweighed the disadvantages of crowded production space.

For example, R. Hoe & Co., manufacturers of printing machinery and steel saws, established a works on a large site in Lower Manhattan during the 1850s that was expanded several times (fig. 3.8). Three sides of the original works were enclosed by narrow loft buildings and a production shed; the foundry was a freestanding structure in the yard. By the 1870s, the facility had grown to enclose the entire block as a quadrangle and included a six-story loft building with a corner tower. Row houses on the expanded site were replaced with another, larger loft structure by the turn of the century. By that time, the works had spread to an adjacent block.[19]

Rather than expanding beyond its original confines, the Novelty Iron Works developed its site quite densely. Around 1840, the works consisted of a range of shops—boiler, blacksmith, and machine—along one side of the yard and a foundry across the rear of a rectangular lot; another group of narrow buildings opposite the shops enclosed the yard. Within a few years, nearly all of the works yard was given over to additional boiler and finishing shops as well as a wareroom, brass foundry, coppersmith shop, and carpenter shop. The loss of the yard must have been compensated for by the ease of shipping from the foot of Twelfth Street on the East River in New York City.[20]

FIGURE 3.9 The Rogers Locomotive and Machine Works was developed in the early 1870s on a site between the lower and upper raceways of the Paterson, New Jersey, waterpower canal. As the site continued to be reworked, the 1831 machine shop and its flume were replaced and a building was constructed behind the blacksmith shop on the former street bed.

Innumerable firms successfully operated works that were not "model" or "best practice" by anyone's standards but were instead the result of years of building on the same site. As structures were added to the Rogers Locomotive works in Paterson, New Jersey, over a period of seventy years, older ones were replaced and streets were closed off to provide additional room for building (fig. 3.9). By the end of the nineteenth century, the works of Harlan & Hollingsworth (Wilmington, Delaware; see fig. 2.6), had expanded by accretion from a single, multipurpose building to a complex of forty-seven structures. The shop foremen and managers devised ways to effectively accommodate both the movement of work through the railroad car department and the more stationary process of shipbuilding. At Harlan & Hollingsworth, standard Tuscan red paint provided visual unity and an identification for the sprawling works (and also reduced maintenance costs).[21] (See figs. 2.2 and 3.1 for views of other accretionary works.)

The Hollow Square or Industrial Quadrangle

Hollow square, or quadrangle, plans were favored for manufacturing works, particularly during the decades following the Civil War. This format was recommended by engineers because it provided the greatest amount of light and ventilation, as well as security for materials stored in the yard and control over employees. It was also considered less vulnerable to a destructive fire, because of the open yard, and convenient for materials handling. Even a loft building, such as that of the Chickering & Sons piano works (rebuilt in 1852; Boston; fig. 3.10), could be arranged as a hollow square. This structure, considered the second largest building in North America during the mid–nineteenth century, was considered an "object of attraction, ornament, and pride for our country." Its main wings were divided by fire walls; a western wing, which housed the steam engine and heavy machinery shop, was only three stories high.[22]

The quadrangle was the form suggested by Charles G. Wilcox, a mechanical engineering student at the Polytechnic College of Pennsylvania, for a model works in 1860 (fig. 3.11). According to Wilcox, the rationale for placing buildings around the perimeter of a site to form a hollow square was based on two systems: millwork shafting that transferred power from steam engines, and industrial rail that connected with a railroad spur line on an adjacent street. Two steam engines were located so that power could be transmitted in more than one direction with a minimum of millwork. Rail entered the works through a central alley, ran past the heavy fitting shop, machine shop, and the coal storage house, and then extended through the yard and into the foundry. Wilcox explained other considerations that also influenced the plan. A two-story machine shop building provided space for light work on the upper level. The foundry was placed at the rear of the yard, where there was space for the storage of flasks and castings. The smith shop was located close to the machine shop, since the machinist frequently required the blacksmith to make and alter tools. The pattern shop required power and also needed to be near the office; its second story was used for pattern storage.[23]

FIGURE 3.10 The Chickering & Sons Piano Forte works, rebuilt in 1852 after a fire, consisted of lofts arranged in a hollow square.

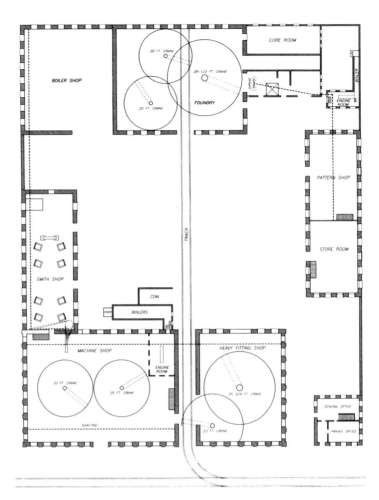

FIGURE 3.11 This layout for an ironworks was a model plan proposed by Charles G. Wilcox. Each function of the operation was housed in a separate building at the perimeter of the quadrangle.

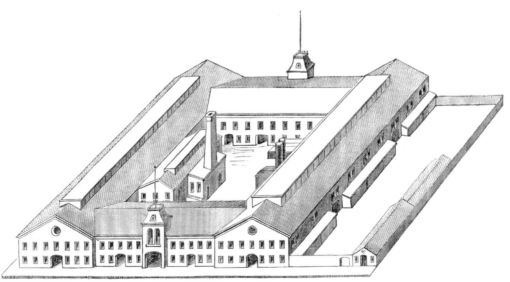

FIGURE 3.12 This "model shop" for the manufacture of architectural ironwork, proposed by architect and engineer William J. Fryer, was laid out in a hollow square form.

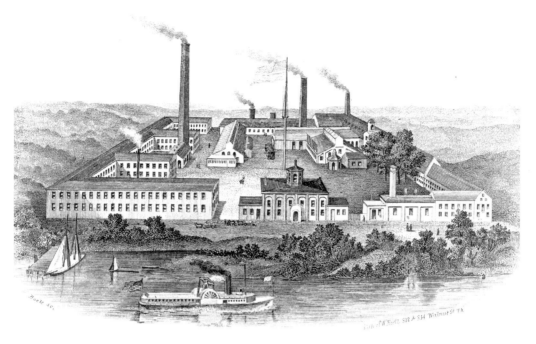

FIGURE 3.13 An imposing office building guarded the entrances to the quadrangle
that comprised the works of the Bridesburg Manufacturing Co. near Philadelphia.

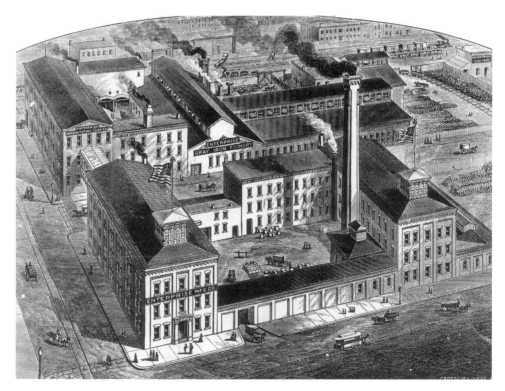

FIGURE 3.14 The works of the Enterprise Manufacturing Co. was located in
Philadelphia, where the urban grid of blocks and streets affected works layout. The
firm expanded its facility in the early 1880s by erecting a second quadrangle (in the
foreground).

A model facility for the manufacture of architectural ironwork proposed by architect and engineer William J. Fryer fifteen years later also had a hollow square layout (fig. 3.12). In Fryer's plan, the works yard was enclosed by nearly identical foundry and erecting shop structures. Two-story loft buildings completed the quadrangle. "Drive-ways" through these buildings gave access to the yard, which Fryer recommended be roofed over where winters were severe.[24]

The quadrangle layout served as a template for positioning various kinds of structures around a central yard at the Bridesburg Manufacturing Co. near Philadelphia (fig. 3.13). By the mid-1860s, the firm had erected a waterfront-oriented works with an office building set between a pair of entrances to the yard. A two-story E-shaped loft building, a gun shop addition to the works (which produced primarily looms and textile machinery), stood on one side of the square. The blacksmith shop and foundry were freestanding structures in the works yard.[25]

One drawback of the hollow square plan was the difficulty of expanding the works. By 1874 the Enterprise Manufacturing Co. (Philadelphia; fig. 3.14), hardware manufacturers, had erected works that consisted of a three-story loft building and a foundry on opposite sides of a yard. Enterprise solved the expansion problem by adding another quadrangle on an adjacent block (c. 1883). An enclosed bridge at the second-story level joined the two portions of the works.[26]

Unit System Plans

By building on a main avenue as proposed, the establishment admits of extension to any degree likely to be required, whereas by building upon the sides of a square, you cannot extend beyond that square, when once completed, without great inconvenience.

GENERAL THOMAS A. RODMAN, 1866

Works consisting of rows of identical loft buildings were considered to be examples of the "Duplicate I" or "unit system" plan by industrial engineers in the early twentieth century. This type of layout was based on standardized buildings and ease in expansion. This layout, which evolved over time to a connected form, usually consisted of a row (or rows) of identical rectangular structures that had the form of a capital letter I. Its advantages included the provision of standardized space in identical buildings, reduced first costs in design and construction, and the use of discrete production units in order to limit loss to fire. This plan was most often utilized for a series of industrial loft buildings that housed light manufacturing.

The Estey Organ works (c. 1870; Brattleboro, Vermont; fig. 3.15) represented the simplest version of the unit system. Eight identical three-story lofts, each 100 feet long and about 35 feet wide, stood side by side in a single row. Two large lumber drying houses, the works powerhouse, a fire-engine

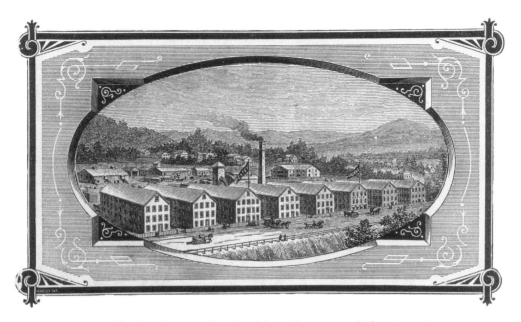

FIGURE 3.15 The Estey Organ works in Brattleboro, Vermont, was laid out in a unit system plan and consisted of eight standardized loft buildings.

house, and other outbuildings completed the complex. This layout was adopted after the firm's works were destroyed twice by fire.[27]

The shops of the Rock Island Arsenal (1866; General Thomas A. Rodman, engineer; Rock Island, Illinois) were laid out in a unit plan and consisted of standardized buildings. The plan positioned rows of five shops on both sides of the main road, near the center of the site, so that the length of the rows could be extended with additional shops as needed. One-story production sheds and three-story loft structures, of uniform plan and construction, accommodated the operation's various components (see fig. 2.11).[28]

The buildings in a unit system plan were sometimes connected with service wings that contained stairs and elevators, supply rooms, and washrooms. These works could easily be expanded by constructing an additional service wing and another loft. Noted examples of this type of unit plan included the United Shoe Machinery Co. (1903–1904; Frank M. Andrews, architect, and Ernest Ransome, engineer; Beverly, Massachusetts), which consisted of parallel reinforced concrete lofts connected by multistory service wings in which toilets, changing rooms, tool rooms, and supply rooms were located. The Remington Rifle plant (1915; Bridgeport, Connecticut) was housed in thirteen identical five-story lofts and several one-story buildings. The loft buildings were connected by service wings and a central corridor that extended through the complex at each story.[29]

A model plan in the Duplicate I form presented in 1907 consisted of two rows of structures through which work progressed from a foundry and wood-working shop through machine shops and then to warehouses. A proponent of this plan described it as a "sausage factory": Raw material entered one end of the plant and proceeded in a direct line, from process to process and building to building, until it reached the other end.[30]

CONSOLIDATED WORKS

Unquestionably the open floor is in every way to be preferred to the separate room-plan for operations which do not interfere with each other.

ENGINEER HORACE ARNOLD, 1890

A new model for the manufacturing works emerged during the last decades of the nineteenth century. It emphasized the proximity of related operations and the connection of the shops that housed them. These layouts demonstrated the advantages of direct communication between various components of the works for ease in materials handling and efficient production flow. In 1882, the Tanner & Delaney Engine Co. (Richmond, Virginia; see figs. 1.5 and 1.6) erected an extensive works to replace a facility destroyed by fire. The new works consisted of an attenuated one-story, E-shaped structure. The erecting shop, boiler shop, and machine shop were in wings of standardized width and were nearly 200 feet long. The foundry was attached at the end of one wing. Industrial rail extended throughout the facility.[31]

The interconnectedness of manufacturing space evident in the Tanner & Delaney works became more common during the late 1800s. Traditional spatial practices—the partitioning of production space into discrete work areas based on trades and materials—gave way to more open layouts housed in large production sheds. This change to consolidated operations on one floor and under one roof was prompted by the use of heavier machinery that was operated at faster speeds and therefore needed to be in ground-story shops. In open and connected shop areas, though, separate rooms continued to be used for such operations as japanning, electroplating, brazing, polishing, and grinding in order to contain, or avoid, dust and the heat of ovens.[32]

The turn-of-the-century move to larger, consolidated, open-plan structures was part and parcel of the changes brought about in industrial architecture by a "technical triumvirate"—electric drive, the powered crane, and the steel frame (examined in chapters 4 and 6). Much larger production sheds were made possible by improved roof lighting and ventilation. Engineers also recognized that large structures with few dividing walls offered ease of supervision and the elastic utilization of space. One large building was generally cheaper to erect and maintain than a number of smaller ones if roof spans were not excessive. Another practical consideration was suitability for reuse by another occupant.[33]

In 1896, engineer and industrial journalist Horace Arnold recommended solving the works design problem by determining a suitable single-story plan and then choosing a form of roof lighting. Following his own advice,

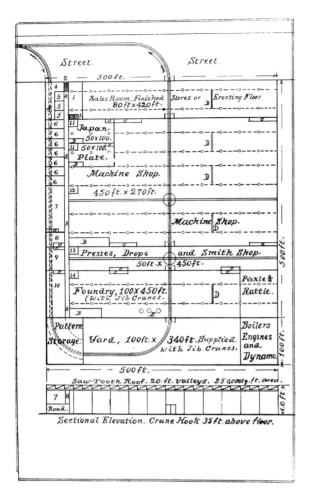

FIGURE 3.16 In 1896 engineer Horace Arnold offered this "machine-shop design" as a model plan that incorporated new ideas about consolidated, open-plan works.

Arnold offered a model shop consisting of a single, unpartitioned one-story space under a sawtooth roof (fig. 3.16). A road and industrial rail passed on one side of the structure to a narrow rear yard. The rail made a loop through the site, bringing raw materials to the yard, and then worked in conjunction with traveling cranes to move components forward through the shop. Operations progressed from the foundry (at the rear) through machine shops to finishing shops and erecting areas near the street.[34]

Horace Arnold argued the case for the open shop, free from partitions, by asserting that the form of machine shop buildings had a great influence on the cost of machine work. He presented the De La Val shop (Frederick Hart; Poughkeepsie, New York), the Straight Line Engine shops (1889; John E. Sweet, engineer; Syracuse, New York), and the Sterling Cycle works (1895; Kenosha, Wisconsin) as noted examples of this new type of works.[35]

There was, however, no immediate abandonment of multishop plans for the works, particularly for large operations. The design of the American Bridge Co.'s new plant (1903; James Christie of the company, designer; Ambridge, Pennsylvania) was based on the premise of separating various kinds of work, assigning a building to each of the more important divisions, and grouping them for ease in materials handling. Writing in 1908, engineer George M. Brill asserted that a group of several detached buildings just might be the best plan for isolating noise, heat, and smoke.[36]

The open, single-story plan of the Foote-Burt Co. (c. 1920; F. A. Barnes, the company's chief engineer, and George S. Rider & Co., architects; Cleveland), characteristic of structures erected after World War I, was planned to take advantage of materials handling methods. The main building, which consisted of a pair of crane-served bays separated by lower service bays, had three main sections separated by transverse aisles. Raw materials were moved in through a "rear aisle," which separated preliminary production areas from the machining department. A "front aisle," between the machining and assembly departments, was equipped with a 10-ton monorail that moved materials between departments and also transferred finished machines to the shipping department at the end of the aisle.[37]

Head-House and Shed Plans

A head-house combined with production sheds was a type of consolidated works used during the nineteenth century that found renewed popularity during the early twentieth century. The name is borrowed from the characteristic form of nineteenth-century armories in which a narrow, multistory building—a head-house—stood in front of a large one-story drill shed. For manufacturing works, the plan combined one-story production areas with loft space for designing and pattern-making operations, light machine or finishing work, and offices. One reason for the popularity of the head-house and shed plan during the early twentieth century was the need for more engineering and administrative offices. The loft structure also screened the lower structures with engineered roofs of unusual form from the view of the general public.

The Davenport & Bridges' Car Manufactory built for the production of railroad cars (c. 1857; Cambridgeport, Massachusetts; fig. 3.17) was of this type. Two very long and narrow shop buildings extended from a three-story head-house. Across the yard, a half-dozen small one-story shops and foundry buildings were positioned in a row, as in a unit plan. A small office building stood next to the main gate. The Detroit File Works (c. 1870) was a more modest version of head-house and shed. There, a two-story loft structure that housed the office fronted a pair of production sheds.[38]

Engineer Oscar Perrigo recommended head-house and shed layouts for their compact form and ease of expansion. He offered a model plan in 1910 that varied the head-house and shed form by incorporating another arrangement common at the time—machine shop wings extending perpendicularly from the main erecting shop. A brick production shed (70 feet wide and 300 feet long) was attached to a three-story head-house. Two machine shops extended from the production shed into the yard. The forge shop and

FIGURE 3.17 The works erected for the Davenport & Bridges' Car Manufactory in Cambridgeport, Massachusetts, incorporated two common types of layouts. A three-story head-house fronted a pair of production sheds. Across the yard, half a dozen small one-story shops and a foundry were positioned in a unit system plan.

powerhouse were freestanding structures in the yard between these wings. Foundry buildings stood on the opposite side of a narrow yard. Integral to the works were the materials handling provisions: A traveling crane commanding the entire length of the main shop was supplemented by overhead trolleys, jib cranes, and hoists.[39]

Although engineers found this type of layout functional and efficient, the architectural profession questioned the ideology it represented. Critic Talbot Hamlin objected to the discrepancy between the appearance of a well-designed head-house, used as an administration wing, and a utilitarian production shed. For him, this was a too visible reminder of the contrasts in the lives of labor and management.[40]

The Manufacturing Unit Plan of Allis-Chalmers

The movement of materials forward through a series of spaces was well accommodated in a plan for the new works of the Allis-Chalmers Co. (1902; Edwin Reynolds, engineer; West Allis, Wisconsin; fig. 3.18). Industrial engineer Charles Day described the plan as a series of shops arranged parallel to one another and connected at one end by a raw materials storage building

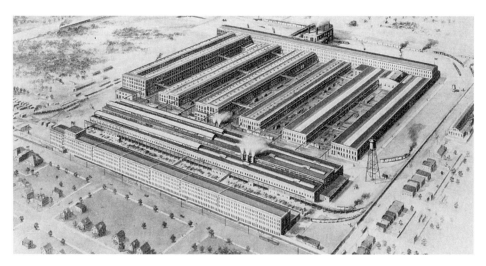

FIGURE 3.18 The manufacturing unit plan adopted for the Allis-Chalmers Co. plant was in an intermediate stage of development in this view of the works, which appeared during the 1910s. The facility was incrementally expanded by adding structures between the foundry (in the foreground) and the erecting shop, which were both elongated at the same time.

and foundry and at the other end by an erecting shop. The Allis-Chalmers plan combined standardized buildings with those tailored for specific operations. A system of traveling cranes, within the structures and commanding the yard space between the shops and the foundry, was the core of the materials handling system. Reynolds based the new plan on the proportion of space devoted to the foundry, machine shops, and erecting shop in the old works, which he termed a "manufacturing unit." An important conceptual element of the plan was that it could be expanded yet maintain the same ratios of space in additional manufacturing units. The foundry and erecting shops could both be extended at one end when a new shop was constructed between the additions.[41]

Industrial engineer William P. Sargent admired the Allis-Chalmers plan to the extent that he adopted a rectangular layout similar to that of the West Allis Plan in his presentation of a model works plan in *Machinery*.[42] Indeed, the only difference between Sargent's plan and the Allis-Chalmers one was the location of the works powerhouse. Sargent noted how the yard space between the machine shops was essential for efficient "side-feeding" of unfinished materials to machine shops with a minimum of crane and truck handling.[43]

As larger and more flexible spaces like the Allis-Chalmers works were planned, operations remained organized by traditional shop divisions (the foundry and machine and erecting shops) even though the spaces were open to each other. By the time continuous process operations and assembly lines came into use, these open-plan, single-story structures could accommodate that type of production. As twentieth-century plants grew in scale, they drew on tried-and-true plans and principles of works layout.

As a manufacturer in such an industrial city (the Bush Terminal) you are relieved of factory cares, you are provided with power at a lower rate, and a hundred and one other advantages are yours at a minimum cost.

THE AUTOMOBILE, 1914

Although industry had long been concentrated along canal and rail corridors and near harbors, almost all works were separate entities. The exception to this practice was the grouping of manufacturing operations in "power buildings" that provided power along with rental space (see chapter 4). Also, large works were subdivided and reused by a number of smaller operations. For instance, when the former Whitely Shops (1883; Springfield, Ohio) were occupied by fourteen firms at the turn of the century the effectiveness of sharing space and services was tested. The intensified stress on efficiency and standardization that infused engineering and manufacturing processes during the early years of the twentieth century helped bring about a new setting for manufacturing that incorporated shared infrastructure: the manufacturing district.[44]

Another important model for these first industrial parks was the union freight terminal served by more than one rail line. It was a means of simplifying rail shipping and eliminating the transfer of freight between various terminals when several rail lines served a city. The Cupples Station in St. Louis, Missouri (established c. 1895), was a union freight terminal that served wholesalers. A common railway terminal and clearinghouse system oversaw the transfer of goods between storage areas of several firms and railcars. Shipping platforms in the basements of warehouses and an extensive elevator system facilitated its operation.[45]

Two large, early industrial parks in the United States—the Bush Terminal in Brooklyn and the Central Manufacturing Districts in Chicago—were laid out during the first decade of the twentieth century. Both developments were based on the idea of improved rail service, but they differed in most other aspects. The Bush Terminal provided a union terminal connection, warehouses, and standardized multitenant industrial lofts that it leased as manufacturing space. In the Chicago districts, individualized facilities with spur rail service were designed and erected for each tenant.

The Bush Terminal (fig. 3.19) was first a union freight depot that facilitated the complicated process of shipping in the New York City harbor. Then, between 1902 and World War I, Irving T. Bush (president of the Bush Terminal Co.) oversaw the transformation of a stretch of the Brooklyn waterfront with the construction of ten manufacturing loft buildings, over a hundred warehouses, several piers, and a freight yard. Bush regarded the lofts as "apartment hotels for factories" that provided tenants with electricity and other utilities, freight transfer, labor from a centralized personnel office, and employee welfare services. Fireproof reinforced concrete loft buildings and a centralized fire sprinkler system enabled tenants to take

FIGURE 3.19 This row of nearly identical reinforced concrete loft buildings was expanded to form the Bush Terminal, a manufacturing district that tested ideas that were exploited in later industrial parks.

advantage of low fire insurance rates. The terminal's slogan, "Triangle of Efficiency," denoted how manufacturing space, storage facilities, and shipping were linked. The separate identity of the place was evoked in the promotion of the "Terminal City."[46]

The Central Manufacturing Districts in Chicago were established by the Union Stock Yard and Transit Co. to attract additional freight for the company's belt rail line. A tract of land adjacent to the stockyard was acquired and laid out as the first district around 1908. Each building site in the district was served by a rail spur, and electric power was provided by a nearby generating plant. The buildings in the district, which were either leased or purchased, included lofts at a uniform height of four stories and production sheds (of various designs) and eventually housed over two hundred operations. In 1910, the development of a nearby parcel as the Pershing Road, or Second, Manufacturing District began. A more comprehensive development plan directed this project. It consisted of complete utilities, including central power and sprinkler plants, a union freight station, a comprehensive system of rail and underground freight tunnels, and street improvements. Architectural and engineering controls included uniform lot size and standardized building design and construction, though the structures were not identical. The district architect, S. Scott Joy, designed all of the reinforced concrete or mill construction structures and detailed their exteriors in brick and light-colored terra cotta (see fig. 5.3 and chapter 11).[47]

The Clearing Industrial District (Bedford Park, Chicago) was a contemporary development of the Central Manufacturing District that introduced another approach to the layout of industrial parks. The large site, near rail and other transportation, was laid out as quarter-mile "superblocks" of 40 acres. Some companies controlled the development of land adjoining their works by organizing a manufacturing district. The Albert Dickinson Co. offered tracts for sale next to its new facility on the Chicago Drainage Canal. During the 1920s and 1930s, a number of railroad-sponsored districts were established, including the Los Angeles Central Manufacturing District (1922).[48]

Irving Bush and his contemporaries brought a new type of order to industrial areas. Several concepts tested in these early projects were incorporated into mid-twentieth-century industrial parks. Restrictive covenants in modern industrial parks engender a uniformity in the physical setting that centralized design and construction programs provided in the early districts. The Pershing Road Central Manufacturing District in Chicago, with its orientation to a prominent highway, pointed to the future importance of freeway access. Attractive landscaping, advocated as part of the model factory movement, eventually led to the aesthetic standards adopted for industrial parks. Such standards, as well as those for building setbacks, height limits, and open space, were intended to make the industrial park a good neighbor to other types of development.

INDUSTRIAL ENGINEERS PLAN THE WORKS

My own high mark to date is the making and testing of thirty-four alternative layouts for one plant before arriving at the one and only one extremely simple and clean-cut arrangement which most nearly harmonized the ideal and practicable layout in all particulars.

ENGINEER H. K. FERGUSON, 1939

As the specialized field of industrial engineering emerged at the beginning of the twentieth century, industrial engineers promoted themselves as uniquely qualified to provide efficient plans for the works. To them, planning the works consisted of "selecting the most effective arrangement of physical facilities to allow the greatest efficiency in the combination of resources to produce a product or service." In addition to the placement of machinery, plant layout addressed the comfort of workers by planning for abundant light, sufficient heat, good ventilation, adequate space for their work, and convenient toilets and washrooms.[49]

The plant layout project of the industrial engineer was a continuation of the type of planning that had been initiated much earlier by mill engineers, who had coordinated the machines and mills of the textile industry for efficient production. The planners of textile mills began by determining the numbers of machines to be housed; then they enclosed the space around the machines, taking into consideration the source of power and its distribution, structural strength and span, and lighting. Mill engineer Stephen Greene asserted in 1889, "The best modern practice in mill engineering follows the true method, namely, that of considering, first and chiefly, the necessary machinery for producing a given product of a desired quality and arranging this in proper order." Industrial engineers often wrote of designing factory layouts in the same way, insisting that the machinery determined the character of the building as well as its size, strength, and general structure.[50]

As industrial engineers working as factory planners thoroughly rationalized the process, information was organized and communicated through outlines of factors, charted production data, machinery and equipment layout worksheets, operations process charts, diagrams of activity and space flow relationships, and detailed floor plans. Materials handling methods were thoroughly integrated into production sequences. Once the process mapping was complete, floor area requirements determined the type of building to be used and its dimensions. Standard building types were preferred because they offered flexibility and adaptability for later occupants. Engineers warned against the extreme adaptation of a space to a specific operation or process that might become obsolete; they preferred the universal space plant.[51]

As factory planners engineered men as well as materials in their plans, they turned to one prominent metaphor that rationalized the modern goals of order, control, and system, writes historian Lindy Biggs. To the industrial engineer, the works became the "master machine," the "master tool," and "the big machine containing and coordinating all the little machines." Engineer Edward Jones expressed the "factory as machine" metaphor as eloquently as any of his contemporaries: "The conception of a modern plant, from the point of view of layout, is of a huge machine or mechanical leviathan; slightly adjusted in the process of fitting it into a series of buildings; designed and assembled much as a machine would be; and performing its function (much as a machine), in so far as it works smoothly, as an intimately coordinated whole."[52]

It is important, though, to recognize this rhetoric as a component of the industrial engineer's professionalization project and its role in characterizing his work as new in scope and essential to the industrialist. Here, however, representation and reality diverge. There was no qualitative difference between the rationale for a model works offered by engineer Charles Wilcox in 1860 and those designed by the first graduates of industrial engineering programs fifty years later. Moreover, the factory building fitted with millwork that linked the structure and powered machinery certainly functioned as a master machine. So did the industrial building that incorporated electric drive, the powered crane, and the steel frame. The boasts of industrial engineers acknowledged this latter type of engineered factory but also attempted to take credit for it. The continuity of the design work undertaken by mill engineers, engineers working before the specialty of industrial engineer emerged, and industrial engineers suggests planners working with all of these titles were responsible for modernizing the factory as the master machine. But the designs offered for industrial buildings and the layout of the works after the establishment of the industrial engineering specialty, around 1910, were primarily revisions and fine-tuning of existing types and plans. The master machine of industry is better thought of as the steel-framed structure incorporating a powerful traveling crane and housing electric-powered machinery than as the product of the industrial engineer's drafting board.

During the nineteenth century, the configuration of the manufacturing works—varied as they were—passed through a four-stage cycle. Begun as a single building, the works expanded into a number of specialized structures. It then contracted to fewer, but larger and connected, machine and erecting shop units. The factories of the twentieth century brought the cycle back to a single structure housing the entire works. Throughout these changes, the arrangement of the works in an efficient and hence profitable manner was the ideal. In part II, we turn our attention again to the buildings that comprised the works and examine the various ways that they were engineered to serve industry.

ENGINEERED FACTORIES | PART II

The industrial structure's problem demands in the first instance an

engineering solution.

ARCHITECT ELY JACQUES KAHN, 1929

4

I have had power in my shop for more than three years, and have found that it is as good as an extra man.

PRACTICAL CARRIAGE BUILDING, 1903

Power generation and distribution[1] were decisive factors in locating, configuring, and operating the works. They also made the factory a master machine. Power generation for manufacturing progressed from waterwheels and turbines, to steam boilers and engines, and then to electric generators. The replacement of the shafting and belting of millwork with individual and group electric drive brought about dramatic changes in the form and use of manufacturing space. Consequently, the age of millwork and the era of electric power are useful categories that reflect the interrelationship between the use of power and industrial building design.

Factory buildings reflect the fact that manpower was a type of industrial power that manufacturing works have always relied on, both in the sense of human physical strength and in the cumulative effect of the labor force. Laborers powered machinery by operating hand cranks, treadmills, treadles and pedals, and levers. Workers at their benches, using tools to shape and fit pieces and guiding the work of belt-driven machinery, occupied most of the space in a manufacturing shop. Human strength was also put to use in materials handling as workers operated hoists and pushed hand trucks.

Developments in the generation and distribution of mechanical power affected the conceptualization of space for manufacturing. Initially, it was the custom to have a waterwheel for each machine and to place the two as close to each other as possible; the gristmill was an example of this practice.

During the early nineteenth century, when power was concentrated in one large wheel, machinery was consolidated in a single large building fitted with millwork. Steam power brought an increase not only in the number of machines but also in their power and weight and led to the use of larger and stronger industrial buildings. It has been suggested that steam power brought all stages of a manufacturing process together under one roof and, in so doing, made greater demands for strength and span in factory construction. Although steps were taken in that direction in the period when the steam engine was the prime mover of industry, most steam-powered operations were, in fact, housed under several roofs. It was electric power that ushered in consolidated, open-plan works with a single roof over everything.[2]

Cranes and other materials handling devices enhanced the ability of a factory building to serve as the master machine of industry. The adoption of the electric-powered traveling crane had a significant impact on the form of factory buildings, the arrangement of equipment within a plant, and the manner in which work was accomplished. The electric-powered forklift truck had a similar effect because it encouraged the construction of one-story plants.

INDUSTRIAL POWER AND FACTORY BUILDINGS

Manufacturers have relied on several types of prime movers to generate industrial power. Water, steam, and electric power have supplied most of the power for manufacturing and left their mark on industrial architecture. Other types of power had less effect on the form of the works.

Horses, and occasionally other work animals, powered enterprises during their start-up phases and were replaced as resources allowed. Benjamin Latrobe's 1813 plan for a steam engine manufacturing works in Pittsburgh demonstrated how a horse mill was incorporated into a facility. Latrobe placed forge, boiler, and filer's shops on three sides of a square area occupied by a "horse walk," where the animals pushed sweeps to turn an upright shaft that was attached to millwork. Horse-powered treadmills were perhaps a more common type of start-up power; during the late 1830s, in Grand Detour, Illinois, John Deere used this system to power his first plow works.[3]

Several types of industrial power had little impact on the design of factory buildings. Gasoline-powered engines, introduced in the late 1880s, were welcomed because they eliminated the need for the steam engine and boiler, along with the half-hour delay to get the steam boiler "up" and high boiler insurance premiums. A number of simple one-cylinder engines, both gasoline- and oil-fueled, were developed for use in small workshops. By 1890, an American manufacturer had two other types of industrial power at his disposal: Hydraulic and pneumatic power, which took advantage of the properties of air and oil under pressure, were ideal for specific applications.[4]

Waterpower

Waterpower played a significant role in the development of American industry. It was essential to the establishment of textile manufacturing, for example, and helped metalworking industries to flourish with powered forging and rolling machines. And it determined the location of industry and stimulated a demand for larger, better-engineered industrial buildings during the early nineteenth century.

When a waterwheel or turbine was the prime mover, the best position for an industrial building was at the edge of the river or canal so that the waterwheel could be incorporated into the base of the structure. When this location was not possible, water was brought to the building by a flume or small canal (see fig. 3.9), or power was brought mechanically from an external waterwheel, perhaps by rope drive (discussed further later in this chapter). The introduction of water turbines during the early 1840s made waterpower more efficient and kept it a viable power source even after the introduction of steam engines. Buildings that made use of waterpower, however, were limited in size by the area available at the edge of watercourses and the capacity of a waterpower.

Steam Power

One of the great excellencies of the steam engine is that its force can be obtained at all times, in all places, and in any quantity.

"IMPROVEMENTS IN MACHINERY," 1820S

The adoption of the steam engine during the 1840s liberated manufacturers from siting their works adjacent to a waterpower and did not limit the size of their enterprises. As steam engines became more widely utilized, however, their impact on industrial architecture was tempered by the more dominant constraints imposed by millwork systems that distributed power to machinery. Many operations actually used a combination of water and steam power. For example, around 1900 the Walter A. Wood Mowing and Reaping Machine Co. (Hoosick Falls, New York) installed a new Harris-Corliss cross-compound condensing steam engine in its powerhouse to supplement two turbines and seven other steam engines.[5]

Steam power influenced the plans of manufacturing works in several ways. If one steam engine powered the facility, it was centrally located for the efficient distribution of power. During the 1880s, the Holyoke Machine Co. (Worcester, Massachusetts; fig. 4.1) used one engine to power two lines of shafting that extended through a two-story structure, as well as a separate line in the blacksmith shop. When more than one steam engine was used, there was much more flexibility in layout. Decentralized steam power permitted buildings to be situated to facilitate the flow of production rather than just be near the engine house. Steam engines were positioned near the

FIGURE 4.1 The Holyoke Machine Co.'s shops erected in Worcester, Massachusetts, in 1882 were powered by a single steam engine and two main lines of shafting. Belting distributed power to each of the machines arranged in rows parallel to the length of the shop.

heaviest work and so that power could be transmitted from them in all directions with the least amount of millwork.[6]

As the size of works grew, so did the number of steam engines. As the extensive car works of Harlan & Hollingsworth (Wilmington, Delaware) were expanded by accretion over several decades, there was no attempt to centralize steam power production. By the 1890s, fifteen steam engines and associated boilers served various departments. The advantage of flexibility in layout afforded by the use of several small engines, however, was offset by the need for extensive millwork and a cadre of steam engineers and assistants to operate a decentralized power plant until improved, shaft-governed, "automatic" engines reduced the demands for personnel to attend each engine. Small steam engines incorporated into machines that could be driven with steam supplied from a central boiler plant offered more freedom in arranging the production sequence.[7]

The Steam Power Building

As important as the use of steam power was in the expansion of American industry, for many years there was no steam engine suitable for small operations. This problem was often solved through the purchase of power from a nearby larger manufacturing operation. Shafting or a wire rope brought power from a neighbor's steam engine.[8]

The unavailability of inexpensive steam engines also prompted the concentration of small manufacturing operations in "power buildings." A manufacturer might erect a loft building that provided more space than he needed, equip it with a large-capacity steam engine, and rent out space supplied with power. *Scientific American* reported during the 1860s that this practice was common in most cities and manufacturing villages. William B. Bement & Sons (Philadelphia), for example, leased out a considerable portion of its machine shop during the 1850s. In 1854, "mechanics' rooms" of various sizes with steam power supplied by steam engines on the premises could be rented in a large three-story brick loft in Cleveland. An old beam steam engine used for nearly fifty years in a power building was recognized as an important economic factor and a local landmark in Worcester, Massachusetts. The Reed Block, a steam power building erected around 1880 in South Boston, housed many firms during its eighty years of operation.[9]

Power buildings continued to be erected during the late nineteenth century, especially in urban manufacturing areas. Known as "loft buildings," they often housed operations in related businesses; there were several printers' lofts in New York City. The Jesse Metcalf Building (fig. 4.2), erected in

FIGURE 4.2 The Jesse Metcalf Building in Providence, developed for the jewelry manufacturing industry, was a "power building" with an electric power plant.

1896 in Providence for jewelry maufacturers, had its own electric plant that powered the machinery in each shop.[10]

THE AGE OF MILLWORK

Water and steam power were mechanically distributed through millwork that unequivocally linked the building and mechanized equipment (see fig. 2.13). Millwork consisted of shafts, gears, pulleys, and belting. Shafting was supported by metal hanger-plates that were attached to the bottom faces of girders, beams, and joists. From a main shaft on each floor, power was distributed to several line shafts. Belts extended downward from a line shaft to machinery below it and also upward through the floor to run machines on the story above (fig. 4.3).

Millwork was a complicated machine and one that was inefficient and expensive to maintain. The system was costly to install, and its arrangement was not easily altered. In many cases nearly a third of the power that entered the system was dissipated. As late as the 1880s, as much as one-fifth to one-third of the power that entered the system was still lost through millwork. Operations such as spinning and weaving, which used multiple machines of

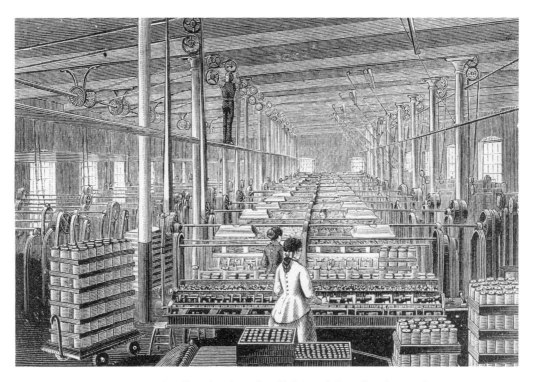

FIGURE 4.3 A millwright adjusted and lubricated the millwork, a machine to transmit motion, in the spooling room of the Clark Thread Co. Works in Newark, New Jersey. A narrow catwalk provided access to pulleys that transferred power from the main shaft to belting that connected with each machine.

the same size, set in rows and driven by parallel lines of overhead shafting, were best served by millwork. In manufacturing works where machines varied in size and time in use and where the location of machines more directly affected production flow, the limitations of millwork were more apparent.

The relationship between millwork and building form is evident in the evolution of the textile mill. In the mills at Lowell, Massachusetts, for example, three large wooden breast wheels were positioned in the basement of each mill erected during the 1820s. Vertical shafts extended up through the four stories of the mill and connected to bevel gear wheels and horizontal shafts that extended the length of each floor. During the late 1830s, the efficiency of the power transfer system was improved by several innovations, including the introduction of the American system of high-speed leather belt main drive. As wrought iron replaced heavier cast-iron sections of shafting, millwork became lighter in weight and could therefore be operated at a higher speed.[11]

This method of power distribution had a direct impact on the form of the textile mill. The vertical shaft and bevel gear system required mills to be tall and narrow because power could not be transferred effectively over 100 feet. Floor areas of limited length were stacked to provide the needed space. Using more efficient water turbines and positioning the main drive shaft in a central location so it could operate two systems of millwork, each half the length of the structure, made it possible to erect mills several hundred feet long and only three stories high.

The link between millwork and the factory building was similar in other types of industries. The need to support millwork, for instance, affected the design of production sheds. It was standard practice to attach shafting and hangers to roof trusses designed to support the weight of millwork (see fig. 2.15). At the C. W. Hunt Co. works (Staten Island, New York; fig. 4.4), a shop erected during the 1880s had roof trusses reinforced with plates enclosing the latticed girder in the area that supported the shafting. Because small changes in the physical dimensions of wood trusses in response to changes to temperature and humidity affected the alignment of millwork, the use of iron trusses was recommended.

The problem of mechanically distributing power over long distances, from 50 feet to three miles, was solved through the use of wire rope (fig. 4.5). Although wire-rope drive was introduced in both Europe and the United States about 1850, it was initially used more widely in Europe. Rope drive was utilized in American works of various types from the 1860s through the end of the nineteenth century. American engineers eventually came to favor the use of a single endless rope that provided uniform power distribution as it wound back and forth to drive pulleys throughout buildings and the works. Wire-rope drive was installed to power the machine shops of the Ohio Falls Car-Works (Jeffersonville, Indiana) during the 1870s and the shops of the Walter A. Wood Harvester Co. (St. Paul) in 1893.[12]

During the nineteenth century, the mechanical distribution of power was a limiting factor in industrial architecture. Millwork furthered the

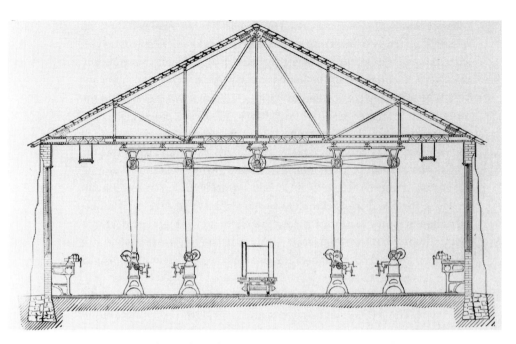

FIGURE 4.4 The machine shop of the C. W. Hunt Co. was set up during the 1880s with four lines of shafting attached to roof trusses. Work benches lined the walls under windows and trucks were pushed on rail that ran down the center of the shop.

FIGURE 4.5 A wire-rope drive extended from a basement engine across roofs and alleys to these structures.

division of labor and the use of separate buildings for machine-powered operations and handwork. It restricted the length of buildings to the distance that shafting could be operated efficiently. The same consideration influenced the layout of the works, since mechanized shops needed to be close to the source of power. As the efficiency of millwork improved, industrial buildings became significantly longer.

THE ERA OF ELECTRIC DRIVE

Electric lighting and electric drive were revolutionary factors in industrial operations. Electric lighting was embraced immediately by the industries that required well-lighted working conditions. Within twenty years from the first applications of electric motors in 1884, the use of individual electric drive—the attachment or incorporation of an electric motor into each machine—became standard practice. The elimination of the mechanical distribution of power through millwork brought a new freedom in production layouts that manufacturers were quick to adopt. These changes had immediate and significant architectural ramifications.[13]

Electric Power

Water and steam power did not disappear with the introduction of electric power; they were the two main sources of electricity for industry. Prior to 1900, manufacturers often combined the oldest and newest forms of industrial power by generating hydroelectricity with waterwheels or turbines. As steam turbines were improved and much less coal was required to generate each kilowatt hour, steam became the most efficient means of producing electricity. The fact that firms could use new electric generators and motors with their existing water and steam-powered prime movers no doubt hastened the adoption of electric drive. The ability to convert equipment for the production of electricity kept many small operations viable even as the much larger works enjoyed economies of scale. However, the introduction of electric power more often brought about the opposite effect: Many older plants were abandoned as more modern works with electric drive were put on line.[14]

Management had to decide whether to generate or purchase electric power when a works converted to electric drive. Extensive use of electricity for heat processes or refrigeration, in addition to operating machinery, pointed to savings realized through the operation of a works powerhouse. A steam-electric plant made sense for operations that used large amounts of steam for heating, drying, cooking, washing, vulcanizing, or other purposes. Consequently, the works powerhouse remained a common component of the works.[15]

The Adoption of Electric Drive

The advantages resulting from the use of electricity are so well known and so universally acknowledged that it is unnecessary to do more than mention them. They may be divided into three classes, as follows: those which affect the senses, those which tend to increase the output, and those which result in important economic gains.

THE ENGINEER, 1903

By the mid-1890s, engineers were evaluating the high first cost of converting to electric drive, as well as the long-term advantages. For a new plant, electric drive often required the construction of a powerhouse equipped with a steam plant and electrical generators and the purchase and installation of electrical motors and wiring. This approach was considerably more expensive than setting up the traditional steam turbine and millwork. Converting an existing facility to electric drive included the same costs, except perhaps the powerhouse and steam plant, and also the abandonment of existing millwork. Electric drive, therefore, had to represent a sufficient recurring savings to offset the extra first cost.[16]

The several benefits of using electric drive also included the availability of the spaces formerly occupied by steam engines and millwork for manufacturing processes, the elimination of inefficiencies due to the mechanical distribution of power, and the economy of a centralized power plant. Moreover, any one tool could be efficiently operated by itself and at a wider range of operational speeds. Electric drive made it easier to produce more uniform goods of a higher quality. And not least important, it was much safer for workmen when an overload occurred: A fuse blew instead of a belt flying off.[17]

The use of electricity in industrial works could be incremental and applied to selected aspects of the operation. Small electric motors were designed specifically for use by the manufacturing operation of limited size, in contrast to the situation with steam engines. Sprague motors of this type were first sold to clothing factories, printing establishments, textile mills, and electrical machinery makers—the industries that were quick to install electric lighting plants. Not surprisingly, electrical-equipment-producing industries promoted the advantages of electric drive. General Electric certainly made it known that it operated its plant in Schenectady with forty-three electric motors. When the firm installed a complete electric drive system in the Columbia Cotton Mills (Lockwood, Greene & Co., engineers; Columbia, South Carolina) in 1892–1893, the event was well publicized.[18]

The adoption of electric drive did not eliminate all millwork in factories. Experts recommended that large machines be supplied with individual electric motors. Smaller tools and machines kept in almost constant use, like textile looms, could be grouped and driven by motor-driven shafts in an arrangement known as "group drive." Although group drive did not offer the flexibility of individual electric motors, it utilized only short lengths of light shafting, and the impact of the millwork was negligible. Motors for

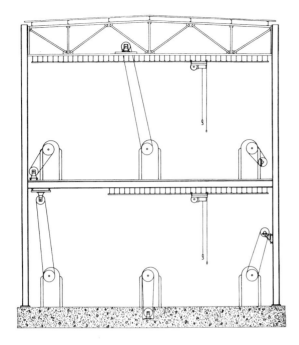

FIGURE 4.6 Shafting and belting for electric "group drive" was attached to floors, walls, and ceilings of industrial buildings, depending on machine location and materials handling methods.

group drive were either supported by brackets on side walls or hung from the ceiling, and they were often connected through the floor to machinery on the floor above (fig. 4.6). The shop built by the Wilkinson Manufacturing Co. (1900; Bridgeport, Pennsylvania) relied on group drive and rather long runs of shafting that extended along the underside of galleries for the length of the 216-foot-long machine and erecting shop. In the new shop erected in 1905 by the Heoffer Manufacturing Co. (Freeport, Illinois), the machinery was arranged in ten groups and run by line shafts that extended across the shop, none longer than 22 feet.[19]

Characteristic of works using individual drive was the Bullock Electric Mfg. Co. (1904; Norwood, Ohio), which was equipped with conduit placed at each side of the middle bay so that only a short length of exposed wire led to each motor. In the new works of the Buckeye Steel Casting Co. (c. 1904; Columbus, Ohio), three generators supplied forty-eight motors that powered electric cranes and machinery in two large shops. An additional feature of this system was automatic signaling to the repair shop that a machine required service.[20]

Electric Drive, Industrial Buildings, and the Works

With the advent of electric transmission all dynamic connection with the power house is at length severed, and the architect is free to group his departments on new principles of arrangement.

THE ADMINISTRATION OF INDUSTRIAL ENTERPRISES, 1926

Electric drive and the elimination of millwork affected industrial operations and the factories that housed them in several ways. Buildings without millwork were not limited in length. Upper walls and roofs became more important than ever as sources for natural light and ventilation once headroom was cleared of millwork; consequently, much wider structures became feasible. The framing of production sheds had to withstand the varying loads of electric-powered cranes rather than support heavy overhead shafting and brace against its vibration. Freedom in the arrangement of equipment, along with more portable tools, focused attention on efficient production layouts and materials handling.

The large corporations that emerged at the turn of the nineteenth century, which had the ability to invest heavily in capital equipment and new facilities, demonstrated in a grand way and a short time the effects of electric power distribution on industry and the configuration of the works. Changes to the physical setting of industry were most visible in the longer, lower shapes of the new works buildings. Historian David Nye argues convincingly that these electrified—and, one must add, steel-framed—works represented a break with the industrial building traditions that preceded them. Electric-powered works, with their vast scale and open and flexible plans, ushered in the era of the modern factory architecture, as well as new production methods and conditions for factory workers.[21]

Electric drive provided new possibilities in the layout of manufacturing works. A single power plant centralized power production and distribution. The works power plant was located to facilitate the receipt and storage of coal, rather than in a central position and close to the mechanized portion of the works. Moreover, electric power placed no limitations on the size of buildings or their arrangement, or on the extent of the works.

It did not take long for the new possibilities for production layouts, building design, and plans for the works to be realized. In 1895 the *Manufacturing Record* noted that electric drive enabled a company to bring together under one roof its erecting, carpentry and cabinet, and metalworking shops, as well as warehouse space. (The configurations used for the new, consolidated plans are described in chapter 3.) The significance of electric drive in the design of the works was suggested by engineer Henry Hess's analogy of "series" and "parallel" electric wiring to describe two plans for advancing work through a plant.[22]

The Traveling Crane

The advent of the electric-driven traveling crane revolutionized shop construction for heavy work. . . . For all shops handling pieces of as little as five hundred pounds' weight even, the traveling crane is needed and, where the work reaches into ordinary steam-engine proportions, this agent is indispensable.

ENGINEERING MAGAZINE, 1896

Electric-powered cranes, along with electric drive and steel framing, revolutionized the physical setting of heavy manufacturing. The elimination of overhead millwork, in fact, made possible the use of traveling cranes in machine shops and other areas previously filled with shafting. Steel framed wide spans and supported heavy-duty cranes. (See chapter 6 for a description of steel-framed production sheds.) New types of spaces—crane-served bays and craneways—became essential components of industrial building design.

The traveling crane consisted of a trolley incorporated into a bridge that spanned a pair of elevated tracks. It had two motions in a horizontal plane: The trolley moved transversely on the bridge, and the bridge traveled longitudinally along the rails (see figs. 4.7, 4.8, and 2.16). Traveling cranes were similar to gantry cranes developed in Great Britain during the 1840s for large civil engineering projects. By the second half of the century, the overhead traveler was a component of well-equipped engineering shops in England and Scotland.[23]

It appears that traveling cranes were not commonly used in the United States until the last quarter of the nineteenth century. A United States Navy report prepared on the dockyards and ironworks of Great Britain and France in 1864 noted the steam-operated overhead traveling cranes used in

FIGURE 4.7 Hand-operated traveling cranes were used to move large pieces of equipment and products through production sheds.

the European shops. It also pointed out that at the New York (Brooklyn) Navy Yard, the service's largest facility at the time, the shop buildings did not have such equipment for materials handling. The reason that cranes were not widely used is revealed in an 1876 advertisement of crane manufacturer J. Henry Mitchell that characterized his hand-operated 10-ton traveling crane as a time- and money-saving device for use in stone and marble yards, foundries, and storehouses—structures without millwork.[24]

Traveling cranes were not cost-effective labor-saving devices for American manufacturers during the mid–nineteenth century for several reasons. Because they could not be used in mechanized operations where headroom was filled with millwork, the jib crane continued to be the most commonly used industrial crane. Timber-framed travelers were limited in capacity and span. They were also primitive in design and difficult to operate effectively; traveling cranes worked well only when they were well balanced, absolutely stable, and free from vibration. According to one crane manufacturer, prior to the 1880s Americans paid little attention to the improvement of cranes for heavy work, and foreign firms provided more advanced products. Engineer Horace Arnold wrote, "It is safe to say that up to 1890 the advantages of the traveling crane and the air hoist were not generally understood by our machine shop managers."[25]

Commercially manufactured cranes available in the 1880s were stronger than earlier models and had more iron components and improved gearing. Still, they were difficult to power. Line shafting was driven by a stationary steam engine or by a steam engine attached directly to the crane. Compressed air-driven (pneumatic) traveling cranes had dragging air hoses, and rope-driven models were quite slow. None of these methods of operation was very satisfactory.[26]

Yet changing economic conditions and keener competition, coupled with improvements in the design of cranes, turned attention to mechanized travelers (see fig. 2.16). At the Tanner & Delaney Engine Co. (c. 1882; Richmond, Virginia), for instance, the erecting shop was commanded by a 15-ton steam-powered traveling crane, managed by only one operator. Three traveling cranes were installed in the fitting-up shop of the Holyoke Machine Co. (c. 1882; Worcester, Massachusetts), although jib cranes remained in use in the machine shop (no doubt because of the presence of millwork). During the late 1880s the erecting shop of the Niles Tool Works (Hamilton, Ohio; fig. 4.8) had a 20-ton powered traveling crane, and there were fourteen travelers throughout that works.[27]

An experimental electric-powered crane installed at the E. P. Allis Co. works (Milwaukee) in 1888 has earned the reputation of being the first of its kind used in the United States.[28] Within two years electric-powered travelers were available from several crane manufacturers. The Baldwin Locomotive Co. (Philadelphia) installed Sellers cranes in an erecting shop in 1890. That same year, the Walker Manufacturing Company of Cleveland, a producer of cranes, hoisting, and other types of machinery, installed electric-powered traveling cranes in its new facility. By early 1893 the

FIGURE 4.8 The main erecting shop of the Niles Tool works in Hamilton, Ohio, was commanded by a traveling crane with a capacity of 20 tons during the 1880s. The crane was powered by a shaft that extended the length of the shop, located above one of the crane girders. The operator rode along with the crane in the cage that hung from the bridge.

Worthington Hydraulic Works in Brooklyn had a Yale & Towne electric traveling crane with a 120-ton capacity in its heavy machine shop.[29]

Traveling cranes affected the way in which work was accomplished in crane-served bays. When a traveling crane was installed, hoists that had served individual machines were often removed. The machinist, then, had less control over his own work. The tasks of supplying materials, moving assemblies along, and positioning pieces at work stations were centralized in the crane operator.

The perfect union of the one-story production shed with a tall central bay and the requirements of traveling crane operation raises the question of whether the crane was adapted to the building, or the building to the crane. The former seems to be the case, since the standard three-bay production shed was developed as a means of framing, lighting, and ventilating a single-story structure of considerable width. The production shed became an important feature of the works during the mid–nineteenth century, when jib cranes, rather than traveling cranes, facilitated the work of the foundry and erecting shop. Nevertheless, the three-bay structure proved to be the ideal form to accommodate the traveling crane because the side bays, or lean-tos, provided space for millwork and machinery adjacent to a crane-served central erecting bay. There is little wonder, then, that production sheds became even more widely utilized after the introduction of electric drive.

The Craneway

These craneways become the common arteries of transportation for all of the buildings and the connecting link between floors.

IRON AGE, 1914

Soon after the electric-powered traveling crane became an essential part of the works, two common types of craneways appeared in order to facilitate materials handling. Horizontal craneways, as transepts or central spines, linked production areas in large plants. Vertical craneways that extended through several stories served side galleries or loft buildings flanking a central erecting space or industrial rail service.

Horizontal craneways were inserted into existing works for ease of materials handling. For example, in 1902 the Baldwin Locomotive Co., located on a constricted urban site in Philadelphia, closed two blocks of a street that passed through the works. Electric traveling cranes were installed to travel above the former street and serve loading platforms at the second stories of buildings next to the craneway. In a similar manner, during the remodeling of the Pennsylvania Railroad Shops (c. 1902; Altoona, Pennsylvania) a craneway was installed in a narrow yard between the erecting and machine shops.[30]

Craneways were soon incorporated into plans for new works as main arteries for the delivery of materials and removal of products from shop areas that met it at right angles. The automobile works of the White Co. (1905–1907; George H. Smitt, architect; Cleveland) featured a 600-foot-long craneway that linked four single-story buildings. Traveling cranes operated 17 feet above the floor, and trucks also used the passageway to move materials between departments. At the time this craneway was considered "one of the most decided novelties in factory construction." A two-story craneway over 300 feet long connected the wings of the Nathan Manufacturing Co. plant (c. 1917; Eugene Schoen, architect; Flushing, Queens; fig. 4.9). The craneway joined six separate two-story wings positioned as a modified unit system plan. Material destined for the second story of the plant was placed by cranes on trucks positioned on bridges that spanned the craneway.[31]

Vertical craneways evolved as the form of production sheds became longer and taller. The Sheerness Boat Store (1858–1860; G. T. Greene, designer; Sheerness Naval Dockyard, England) may have been a prototype for this type of craneway. It consisted of a central bay spanned by traveling cranes that served the flanking four-story sections. But this building seems not to have been widely replicated until the introduction of electric-powered traveling cranes. We begin to see vertical craneways in factories like the Triumph Electric Co.'s new plant (1909; Cincinnati), which was erected with a vertical craneway that served side galleries at three levels. The scale of these spaces was sublime. A four-story-high craneway, an 800-foot-long erecting bay, in the General Electric Co.'s plant was christened the "Grand Canyon of Schenectady" by an enthusiastic journalist. The Studebaker Plant (designed

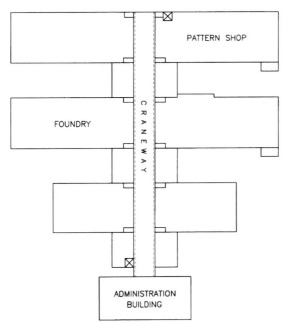

FIGURE 4.9 A plant layout dominated by a craneway was adopted for the works of the Nathan Manufacturing Co. in Flushing, New York.

in 1916 but not erected until after World War I; South Bend, Indiana; fig. 4.10) included buildings with exceptionally wide and long central bays in which cranes served three gallery levels.[32]

Galleries next to vertical craneways were designed to facilitate materials handling. In the Pfannmueller Engineering Co.'s warehouse (c. 1910; Alfred S. Alschuler, architect; Central Manufacturing District, Chicago), gallery floors were cantilevered beyond the column line framing the craneway. The machine and erecting shops of the Barry-Wehmiller Machinery Co. (c. 1913; Widmann & Walsh, designers; St. Louis) had a similar arrangement. Cantilevered second-story galleries, used as metalworking shops, had loading platforms that projected even farther. Raw materials were brought into the building in railroad cars, unloaded at one end by the crane, and lifted to the upper galleries to begin their movement through the shop toward the other end.[33]

It was a short step from a vertical craneway serving galleries to one serving adjacent loft buildings, as demonstrated by the Ford Motor Co.'s Highland Park Ford Plant (1914–1915 expansion; Albert Kahn, architect; Highland Park, Michigan). Six-story loft buildings flanked craneways that commanded rail spurs and raised raw materials to staggered cantilevered landing platforms on the upper stories. Other Ford Motor Co. facilities, including those in Chicago and Kearny, New Jersey, also made use of this configuration. A very similar craneway—no doubt inspired by Ford's—was built into the Brooklyn Army Supply Base (1918; Cass Gilbert, architect; Brooklyn). There the craneway served landing platforms that projected from a pair of eight-story lofts.[34]

FIGURE 4.10 The Studebaker Plant in South Bend, Indiana, incorporated vertical craneways that served four-story reinforced concrete loft buildings. Staggered balconies facilitated the transfer of materials at the upper levels.

The craneway and loft combination evolved at the time when movement of materials vertically was more efficient than horizontal transport. Some industrial engineers considered it a mistake to use large one-story buildings in which goods had to be moved over great distances. Engineers enthusiastic about vertical craneways predicted that crane service would relegate elevators to an auxiliary role. Instead, another innovation in materials handling pointed the way to the future.

The Electric Forklift Truck

During the first half of the twentieth century, both materials handling and the ideal form for a factory building were significantly altered by the electric forklift truck. Battery-powered tractors and trucks were introduced for industrial use to avoid the exhaust and noise of internal-combustion and steam engines. Trucks with self-contained power systems became available around 1914. The Elwell-Parker Co. soon developed a truck with a built-in lifting mechanism, and by 1917 several competitors had entered the field.

A forklifting device was a 1919 Elwell-Parker improvement to its elevating-platform, or "high-lift," truck. The high-lift truck (also called a tiering truck and pallet truck) was a common tool of industry by the late 1920s. Skids, or racks, had long been in use, but around 1930 they were transformed into standard 4-foot-square pallets with openings for the fork. Pallets prompted changes in packaging and lot size, and the cubical pallet unit became a standard module for storage and shipping.[35]

Electric-powered trucks required smooth floors, but they could maneuver in narrow aisles and needed little turning room. They worked most efficiently in one-story structures with 20-foot-high ceilings. The trucks could be used in lofts, but older structures often needed to have their door openings enlarged and smoother flooring installed. A loft intended for storage and service by a forklift truck carried higher construction costs due to the required additional headroom and floor strength. Consequently, the forklift truck had a strong bearing on the type of industrial building that manufacturers preferred. New construction more than ever was likely to be production sheds, even for operations otherwise well suited for multistory lofts.

POWER FOR HEAT AND LIGHT

The power that operated the machinery in the manufacturing works also made possible the engineering of the works for the comfort of the workforce and improved conditions for production. Steam heating of works buildings became common once the steam engine became an auxiliary or primary source of power. Artificial lighting, in the form first of gas lighting and then, during the 1880s, electric lighting, supplemented rather than replaced daylight for quite some time.

Steam Heat

Heating systems were introduced into industrial buildings when exhaust steam from the boiler could be trapped and used for this purpose. Both direct steam systems, in which heat radiated from steam pipes, and indirect systems, which circulated hot air through the building, were used in factories. Radiant steam heat was a great improvement over the use of isolated stoves and was a relatively safe way to heat industrial buildings. Although Americans usually installed small steam pipes along the perimeter of the building underneath windows, they also adopted the British practice of placing steam pipes overhead. These pipes, however, tended to overheat the ceiling area or workbenches near the windows and were difficult to locally control for a uniform supply of heat.

Hot air systems of heating and ventilation used steam-heated coils and a mechanically driven fan or blower to move warmed air throughout buildings. The heated air moved through a system of underground and pipe ducts to sheet-metal flues and entered work areas through openings near the floor level. Metal flues could be eliminated when heated air was conveyed through the pilasters of mid-nineteenth-century textile mills, through steel columns (in the 1902 Lunkenheimer Co.'s Fairmount Works, Cincinnati), or through reinforced concrete columns (in the Ford Motor Co.'s Highland Park loft buildings). During the 1870s, the B. F. Sturtevant Co. developed mechanical components utilized in such systems, initially for drying purposes in manufacturing. Sturtevant systems were first installed in many textile mills, and by 1890 they were used widely throughout industry.[36]

The hot blast system was well suited for heating production sheds. Its components, heating coils and fans, could be mounted out of the way, either on the upper portion of the wall or from floor or roof framing. This type of heating also eliminated overhead pipes that obstructed the movement of traveling cranes.

Electric Lighting

Electric lighting had a significant bearing on industrial production. It affected both the quantity and quality of manufactured goods, permitted longer hours of operation, and made the night shift possible. But since artificial lighting did not replace daylight as the main source of light in most manufacturing operations until the adoption of controlled conditions plants around 1940, it had less of an impact on industrial architecture.[37]

Manufacturers quickly embraced the new technology, and many of the first electric lighting systems were placed in industrial buildings. Edison "isolated plants" were available with dynamos suited to various sizes of operations. Electric lighting plants were installed in the textile mills of Lowell just after 1880 and soon thereafter appeared in many textile mills and newspaper plants.[38]

Illuminating engineers began making recommendations for factory lighting during the early twentieth century. But since the amount of light required varied with the size of rooms, the character of work to be accomplished, the positioning of machines, and shop conditions, general standards for factory lighting were difficult to establish. Illuminating engineers had five types of electric arc lamps from which to choose as they designed both general and task-directed lighting over benches and machines. The goal was an evenness of illumination without glare and with "easy" shadows. The "searching quality" of light produced by mercury-vapor lamps made them especially suitable for factory lighting.[39]

Flaming or enclosed arc lamps were recommended for forges, steel mills, structural ironworks, and boiler shops that needed good general illumination rather than concentrated light. Among the most difficult spaces to properly light were foundries and shops with traveling cranes. The presence of traveling cranes required the placement of all light fixtures 20 to 30 feet above the floor or at the sides of the space. One solution for foundry lighting was the use of "Lucigen" lights (burning jets of kerosene oil) mounted near eye level on the terminations of fuel-conducting pipes that rose from the floor.

High-wattage, high-pressure mercury lamps developed in 1935 could be effectively mounted at heights of 20 to 40 feet above the floor. Fluorescent lamps, introduced in 1938, became another popular source of artificial illumination. Continuous rows of fluorescent lamps soon brought new economies in wiring and installation costs, as well as better lighting conditions. These improvements in lighting fixtures ultimately led to a total reliance on artificial light and a controlled atmosphere in buildings without windows and skylights. (See chapter 7 for the introduction of controlled conditions plants.)[40]

Power generation and distribution have been intertwined with industrial building design and the layout of the works. With structures, power sources, and machinery working together as a master machine, factories were powered for profit. Their productive operation, however, also depended upon designs that could meet the engineering demands of powered manufacturing operations and limit fire losses.

ENGINEERING CONSIDERATIONS   5

The buildings must be strong, if fireproof so much the better.

THE MANUFACTURER AND BUILDER, 1869

I n 1869 an engineer made recommendations for the construction and arrangement of a wood-working establishment. The building, constructed of stone, brick, iron, and slate, had to be strong and should contain no wood so it would be fireproof. The three- or four-story structure, with brick walls at least 18 inches thick, was to have door and window openings as large as possible without compromising the strength of the walls. The first floor, where the heaviest machinery would be placed, should be flush with the ground.[1]

As this example illustrates, the design problem of a sturdy industrial building was well understood by the mid–nineteenth century. Factories needed to be fireproof and strong enough to bear the weight and withstand the strain of both the machinery operated in them and the varied and shifting loads of the materials used in manufacturing. Of all the demands that industry placed on factories, the mandate for maximum strength and stability was dominant.

ENGINEERED FOR STRENGTH

In ordinary mills, the stability of the building limits the speed of most textile machinery, but when vibration is reduced to a minimum, as in the case of a one-story mill, the limit of speed is a question of machine construction.

MILL ENGINEER C. J. H. WOODBURY, 1882

Industrial buildings that housed mechanized equipment had to withstand both vibration and oscillation. Vibration, the shaking of a building due to the movement of its elastic floors and beams, was not caused by a lack of structural stability. It was reciprocating machinery that put walls in motion and could shift buildings off their foundations. In textile mills and machine shops, vibration was produced by machinery, or perhaps by water flowing over waterpower dams, and could be reduced by altering the speed of machines. The excessive vibration of multistory buildings could limit the speed with which its machinery could be operated; but occasionally increasing the speed solved the problem. The interior framing of textile mills and machine shops had to be designed to be strong and stiff enough to provide solidity and steadiness but also elastic enough to withstand vibration. Production sheds where large cranes and machinery were operated also had to resist vibration and oscillation. Shops housing light machinery that operated at high speeds required great strength in wall construction to absorb the vibration.[2]

Oscillation, the swaying of the entire building, resulted from the movement of cranes or machinery and insubstantial construction. It could cause windows and skylights to break, even in steel-framed structures. Reinforcement of structural elements and buttressing of exterior walls often reduced oscillation. To minimize it in loft structures, mill engineers placed Pratt trusses under floors and roof planks; they also laid the top layer of flooring diagonally to make the two floor layers act as a horizontal lattice.[3]

Architects and engineers came to understand that thick load-bearing walls alone could not limit the effects of oscillation and vibration. They engineered industrial buildings to limit and diffuse such forces. Properly balanced and bonded walls served better if there were pilasters and offset sections of long walls (projecting pavilions, for example) to disrupt vibratory motion (see figs. 1.2, 3.7, 8.4, and 9.1). If the design of roof and interior framing transferred weight to concentrating bearings, rather than dispersing it, the effect of vibration was reduced. Roofs also vibrated and had to be supported properly or they would cause walls to bulge.[4]

Floor construction was tailored to the intended use of the building. The jarring and reciprocating pounding movements of machinery in wood- and metalworking machine shops required floors with properties that were different from those used in lofts filled with steadily operated textile spinning and weaving equipment. Joist-framed floors were stiffer and less yielding than more elastic mill floor construction. One of the reasons the heavy timbers and planks of slow-burning construction were combined with steel framing for industrial loft buildings was to reduce problems with vibration.[5]

Floor Load Capacity

Every wall, pier, column, or beam in a building can be calculated, the maximum strains determined and such dimensions given to each detail of construction that the building shall not only be secure against accident, but shall be a homogeneous whole; that is, every part strong and no material wasted.

WILLIAM LE BARON JENNEY, 1877

During much of the nineteenth century, the problem of moving materials to upper stories checked the need for great strength in commercial and industrial building construction. The introduction of the elevator, however, changed this situation. Suddenly it was easy to move heavy goods to upper floors, where previously only the lightest materials had been stored. During the 1870s, architect William Le Baron Jenney (who had extensive engineering training) expressed concern over the strength and overloading of loft buildings with elevators. Structures that could safely carry only 70 pounds, he asserted, were being loaded with 100 to 200 pounds per square foot. Jenney confidently pointed out, though, that since the engineer had the ability to calculate the strength of every element in the structure, this should be an easy problem to correct.[6]

The computation of live load capacity soon led to the establishment of standard, and even required, floor load strengths. Building codes like that of New York City, first adopted in 1862, required a minimum floor load capacity of 150 pounds per square foot in new construction, a standard that remained unchanged throughout the nineteenth century. New York City also dictated that the capacities for existing buildings used for storage be posted in them; this emphasis led works owners to rebuild structures' interiors to enable them to better serve their purpose. Yellow-pine girders were replaced with steel ones in some buildings used as warehouses. For instance, after a fire in 1897, the Dietz lantern factory (1887; R. W. Tieffenberg, architect; New York City) was rebuilt with a combination of cast-iron columns and steel beams. Henry Grattan Tyrrell presented the New York City standards for floor load strength in his 1901 volume on iron mill building construction. He recommended that structures housing heavy machinery have floors with a capacity of 250 to 400 pounds per square foot, and he reproduced a table of weights of various types of merchandise.[7]

Floor load requirements for buildings used primarily as warehouses added considerably to the cost of the structures and determined the type of construction used. For example, the developer, architect, and construction contractor discussed at length the floor strength suitable for the Austin Nichols Warehouse (1913; Cass Gilbert, architect; Brooklyn), which was designed to house a wholesale grocery warehouse and food processing operation. A compromise capacity of 300 pounds per square foot influenced the selection of reinforced concrete as the building material. The Turner Construction Co. later recommended reducing the capacity to 250 pounds to achieve a savings of $10,000.[8]

Column Spacing

In the factory building, high or low, column spacing seems to be the most important consideration. When bays become too large, excess cost of columns and steel framing appears. The column arrangement must fit properly the lines of machines, the receptacles for merchandise, the handling of goods for packing or shipping.

ARCHITECT ELY JACQUES KAHN, 1929

The desire for floor space as unobstructed as possible with columns and for corresponding large bays (the space between columns) complicated efforts to build economically for strength and stability. The problem was not framing large bays; it was doing so without adding inordinately to the expense of the structure. Extra-long girders of wood, iron, steel, or concrete—those more than 25 feet in length—had to be of increased depth. Hence, they added to the height required for each story, and the resulting structure was taller and more expensive than one with an equal number of stories and standard column spacing. The trade-off was between a higher first cost of wide-span construction and any savings in production that might be realized through more flexible machinery layout in large bays. The construction of bays of above-average dimensions was often limited to specific portions of a manufacturing building, such as a ground story where shipping tracks and platforms were located.

Generous column spacing that offered the most flexibility in machinery layout was especially valued by manufacturers who used machines of various sizes. Engineers considered a column to nullify as much as 9 to 16 square feet of the floor area around it for machinery placement. The challenge of positioning machinery led to the practice of using only two rows of columns extending the length of industrial loft buildings, and sometimes placing them close together to define a narrow transportation corridor (see fig. 2.1).[9]

The need for unobstructed space also prompted the construction of floors supported from above by rods or trusses. The ground floor, where large and heavy machinery was apt to be located, or a floor near the top of the building, where the lighting conditions were good, were sometimes freed of columns in this way. For example, the first and fourth floors of an American Express stable (New York City) were kept clear of columns for wagon storage with the use of "hung floor" construction. In a three-story loft building of the Detroit Shipbuilding Co. (1902; Detroit), the second-story floor was attached to the lower chord of a truss formed by the upper floors and roof trusses of the steel-framed structure, thereby eliminating columns on the ground floor.[10]

ENGINEERED FOR THE CONTAINMENT OF FIRE

Careful attention has been given to the fire hazard. An engineer trained in the inspection of manufacturing properties devotes his entire time to the fire protection devices and to the safeguarding of all of the processes of manufacture.

THE WESTERN ELECTRIC CO., 1906

A three-story loft building that housed the Goold Coach Manufactory (1841; Albany, New York) was carefully planned to limit the spread of fire. It was divided into four sections by fire walls, and each portion was further separated from adjacent ones by service bays. In those areas, cisterns that provided water for fire-fighting, carriageways, and hoistways (which could act as flues) were isolated from production shops. In the blacksmith shop, the floor was brick; wood benches (the only combustible material in the shop) were considered to be low enough that if they burned the fire would not reach the high ceiling.[11]

The careful attention given to the fire safety program at the Western Electric Co.'s Hawthorne works near Chicago (1906) was characteristic of efforts at large manufacturing plants during the early twentieth century. An engineer whose time was devoted to the supervision of the fire prevention program was the counterpart of the modern-day safety engineer. Production sheds were spaced far enough apart to reduce the danger of fire spreading from one to another; production space within them was compartmentalized by heavy fire walls with tin-clad doors at their openings. The steel-framed structures had brick walls, window sash with wire glass, floors of concrete, and tile roofs. An automatic sprinkler system that extended throughout most of the works was considered unnecessary in the foundry, the forge shop, and the main portion of the machine shop because of the absence of combustible materials. Nevertheless, the steel structure of the machine shop was protected with rings of sprinkler heads attached to the columns 15 feet above the floor. A water tower housed several tanks connected with the water sprinkler system. The Western Electric works was equipped with numerous hydrants; several caches of hose, axes, and lanterns; and fire alarm boxes. The company also maintained a brigade of trained firemen and two fire pumps.[12]

The measures taken in the designs of the Goold Coach Manufactory and Western Electric's Hawthorne works illustrate how "fireproof" factories have been an ideal that, though seldom achieved, has long had a bearing on architecture and the layout of manufacturing works. Many factory construction projects took place in the aftermath of a fire. Rebuilding at such a time certainly provided an opportunity to consider the relative fireproofness of building materials and to incorporate design features that limited the spread of fire.

Fire was a constant threat to factories, especially during the nineteenth century, because of the combustibility of building materials and contents. Many types of industrial operations had to contend with the most common sources of fire: sparks, defective chimneys, the friction generated by machinery in motion, and the spontaneous combustion of oil, as well as the use of matches and lighting fixtures. The combination of dust-laden air with a spark could result in an explosion and fire in such diverse industries as breweries, flouring mills, and candy factories (where sugar and starch became airborne particles). Lumber drying kilns, as well as the presence of sawdust throughout the premises, created hazardous conditions in woodworking operations.[13]

Nevertheless, manufacturers seldom built "fireproof" factories. The fireproof construction used in well-financed British textile mills—usually brick-arched flooring supported by iron interior framing members—was considered too expensive and heavy for textile mills and other industrial buildings in the United States. Indeed, an 1849 report on the warehousing system of Great Britain prepared for the American secretary of the treasury admitted that there was scarcely a single absolutely fireproof storehouse, one with no combustible materials, in the United States. Instead, noncombustible materials and wood were combined in various types of "semifireproof" construction. In the practice known as "fire-resistive construction," industrial facilities were engineered to contain and retard the spread of fire. Pragmatic industrialists unquestionably wanted to limit their losses to fire, a hazard that seemed unavoidable.[14]

This attention to the threat of fire unquestionably affected the architectural appearance and engineering of factory buildings. It influenced the choice of building materials and the way that some materials, like sheet metal, were used. The size and shape of buildings, their internal compartmentalization, roof form, and construction, were aspects of fire-resistive construction. The use of a fire-resistant envelope of sheet metal, concrete stucco and metal lath, and steel-framed sash also affected the aesthetic development of industrial architecture as enclosing walls were articulated in ways that departed from the traditional load-bearing masonry wall. These materials and forms became part of the language of an industrial architectural modernism (see chapter 11).

Fire Safety Programs

The buildings of this company are all of brick, with heavy walls and floor beams, and are covered with slate roofs. Water mains from the city traverse the yards of the company, with hydrants at convenient places. No combustible material is allowed on the premises, and this establishment is considered by insurance surveyors as the best machine-shop risk in the country.

THE NEW-YORK STEAM ENGINE CO., 1874

By the mid–nineteenth century manufacturers had developed integrated programs, based on empirical observation, to prevent, detect, contain, and suppress fire in manufacturing works. This multifaceted approach to the threat of fire, however, resulted in imprecise and varied meanings for the term *fireproof*. For example, this description of the works of the New-York Steam Engine Co. (Passaic, New Jersey; see fig. 1.4), a facility that was considered fireproof, noted the various measures taken to limit loss to fire. In this case, fireproofness was based on the elimination of fuel in the contents of the building and on the use of fire-resistant materials in building construction. The provision of fire-fighting equipment was another part of the strategy.

A factory building considered fireproof might be erected primarily of noncombustible or fire-resistant materials or might incorporate elements of fire-resistive construction. In fact, fireproof construction was always a relative characteristic that changed as building technology and the understanding of building materials' performance evolved. Fireproof construction generally referred to assemblies that eliminated wood and were of masonry, metal, and cement (mortar and eventually concrete). Nineteenth-century fireproof construction relied on the use of noncombustible materials in sufficient quantity that a fire might damage their surfaces but not compromise structural integrity. Heavy timber framing in mill construction (discussed later in this chapter) was based on this rationale. During the late nineteenth century, the need to protect iron and steel framing became evident. "Fireproofed" construction methods were developed in which outer, exposed fire-resistant portions of assemblies protected more vulnerable structural elements.[15]

A manufacturing works described as fireproof might consist of buildings of "fireproof" construction divided by fire walls. Timely fire detection and rapid fire suppression were integral aspects of the works' fire safety program, and one of the main duties of the factory night watchmen was to be on the lookout for fire. Many works had trained fire brigades. The owner of the Oswego Starch Factory was at least the titular head of a 100-man company that was "fully equipped and thoroughly drilled."[16]

Manufacturing works were laid out to retard the spread of fire and facilitate its suppression. One of the functions of yard space between buildings was keeping fire from extending from one structure to another; it also provided staging areas for fire-fighting. Office and pattern storage buildings (often built of more fire-resistant materials and with additional elements of fire-resistive construction than the other structures in the works, as described in chapter 2) were sometimes located across the street or the works yard from other buildings. Freestanding powerhouses isolated the boilers and steam engines, and later electric equipment, from other sources of fire and offered some chance for containing fires that originated there. Buildings housing hazardous operations and used for the storage of flammable materials were removed from other structures to the extent possible. Oil storehouses were sometimes erected with their floors below the level of the yard to prevent the spread of burning oil. Where space allowed, a pond was maintained as a source of water for fire-fighting. A more common procedure was storing water in tanks elevated in towers that rose above the pattern storage, warehouse, and main production buildings. Brick walls around the works also served as fire walls and protected the operation from external sources of fire.

Automatic sprinkler systems combined aspects of fire suppression, containment, and, eventually, detection. Early sprinkler systems developed for use in textile mills consisted of ranges of perforated pipe placed under ceilings. The pipes were supplied with water from a tank or reservoir, and the system was operated by controls located on the exterior of the building (fig. 5.1). In 1874 the Parmalee Co. perfected an automatic sprinkler head in which heat melted the solder joints that kept its cap in place and the water contained. By the mid-1880s, numerous types of automatic sprinklers had

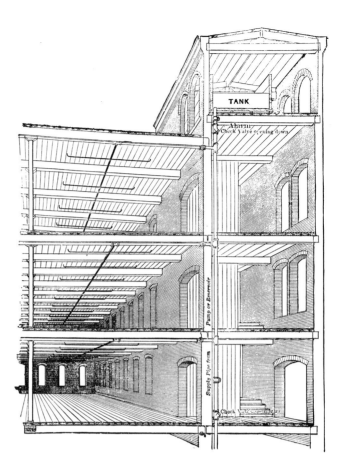

FIGURE 5.1 Automatic sprinklers, in general use by the mid-1880s, were installed in industrial buildings as shown in this sectional view of a textile mill. The water tank for the system occupied an elevated position at the top of a stair tower.

been installed in many textile mills, and manufacturers of other types of goods soon adopted the technology.[17]

Another aspect of fire safety—provision for quick exit by factory workers—also received some attention. Municipal building codes required the use of fire escapes, which were either interior stairwells or iron platforms and stairs attached to the exterior of structures. In New York City, an 1871 revision of the building code required fire escapes on buildings used as factories that were three or more stories in height.[18]

Industrialists who joined a mutual fire insurance company, like those established in New England, had support for their efforts to limit loss to fire. The Factory Mutuals (as they were known) advocated fire-resistive construction and the use of slow-burning mill construction (discussed later in this chapter), instituted a program of inspections, offered technical advice to policy holders, and researched ways to prevent loss. In these efforts they pioneered the field that became insurance engineering, or safety engineering.

The majority of manufacturers, however, insured their property with the so-called stock fire insurance companies, which underwrote most fire insurance in the United States. Unlike the Factory Mutual companies, which were owned by their members and therefore had an interest in reducing loss, stock companies accepted loss and sought to collect enough premiums to be able to pay claims and make a profit. Most industrial works owners who erected fire-resistive buildings and established fire prevention programs did so mainly on their own initiative. Not until the Universal Mercantile Schedule was developed, during the early 1890s, did the stock companies collectively attempt to "scientifically" analyze all aspects of the fire hazard of commercial and industrial structures. The mercantile schedule helped manufacturers and businessmen identify and eliminate hazards. The rates it established used lower premiums to reward fire-resistive building construction. Stock insurance companies also began to provide standards for the use of fire detection equipment and the storage of hazardous materials, as well as for fire-resistive construction.[19]

Even after the modernization of the fire insurance industry during the early twentieth century, management's interest in fireproof and fire-resistive construction determined its use in factory construction. The higher initial first cost of building a factory of fireproof construction was offset, though not fully compensated, by lower fire insurance premiums. Savings in fire insurance premiums, nevertheless, represented one reason that manufacturers were willing to spend the extra money to erect fireproof reinforced concrete buildings.

Fire-Resistive Construction

Every precaution has been taken to prevent the occurrence of fire, or its extending if once begun. . . . It is believed that a fire could not spread beyond the part in which it might originate.

NEW YORK STATE MECHANIC, 1841

Fire-resistive construction, though that term was not yet in use, was much in evidence in the design of the Goold Coach Manufactory (described earlier). Based on the realistic assumption that the occasional fire was inevitable, fire-resistive construction embraced specific features that isolated and contained fire. Elements of fire-resistive construction were incorporated into the municipal building codes adopted in cities during the second half of the nineteenth century and thereby became required in many factories in urban settings.[20]

Isolation was a dominant principle in fire-resistive construction. Industrial buildings and works of fire-resistive construction were arranged to segregate sources of fire and to limit their spread. Factory fire hazards included furnaces and boilers, forges, lumber-drying kilns, and any dust-laden operations. The most common method of isolation was to house these activities in freestanding structures.

The fire wall, or fire stop, was another isolation and containment tool. A fire wall extended from the foundation level through all stories to the roof and above. As was typical, fire walls extended through the roof of the paint

FIGURE 5.2
Fire doors of thick
wood planks were
lined on both sides
with sheet iron or tin.
They were considered
automatic, or self-
closing, if they
moved back into a
closed position after
being opened.

shop of the Wason Car Manufacturing Co. (1872–1873; George C. Fisk, proprietor and designer; Springfield, Massachusetts; see fig. 2.8). In addition to being constructed of non-combustible brick, fire walls had to be thick enough to prevent the transmission of heat and to resist the tendency to bulge and collapse during a severe fire. Fire walls were used in buildings of both ordinary and mill construction. Openings in them were limited in number and staggered in large structures with several divisions. Double sets of tin-lined doors were hung on hardware that caused them to close automatically after each opening (fig. 5.2). Vertical flues, such as stairways, through which fire readily spread, were isolated to the extent possible. Industrial lofts often had stairs, hoists, and power transmission systems positioned in towers that acted as flues and were consequently placed on the exterior of the rectangular mass (see figs. 1.2, 1.7, 3.6, and 6.3).

The Factory Tower: A Legacy of Fire-Resistive Construction

George C. Nimmons, the architect of these and many other factory buildings, . . . often gives a fine dignity and a dominate note of *design* by insistence on a great, massive, square tower, with buttresses.

CRITIC C. MATLACK PRICE, 1917

A tower rising along the side of a factory building, or from its roof, has become a distinguishing characteristic of industrial buildings. Architectural historians have asserted that these towers became standard elements of textile mill architecture because they provided a civic presence that coincided with the mill's dominant role in a new industrial order. Indeed, the prominence of towers and cupolas, often with bell towers or clocks, supports that argument. The star-studded royal blue onion dome of the Colt Armory (both the 1855 and 1866–1868 structures; Hartford, Connecticut; fig. 3.7) was one of the most distinctive interpretations of the industrial building tower and certainly established a public stature. In fact, the presence of the tower can best be accounted for by the pragmatism and profit motive that drove the design of industrial buildings.[21]

Stair towers adjacent to textile mills and freestanding lofts in works were components of fire-resistive construction. They often extended above the roofline with a belfrylike termination and, consequently, replaced cupolas that had held the factory bells that regulated the workday. Stair towers articulated the long facades of textile mills and added to their overall architectural character. Many exhibited a kinship to Italian campaniles, with their varied window openings, detailed brickwork, and decorative roofs (see figs. 1.2, 1.7, 3.6, and 6.3). Service towers that housed toilets and power transmission shafts were likely to extend from the rear of structures and were more utilitarian in design.

The tower became a more standard element of industrial architecture and works iconography at the time that automatic sprinkler systems were widely adopted during the late nineteenth century. Although water tanks could be placed on the roof, elevated on a framework of timber or angle iron (as was common in urban areas), manufacturers often chose to use masonry towers to protect their sprinkler system tanks from the weather and fire. The role of the tower was occasionally expanded: Some towers housed steam whistles or chimes and supported clock faces. Towers were detailed as forms rising through the facade and positioned to emphasize prominent corners or main entrances; they were often terminated by a decorative roof form. Sometimes they were more isolated features on the rooftop.

Water tank towers were incorporated also into works housed in production sheds. A freestanding brick water tank tower stood next to the Green Island Shops of the Rensselaer & Saratoga Railroad (1872; Green Island, New York; see fig. 10.7). The works of the Tanner & Delaney Engine Co. (1882; Richmond, Virginia; see fig. 1.5 and 1.6) featured two towers. Probably both the tower above the pattern storage building and the more ornamental, mansard-roofed tower rising from a corner of the office block enclosed water storage tanks.[22]

Architects, in particular, made the factory tower a focal point of industrial architecture. Architect George C. Nimmons considered the tower an essential element of factory design that vastly improved the silhouette of industrial loft buildings. He often placed the main entrance in the base of a

FIGURE 5.3 The prominent tower, powerhouse, and chimney of the Pershing Road unit of the Central Manufacturing District in Chicago represented an emphatic synthesis of centralized power and fire protection.

tower that rose from ground level to above the flat roof (see fig. 9.10). Architectural critic C. Matlack Price affirmed the architect's devotion to the tower and suggested that the tower of Nimmons's Liquid Carbonic Plant (c. 1915; Chicago) elevated the structure from a utilitarian building to "architecture." The Hawthorne Shops of the Western Electric Co. (1906; Chicago) had a tower of "artistic design." According to the architect, H. Black Co. officials specifically requested that a freestanding tank tower be an ornamental feature of their Wooltex plant (1909; Robert D. Kohn, architect; Cleveland). The tower rising above the American Bank Note Company Building (1909–1911; Kirby, Petit & Greene, architects; the Bronx) was terminated as a crenelated parapet that reinforced the fortresslike quality of the structure. In addition to housing the water tank, the tower provided secluded and secure quarters for the company counterfeiter, who insured that the firm's printed money and financial documents could not be replicated.[23]

The imposing tower of the Pershing Road unit of the Central Manufacturing District (c. 1917; S. Scott Joy, architect; Chicago; fig. 5.3) was an emphatic synthesis of centralized power and fire protection. Prominently located, the tower housed the tanks and other components of the sprinkler system that extended to all of the buildings in the development and the offices of the industrial district's architect and construction staff. Electrically lighted clock faces, set in each side of the tower, incorporated the seal of the Central Manufacturing District and served as an ever visible reminder of the need for fire safety.[24]

Fire-Resistant Materials

If a manufacturer can build a plant that is absolutely fireproof, that is well lighted and well ventilated, notwithstanding the expense of a trifle more than a wooden building, is it not a prudent expenditure?

THE BERLIN IRON BRIDGE COMPANY, C. 1892

Toward the end of the nineteenth century, incombustible or fire-resistant materials began to be more effectively utilized in factory construction. Fire-resistant materials of the highest grades were placed in areas that held the greatest hazards or the most valuable resources. Experience had clearly demonstrated that the qualities of noncombustibility and fire resistance, particularly when applied to building materials, were not the same. Indeed, the materials and type of construction considered fireproof changed over time. Gradually, empirical notions of relative fireproofness were replaced with a more definitive and standardized attribute of fire resistance. When the performance of building materials became "scientifically" rated, fire resistance became a measurement of the time (in hours) that a building material or assembly would not structurally fail when exposed to fire.

New materials such as terra cotta provided inexpensive yet fire-resistant protection for wood and steel during the last decades of the nineteenth century. Many composite assemblies (often proprietary or patented) were introduced. Wire or expanded metal lath and plaster sheathing systems were recommended for interior partitions and ceilings. Composite floors that incorporated a fireproof layer of cement also became common. Some of these materials, such as metal lath and stucco, were adapted for the exterior cladding of production sheds.[25]

Similar types of products incorporated asbestos for fire resistance. The Mattison Co. offered a fireproof building material that consisted of asbestos fiber and hydraulic cement; it was marketed as "Century shingles" and later as "Ambler asbestos corrugated sheeting." The Johns Mansville Co. offered "Asbestoside," sheets of asbestos fibers and asphalt cemented together, and "Asbestosteel," sheet steel strengthened with rectangular corrugation and protected with a coating of asphalt and asbestos felt. By the 1920s, asbestos fibers were combined with Portland cement to form corrugated sheets that were recommended as roofing and siding material for factory and farm buildings. An industrial flooring of asbestos material heated and mixed with an aggregate was poured as a monolithic sheet at the building site.[26]

As noted in chapter 2, urban store and loft buildings and textile mills were similar types of multistory factories that served as models for buildings in a variety of industries. The two archetypes, however, were engineered differently to provide strength, stability, and resistance to fire. The setting for the urban loft was different from that of the textile mill or loft building in a manufacturing works with surrounding yard area. Also, textile mill engineers designed structures to meet the standards of the Factory Mutuals for optimal insurance rates. Architects, engineers, and builders had to conform to the specifications of municipal building codes in the design of urban lofts. The two approaches to construction certainly were not mutually exclusive; one could find a textile mill type of loft in a city. The adoption of one or the other depended on location and local building practice.

The Urban Industrial Loft

The essentials of the model loft building are (1) light and air, (2) heavy construction, (3) large single areas that can be easily adjusted to the needs of tenants, (4) the elimination of columns, (5) ample utilities such as elevators, etc., properly arranged, (6) fire protection.

REAL ESTATE RECORD AND GUIDE, 1914

Industrial loft buildings erected in urban areas were governed by municipal building codes that mandated certain materials, dimensions, and fireproof design practices. The stipulations of the New York City code serve as an example of how these statutes determined both general characteristics and the detailing of factories.

Because pilaster wall construction was allowed in the earliest code (1862) and wall thickness requirements could be met in piers or buttresses, masonry commercial and industrial buildings were likely to be constructed with pilasters and panel walls. An 1866 revision of the code dictated that the exterior walls of buildings used for storage be four inches thicker than the walls of residences. At the same time, requirements for fire walls encouraged the construction of groups of narrow buildings unified on the exterior to look like one large structure.[27]

In the urban lofts of New York City, interior structural systems of exposed cast-iron columns, yellow-pine beams, and joisted floors predominated. Although the building code did not encourage or prohibit the use of slow-burning, or mill, construction, only a small number of buildings were built to the standards of the Factory Mutuals. A mill engineer writing in 1890 about factory construction offered one explanation for this. He maintained that architects in Philadelphia, New York, and Boston did not use mill construction because of force of habit and inattention to anything except the ground plan and elevation. Actually, during the nineteenth century the use of many urban lofts for light manufacturing (which was often handwork aided by relatively small machines) and storage was different enough from that of the textile mill that there was no real reason to use heavy timber floor construction. Urban lofts required stiff, strong floors framed by cast-iron columns and joists more than they did the elasticity of mill construction. Besides, cast-iron columns were of smaller diameter than wood ones and consequently blocked less light in urban buildings with no windows in their side walls.[28]

Fire-Resistive Construction and Building Codes

Stopping the spread of fire in densely built up manufacturing districts was a municipal concern addressed through fire-resistive construction. A 75-foot cap for nonfireproof construction set by the New York City code effectively limited the height of industrial loft buildings to six or seven stories, though five stories were more common. Production and storage areas were to be isolated by fire walls, and each floor was to be sealed off from the others. An 1871 revision of the New York City code required fireproof partition walls every 50 feet in factories and warehouses; in 1882 the distance between fire walls was extended to 75 feet. Consequently, industrial (and commercial) loft buildings were limited to floor areas of 50 or 75 feet by 200 feet deep, though many buildings extended only halfway through the block.

This division of urban lofts into narrow, vertical units enclosed by fire walls was mandated by the internal location of stairs and vertical flues. In the city, industrial lofts covered virtually all of their narrow, deep lots. Because of this dense development, municipal building codes required that vertical shafts for hoists, elevators, and stairs be placed on the interior of buildings and enclosed by brick or tile fire walls. Self-closing trap doors and fire doors sealed openings in shafts and stairwells. Openings through floors for millwork and utilities were kept as small as possible and were sometimes fitted with small shutters and hoods that minimized air movement through them.[29]

Fire-resistive construction also addressed the threat of external sources of fire and limited the spread of fire from building to building. Rolling iron shutters were required to seal large openings in storefronts and loading bays on the first story. *When closed*, the iron or tin-clad wood shutters (fig. 5.4) that were required at window openings facing other structures helped to make exterior walls act as fire walls.[30]

The Harper's Publishing Co. (1855; Manhattan) was noted for the unusual steps taken in the fire-resistive construction of its works. The floors of the pair of brick loft buildings consisted of iron girders and beams supporting brick arches; hardly any wood was used in the structures. A single stairway and a hoistway positioned in the interior courtyard served all floors and eliminated vertical shafts and openings between floors.[31]

A warehouse erected in Philadelphia in 1874 (fig. 5.5) incorporated an assortment of fire-resistive construction elements that was typical of urban

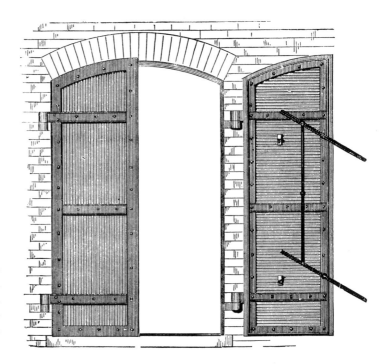

FIGURE 5.4 Iron-clad shutters installed on window openings added to the fire-resistive construction of industrial and commercial buildings.

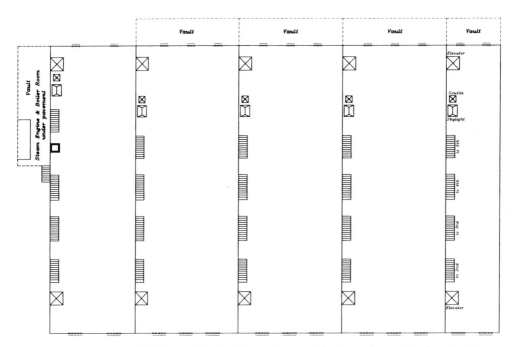

FIGURE 5.5 Fire walls divided the warehouse of the Pennsylvania Warehousing Co. into five separate compartments. This fire insurance survey combines features of all stories of the building and the roof onto a single plan.

building projects. The five-story building that extended through the block was divided by fire walls with no openings into several completely separate sections. Cast-iron columns on the lower three floors, and wood ones above, supported double wood-plank flooring. Window and door openings were fitted with iron-lined wood shutters; gas lighting was limited to the office. The steam boiler and engine (for powering platform elevators in each section of the building) were isolated from the warehouse by a fire wall. Despite all of these measures, unenclosed stairways were positioned along one wall of each compartment, and the floor openings through which the elevators passed were not fitted with trap doors that would have sealed off each floor. Hence, fire easily could spread vertically throughout any one compartment of the structure.[32]

The degree to which building code requirements could be manipulated and an urban loft engineered like a textile mill are highlighted in the unusual design of the Joseph Loth & Co. silk mill (1885; Hugo Kafka, architect; New York City). Kafka successfully worked within the strictures of the city building code to design a structure that was neither a conventional urban loft nor a standard textile mill. The city's requirement of interior fire walls led to the use of an idiosyncratic floor plan. A K-shaped form kept the width of the structure, both the main stem of the K and the angled wings, less than 30 feet; therefore, no fire walls or even interior columns were required. Of all the manufactories and warehouses erected in Manhattan and the Bronx during 1885, the Loth mill was the only building that had floors of mill construction, rather than the usual joisted ones.[33]

The Textile Mill Model

The New England mill is one of most complete works of engineering, as far as the fitness of means to ends [and] an economy of material [are] concerned, and its radical difference from all other buildings is that of the floor, constructed by laying thick plank upon heavy timber beams.

MILL ENGINEER C. J. H. WOODBURY, 1889

Textile mills were a specialized type of loft building engineered to serve a specific industry. They were designed to minimize the effects of vibration and retard the spread of fire. Mill engineers and the Mutual Fire Insurance Companies dominated this field and worked together to improve the design of mills during the nineteenth century.

Floor load capacity was not as critical a factor in textile mills as it was for other industrial loft buildings. Floors of mill construction were considered capable of carrying a live load of 150 pounds, though that burden rarely exceeded 50 pounds per square foot. Theoretically, the floor timbers could be varied in size; smaller members could be placed in upper stories, where less strength was needed. It was common practice, however, to use floor framing members of the same dimensions throughout the mill.

The span of bays and the width of textile mills was based on a fairly standard module determined by the properties of mill construction and the dimensions of machinery. Space between the columns running the length of the mill was limited, usually 8 or 10 (or possibly 12) feet. The bay dimension across the mill was always between 20 and 25 feet. The constant transverse bay dimension meant that the width in mills grew in standard increments. There was a jump from three 20-foot-wide bays in a 60-foot-wide mill to four 20-foot spans in an 80-foot-wide structure, or to four 25-foot spans in a 100-foot-wide mill. In the early twentieth century, mills with five 25-foot-wide bays appeared. Story height increased with the width of the mill and ranged from 12 to 14 feet.[34]

Mill engineers tried various means of securing additional strength for the exterior walls so that window openings could be larger. As early as the 1850s, vaulted brick walls were erected with a 4-inch air space between their interior and exterior portions. The vault was thought to facilitate the drying of mortar and thereby to ensure that the masonry assemblage achieved its maximum strength. More attention was directed to designing brick mill walls with their strength concentrated in piers and to manipulating the panel walls between them to create maximum window openings. Interior framing was designed to support most of the floor load, so exterior brick walls needed to support only their own weight. The more they were like curtain walls, the larger the window openings could be.[35]

Vibration generated by power looms and the need for elasticity in the structure argued against the use of cast-iron columns (the strength of which was compromised by incessant vibration) and rolled-iron beams because wood members could better absorb the movement. As hard as mill engineers tried to engineer the multistory textile mill to withstand vibration, that factor was the main reason for the eventual adoption of the one-story "weave shed" in the United States. The placement of machinery on only one level, with its millwork under the floor in a crawl space, created a new set of operating conditions. One promoter of these new weave sheds suggested that looms could be operated in them at a speed 12 percent higher than was possible on the second floor of an old mill. Needless to say, higher operating speeds translated into greater profits.[36]

Fire-Resistive Construction in Textile Mills

The concept of isolation in fire-resistive construction prompted the removal of operations that carried extra risk from the main mill building. Because of the danger of explosion presented by the dust released as the cotton bolls were opened, coupled with the fact that foreign objects in the picker apparatus could produce sparks, the picking operations of cotton manufactories were often housed in freestanding structures. "Picker houses" were described as "like guard houses," set 20 or 30 feet away from the main building. Some were built using the British type of fireproof floor construction, and most had door and window openings fitted with iron shutters.[37]

Because textile mills were freestanding structures, even if clustered along a waterpower canal, their fire-resistive features were different from those of urban lofts. The stair and service towers, which tended to act as flues during a fire, could be attached to the exterior of the main structure. These external stair and utility towers also kept loft floors free for the optimal arrangement of machinery (see fig. 5.1).

Textile mills were traditionally compartmentalized more as horizontal units, floor by floor, than as small vertical sections separated by fire walls. As mill engineer C. John Hexamer put it,

> The great principle in fire construction is to divide the building into numerous parts, and then to construct these parts in such a manner and of such a material that a fire originating in any one part may be restricted to it. . . . It becomes our problem then to construct each story so that a fire starting in one, may be restricted to that story; so that smoke, fire and water used to extinguish the flames may not harm other stories and their contents.[38]

Each floor was sealed off from all others by self-closing fire doors to stair towers. Flooring was made watertight so that if the automatic sprinklers were activated, a shallow pond of water held on the floor would keep it from burning; the water could be released through scuppers in the walls. To reduce the chance of a fire gaining a foothold, inaccessible air pockets in hollow walls, ceilings attached to the underside of floor beams, and attics under pitched roofs were eliminated. The use of varnish and combustible interior fittings, such as shelving and partitions, was avoided.

The components of fire-resistive construction in textile mills were modified during the early twentieth century. More reliable fire walls allowed mill designers to incorporate the picking operation, the boiler and engine house, and the stair and belt towers into the main block of the building.[39]

Slow-Burning Construction

The mass of such construction, the small amount of surface, and the smoothness of the surfaces make this type of construction fire-resisting, and merit the name often applied to it, of being 'slow-burning.' Compared with this, the floor and roof construction consisting of planks on edge for beams and a foot or two apart are kindling wood.

ENGINEER FRANCIS W. DEAN, 1917

Textile mills were erected with a particular type of fire-resistive construction, heavy timber framing that became known as "slow-burning construction" or "mill construction" (figs. 5.6, 5.8). It was considered not fireproof, but fire-resistant enough not to fail before a fire was contained and suppressed. Hence the name *slow-burning*, a term first used during the 1870s.[40]

The rationale of slow-burning construction was using wood for columns, floors, and roofs but shaping and placing it to produce the least favorable conditions for fire. Experience demonstrated that though the outer

FIG. 33.

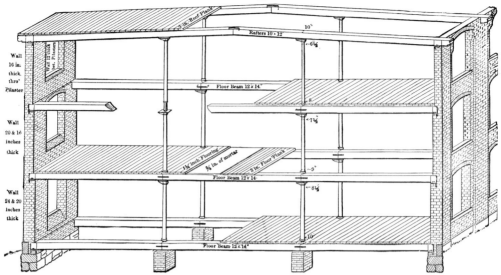

FIGURE 5.6 The "proper construction of one bay of a three-story mill" was detailed in this drawing published by mill engineer C. J. H. Woodbury in 1882; it subsequently appeared in many engineering and building treatises.

few inches of timber posts (commonly 12 by 14 inches) and beams (10 by 12 inches) became charred during a fire, the inner wood retained its strength and continued to support the floor or roof above (fig. 5.7). Another distinctive element of slow-burning construction was thick plank flooring laid directly on beams without any accompanying joists. This type of floor was slower to burn than a joisted one, where the larger number of smaller wood members were surrounded by pockets of air. Construction was detailed to let the interior wood framing members, if damaged by fire, fall away from exterior brick walls without damaging them. Flat roofs not only burned slowly but also eliminated inaccessible attic spaces filled with dust where a fire could smolder unnoticed and easily spread.[41]

The name *slow-burning construction* has obscured other reasons why the construction method was adopted for textile mills. Wood columns were used not only because they performed better during a fire but also because they were more appropriate for the task at hand than iron ones. A piece of timber was less likely to be defective than a cast-iron column, and more resistant to vibration as well. James Montgomery's description of the construction method in 1840 concluded, "The floor being in all four inches thick, is very strong and stiff." The floors were both strong and elastic enough to withstand vibration unless bay dimensions were increased and the middle of each bay became too flexible. Mill construction did lack stiffness at the points were columns of adjacent floor levels met and the weight of outside piers and walls contributed to the rigidity of the structure. To further stabilize mills, flat roofs were constructed in the same manner as floors. Moreover, when John Ripley Freeman compared English and American textile

FIGURE 5.7 The rationale for "slow-burning construction" was demonstrated in a structure that incorporated both wood timbers and steel I-beams and caught fire. Although the 8-by-10-inch timbers were charred on the surface, they continued to retain structural integrity, while the unprotected steel beams sagged and twisted.

mill construction in 1890, he found that mill construction still predominated because it was inexpensive; it also afforded low fire insurance rates from the Factory Mutuals.[42]

A Wider Application of Slow-Burning Construction

As noted earlier, only a limited number of industrial buildings—mainly textile mills—were insured by the Factory Mutual companies. Nevertheless, the Factory Mutuals influenced fire-resistive construction far beyond the sphere of their direct control. Edward Atkinson, president of the Boston Manufacturers' Mutual Fire Insurance Co., actively promoted the use of slow-burning construction as a method with proven success. Information on the method of building was disseminated through such drawings and descriptions as those in C. J. H. Woodbury's *The Fire Protection of Mills* (1882; see fig. 5.6) and the 1885 edition of Frank Kidder's general construction manual, *Architects and Builders Pocketbook*. Engineers trained in the Northeast and exposed to the textile industry undoubtedly extended the use of mill construction as they moved to other regions of the country. By the late nineteenth century, slow-burning or mill construction and elements of fire-resistive construction long used in textile mills had become one of the standard methods of building construction.[43]

FIGURE 5.8 Mill construction was modified through the insertion of additional floor framing members and metal post caps and joist hangers that distributed weight on bearing surfaces and accommodated the shrinkage of timbers.

Slow-burning construction was considered appropriate for storehouses but had to be modified to sustain particularly strong floors. Beams of paired timbers of southern pine with a 20-foot span, 8 feet on center, could sustain a load of 180 pounds per square foot. Modified mill construction, with either supplemental girders (fig. 5.8) or paired beams for additional strength, was used for lofts constructed as warehouses in the parts of the United States where timber was readily available and where floor load demands were high. Slow-burning construction was suitable for production sheds as well (see fig. 4.8). Edward Atkinson recommended it for the new single-story weave sheds of the textile industry, and engineer Oscar Perrigo presented a model production shed of mill construction.[44]

In a 1904 issue of *Machinery*, an editorial asserted that mill construction probably combined more desirable and necessary features than any other type of construction for industrial lofts. Historian Sara Wermiel, though, points out that mill construction was not considered an ideal type of construction in densely developed urban areas, where the greatest threat of fire came from exposure to other structures. Nevertheless, in Chicago, where mill construction was quite popular, the building code permitted its use for office buildings, stores, and warehouses much taller than those of ordinary, nonfireproof construction. During the 1910s, mill construction represented a savings in construction cost that varied from 5 to 15 percent over that of a reinforced concrete structure. But by the 1920s, mill construction was only slightly less expensive than other construction with noncombustible materials, and it began to seem old-fashioned.[45]

Industrial buildings were carefully engineered to be commodious, well adapted to their purpose, and substantial, strong, and solid enough to house machinery in motion. Although most industrialists considered fireproof construction too expensive to be cost-effective, the works and individual buildings were designed to be fire-resistive. American engineers and builders used a variety of building materials to meet these goals, as detailed in the next chapter. They were particularly receptive to new materials that offered both greater strength and resistance to fire.

MATERIALS OF CONSTRUCTION

6

For manufacturing buildings, probably no construction is more satisfactory in every respect than brick walls and an iron roof.

ENGINEER OSCAR PERRIGO, 1906

Building materials used in factories were selected and utilized to provide maximum strength and stability, at reasonable cost and with an acceptable degree of fire resistance. Builders relied on traditional building practices and used locally available materials until the engineer was able to calculate the strength of materials in compression and tension. Such advances in engineering permitted building designers to meet the greater demands that were placed on the structural frames of industrial buildings as machines became larger and heavier and operated at higher speeds. Manufacturers were aware of the importance of matching material, method of construction, and manufacturing requirements and were willing to pay for high-quality construction.

THE VERSATILITY OF THE WOOD FRAME

Wood-framed structures offered technological and economic advantages that were exploited in industrial building construction. Indeed, several physical properties of wood recommended its use in factory buildings. It was valued for its high tensile strength (resistance to bending and breaking) and elasticity. Compared to stone and iron, wood was easier to work. Wood posts were utilized instead of masonry interior bearing walls because they were more efficient in resisting loads and allowed for greater flexibility in the use of space. Skeletal wood frames lent themselves to rational design and the use of engineered curtain walls. Not surprisingly, the ranges of continuous sash first appeared in wood-framed industrial buildings, as explained in chapter 7. Wood comprised the interior framing of both urban industrial lofts and textile mills, as discussed in chapter 5. It was also used to sheath factory buildings (fig. 6.1). These advantages were offset by wood's limited strength and combustibility. Wood siding, though prohibited by many municipal building codes for urban factory buildings, was used throughout the nineteenth century in rural settings, towns, and smaller cities.[1]

Wood framing was used in production sheds to reduce the effects of vibration (see fig. 4.8). Many of the buildings of the Walter A. Wood Harvester Co. (1892–1893; St. Paul, Minnesota) were constructed of brick with interior posts and roofs of wood; single pieces of Oregon pine 40 to 60 feet in length formed the roof-framing members. In this works, the use of iron was limited to cast columns in the foundries and noncombustible roof trusses for the boiler and engine rooms. The De La Val shop (c. 1896; Frederick Hart, designer; Poughkeepsie, New York), which combined an open plan and an early sawtooth roof with traditional wood framing, was considered a model example of shop design and construction.[2]

By 1910, the use of wood in industrial building construction had become more limited, primarily because wood had become difficult to procure in longer lengths. Much of the old-growth forest that provided timbers of considerable size had been harvested. When timber framing members were used, they were likely to be carefully proportioned (based on the engineer's calculations) to eliminate the cost of extra material. Where strength and

FIGURE 6.1 During the 1850s the main building of the Kensington Iron Works and Rolling Mills in Philadelphia was framed and sheathed of wood. Vertical board sheathing was replaced, where needed, by window openings and louvers. The works office was distinguished by a better grade of siding.

span were dominant requirements, wood was either no longer the material of choice or was used in different ways to achieve strength. Wood beams, rectangular in section and limited to 12 to 16 feet in length, were joined to make timbers of sufficient size.

The cost of timber-framed construction varied by location and was influenced by availability and shipping costs. The low first cost of wood construction made it a popular material in areas of the country where timber was plentiful. Wood roof trusses, easily framed of laminated chords (several layers of planks glued and spiked together) and web diagonals of solid timber, remained popular during the early twentieth century. Standard size lumber and simple, repetitive framing plans helped to keep the cost of wood construction reasonable.[3]

SUBSTANTIAL AND INCOMBUSTIBLE MASONRY

The best fire-resisting material for walls, it may safely be asserted, is hard-burned brick.
FIRE INSURANCE EXECUTIVE FRANCIS C. MOORE, 1903

Masonry construction materials—stone, brick, and tile—were utilized in factory construction because of their strength and fire resistance. The popularity of stone construction reflected regional resources and traditions. Textile mills of local stone represented common building practice in Fall River, Massachusetts; Willimantic, Connecticut; the Berkshires area of Massachusetts and Connecticut; and throughout Rhode Island. Other examples of stone factory buildings were more isolated. A group of buildings for the Brooklyn Clay Retort and Fire Brick Works (1850s) constructed of common schist were unusual for that locale. A machine shop with wood interior framing at the Du Pont Powder Works (c. 1903; Wilmington, Delaware; fig. 6.2) was the last of a series of industrial buildings at that facility erected of local stone.[4]

Locally available granite, schist, sandstone, and limestone were noncombustible and inexpensive building materials. The strength and hardness of granite recommended the material for industrial use, particularly for foundations. The style of masonry for industrial buildings ranged from roughly cut and barely coursed work to cut and coursed ashlar (see fig. 2.11). In many cases, only the main facade of an industrial building was laid of cut stone, and the other sides of the structure had a rougher finish.

During the early nineteenth century, building stone, mortar, and slate for roofs were among the most fire-resistant building materials available. However, stone did fail when exposed to high heat and water during a fire. Granite performed poorly once a fire started because water poured on a blaze during a fire entered its intermolecular spaces, vaporized into steam, and caused disintegration.

Brick pressed by machine became the masonry material of choice for fire-resistant construction around 1860 because it was denser than

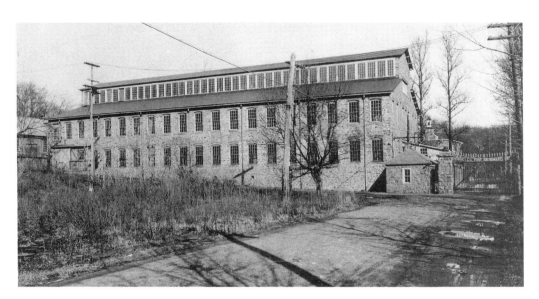

FIGURE 6.2 Local stone formed the walls of a new machine shop erected at the du Pont Powder works near Wilmington, Delaware, during the first years of the twentieth century. Except for its stone walls, this structure was characteristic of other machine shops of its era.

hand-molded brick and had a greater resistance to high temperatures. Standard brick stood long after granite had disintegrated and marble had been burnt into lime. Brick and other clay products—ornamental terra cotta and hollow tile—remained the most fire-resistant building material available prior to the widespread use of concrete.[5]

There were other reasons to build factories of brick. It could be engineered to meet various requirements for strength and elasticity (which was provided by the mortar joints). For industrial buildings, builders converted masonry load-bearing brick walls into a quasi-framed system. As noted earlier, the strength of the wall was concentrated in brick piers that projected from flanking sections of panel walls as pilasters and supported the heavier roof-framing members. Pilaster brick wall construction became standard practice during the mid–nineteenth century. It appeared in American textile mills by the mid-1840s; the Atlantic Cotton Mills (1846; Charles Bigelow, engineer; Lawrence, Massachusetts; fig. 6.3) was an early example.[6]

The search for inexpensive and fire-resistant materials to enclose steel-framed production sheds led to the use of fire-resistant, unglazed, hollow terra-cotta tile (see figs. 6.4 and fig. 8.5). Builders had begun to use hollow terra-cotta tile during the 1870s for the construction of partition walls and floor arches and as a protective covering for iron and steel elements. In 1898 civil engineer O. Benson wrote of using hollow tile to fill in the walls between the steel columns of his "incombustible foundry buildings." A New Jersey brick and terra-cotta manufacturer, Henry Maurer & Son, developed a "Phoenix" system of hollow tile construction, in which upright I-beams set 15 feet apart reinforced the walls. During the first decade of the twentieth

FIGURE 6.3 The Atlantic Cotton Mills, designed by engineer Charles Bigelow and erected in two building campaigns (1846 and 1852) at Lawrence, Massachusetts, was an early textile mill with brick panel walls spanning pilasters.

FIGURE 6.4 Hollow terra-cotta tile formed the enclosing walls of a steel-framed foundry building of the Westinghouse Electric Co. Essington works.

century, hollow tile appeared in exterior curtain wall construction, sometimes exposed to view, but often covered with stucco or brick. The tile was more heat- and moisture-proof than brick, and its interior air spaces served as insulation. Compared with brick walls of the same type, tile walls were less expensive because the larger unit size of tile reduced labor costs during construction, particularly when the position of steel frame members eliminated the need to cut the tile.[7]

A building designed by mill engineer John O. De Wolf around 1910 was specially detailed for the use of steel framing and hollow tile curtain walls. The tiles fit into the 8-inch channels of the steel columns, which were spaced to carry uncut tile. The grooved sides of the tile were placed on the exterior to receive cement plaster; on the interior, the tile was left exposed. The foundry and machine shop buildings erected by General Electric Co. (c. 1911; Erie, Pennsylvania) were of steel and hollow tile construction, though the walls were faced with brick. Hollow tile was left exposed as the curtain walls of several structures at the Essington works of the Westinghouse Electric Co. (1918–1919; Westinghouse, Church, Kerr & Co., design and construction; South Philadelphia; fig. 6.4).[8]

IRON AND STEEL FOR STRENGTH

Iron and steel framing in industrial buildings allowed for increases in both span and strength. In fact, these considerations far outweighed the risk of exposing iron and steel frames to fire in production sheds. The forms developed to take advantage of these materials evolved jointly with consolidated, open plans for manufacturing works.

Structural Iron

Iron was incorporated into industrial buildings in an incremental manner. It was used first as the tie-rods that braced brick structures and as discrete elements in timber roof trusses. The next steps included the use of iron roof trusses and cast-iron bearing plates and columns to support the heavier loads of machinery in multistory lofts. Combination framing systems of cast-iron columns (in compression) and wood (in tension) in beams and rafters capitalized on the properties of both materials. Wrought-iron beams and lintels were introduced as an alternative for spanning large bays and framing wide window and door openings. Finally, structural frames of iron and steel became standard in production sheds.

The use of iron components in European industrial buildings, which began at the turn of the eighteenth century, included some notable examples that may have influenced construction in the United States. Textile mills incorporated iron framing elements at an early date, and British engineers Boulton and Watt designed a cast-iron roof truss for the Twist Mill in 1801. Within a few years iron trusses were spanning the brick walls of production sheds like that of Maudslay Sons & Field (1834; London). In contrast, the casting shed of the Sayn Foundry was an all-iron tour de force (1830; Karl Ludwig Althans, engineer; Bendorf, Germany).[9]

The use of iron structural elements in American industrial buildings seems to have been the exception, rather than standard practice, during the first half of the nineteenth century. High cost and questionable quality limited the popularity of cast-iron columns, though surely many early instances of their use remain unknown to historians. Cast-iron columns, cruciform in section, in the Springfield Armory's East Arsenal (1824; Springfield, Massachusetts) are considered among the earliest in industrial buildings. Cast-iron framing elements appeared in structures erected at the Harpers Ferry Armory (Harpers Ferry, West Virginia) between 1845 and 1854. Beginning during the 1830s, iron was used to frame storefronts; soon thereafter, cast-iron facades were applied to commercial buildings in urban areas. Though neither of these applications was common in industrial buildings, they both increased the demand for structural iron components and the familiarity of builders with the material.[10]

Mill engineers experimented with the use of cast-iron columns in textile mills as early as the mid-1820s; the framing of the oldest portion of the Middle Mills (1825; near Utica, New York) was a combination of cast-iron columns and wood girders and joists. However, the spectacular failure of the Pemberton Mill (1852–1853; Charles Bigelow, engineer; Lawrence, Massachusetts) in 1860 instigated a reevaluation of the use of cast-iron columns in textile mills. In the design of the Pemberton Mill, Bigelow increased the width of the structure to 84 feet to allow spinning mules to be placed perpendicular (rather than parallel) to the length of the building. He departed from common building practice with the use of cast-iron columns, vaulted brick walls, and particularly large window openings. James Francis, the engineer who investigated the Pemberton's collapse, pinpointed causes for the failure and published his study of cast-iron columns in 1865 as *On the Strength of Cast Iron Pillars*. He provided rules for calculating the size of columns and offered evidence that the strength of cast-iron columns was compromised by vibration. Wood posts returned to favor, except in damp mill basements. Hence, mainly because of iron columns' susceptibility to vibration and loss of structural integrity during a fire, mill engineers turned their attention to the perfection of a wood interior structural system for textile mills (see chapter 5).[11]

Cast-iron columns were nevertheless utilized in other types of factories, even after rolled-iron and steel elements became available. Henry Grattan Tyrrell preferred cylindrical cast-iron columns over built-up steel columns because they occupied a smaller space, had a better appearance, and didn't fail as quickly. To add stiffness to a frame for a warehouse, he extended its columns through at least two stories and staggered their splicing. Another reason for the continued use of cast-iron columns was that this material developed a patina of rust that did not compromise its strength; wrought iron, on the other hand, would rust to the point of danger.[12]

Wrought, or rolled, iron was utilized in beams and also as an alternative for cast-iron columns because of its greater tensile strength. Machine-fabricated wrought-iron plates, channels, and angles could be joined into various configurations of built-up shapes that could be easily inspected for flaws and checked for proper thickness. The material was often utilized to frame noncombustible roofs sheathed with corrugated sheet iron. By the 1870s, buildings framed entirely of wrought iron and sheathed with corrugated sheet metal, with clear spans of up to 150 feet, were recommended for use by railroads and industry.[13]

The work of Major Theodore Laidley suggests how engineers experimented with iron in industrial buildings. Laidley, a graduate of West Point, oversaw the construction of a group of buildings at the Frankford Arsenal (Philadelphia) during the 1860s. He designed structures with wrought-iron frames and brick curtain walls that could be rebuilt quickly if damaged by an explosion; this type of wall later became common in factory construction. Laidley was also an early purchaser of iron Phoenix columns (originally patented by the Phoenix Iron Works and later produced by other manufacturers), which consisted of curved sections bolted together. Phoenix columns were commonly utilized in industrial building projects throughout the period before steel columns became standard.[14]

Iron frames were generally not exposed on the exteriors of industrial loft buildings; instead, perimeter columns were embedded in masonry pilasters.

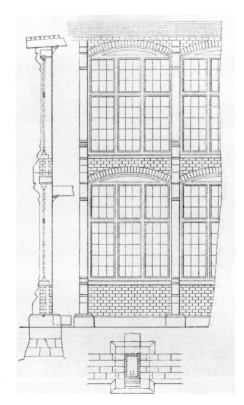

FIGURE 6.5 In 1889 foundry owner Edmund Grinnel proposed replacing masonry piers with cast-iron ones to increase the window area of textile mills.

But builders sought ways to decrease the dimension of piers and increase window size. In 1889 Edmund Grinnel, the proprietor of the New Bedford Iron Foundry, proposed adapting for textile mills the method of construction used for the cast-iron fronts of commercial buildings (fig. 6.5). He pointed out that 12-inch-wide cast-iron columns, rather than 4-foot-wide masonry piers, framing bays in the exterior walls would provide half again as much area for glazing. This idea found practical application within a few years (discussed later in this chapter).[15]

Structural Iron as a Fire-Resistant Material

The incombustibility of iron framing elements and sheet metal led builders to consider them fireproof during their first years of use. The increasing use of iron generated interest in the type of iron beam and brick-arched floor construction long used in England. An early application of this type of construction was the group of three-story loft buildings erected at the Rock Island Arsenal (1866–1872; Thomas A. Rodman, engineer; Rock Island, Illinois). These floors were depicted in views of the shops of the Singer Sewing Machine works (1872–1873; Elizabeth, New Jersey; fig. 6.6). They were first used about the same time for industrial loft buildings erected at the machine and tool works of Brown & Sharpe (1872; Providence).[16]

The vulnerability of iron structural elements to fire, however, became very apparent. Cast iron softened and warped upon exposure to high tem-

FIGURE 6.6 "Fireproof" brick-arched floor construction is visible in this view of the assembling room of the Singer Sewing Machine works erected in 1872–1873.

peratures, and the changes in its physical form caused the collapse of burning buildings (see fig. 5.7). Steel, like wrought iron, lost its elastic limit and ultimate strength at temperatures reached in ordinary fires. Numerous types of assemblies were devised to protect iron and steel columns and beams with more fire-resistant materials. This expensive construction could be justified in tall office buildings and public buildings like hotels and theaters. However, it saw only limited use in industrial loft buildings, as did the type of construction that incorporated hollow terra-cotta, or structural tile, or floors.

Standard practice sanctioned the use of unprotected iron and steel in production sheds that housed metalworking industries because of the limited amount of combustible material on the premises. Though the perimeter framing members might be protected by brick or tile curtain wall construction, the interior columns and roof-framing elements were nearly always left exposed. The faith that was placed in the "fireproof" character of these structures was demonstrated by the Berlin Iron Bridge Co. when it erected a new building for its own use (1890–1891; East Berlin, Connecticut; see figs. 6.10 and 6.11). No fire insurance was carried on the brick, iron, and glass shop, since there was "nothing about the building which can in any way take fire and burn." Walter Berg, chief engineer of the Lehigh Valley Railroad, considered metalworking shops with brick walls, unprotected iron columns and trusses, and floors of solid planks on concrete to be "practically fireproof." Berg also pointed out that sprinkler systems were ineffective in large-scale production sheds.[17]

Sheet Metal: "The Best Protection against Fire"

By the last quarter of the nineteenth century, corrugated sheet metal had become an important component of factory construction. It was an inexpensive material that could be quickly applied to walls and roofs. However, the fire-resistant quality of sheet metal was the main reason for its popularity and also influenced the manner in which the material was utilized.

Sheet metal, corrugated to increase its rigidity, was introduced in England during the 1820s. Curved sheets of corrugated sheet iron were soon available. The process of galvanizing, coating iron with zinc to prevent rusting, became more affordable in the mid-1840s. Soon after that development, corrugated, galvanized sheet iron was utilized on industrial buildings and structures for railways and gasworks. The British production and use of corrugated sheet metal was detailed in an 1833 *Journal of the Franklin Institute* report. British manufacturers exported galvanized iron to the United States during the 1840s and filled many orders for roofing, though American manufacturers soon began providing the material.[18]

A storehouse erected at the Watervliet Arsenal (1859; Watervliet, New York) was an iron-framed and -sheathed industrial building that was similar to the type developed in England. The design of the one-story warehouse, provided by the Architectural Iron Works of New York City at the request of Major Alfred Mordecai, was similar to the ornamental iron fronts that firm supplied for commercial buildings. The warehouse was constructed with a cast- and wrought-iron frame and a roof supported by Fink trusses. Bays articulated with paired pilasters were filled with either rusticated sheet metal or arched door and window openings. Neither this method of exposed-frame construction nor the formal architectural character of the storehouse enjoyed any degree of popularity in American factory buildings.[19]

In 1872 the *Industrial Monthly* reported on the extensive use of corrugated iron in the United States for the construction of depots, station houses, storehouses, buildings for commercial and mechanical purposes, and even churches. Interest in the material escalated during the 1880s, as the cost of lumber increased. Sheet-metal-clad buildings were promoted as the "best protection against fire" and a less expensive alternative to brick construction. To capitalize on their fire-resistant quality, metal sheathing materials were used to create an enveloping, noncombustible shell—a metal curtain wall.[20]

The Canton Iron Roofing Co. presented views of its works during the 1880s to demonstrate the use of its products (fig. 6.7). The buildings were rendered to emphasize that metal sheathing provided a protective envelope, a curtain without any structural function. The main building, a three-story loft, had walls sheathed with corrugated sheet metal and a standing-seam metal roof. The artist's cutaway indicates that this sheathing was applied to wood framing and horizontal sheathing.[21]

FIGURE 6.7 The Canton Iron Roofing Co. works were presented in an 1888 catalog to illustrate how the firm's sheet-metal products could be used to form protective envelopes around wood-framed structures.

Views of sheet-metal-clad structures in trade catalogs illustrated the conventions adopted for the material's use that were based on the concept of a protective, tightly drawn metal curtain wall. In some cases, smooth metal sheathing on flush corner posts, baseboards, and window frames protected wood framing members and provided slight relief from uniform corrugated wall surfaces. A ridge roll, molded gutters, and downspouts necessary for the removal of water from the roof were often the only other details.[22]

Early twentieth-century developments in the use of sheet metal included the introduction of a "weatherboard siding," molded to look like clapboards. Aluminum siding, which offered superior resistance to corroding sulphurous gases, became available during the 1920s and was recommended for use in heavy industry.[23]

Structural Steel

Along with electric drive and the powered traveling crane, steel framing transformed industrial architecture. It changed the way engineers conceived of industrial buildings. The design of an industrial building had long begun with a plan that detailed dimensions, exterior wall construction, and interior column spacing. In contrast, an initial scheme for a steel-framed production shed was represented by a section drawing that delineated the bents (the columns and truss) that would frame the structure. The uniform quality and standardized forms of steel, which could be accurately specified for strength and dimension, contributed to an increasingly systematized approach to industrial building design and construction. Steel also introduced a new scale into building that seemed limitless, restrained only by costs, not by the strength or availability of materials.

During the last two decades of the nineteenth century, cast iron, wrought iron, and steel were all used in industrial building construction. The practice of forming built-up shapes in machine-fabricated iron and steel and their superior strength led to the more limited use of cast iron. Wrought iron and steel had almost identical material properties in tension and compression; but steel had an elastic nature when stressed almost to its breaking point that made it the superior building material. The forms of the plates, channels, and angles introduced in wrought iron became the templates for structural steel members. Hence, there was little difference in the detailing of structural frames as steel replaced iron during the 1890s. Indeed, in 1892 engineer John Seaver recommended that the designer of a one-story mill building specify maximum strains before the kind and quality of iron or steel were chosen. Seaver thought it best to let the builder specify the material, depending on the market price.[24]

Steel's tensile and compressive strength provided the stability and spans desired in industrial buildings, and its ductile and elastic nature gave it the ability to withstand the pounding and jarring of machinery without fracturing. The ability of steel to endure strain when approaching its elastic limit diminished the immediate seriousness of errors made in the design of framing and bracing. However, insufficient stiffness in steel framing caused damage to wall coverings and glazing, as well as problems with alignment for cranes and shafting, and ultimately compromised the frame. The speed with which steel-framed buildings could be erected from factory-fabricated members also recommended its use. In comparison to those of wood and iron, steel framing members could be smaller in section; therefore they were lighter in weight, took up less room, and did not obstruct as much daylight from skylights, monitors, and windows. Steel did not shrink or rot, and when properly protected with paint or treated to produce a protective oxide coating, it required little maintenance.[25]

The American Standard I-beam, and columns built up into I, T, H, and box shapes from angles, plates, and webs, were the usual components of the steel frame. Riveting provided a connection that was much stronger than bolted cast-iron and wrought-iron joints. It was used extensively for connections in wrought-iron and steel framing; cast iron could not be riveted (another reason for its limited use). Although the forms of steel framing elements, like the I-beam, were standardized, engineers and steel frame shops developed their own preferred built-up column forms and framing configurations. Engineer Henry Grattan Tyrrell noted in 1901 that the form and section of columns varied greatly, though the use of four angles, latticed together, was common in structures for light loads. I-sections were used both as the columns that supported traveling cranes and the girders on which they traveled; those carrying very heavy cranes were braced transversely.[26]

Steel columns that were round in section occupied a smaller space than built-up columns of comparable strength. They were recommended when size (as in partition walls) and appearance were considerations. Filling steel columns with concrete provided protection from fire and oxidation. Several patented versions of this element appeared, including the Lally column, introduced around 1900.[27]

Steel-Framed Industrial Loft Buildings

Steel-framed loft buildings represented the most expensive way to build because their steel members had to be protected with fireproofing materials. Steel-framed industrial lofts, therefore, had to be justified by programmatic and economical considerations. The selective use of steel took advantage of its strength without adding the cost of an entirely steel-framed structure. For example, steel I-beams were incorporated into the wood mill-type floor construction of the Frances Building, an industrial loft erected in 1889 (Treat & Foltz, architects; Chicago). Steel also appeared in industrial buildings as a substitute for reinforced concrete construction when columns of the latter material on lower stories would have been too large to be practical. Steel columns and beams, encased in poured concrete or fireproofed with concrete sprayed onto them (this type of concrete was known as Gunite), sometimes framed a lower story of a loft building in which wide spans were needed for rail-served shipping platforms.[28]

By the turn of the century, multistory steel-framed structures were being erected in industrial works. Steel was used in an addition to the Brown & Sharpe Mfg. Co. works (1896; Providence), a four-story loft designed by company engineers. Steel columns flanked by a pair of flues were set into brick pilasters. A machine shop erected at the Jones & Lamson works (c. 1908; Springfield, Vermont) was a three-story structure with a concrete-fireproofed steel frame, reinforced concrete roof and floors, and brick curtain walls. A shop building of the Pratt & Whitney Co. (c. 1908; Hartford, Connecticut) was an extremely rigid structure with a steel frame and concrete floors supported by concrete-covered I-beams. It seems likely that steel framing was considered necessary to support a craneway in the first story of this structure. Perhaps because the production sheds of the extensive Remington Arms Co. plant (1914–1915; Bridgeport, Connecticut) were framed of steel, the loft buildings at that works were erected of the same material.[29]

Steel construction was slow to be adopted for textile mills because of its high cost. The situation changed during the first decades of the twentieth century, as timber became more scarce, and by the 1910s, the use of steel beams with wooden or concrete floors had greatly increased. Steel trusses supporting sawtooth roofs made possible the large weave sheds of the early-twentieth-century textile mills; for example, the Chicopee Mfg. Co. weave shed (c. 1911; Chicopee, Massachusetts), had bays wide enough for six rows of looms.[30]

The "Steel Mill Building"

Mill buildings are long structures, usually one story in height, whose distinctive feature is their one or more broad bays free of posts. This type of building is used for heavy metal-working shops such as foundries, boiler shops, etc., where cranes are necessary for handling heavy or bulky work, and where large spaces clear of columns are required. For this type of building steel framing is practically a necessity.

ARCHITECTURAL FORUM, 1923

Just before the turn of the nineteenth century, engineers turned their attention to a type of production shed known as an "iron mill building" or "steel mill building."[31] (As noted in chapter 2, these structures are referred to in this study as "production sheds" to avoid confusion with those erected to house steel mills and textile mills.) Factories of this kind were valued for their strength, simplicity, and economy. Steel was the ideal structural material to support the long spans and high walls exposed to wind pressure, as well as the lateral forces of moving cranes. Steel framing was especially suited for buildings with trussed roofs that incorporated monitors.

Many of the iron and steel mill buildings erected during the 1890s were transitional in their design. Engineers took advantage of steel framing to provide interior spaces with crane service and experimented with the layout of the works in wider structures of parallel crane-served bays. It took a bit longer for them to convert brick enclosing walls into engineered curtain walls filled mostly with window sash.

Around the turn of the century, handbooks that codified practice in the construction of iron and steel mill buildings became available. Even as considerable latitude in the form and size of these structures was exercised, standardized construction methods emerged. Load-bearing brick walls were combined with iron trusses and interior framing when inexpensive structures of moderate height were needed. Structures of that type were described by one author as most satisfactory in every respect for manufacturing buildings. When they were strengthened by piers that served as buttresses between windows and perhaps steel columns at the corners, load-bearing masonry walls were stronger and more rigid. Therefore, buildings of that type of construction were well suited for operations using heavy machinery, light jib cranes, and traveling cranes suspended from the roof trusses.[32]

A third common method of steel mill building construction utilized iron or steel framing and masonry curtain walls of brick, tile, or concrete (fig. 6.8). The cost of expensive steel columns was offset by savings in the cost of thin curtain walls. Brick curtain walls were preferred because they were relatively inexpensive and better-looking than stuccoed tile or concrete walls, though all of these materials were used. Curtain walls, which were self-supporting but carried no load, did brace structures and often provided fireproof protection for steel columns. When traveling or jib cranes were to be installed, it was recommended that all bracing for the cranes be incorporated into the structure's framing and that the cranes be installed and operated prior to the construction of the curtain wall. In these production sheds, the strength of the structure was concentrated in the steel frame that supported the crane girders (fig. 6.9).[33]

Two railroad car shops illustrate steel mill building practice at the turn of the century. A shop of the Lehigh Valley Railroad Co. (1903; D. C. Newman Collins, Walter C. Berg, E. D. B. Brown, designers; Sayre, Pennsylvania) was erected with brick walls on their own foundations and independent of the steel frame except where anchored to the heavier posts. Steel construction was standardized in the shops erected by the American Locomotive Company (1902–1903; A. J. Pitkin of the company, designer; Sche-nectady, New York). All five structures had identical steel frames; end walls of brick, 20 inches thick at their bases, were self-supporting and were not tied to the columns.[34]

More steel mill buildings had engineered curtain walls as the first decade of the twentieth century drew to a close, although the use of window openings of traditional size and proportion persisted. It became common to use a low wall of brick, 3 to 4 feet in height, as a moisture-proof raised foundation, regardless of the sheathing of the rest of the frame. Above this, the structure was enclosed by a combination of window sash and corrugated

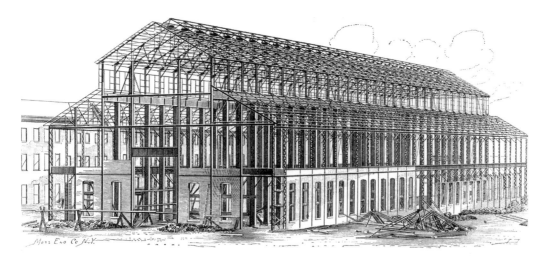

FIGURE 6.8 The machine shop designed and erected by the Berlin Iron Bridge Co. for the Newport News Ship Building and Dry Dock Co. at Newport News, Virginia (c. 1890), was an iron- or steel-framed structure. The rendering suggests that the brick enclosing walls were set between the latticed columns.

FIGURE 6.9 This 1919 construction photograph of the foundry building at the Essington Works of Westinghouse Electric Co. in South Philadelphia invites comparison of the scale of the framing elements that supported the traveling crane to the less-substantial ones that held up the roof.

sheet metal or some type of fireproof sheathing material. Panels of corrugated sheet steel coated with asbestos or cement were easily installed as siding materials. Walls were also formed of expanded metal lath hung on the steel frame and covered with a coating of cement stucco on the exterior and plaster on the interior. Wood sheathing was also used.[35]

The all-metal production shed, with an exterior entirely of corrugated sheet metal and sash attached to the frame, was suitable for only some manufacturing works. It was best for metalworking operations that generated their own heat (like steel mills and foundries) and storage buildings, since heat loss and condensation were problems in heated structures of this type. Some engineers considered the use of sheet-metal sheathing on steel mill buildings of doubtful economy because it added no bracing and stability to the structure; the cost of the additional bracing of the steel frame canceled any savings realized in the sheathing material. This type of curtain wall, however, helped to usher in the engineered curtain wall.[36]

Bridge Shops Experiment

The general design of these structures is the result of long experience and much study on the part of the Berlin Iron Bridge Co. to produce an economical building to meet the requirements of foundries and manufacturing establishments where buildings of considerable width are used, necessitating strength and plenty of light, and the design has met with popular favor among the manufacturing men of New England and other sections.

IRON AGE, 1895

The companies most closely associated with the production of structural steel were known as "bridge shops" because much of their product was used for bridge construction, even though they also provided steel for building construction. These firms were responsible for innovations in the steel framing of industrial buildings. Projects of the Berlin Iron Bridge Co. and the American Bridge Co. represent the experimentation that was undertaken by such firms during the first years of use of the steel frame. The Berlin Iron Bridge Co., which erected several hundred patented lenticular truss bridges during the 1880s, became one of the largest structural iron fabricators in New England around 1890. Prior to its incorporation into the American Bridge Co. in 1900, the Berlin Iron Bridge Co. was active also in the design of iron and steel structural systems for industrial buildings.[37]

Traditions of building with cast-iron columns influenced the earliest shops designed by the firm. Cylindrical iron columns became massive, 3 feet in diameter, to support latticed girders that served as crane rails in a production shed erected for the Farrel Foundry and Machine Works (c. 1890; Ansonia, Connecticut). The Detroit Dry Dock Co. (1892; Detroit) represented a relatively conservative approach to design. Steel was used to frame an erecting bay (with a height equivalent to three stories) commanded by a traveling crane. The brick curtain walls that enclosed the steel frame (and left it exposed on the interior) were detailed as load-bearing walls. Traditional fenestration patterns prevailed: Each bay was pierced by two windows of standard size.[38]

When the firm turned its attention to expanding its own shops in 1890–1891 (East Berlin, Connecticut), it attempted to reduce the cost of manufacturing its products, minimize the expense of maintenance and repairs, and reduce the first cost of building. The main building of the new works, 80 feet wide and 400 feet long, was constructed entirely of brick, iron, and glass (fig. 6.10). Its engineered curtain walls featured a 10-foot-high expanse of iron-framed sash above a lower wall that consisted mostly of doors. Iron trusses were designed to support both the roof and the loads carried by traveling cranes that ran on their lower chords to move material in conjunction with industrial rail (fig. 6.11).[39]

The company's design for the Fuller Iron Works (1893; Providence; fig. 6.12) was another definitive step in the direction of engineered curtain walls. Buildings like this one demonstrate that industrial building designers were experimenting with window walls long before steel sash became widely available during the 1910s. In this case, the Berlin Iron Bridge Co. made the leap to a window wall; the walls were enclosed with uninterrupted expanses of sash. The Fuller company's satisfaction with this structure, considered to be the first of its kind in Providence, led to the construction of a similar foundry in 1901.[40]

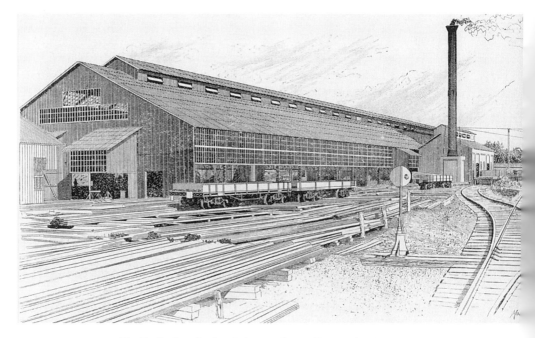

FIGURE 6.10 The Berlin Iron Bridge Co.'s own shop in East Berlin, Connecticut, was characteristic of the new type of one-story production shed with specialized curtain walls. (See fig. 6.11 for an interior view.)

FIGURE 6.11 Several hoists were supported by roof trusses and industrial rail facilitated the handling of long, heavy structured iron and steel pieces in the shop of the Berlin Iron Bridge Co. in East Berlin, Connecticut (see fig. 6.10).

FIGURE 6.12 The steel and glass machine shop (on the right in this view) was designed and built by the Berlin Iron Bridge Co. in 1893 for the Fuller Iron Works in Providence. The older brick building was erected in 1869.

During the mid-1890s, the Berlin Iron Bridge Co. experimented with iron and steel framing in loft buildings in order to provide better natural lighting and greater resistance to vibration. The company turned to brick walls that were self-supporting, not load-bearing; these thinner (8-inch-thick) walls were cheaper and could be pierced with larger window openings. A "composite construction" was developed that consisted of an iron or steel frame, self-supporting brick walls, and mill floor construction. The iron frame was stiffened by several types of bracing, including rods that extended across the building and could be adjusted by turnbuckles.[41]

During the late 1890s, the Berlin Iron Bridge Co. exploited Edmund Grinnel's idea (discussed earlier in this chapter) for eliminating masonry exterior columns. The steel framing of a three-story loft building to be used as a machine shop by the Veeder Manufacturing Co. (1898; Hartford, Connecticut; fig. 6.13) was left exposed and enclosed with sash set above brick spandrel walls at each story. The significant increase in the area of glazing raised questions about adequate ventilation and cooling of the shop floors during warm weather and the loss of heat through the glazed walls during the winter. Pivoting window sash and the installation of a forced-air blower system addressed these issues. On the interior, steel girders spanned the 30-foot width of the building; hence, the floors were unobstructed by columns.[42]

The American Bridge Co., into which the Berlin Iron Bridge Co. was folded, continued the practice of innovative design. American Bridge's own works (c. 1902; James Christie of the company, designer; Ambridge, Pennsylvania) certainly took advantage of the firm's products. The layout of

FIGURE 6.13   At the time of its construction, a loft building designed to house a machine shop for the Veeder Manufacturing Co. (1898; Hartford, Connecticut) was noted for the exposure of its steel framing and the large proportion of walls devoted to windows.

the facility was governed by interrelated systems of surface tracks and traveling cranes for materials handling, the minimum obstruction of the interior space by columns, and the use of the roof trusses to support the crane girders. This scheme was a mature version of the truss-supported hand-operated trolleys and traveling cranes of earlier shops, such as that of the Berlin Iron Bridge Co. The design of the main bridge shop at the Ambridge works can serve as an example. Its 270-foot-wide and 648-foot-long interior had unobstructed floor areas interrupted by a minimum number of columns that supported a dual system of trusses with 90-foot and 120-foot spans. Transverse roof trusses supported runways for about sixty traveling cranes. Short, narrow traveling hoists, called jacks-in-the-boxes, were placed between those cranes; they ran on tracks secured to lower chords of pairs of transverse trusses and therefore worked at right angles to the larger cranes.[43]

The Welded Steel Frame

It will follow as the night follows the day that welded steel will be quickly and universally accepted by the owner and the public, and we will have welded structures rising in all sections of the country.

ENGINEER J. E. FERGUSON, 1931

By the early twentieth century, the production shed had become a series of parallel crane-served bays that housed machines operated by electric drive, and the advances made in its design and construction during the next thirty years were less dramatic. After the introduction of steel sash, the next significant breakthrough in the engineering of such buildings occurred with the welding of steel.

Electric arc welding of steel members produced much more rigid connections than those achieved by riveting. Since welded joints acquired the strength of the members connected, beams and girders could be made continuous. A steel I-beam of given section and length, fixed at its ends by welded joints, could sustain a load up to 25 percent greater than the same beam connected by rivets. Not surprisingly, the earliest applications of welding to structural steel frames were made by firms in the electric equipment and welding fields. The Lincoln Electric Co., the General Electric Co., and Westinghouse used welded construction in their own facilities as a means of promoting the new method of joining steel.[44]

As early as 1916, welded columns were utilized in a four-story structure. In the construction of a building for the Electric Welding Co. of America (1920; T. Leonard McBean, engineer; Brooklyn) welding was limited to the triangular Pratt trusses that were attached by rivets to columns. Such substitution of welding for riveting characterized several early projects, though engineers soon designed frames specifically for welded construction. The possibilities of the new construction method were more fully developed in the design of a building for the Westinghouse Electric and Manufacturing Co. (1926; Sharon, Pennsylvania). The loft was the first to incorporate a multistory, completely welded steel frame in which the beams and girders formed a continuous grid. Although considerable savings had been realized in the amount of steel used in the structure, the cost of the building was still higher than if it had been erected with standard riveted construction.[45]

By the late 1920s, electric welding had passed an experimental stage. The expense of shop welding was contained through the use of semi-automatic welding machines and templates for laying out truss forms. Members of trusses were formed of small section angles and tees and were welded directly to one another without the use of gusset plates. Welded trusses consequently had a strikingly light appearance, in comparison to riveted ones, and were ideal for the wide spans of production sheds (fig. 6.14). Welding made practical the use of "battleship deck floors" of steel plates that were too costly to rivet. Welded "bar joists," where bars connected top and bottom chords in a truss form, were lightweight and permitted pipes and conduits to be run in any direction under floor assemblies.[46]

Through stronger connections and reduced sections of steel members, welded steel construction made a significant difference in the cost and types of spaces possible in the ever larger production sheds of the 1920s and 1930s. The scale of welded steel construction was advanced in the Electro-Motive Corp. plant (1935; The Austin Co., designer and builder; LaGrange, Illinois), in both the scope of the project and the dynamic loads placed on welded crane girders. In the main erecting shop, tripartite welded columns supported plate girders that carried a 200-ton crane, which was also of welded assembly.[47]

FIGURE 6.14 Welding was used in 1932 throughout the construction of the Spring Perch Company plant at Lackawanna, New York, and its frame appears insubstantial and attenuated in comparison to riveted steel structures.

Reinforced concrete has provided for the manufacturer an entirely new building material. Indestructible, economical and fireproof, it offers under most conditions features of advantage over every other type of construction.

Industrial lofts and production sheds were among the first buildings erected of reinforced concrete when the material was introduced at the turn of the twentieth century. Concrete embedded with steel reinforcement remained a common choice for factory buildings throughout the pre–World War II period. Like steel, reinforced concrete offered great tensile and compressive strength; it had three times the working strength of the best brickwork and seven times that of common brick. The material permitted the use of panel enclosure walls and large windows for maximum daylighting and good ventilation. The lack of joints in monolithic construction and the weight of the material allowed reinforced concrete to absorb and deaden vibration.

Moreover, reinforced concrete was fireproof. Although intense heat affected the surface of concrete, the nonconductive qualities of the material protected the steel reinforcement, and structural integrity was not compromised. Concrete, which had been used in foundations and as the floors of cellars for some time, began to dominate fireproof construction around 1890. It was used to level brick-arched floor construction and was poured over corrugated sheet-metal arches (fig. 6.15), as that type of floor construction found favor. Cement stucco was applied to metal lathe to form a fireproof material. These applications foreshadowed a revolution in fireproof construction brought about by the use of reinforced concrete.[48]

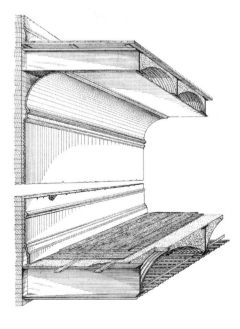

FIGURE 6.15 A system of "fireproof" floor and ceiling construction was offered by the George Hayes Co. The assembly consisted of wrought-iron beams and corrugated sheet-metal arches, concrete, and wood plank wearing surfaces and metal lathing for ceiling plaster.

A New Material

The time is so recent and reinforced concrete buildings are now so common that it is difficult to appreciate the boldness of the conception to construct a four-story building to sustain actual working loads of 400 pounds per square foot besides heavy machinery . . . out of a material until recently used almost exclusively for foundations, and considered capable of resisting only compressive loads.

REINFORCED CONCRETE IN FACTORY CONSTRUCTION, 1907

Reinforced concrete was adopted for industrial buildings in the United States at the beginning of the twentieth century, even though a few experimental buildings had been erected during the 1890s. An important impetus for the development of the new material was the improvement of processing methods for Portland cement that took place during the 1880s and 1890s. By 1900, engineers were discussing the advantages of reinforced construction; it didn't take them and the cement manufacturers long to convince industrialists to try the new material. By 1905 reinforced concrete construction had moved out of the experimental stage. In that year the New York City Department of Buildings approved the use of the Ransome system of reinforced concrete construction.[49]

Most factory buildings of reinforced concrete were monolithic structures. The first step in their construction involved the construction of "formwork," into which reinforcing rods were placed and wet concrete was poured and allowed to set. Then the forms were repositioned, new reinforcing bars were connected to those already embedded, and pouring continued so that the structure was, in a sense, cast as a single entity.

Ernest L. Ransome undertook groundbreaking work in the design and construction of reinforced concrete in the United States. After experimenting with twisted reinforcing rods during the 1880s and constructing several buildings of reinforced concrete in the San Francisco area, Ransome moved his business to the East Coast. As he erected buildings of the new material, Ransome Americanized the construction process by developing a system of reinforcement that was simpler (and therefore cheaper) than the French Hennebique method. He seems also to have introduced American builders to the use of reinforced concrete in a skeletal form.[50]

A demand for fireproof construction and the strength to support excessive loads led to Ransome's first major building project in reinforced concrete. At the edge of the New York City harbor in Bayonne, New Jersey, Ransome oversaw the construction of the Pacific Coast Borax Refinery (fig. 6.16). A loft building erected in 1897–1898 had originally been planned as a structure of mill construction with brick walls, but heavy tanks and large machinery required very strong floors. After deciding to use fireproof construction and evaluating the bids it received for the project, Pacific Coast Borax awarded a contract to Ransome. The first portion of the four-story structure utilized beam-and-girder floor construction, which was to become standard practice. The exterior walls of the structure, however, were

FIGURE 6.16 By the time engineer Ernest L. Ransome oversaw the construction of an addition to the Pacific Coast Borax Refinery in Bayonne, New Jersey, in 1903–1904, he had adopted the skeletal form of construction that characterized concrete factory buildings during the following decades. The original 1897–1898 building is just visible at the right side of the photograph.

conceived as self-supporting masonry walls and were pierced only by small window openings. Many of the engineers, architects, and industrialists who visited the construction site were especially interested in how the heavy machinery was supported by the floors of the concrete structure. The Pacific Coast Borax facility also demonstrated the fireproof qualities of reinforced concrete construction when it withstood a fire in 1902 that destroyed its contents and wood elements.[51]

By 1902 Ransome's method of reinforced concrete construction had advanced to a more skeletal form, and that year he patented a system of extending the floor slab beyond the face of the building to support brick panel walls and large windows. Ransome is believed to have introduced this method of construction, and its expression in gridlike exterior walls, in the United States. The new skeletal form appeared in an addition to the Pacific Coast Borax building (1903–1904) and the four-story Kelly & Jones Co. factory (c. 1903; Greensburg, Pennsylvania). The contrast between the two sections of the Bayonne complex demonstrates how, in literally one step, Ransome advanced American reinforced concrete construction to the skeletal forms used for decades.[52]

With the contemporary United Shoe Machinery Company project, Ernest Ransome made advances in the standardization and refinement of detailing. The concrete expert convinced the managers of the United Shoe Machinery Company to use reinforced concrete for its new plant (1903–1904; Beverly,

Massachusetts) that had originally been planned as a group of steel-framed structures. The switch to Ransome's reinforced concrete resulted in one of the largest collection of buildings in the new material: a row of identical four-story loft buildings, joined by connecting wings of equal height, and a production shed. Windows—each bay had one pair separated by a narrow concrete mullion—comprised 90 percent of the wall area. When the facility was enlarged during 1906 and 1907, few alterations to the original design of the buildings were made.[53]

Reinforced Concrete Lofts

When constructed of reinforced concrete, the industrial loft attained a third reincarnation (following a second period of effectual service made possible by the elevator) as a fireproof, vibration-free alternative to the production shed. Reinforced concrete was particularly suited for the construction of industrial lofts for many reasons, not the least of which was its strength. Though the floor load capacity of many reinforced concrete floors was as much as 500 pounds per square foot, special floors were designed to carry much greater loads. Long spans could be erected more economically in reinforced concrete than in steel-framed construction; for the relatively light loads of roofs, reinforced concrete girders from 70 to 115 feet in length were feasible. The extensive window area and good lighting possible in concrete lofts were used to advantage (as described in chapter 7).

Initially, reinforced concrete floor construction was based on traditional beam-and-girder framing elements. The expense of the formwork necessary for pouring floors of this type and the manner in which the beams and girders blocked light that entered the structure through windows that extended to the ceiling, however, led to the exploration of other ways to form floors. Engineers began placing beams the length of the building and using ribbed slabs to reduce the depth of the shadows in the ceiling area. They also developed a single system of beams set transversely, without intersecting members that would block daylight.

Early construction in reinforced concrete was by no means limited to the work of Ransome and others on the East Coast. Civil engineer C. A. P. Turner, who had erected reinforced concrete buildings by 1905 in the Minneapolis area, turned his attention to an improved form of floor construction. Turner thought that beams could be eliminated from floors designed to carry light loads (from 200 to 400 pounds per square foot) if reinforcement was placed in the floor slabs, extending from column to column. His first structure to use such "flat slab" construction was the Johnson-Bovey Building (1905–1906; Minneapolis). Turner extensively promoted his "Mushroom System" (fig. 6.17), named for the shape of the column heads that enclosed the reinforcement tying the column and floor slabs together (and for the remarkable rapidity with which they could be erected). According to Turner, flat slab construction allowed for the better distribution of light and the

FIGURE 6.17 The lighting conditions for the Union Switch & Signal Co. in Swissvale, Pennsylvania, were improved with the use of flat slab construction (here with drop panels above the column heads).

easier placement of shafting and sprinkler systems. It was also more resistant to vibration.[54]

The textile industry was not particularly quick to adopt reinforced concrete construction; the method was used first in discrete portions of facilities. In the Wood-Worsted Mills (1905; Dean & Main, engineers; Lawrence, Massachusetts) reinforced concrete was combined with exterior walls of brick and ordinary slow-burning mill construction. Relatively waterproof concrete was used to advantage for the wool-scouring floor and in the dye house. The Maverick Cotton Mills (1910; East Boston) was the first textile mill entirely of reinforced concrete erected by the prominent firm Lockwood, Greene & Co.[55]

Reinforced Concrete Production Sheds

The properties of reinforced concrete that recommended it for use in loft construction also applied to production sheds. The tensile strength of the steel reinforcement in concrete enabled the use of long roof spans; its compressive strength allowed it to support heavy traveling cranes.[56]

Reinforced concrete production sheds with crane-bays had a period of popularity before 1910. Some of them combined concrete structural members with exterior walls and window openings based on the forms of traditional masonry load-bearing construction. Reinforced concrete was selected as the material for the erecting shop of the Ingersoll Milling Machine Co. (1906; W. W. Crefore, designer; Rockford, Illinois) because sand and gravel were available on site. Panel walls pierced only by small windows and timber roof trusses suggests an unfamiliarity with the material. Unusual proportions distinguished the machine shop of the Bullock Electric Mfg. Co. (1906; Norwood, Ohio), which consisted of a narrow central craneway flanked by wide side bays. For aesthetic reasons, the wall columns were tripled in width on the exterior to create vertical bands that corresponded in width to the horizontal bands of the floor slab and panel walls.[57]

Automobile manufacturers built one-story assembly spaces of reinforced concrete construction during this early period. Local materials were used in the construction of an addition to the Rambler Automobile shops (1906; Kenosha, Wisconsin), which had reinforced concrete walls and steel pipes filled with concrete to support the sawtooth roof. Rambler was in the process of adding to its manufacturing space by constructing, in increments, assembly areas 257 feet square.[58]

The Geo. H. Pierce Co. plant (1906–1907; Albert Kahn, architect, and Lockwood, Greene, engineers; Buffalo, New York) was one of the new integrated, open-plan works. The roof-lighted manufacturing spaces with wide spans were constructed entirely of reinforced concrete. The brazing building and powerhouse were production sheds with monitor roofs. The walls of the one-story manufacturing building were filled with sash set between concrete piers, and its sawtooth roof was supported on concrete bents. The assembly building was a much taller one-story space and also had a sawtooth roof. In this structure only one row of columns divided the interior, and wide-span beams (93 inches deep) created two crane-served bays 60 feet wide and 400 feet long.[59]

The strength and flexibility of steel-framed production sheds and the speed with which they could be erected led companies to prefer them over reinforced concrete ones during the 1910s. The introduction during the late 1930s of wide-span reinforced concrete forms, such as rigid frames and butterfly and barrel shells, renewed interest in the reinforced concrete production shed.[60]

The fact that engineers often categorized industrial buildings only by building material and number of stories is testimony to the importance of using the right components. After this choice was made, attention turned to the form of two important elements of industrial buildings: their walls and roofs.

FACTORY WALLS

7

The success of an industrial building, given a column spacing that is adequate for the manufacturing process, depends mostly on the efficiency of its skin—walls and roof—to cope with wind and weather.

ENGINEERING NEWS-RECORD, 1936

The walls of industrial buildings, as well as their roofs, were engineered to provide light and ventilation for manufacturing space. Invariably, the goal was to replicate ideal outdoors conditions—the brightness and comfortable temperature of a June day.

Daylight, especially northern light, was preferred for manufacturing space because of its high quality and low cost. Even after the introduction of gas and electric lighting, natural light was cheaper and better for close work and matching colors. Artificial light was used to supplement daylight during the early morning and late afternoon hours only as necessary. The term *daylight factory* became prevalent when reinforced concrete and steel-framed construction nearly doubled the amount of wall space that could be devoted to window openings. The large windows that extended from pier to pier and nearly from floor to ceiling created previously unimaginable lighting conditions in loft buildings.[1]

The need for natural light influenced many aspects of the design of manufacturing works. If possible, buildings were positioned so as not to block the light of neighboring structures. The maximum width of industrial buildings was determined by the extent to which light could penetrate into the interior. The quality of light in various areas determined the positioning of operations in factories. Handwork, as well as fine machine work, was undertaken at benches placed directly below or perpendicular to window openings. Industrial lighting also relied on the installation of specially designed lighting fixtures (discussed in chapter 4).

During the early twentieth century, engineers began to think of large buildings as "enclosed acreage."[2] As the scale of these plants increased to include as much as 40 acres under a single roof, they considered more seriously the notion of artificial manipulation of light and ventilation. The concept of the "controlled conditions" plant was adopted as defense plants were erected before World War II. This change ushered in a new era of industrial architecture.

FACTORY WINDOWS

The general character of the walls and roof is dependent upon the question of natural lighting, which, however, is comparatively simple. Daylight is the cheapest possible illuminant and this is an important factor during much of the year.

ENGINEERING RECORD, 1909

The dimensions of an industrial building were influenced by the need for daylight to penetrate its interior. Common practice throughout the nineteenth century assumed that good lighting could not be had in factory buildings over 60 feet in width; many structures were considerably narrower. Wall construction determined the maximum size of windows and hence the quality of interior lighting. Load-bearing masonry walls generally supported a portion of the floor-load in addition to their own weight and the width of window openings in them was limited by the strength demanded of the wall. The concentration of the strength of the wall in pilasters allowed for larger openings and this was one reason for the popularity of pilaster and panel wall construction. The size of window openings was also influenced by the type of sash available to fill them. Window sills were positioned just above radiators and workbenches placed along the outer walls. The amount of light entering through windows was maximized through the use of splayed, or angled, openings. At best, the windows in a brick multi-story building could constitute 30 to 35 percent of the wall area.

Regularity in the size and placement of window openings in industrial buildings was engendered by the identical dimensions of the bays within and the need for even interior lighting. Uniform fenestration was also a means of providing a sense of organization and, by extrapolation, dignity for the factory exterior. In most cases, a range of windows was broken only by hoistway doors and vehicle passageways, or perhaps by areas of more extensive glazing. Variations in window size might reflect changes in story height or the shape of the gable end wall (see fig. 8.6). The fenestration of the top story of a loft building was often different from that below, since larger or more numerous openings were possible where demands for wall strength decreased.

For aesthetic and pragmatic reasons, regular fenestration prevailed even when the demand for good lighting was not a dominant consideration. Warehouses erected during the nineteenth century suggest how limited the use of blank expanses of wall and irregular fenestration patterns were. These structures nearly always had window openings to limit the need for any costly and potentially hazardous artificial lighting and to provide ventilation. Moreover, a building with regular fenestration could be readily converted for manufacturing or other uses. A facade relieved by window openings or even by blank windows (with a lintel and sill framing a thin panel of brickwork that could be removed) was not only adaptable but also more acceptable aesthetically. Around the turn of the century, it became common practice to use windowless walls for cold storage facilities and other types of warehouses equipped with electric lighting.[3]

Window Sash for Factories

In most every case steel sash is the most economical and practical for the modern factory, and it is also possible to obtain maximum light and ventilation—which cannot be accomplished by using double hung or counterbalanced wood sash.

ARCHITECTURAL FORUM, 1919

During the mid–nineteenth century, standard units of multilight wood sash, either double-hung or fixed, were placed in industrial buildings. Gradually, window sash was engineered for factory conditions through the adoption of various types of glass, sash that operated in different ways, mechanical operating devices, and noncombustible framing elements.

By the late nineteenth century, several types of glass were available for factory sash. Opaque glass admitted a soft, diffused light into work areas. Prismatic glass, with parallel ribs, bent rays of light and projected them deeper into the interior. However, it was recommended that clear glass be used at eye level and below in order to avoid a prisonlike effect (see fig. 7.2).[4]

Counterbalanced double-hung sash allowed large windows to be opened with ease. The lowering of the top sash in unison with the raising of the lower one facilitated the movement of air by providing an outlet for hot air near the ceiling. Some engineers favored counterbalanced sash because it did not create a cross wind and could ventilate a wider building than pivoted sash. When the height of the window opening demanded triple-hung sash, counterbalanced sash was often used; the center section could be fixed to stabilize the opening and the other sash units. Horizontal and vertical pivoting sash offered various ways to control ventilation.

The introduction of mechanical sash control devices during the 1880s transformed window sash into ventilating equipment. Fixed sash that had been used in roof monitors, or clerestories, could be replaced with horizontally pivoting sash that was easily operated from the shop floor. The new ways to open windows beyond reach permitted designers to commit more of the wall space of production sheds to windows without creating a greenhouse effect.

In addition, advances were made in the engineering of sash because the windows of factory buildings in densely developed works and urban areas limited the effectiveness of fire-resistive construction. Windows were not fire-resistant for two reasons: the poor heat resistance of glass and the combustibility of wood frames and sash. Once heat caused window glass to break, drafts were created that carried fire through otherwise fire-resistant walls. The iron shutters required by municipal building codes were only a partial solution to the problem. The need for a more fire-resistant window sash was underscored by the fact that the window area in industrial buildings steadily increased and could constitute as much as 70 percent of the wall surface in reinforced concrete structures.[5]

"Fireproof" Windows

The Knisely Fireproof Window is especially adapted for use in large factory buildings and warehouses where adequate ventilation must be combined with fire protection.

SWEET'S CATALOG, 1906

The problem of the poor fire resistance of glass, its structural failure, and the resulting exposure of the interior of a building to a spreading fire was solved in part through the introduction of wire glass. This shatter-proof material, which consisted of wire mesh embedded between layers of glass, became available during the 1880s. Because the wire provided additional strength and held glass in position after it was broken, wire glass slowed the spread of fire through window openings. The fire resistance of the reinforced concrete C. Kenyon Company building (1905; Brooklyn), 50 percent of which was glazed, was dramatically altered by its windows of Mississippi brand wire glass in hollow metal sash frames.[6]

The replacement of wood in window frames and sash was more of a challenge. Although both cast-iron and rolled-iron window frames and sash were available in the United States throughout much of the nineteenth century, they saw limited use. Expensive iron sash was not without problems; it twisted upon exposure to fire and released its glass panes. Wood windows and doors were eliminated in only one building of the Pennsylvania Railroad Car Shops (c. 1873; Joseph Wilson, engineer; West Philadelphia): A small oil storage house was fitted with cast-iron window and door frames and wrought-iron shutters and doors.[7]

Around the turn of the century, the use of metal window frames and sash became more common, though by no means universal. For instance, cast-iron window sills and frames were used in the construction of the Semi-Steel Co. foundry (1898; J. L. Silsbee, architect; Chicago Heights). The Brooklyn Navy Yard Steam Engineering Department shops (1902) were fitted with steel-framed windows to avoid the use of wood. About 60 percent of the total wall area of the Brown Hoisting Machinery Co. works (1903; Cleveland) consisted of ribbed glass set in steel angle frames.[8]

FIGURE 7.1 Hollow-metal and wire-glass window sash units, like those offered by the George Hayes Co. during the 1890s, replicated the forms of wood sash.

Sheet metal was pressed into service in metal-clad and hollow metal window frames. The metal-cladding of window frames was effective only if fire did not reach the wood under the sheet metal; hollow metal units had no wood components. Both types of sash were available with an additional fire prevention feature: an automatic closing device that was activated by high temperatures. The New York City Department of Buildings began to approve the use of metal-clad window frames and sash glazed with wire glass as an alternative to the previously required iron shutters just after the turn of the century.[9]

Around 1894 the George Hayes Co. introduced a sheet-metal window that was glazed with wire glass (fig. 7.1). The "fireproof windows" offered by window manufacturers in the 1906 *Sweet's Catalogue* were hollow metal products that replicated the form of traditional wood sash units—a single frame holding double-hung, pivoting, or casement sash. They were described as being "hardly detected from wood by casual observation." James A. Miller & Bro. asserted that the cost of their sheet-metal window frames and sash of galvanized iron was about the same as that of ordinary wood sash and iron shutters.[10]

The extent to which hollow metal window sash was used in industrial building construction during the period from 1890 to 1910 is difficult to determine. It was used in some warehouses, breweries, and industrial loft structures intended to be fireproof and certainly was placed in many reinforced concrete structures. Voightmann brand hollow metal sash was used in an addition to the Pacific Coast Borax Refinery (1903–1904; Ernest Ransome, engineer; Bayonne, New Jersey; fig. 6.16) and in the first reinforced concrete loft buildings erected by the Bush Terminal Co. (1904–1908; Brooklyn).[11]

Industrial Steel Sash

One error revealed was not using steel window sashes and trim and wired glass that withstands great heat. We will certainly have to use that finish henceforth. My friend, Henry Ford, tells me that all his automobile factories have this steel trim and wired glass.

THOMAS EDISON, AFTER HIS WORKS
WERE DESTROYED BY FIRE IN 1914

As the construction of fireproof reinforced concrete industrial lofts proliferated between 1905 and 1910, the need for rigid and fire-resistant metal sash to fill pier-to-pier window openings became more urgent. Indeed, the first two sections of the otherwise fireproof reinforced concrete structures of the United Shoe Machinery Co. plant (1903–1904 and 1906–1907; Ernest Ransome, engineer; Beverly, Massachusetts) were fitted with wood sash.[12]

Imported British steel sash appears to have been used in the United States to some extent prior to the introduction of American products. An American journalist noted that the advantages of steel windows had been recognized in European countries, especially England and Germany, before they were acknowledged in his own country. It seems that American factory owners avoided the expense of iron and steel window frames and sash—as they did other expensive types of construction methods and materials— until fireproof reinforced concrete construction and the need for the maximum amount of glazed surface altered their perception of economical building.[13]

Around 1910 several American manufacturers began to offer lines of steel sash. Almost immediately it became the standard in industrial buildings. The *American Architect and Building News* noted the remarkable growth of the use of steel windows between 1909 and 1911. There were several good reasons for the popularity of steel sash: It was noncombustible and admitted more light than wood sash because its framing members were of smaller section. It was considered to provide healthier conditions for workers. And it was projected to be less expensive to maintain than wood sash.[14]

Industrial steel sash was made of rolled-steel sections (often T-shaped) designed to provide the greatest strength with the smallest dimension in order to afford the maximum glazed area (fig. 7.2). The framing elements also were engineered to be air- and watertight. Steel sash originally had

FIGURE 7.2 United Steel brand industrial steel sash in an addition to the United Shoe Machinery Co. loft buildings extended from floor to ceiling and pier to pier. There was a row of clear glass near eye level.

relatively small panes. These were less expensive, but by the late 1910s, larger panes were preferred because windows were easier to keep clean when they didn't have so many dirt-catching horizontal muntins. From the time that steel sash was first offered by American manufacturers, pivoting sections of sash, which provided ventilation without admitting precipitation, were popular (fig. 7.3; see also figs. 6.4 and 10.2). Units of steel sash—in various combinations of fixed and pivoting sash—came in standard sizes that were placed side by side to fill large openings or expanses of walls.[15]

Top-hung continuous sash, operated in long sections by mechanical or electrical operating devices, was used first in roof monitors and sawtooth roofs and later in window openings. Continuous sash was placed on the exterior of some columns of loft buildings, creating expanses of sash that spanned two or three bays. Long sections of the sash were attached to the exterior of the framing of production sheds. The shop of the Detroit Steel Products Co., which had walls entirely enclosed with the continuous sash the firm manufactured, was featured in the company's catalog to promote a "window wall" approach to glazing.[16]

A few large manufacturers dominated the steel sash industry. The firm of David Lupton introduced its "Pond continuous top-hung" steel sash in 1909. One of the first large installations of Lupton sash was in the General Electric Co.'s Erie Works (c. 1910; Harris & Richards, consulting engineers and architects; Erie, Pennsylvania), where it was used in window openings

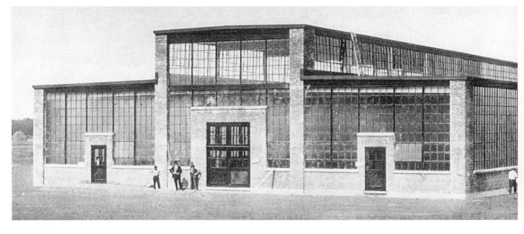

FIGURE 7.3 Pivoting sash, set low in the walls of the New York Air Brake Co. building in Watertown, New York, and in the side walls of the roof monitor, enhanced
natural air circulation in this standard building erected by The Austin Co. during the
1910s.

and on the Pond truss roof monitor. Fenestra brand steel sash was offered
around the same time by the Detroit Steel Products Company, which
claimed to be the "makers of [the] first steel sash manufactured in America." Fenestra sash replaced the hollow metal windows that had been used
in earlier structures in reinforced concrete lofts erected at the Bush Terminal
(1909–1910; Brooklyn). It was also the steel sash that Thomas Edison's
friend Henry Ford used at the Highland Park Ford Motor Co. plant (1909–
1910; Albert Kahn, architect). In 1910, Julius Kahn's Trussed Concrete Steel
Co. (Detroit) began to market its United Steel Sash line. Advertisements of
the Patented Specialties Manufacturing Company (Cincinnati) headlined
"Daylight Unit Fireproof Steel Windows" helped to coin the term *daylight
factory*, which was applied to reinforced concrete loft structures with steel
sash.[17]

THE WINDOW WALL

A view of the Nelson Gavit Machinist and Manufacturing works (established in 1854; Philadelphia; fig. 7.4) published during the 1870s suggests
that by midcentury manufacturers were experimenting with the window
wall.[18] The Gavit works included two buildings facing the street: One was a
conventional two-story structure with tall window openings. The other was
a three-story structure whose street wall was depicted as being entirely
enclosed by window sash. This type of wall probably evolved from a more
selective use of extensive glazing. The varnishing room on the third story of
the Goold Coach Manufactory (1840s; Albany), for example, was enclosed
with sash set at an angle. In a similar fashion, a bank of closely set double-
hung windows interrupted the fenestration pattern of the Turner Machine
Company (Danbury, Connecticut).[19]

FIGURE 7.4 In one of the buildings in the Nelson Gavit Machinist and Manufacturing works, window sash was placed side by side to form the front wall. The artist's cutaway of the ground-story walls reveals the activity within.

FIGURE 7.5 The exposure of the steel frame of the Fischer Marble works was prompted by the desire for maximum window area.

Engineers and builders understood that the walls of wood-framed industrial buildings were enclosing walls. During the nineteenth century they usually employed fenestration patterns dictated by common building practice rather than taking advantage of the freedom the construction method offered in the placement of windows. Nevertheless, when dramatic increases in the ratio of window to solid wall and early examples of window walls first appeared, they were in wood-framed buildings in which pairs of wood sash were set between vertical posts. When the sections of wall above and below the sash were sheathed with horizontal wood siding or shingles, the result was alternating horizontal bands of sash and siding, as in the production shed of the Herreshoff Manufacturing Company (1870s; Bristol, Rhode Island). This method of construction seemed to have been popular in Rhode Island. Benjamin Wilbur, not deterred by twice losing his factory to fire, rebuilt a "substantial wooden building" (1883; South Scituate) whose lower story had a long wall filled with double-hung sash.[20]

The desire to gain as much window area as possible in steel-framed loft buildings led designers to experiment with eliminating piers and panel walls and exposing the steel frame. In the Veeder Building (1898; Hartford, Connecticut; see fig. 6.13) and the Fischer Marble Works (1904; Charles H. Caldwell, architect; the Bronx; fig. 7.5), steel frames were used to advantage in this manner. Architectural critic Russell Sturgis noted that these buildings heralded new possibilities and "novel motives" of design. Nevertheless, for production sheds, this was the approach not taken.[21]

Engineered Curtain Walls for Production Sheds

Sash Makes the Factory.

AIR AND LIGHT IN MACHINE SHOPS, 1920

Production sheds with load-bearing brick walls had the same limitations on the size and number of window openings noted earlier; relatively tall, narrow openings, single or paired, were set in each bay. As larger products were assembled with the assistance of cranes and the height of the one-story space increased, window openings were often set in tiers that gave the structure's exterior the appearance of a two- or three-story building. Window openings were also placed in the upper portion of the gable face for additional light and ventilation. Round bull's-eye openings fitted with tilting sash, or groups of arched windows with taller openings under the peak of the gable, were common arrangements (see figs. 2.9, 2.14, and 3.12).

Around 1880, wood-framed window walls (described earlier) were first used to enclose production sheds, especially those used as foundries. Low brick walls, 3 to 4 feet in height, provided damp-proof foundations; upper walls consisted of sash attached to wood framing members. The Corliss Steam Engine Co. (Providence) was considered one of the first firms to build a one-story shop of this type. A foundry erected by the nearby Brown &

Sharpe firm (1880; Providence; fig. 7.6) also had walls of double-hung sash above a low brick wall. Timber framing described as "although of an inexpensive character, exceedingly strong and durable," surrounded windows set into 4-foot-wide, 11-foot-tall openings in a foundry at the Yale Lock Manufacturing Co. (c. 1882; Stamford, Connecticut). As many production sheds were erected during the 1880s, the idea of the window wall gained popularity and a secondary system of wood framing was used to support wood sash and corrugated-metal siding.[22]

Meanwhile, the window area of production sheds with brick enclosing walls was increased only gradually as the traditional forms of masonry construction prevailed. The machine shop and other buildings erected at the Kinkora works of the John A. Roebling's Sons Co. (1905–1907; Charles Roebling, engineer; Roebling, New Jersey), demonstrated the strong influence asserted by the forms of load-bearing brick construction and the familiar elements of the firm's first Trenton works (begun during the late 1840s). Charles Roebling retained individual segmentally arched window openings of traditional proportion, some of which were quite large. When the height of the window was limited, he placed sets of three narrow windows separated by brick mullions in each panel, rather than one opening with a horizontal orientation.[23]

Engineers and structural steel firms began to replicate the window walls of wood-framed structures in steel-framed ones during the 1890s. (See chapter 6 for a discussion of how the Berlin Iron Bridge Co. designed steel-framed buildings to maximize window area.) It was soon recommended that one-fifth of the wall, or one-tenth of the total area of production sheds, be devoted to windows and skylights. But often the entire upper half of side walls were enclosed with window sash bolted to framing. Some engineers asserted, however, that window walls were not really necessary and might make factories too bright and hot in the summer and expensive to heat

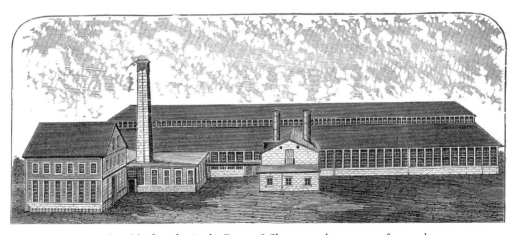

FIGURE 7.6 An 1880 foundry in the Brown & Sharpe works was one of several buildings erected at that time with window walls.

FIGURE 7.7 The Buffalo Foundry Co. plant seemed "to be made largely of glass when viewed from outside," particularly at nighttime.

during the winter. Nevertheless, every vertical surface of the main foundry building of the Buffalo Foundry Co. (c. 1903; Buffalo, New York; fig. 7.7) was glazed with translucent glass. The next stages in the evolution of production shed walls are described in chapter 10.[24]

Continuous Sash Transforms Industrial Lofts

Thus the old process is reversed; while formerly the walls supported the floors, in "Daylight" buildings the floors support the walls!

BUILDINGS FOR COMMERCE AND INDUSTRY, 1924

In industrial loft buildings, reinforced concrete construction introduced not only larger window openings but also window walls. It became common for at least 50 percent—and up to 80 percent—of the wall area to be windows that filled the grid established by vertical piers and horizontal floor slabs and panel walls. The goal of increasing even further the amount of glazed wall area led building designers to place window sash on the outside of the perimeter columns. The Winston Building (1917; Paul Gerhardt, architect; Chicago) was considered one of the first structures of this type. Its floor slabs were extended 6 inches beyond cylindrical columns to support panel walls and sash. An eight-story reinforced concrete loft structure erected for the William Wrigley, Jr., Co. (c. 1921; S. Scott Joy, architect; Chicago) was of similar construction.[25]

The Ballinger Co. of Philadelphia promoted such structures as its "All-Window 'Daylight' Buildings." A Ballinger "Daylight Building" admitted 15

FIGURE 7.8 The Ballinger Co. promoted its design for the James Lees & Sons Co. yarn mill as an "All-Window 'Daylight' Building."

percent more light than an ordinary reinforced concrete loft and was less expensive to build, since exterior piers and paneled walls were omitted. The first building of this type that the Ballinger Co. erected was a textile mill for James Lees & Sons (1922; Bridgeport, Pennsylvania; fig. 7.8). Piers and corner pylons rose through the facade to provide "architectural effect." This concept was interpreted in a building for the Firestone Tire & Rubber Co. (1922–1923; Ballinger Co. and Osborn Engineering Co.; Akron, Ohio), where every third column broke long expanses of continuous sash.[26]

CONTROLLED CONDITIONS

Incidentally, it is a significant index of our present state of mind in architectural matters that we are trying out the windowless building at the same moment that we build structures of steel and glass that are practically all windows.

ARCHITECTURE, 1931

The idea that windows might be unnecessary for a well-lighted factory but could be used for sentimental and psychological reasons was suggested by improvements in roof lighting (described in chapter 8). During the 1920s, engineers began to consider a new model for industrial building design, one that abandoned the goal of replicating ideal outdoor conditions and the use of windows. Instead, they would create and control the conditions for industry. After all, artificial light could be uniform in color and intensity, and air quality could be regulated through the monitoring of moisture and temperature and the frequent exchange of air.[27]

The Simonds Saw & Steel Co. plant (1930–1931 and 1939; The Austin Co., architect; Fitchburg, Massachusetts; fig. 7.9) is considered among the first windowless, or controlled conditions, plants erected in the United States. Simonds decided to consolidate several plants and introduce a straight-line production operation in a modern one-story facility. The Simonds and Austin companies planned a building that had a footprint of five acres. Windows were eliminated; lighting, ventilation, heating, and cooling were to be controlled mechanically. The carefully planned interior environment made use of a paint scheme of blue, green, and white. Illumination was provided by hundreds of specially designed 100-watt lamps. A complete exchange of humidified and heated or cooled air was to take place every ten minutes, while acoustical wall, ceiling, and floor coverings would reduce noise levels. The windowless factory presented a challenge for "architectural effect." The

FIGURE 7.9 The Simonds Saw & Steel Co. plant was among the first windowless, or controlled conditions, plants erected in the United States.

exterior walls of the steel-framed structure were faced with two shades of brick. Horizontal bands of light-colored brick that extended from its corners were intended to emphasize the horizontal sweep of the structure; door enframements that rose to the roofline provided some contrasting expression of height.[28]

The notion of controlled interior conditions became more popular during the 1930s than the elimination of windows in factories. Glass block was utilized instead of sash, beginning in the mid-1930s, to create insulated, airtight walls, particularly for air-conditioned buildings. The plant of the Industrial Rayon Corporation (c. 1939; Wilbur Watson & Associates, engineers; Painesville, Ohio; fig. 7.10) was an air-conditioned factory that housed continuous spinning processes. Glass block filled all window openings and monitor walls in one of the largest installations of that material to date. As air-conditioning became more common in plant offices, administrators were often housed in separate buildings that had few windows or openings filled with glass blocks. An office with unpierced limestone walls was constructed by the Hershey Chocolate Corp. (c. 1936; Hershey, Pennsylvania), though a nearly opposite approach was taken with the glass block walls of the office building of the Owens-Illinois Glass Co. (c. 1936; Toledo, Ohio).[29]

FIGURE 7.10 Glass block filled the side walls of the "high and low bay" roof and window openings of the Industrial Rayon Corporation plant.

When the pace of industrial building quickened during the late 1930s, the debate over whether factories should have windows resumed. Controlled conditions were valued in process industries such as chemical, textile, and printing. They facilitated precision work because expansion and contraction of materials due to temperature changes was eliminated. The windowless plant also simplified production layout, since all areas were equally well lighted and wall space could be used for shelving; it was particularly adapted to assembly-line production and better suited for shift work. Those who favored controlled conditions asserted that total artificial illumination cost little more than the lighting needed for plants with windows and that fluorescent lamps introduced little heat and therefore limited the demand on air-conditioning equipment. An analysis of conditions in Detroit revealed that artificial light was required over 70 percent of the time. Consequently, the Bundy Tubing Co. decided against the "so called 'greenhouse' style [of plant] with an over-abundance of glass side walls and monitors." The subjective arguments for windows that gave architecture its human scale and linked production space to the world beyond were apparently not convincing.[30]

During the long period when the conditions of a June day seemed ideal for manufacturing, the walls of a factory did more than enclose production space. They also helped provide light and ventilation for profitable manufacturing. But walls had a partner in this task—the factory roof, to which we turn next.

FACTORY ROOFS

8

On the basis of the functions that it has to perform, the roof of an industrial building is more important than the walls. In addition to providing weather protection, it usually serves as both lungs and eyes of the structure.

ENGINEERING NEWS-RECORD, 1936

Perhaps more than any other aspect of the industrial building, the roof was engineered to serve industry—to provide ventilation and light, resist fire, span large areas, and support equipment. Engineered factory roofs also gave industrial buildings, particularly production sheds, their distinctive form and character. American engineers adapted European roof forms and methods of roof lighting for the harsher climate of North America and developed new ones as well. Roofs engineered to provide light varied from the gable roof pierced by skylights to roofs that *were* skylights: the sawtooth roof. The monitor roof, with its clerestory of sash elevated above adjacent portions of the roof to provide both light and ventilation, saw extensive use and was engineered to be even more effective during the first half of the twentieth century.

ROOF FORMS FOR FACTORIES

The various types of roof forms used for industrial buildings during the nineteenth century were chosen for functional reasons. A gabled roof provided attic space. A flat roof could increase a structure's stability. A roof with ventilators dissipated heat. As noted in chapter 5, roof forms and their materials were also aspects of fire-resistive construction.

The Gable Roof

During the nineteenth century, many factories had gable roofs. Initially, the scale of industrial operations was well matched with the limitations of the span of roof rafters, and a 25- to 30-foot width for factories prevailed. These gable roofs were framed in various ways that reflected regional and ethnic building practices.

During the midcentury, though, industry began to require larger spaces, and two methods of spanning somewhat wider industrial buildings with gable roofs became standard practice. Traditional rafters and purlins could be used to support the roof of a wide building if two rows of columns were used to divide the interior into thirds. The central bay of the building was then raised above the shed roofs covering the side bays: This form became known as a "monitor" (discussed later in this chapter). The clerestory walls of the central bay were filled with windows that provided light and ventilation. This roofing solution—the advantages of which had been demonstrated in cathedrals—was well suited for industrial buildings and market enclosures. Alternatively, roofs supported by trusses eliminated the need for (or limited the number of) interior columns as they spanned wider structures.

The pitch of a gabled factory roof was a compromise between the rise needed to keep wind from driving rain under roofing materials and the flatness that minimized the wind load and limited the area of the roof. Gable roofs were often divided by fire walls that extended above them for a few feet and edged with parapets to protect them from fire spreading from adjacent structures. They were covered with a variety of roofing materials, the choice of which depended on cost, degree of fire-resistance required and the pitch of the roof. The use of wood shingles on industrial buildings was avoided, although wood sheathing was often laid under more fire-resistant sheathing. Slate shingles and sheet metal were the fire-resistant roofing materials of industry until the 1890s, when concrete roofing tiles, slabs, and shingles became available. By the time asphalt shingles were introduced in 1916, when the National Board of Fire Underwriters called for a ban on the use of wood shingles, few new factories had gabled roofs, though many older ones were still in use.[1]

American builders almost always covered an industrial building with a single roof gable and placed its ridge parallel to the length of the rectangular structure. They did not often utilize the "ridge and furrow" roof of multiple gables that was popular in England, even though it weighed less and was consequently less expensive, less subject to damage, and less inclined to spread the walls of the structure. Engineer Alexander Holley explained that in the northern areas of the United States, the potential for snow and ice accumulation in the valleys of roofs of this type limited the use of the "MM arrangement of roofs."[2]

The Flat Roof

The elimination of spaces that easily caught fire and the stability gained from a roof of mill construction led to the use of nearly flat roofs on industrial loft buildings during the mid–nineteenth century. This change was made possible by the built-up roofing, developed during the 1840s, that could be used on flat and very low-pitched roofs; in the following decade flat roofs became standard for urban industrial and commercial buildings. Several types of proprietary systems, such as Carey and Barrett, were so popular that the brand names were used to refer to this type of roofing. Tar and gravel roofing, another common type of fire-resistant covering, could be used only on a flat or very low-pitched roof with a rise of not more than one inch per foot. Slag (the fire-resistant residue from the blast furnace) was introduced as a wearing surface for flat roofs during the late 1860s.[3]

Flat roofs were popular on lofts because they provided outdoor areas for drying materials and processes that produced offending odors. For example, a platform that held drying racks was affixed to a roof (in this case, a pitched roof) of the Quaker City Dye Works (Philadelphia; fig. 8.1). Flat factory roofs were also spaces that employees utilized for rest and recreation. During the model factory era at the end of the century, factory roofs were occasionally turned into appealing gardens.[4]

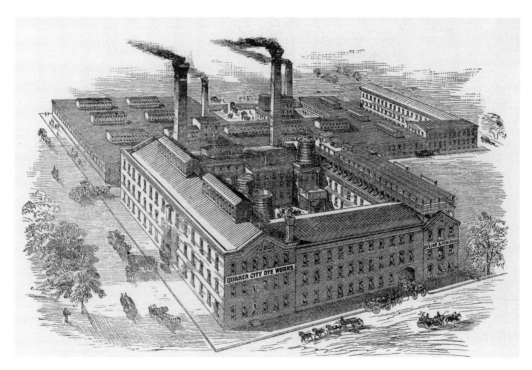

FIGURE 8.1   The roofs of the Quaker City Dye Works featured various types of roof monitors, water tanks, and racks for drying yarn.

After the turn of the twentieth century, large production sheds more often had flat roofs. As these types of buildings came to enclose acres, flat roofs eliminated deep valleys and snow and water shedding problems. But the manner in which areas of flat roofs were combined with various types of roof monitors led to even more roof varieties.

The Mansard Roof

The construction of industrial buildings with mansard roofs was limited to a short period during the 1860s and 1870s. The enclosed attic space of a mansard, with its numerous small framing members, burned with remarkable ease, as was demonstrated by the great Boston fire of 1872. Urban building codes soon thereafter required that mansard roofs be erected with iron framing and that a layer of noncombustible mortar be placed under metal, slate, or tile roofing. The roof's brief popularity coincided with a building boom in factory construction, though, and late-nineteenth-century views of works depict many buildings with this type of roof.[5]

Mansard roofs allowed the introduction of light into the attic story through dormers that projected from the lower slope of the roof, and possibly from skylights set in the upper, flatter portion of the roof. A truncated hipped roof with projecting dormer windows and skylights on the flat upper portion covered the loft buildings of the Mason Machine Works (1845; Taunton, Massachusetts; see fig. 3.6) during the 1870s. In Worcester, Massachusetts, where the mansard roof was popular, it appeared on both the main building and the tower of the new L. Coes works (1869) and on the main building of the Washburn & Moen Manufacturing Co. works (c. 1871; see fig. 9.7). The immense loft building erected for the Singer Sewing Machine Co. (1872–1873; Elizabeth, New Jersey) had a mansard roof with a prominent hipped upper portion; the attic story was lighted by large dormers.[6]

Mansard roofs were often used to give certain structures a more formal appearance. The office buildings of Parke, Davis & Co. (c. 1872; Detroit) and the Hartford Machine Screw Co. (1880; Hartford) were treated in this way (see also figs. 2.8 and 8.10). And mansard roofs often served as distinctive caps for water tank towers, where their potential as a fire hazard was minimal (see figs. 1.5, 1.6, and 3.12).[7]

TRUSSED ROOFS

Builders turned to trussed roofs to span wider areas and to eliminate interior columns. Most trusses used in American industrial buildings were simple ones, and many were constructed with both timber and iron elements. Even after the introduction of iron roof trusses, timber trusses remained in common use because many builders knew how to erect them and the small pieces of lumber that comprised trusses were inexpensive.

By the 1840s, iron rods had been introduced into roof trusses as auxiliary tension members. All-iron trusses were soon used because they were non-combustible and had members that were smaller in section and therefore weighed less and blocked less light entering the building through skylights and monitors. The common practice of using roof trusses to support shafting demonstrated another advantage of iron trusses: They did not shrink and swell, as wood trusses did, and thereby cause misalignment of millwork (see fig. 4.4). Iron, and later steel, roof-framing members were often T-sections, made up of two angles attached back to back and to gusset plates.[8]

During the mid-1850s iron trusses appeared in large production sheds erected in ironworks and government facilities. A building in the Albany Iron Works (c. 1853; Albany) had a sophisticated cast- and wrought-iron roof with a ventilating monitor. By 1855 a trussed roof of cast- and wrought-iron components and corrugated sheet-iron sheathing had been installed on a blacksmith shop in the Brooklyn Navy Yard. The use of iron roofs spread, and during the 1880s the demand for them increased further due to the scarcity of good timber and the vulnerability of wood buildings and roofs to fire.[9]

The form of the roof truss was determined by the length of the span and the number and spacing of supporting columns. The bracing of roof monitors and the accommodation of wind and snow loads were taken into account, as were the slope of the roof and type of covering to be used. Trusses were designed with a panel point under each purlin so that a diagonal member of the truss could carry the direct load from the purlin. Because standard practice limited the distance between panel points and purlins to 8 feet, truss design was related to the length of the span (fig. 8.2). For narrow roofs of 20 to 30 feet, a king-post or king-rod-and-queen-rod truss was recommended. Two truss types were commonly used for the wider gable roofs of industrial buildings. Variations of the Fink and fan trusses, including their compound versions with subdivided panels, worked well for spans up to 100 feet. The Fink truss was preferred because of its simplicity and low cost. Arched roof trusses could support spans of more than 100 feet. For nearly flat roofs, flat Pratt, flat Warren, and flat Howe trusses—which could be used for spans of various lengths up to 80 feet by varying the number of panels—were favored.[10]

The spacing of roof trusses was a matter of preference and changed over time, even though bay width and truss dimensioning was interrelated: The wider the spacing, the heavier the trusses had to be. Positioning trusses 10 to 16 feet on center was considered most economical for spans up to 50 feet. For longer spans, a distance of from one-fourth to one-eighth of the span length was suggested. If trusses were only 8 to 10 feet apart, planking could be placed across them, eliminating the need for rafters and purlins. During the early twentieth century it became common practice to place roof trusses 20 to 30 feet apart. In addition to carrying its covering, roof framing supported shafting, hoists, tramways, and cranes (see figs. 4.4 and 6.11).[11]

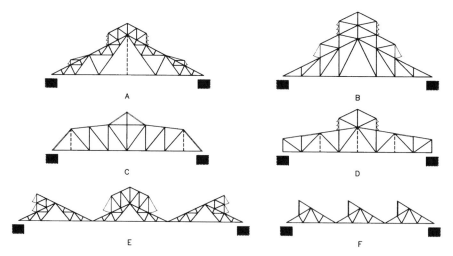

FIGURE 8.2 Common roof forms for industrial buildings: (a) Fink truss with monitor; (b) Pratt truss with double monitor; (c) flat Pratt truss with flush skylight in angles chord of end panel and A-frame monitor; (d) flat Warren truss with flush skylights and monitor; (e) silk mill roof with Fink trusses; (f) sawtooth roofmodified to place glazing in a vertical plane.

The Arched Truss

The best-known large arched truss roofs erected in the United States during the mid–nineteenth century are those of railroad train sheds, which have been documented by historian Carl Condit. These buildings and their specialized roof structures, designed by civil engineers working for the railroad companies, must have served as models for industrial buildings that had similar demands for space. Since many train sheds and car shops with arched roofs had monitors for lighting and ventilation, they may have served as models for that feature as well.

Arched trusses—often webbed bowstring trusses—were used to roof not just particularly wide industrial buildings but also, occasionally, some structures of more common dimensions. The distinctive shapes of production sheds with arched roofs make them easily identifiable in views of industrial works. The Commercial Point Forge (Dorchester, Massachusetts) was enclosed by a pair of parallel arched roofs during the 1850s. The Milwaukee Iron Co. Works (c. 1870) erected a large, nearly square building with an arched roof from which a wide monitor rose. Both large production sheds and smaller buildings in the National Tube Works (c. 1874; McKeesport, Pennsylvania) had arched roofs. The 110-foot-wide production shed of the Kieghler Manufacturing Co. (Cincinnati; fig. 8.3) was depicted in 1891 as having a roof supported by double-webbed arched trusses and crowned with a central monitor. A timber-framed bowstring truss system supported the roof of the foundry of the Semi-Steel Co. (c. 1898; J. L. Silsbee, architect; Chicago Heights).[12]

FIGURE 8.3 Double-webbed arched trusses supported the roof of a production shed of the Kieghler Manufacturing Co.

The use of arched trusses in roofing industrial buildings may have been limited because of the same disadvantages encountered in their use for railroad train sheds: A large arched roof was relatively expensive to construct and difficult to maintain. Though it was hoped that the high vault and monitor ventilator at its apex would exhaust smoke and hot air, the large space tended to diffuse rather than draw air currents.[13]

The small, iron-framed sheds with arched roof trusses to carry corrugated sheet-metal roofing, buildings promoted during the 1870s, would not have had the same drawbacks. Their roofs could be supported with "light ribs of iron or wood pass[ing] from column to column" because of the stiffness and strength that corrugation gave to iron sheets. A "continuous skylight, rising to a ridge," was recommended, in part, to provide a peaked roof and ridge to shed water.[14]

SPECIAL FORMS FOR LIGHT AND VENTILATION

The natural result has been the development of all sorts of methods of roofing over large areas of ground in such a way that light may penetrate the entire building, and the consequent development of sawtooth, monitor, and clerestory roofs of various kinds.

CRITIC TALBOT HAMLIN, 1940

The engineering of factory roofs for light and ventilation dates from the earliest years of the nineteenth century. This effort expanded from the use of simple skylights to specialized roof forms. Once electric drive cleared the headroom of millwork, engineered factory roofs became even more effective.

Attic Lighting

Whether covered by a flat, gabled, or mansard roof, the top floor of a manufacturing loft was valued as a well-lighted space above the shadows cast by neighboring buildings. It often had larger or more numerous windows and might be unobstructed by interior columns under a trussed roof. Before the adoption of top-down production layouts, the operations that required the best lighting conditions were housed on the top story.

The limited size of early waterpowered manufacturing operations directed attention to the attic under the sloping gable roof as potential manufacturing space. The dormers used on residences were borrowed as a means of admitting light into garrets of textile mills and other types of industrial lofts. Low-pitched shed dormers introduced just a bit of light into the attic spaces of the Providence Tool Co. buildings during the 1850s. Dormers used to better advantage, one above every window bay, projected from a roof of the main building housing the machine works of the Atlas Manufacturing Co. (c. 1881; Newark, New Jersey).[15]

Mill engineers adapted the "lantern roof" or "double roof" to textile mills to better light their attics. Both clerestory and trap-door monitors, which had been employed to some extent in England, became common elements in American mill buildings during the early nineteenth century. The trap-door, or eyebrow, lantern was formed by raising a section of a sloping roof to a flatter angle and inserting small windows in the gap. It offered only slightly improved lighting for the attic loft. Trap-door lanterns on the machine shops of the Crown and Eagle Mills (1825–1830; North Uxbridge, Massachusetts) and the Phoenix Iron Foundry (1848; Providence) indicate that other industries made use of the roof form as well.[16]

A clerestory lantern, formed by raising the roof on both sides of the ridge to allow for the insertion of a range of windows, was a more effective solution to the problem of lighting the attic. This type of roof modification, quite similar to the roof monitors of production sheds (discussed later in this chapter), was used as early as 1806–1807 for the roof of the machine shop of the Hope Manufacturing Company (Hope, Rhode Island). The double roof was one of the features that distinguished American textile mills from British ones during the mid–nineteenth century. The preference for flat roofs for textile mill construction after the 1860s led to the removal of many older monitor roofs. The construction of lofts with clerestory lanterns persisted in some areas, though, as demonstrated by silk mills in Paterson, New Jersey, and Allentown, Pennsylvania, erected during the 1880s (fig. 8.4).[17]

The practice of providing good lighting on the top floors of industrial lofts continued during the twentieth century. For example, an addition to the works of Northwestern Terra Cotta Co. (c. 1911; Peter B. Wight, architect; Chicago; fig. 8.5) had sawtooth skylights set at three different levels over the clay modeling room. In a similar manner, the top floor of the B. F. Goodrich plant's five-story Building No. 40 (c. 1917; Akron, Ohio) was "transformed" by a sawtooth roof with mechanized continuous sash.[18]

FIGURE 8.4 The top stories of the Adelaide Silk Mills in Allentown, Pennsylvania, erected c. 1882, were lighted by roof monitors.

FIGURE 8.5 The roof transformed the top story of a portion of the Northwestern Terra Cotta Co. works into a production shed. Sawtooth skylights at three different levels enclosed the clay modeling room; the end wall is formed of hollow clay tile.

Skylights

The tall loft, yawning with overhead space, was strung with pulley ropes like bull-lines in a mining pit and, when jerked at, a section of skylight would drop like a weighted jaw, disclosing a smoky square of city sky.

THE FOUNDRY, 1934

Skylights were the most common means of lighting the top story of industrial lofts during the nineteenth century and were also used extensively on production sheds. The shape of skylights, as well as their form, varied over time, culminating in large expanses of continuous skylights. They offered both better lighting and some disadvantages. Skylights were likely to leak, were prone to glass breakage, and could be obstructed by snow. When they admitted too much direct sunlight, the use of ground or yellow glass or translucent cloth shades was recommended (see fig. 8.7). Skylights could be purchased from builder's suppliers and sheet-metal works, or they could be crafted by the local carpenter. The latter, no doubt, was responsible for the pyramidal shapes covered with panes of glass laid as shingles that extended from the roof of the Hanford woodworking mill (East Meredith, New York).[19]

Some of the skylights pictured in early views of works are turret- or lanternlike structures perhaps 2 feet tall; vertical walls filled with sash were set under sheathed (not glazed) roofs. This type of skylight, with operable sash that also ventilated, rose from the roofs of the one-story foundry and a two-story loft of the Snow, Brooks & Co. Machine Works (West Meriden, Connecticut) during the 1850s. Ornate lantern skylights, in two sizes, lit the production shed of the Thomas Manufacturing Co. (Plymouth Hollow, Connecticut; fig. 8.6) in 1860. Once the roof of the lantern was glazed, its height was reduced, and it assumed the shape more characteristic of late-nineteenth-century boxed skylights.[20]

Though the advantage of a centrally located overhead light source was obvious, there was a striking similarity between these lantern skylights and the cupolas that terminated the low-pitched roofs of Italianate villas popular during the 1840s. Wire-rope manufacturer and bridge engineer John A. Roebling rebuilt his house in such a style in 1855 and soon thereafter erected a nearly square building in his adjacent works (Trenton, New Jersey). The similarity between the roof forms—a low-pitched hipped structure with a central cupola or lantern—suggests how features were adapted from one type of building to another.[21]

Views of industrial works indicate that skylights were also placed flush with the surfaces of pitched roofs (see fig. 3.3). Historian Richard Candee has documented how the textile industry turned to this type of roof lighting in 1825 with the decision to use flat skylights "like the roof of the Ship House" at the Charlestown Navy Yard in the roof of the Dover Manufacturing Co.'s No. 4 building. The skylights were found so satisfactory that they were immediately used in nearby mills and in 1831 were adopted in Lowell

FIGURE 8.6 Lanterns that served as skylights and ventilators rose from the roof ridges of the Thomas Manufacturing Co. works.

mills.[22] That this method of roof lighting headed westward with the industry was demonstrated by the two rows of flush skylights lighting the weaving room on the top floor of Adolphus Meier & Co.'s St. Louis Cotton Factory (1849–1850; St. Louis).[23]

British engineers extended the form of flush skylights to glazed roofing. As early as the 1850s, they installed heavy plate glass to form part of the roofing of sheds covering shipbuilding slips. By 1873 the Pennsylvania Railroad had begun to use continuous skylights up to 13 feet wide on some of its large shops. Around 1880 the Rendle system, an improved method for holding the glass sheets in place, was introduced in the United States. Early installations of Rendle skylights included the New York Central & Hudson River Railroad Co.'s Buffalo, New York, depot and the machine shop of the Flint & Père Marquette Railroad Co. (East Saginaw, Michigan). When Americans began using extensive flush skylights on production sheds, they became known as "continuous skylights" (fig. 8.7).[24]

Low, boxed skylights with hipped or single-pitch roofs were also common. Their bases could be fitted with louvers that provided ventilation as well. The standard boxed skylight of the early 1900s was 12 by 6 feet. The number of boxed skylights in the roofs of industrial buildings varied, ranging from a select few, set to light a certain process or portion of the top floor, to long rows of them (of one or more sizes) positioned over large expanses of roof area. The production sheds of the Detroit Car Works (1872; Detroit), for instance, had flat roofs with numerous skylights placed at regular intervals to give uniform lighting. In a similar manner, production sheds that housed

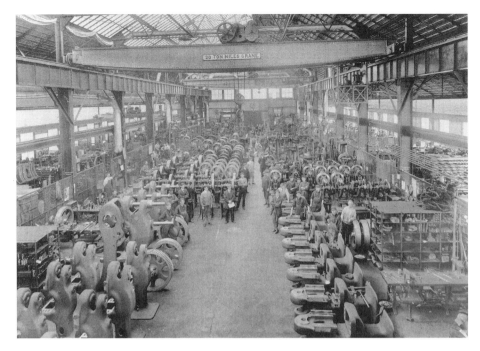

FIGURE 8.7 A continuous skylight formed the upper portion of one plane of the roof of the production shed erected in 1902 at the Ferracute Iron Works in Bridgeport, New Jersey. Cloth shades that could be pulled upward to soften the light are visible at the bottom edge of the skylight.

the Ohio Falls Car-Works (1873; Jeffersonville, Indiana) had rows of narrow skylights set perpendicular to the roof ridge.[25]

Around the turn of the century, industrial and illuminating engineers codified common practices of roof and window lighting as recommendations based on a calculation of the percentage of the wall and roof areas devoted to glazing. At that time, engineers preferred for at least half of the glazed surfaces to be in the form of skylights. A later guideline urged the use of roof lighting if the width of the structure exceeded its height by five times. In some cases, 50 percent of the roof surface was glazed, but more representative of engineers' recommendations were the Atchison, Topeka and Santa Fe Railroad shops (Topeka, Kansas), in which skylights comprised 20 percent of the roof surface. Nevertheless, a full 60 percent of the envelope of the Steam Engineering Building at the Brooklyn Navy Yard was glass; most of the roof consisted of continuous skylights.[26]

Roof Monitors

By raising the center span a ventilator is formed the whole length of the roof except on the end panels, the sides having glazed sash.

ENGINEER JOSEPH M. WILSON, 1873

One of the defining elements of the nineteenth-century production shed roof was the monitor, which provided both ventilation and lighting for the interior. This monitor, or superstructure gable roof, frequently extended most of the length of the main roof. Because monitors drew hot air currents upward and allowed them to escape, they helped tall, one-story spaces function as chimneys. Monitors were preferable to skylights because they provided good ventilation and eliminated skylights' usual leaking and dripping. They did admit bright sunlight that contrasted sharply with dark shadows, and the heat of the sun; for those reasons, opaque glass or shades were recommended.[27]

The first type of roof ventilator was a turret or lantern shape that rose above both pitched and flat roofs (see fig. 3.3). During the early nineteenth century the millwright and blacksmith shops in the West Point Foundry's New York City shops were depicted as having lantern ventilators with slatted sides and pyramidal roofs. A turret ventilator rose above the foundry portion of the Dale Scale factory (c. 1847; Lansingburgh, New York; see fig. 1.3).[28]

The next generation of monitors, those of the 1870s, tended to be larger boxlike forms. Three box ventilators surrounded the chimneys on the roof of the blacksmith shop of the G. A. Ainslie & Sons Carriage Factory (Richmond, Virginia). Several rows of monitors of this type lighted and ventilated production sheds of the Quaker City Dye Works (Philadelphia; see fig. 8.1). The rolling mill of the Phoenix Iron Company (c. 1880; John Griffen, engineer; Phoenixville, Pennsylvania; see fig. 8.11) had iron-framed roof ventilators 16 feet square and 12 feet high.[29]

The monitor roof is an adaptation of the raised central area of a cathedral clerestory, as noted earlier. It appeared on engineering shops in Europe during the early nineteenth century. By the 1850s the monitor roof was in use in the United States as well. Roof ventilators, or lanterns, became more commonly called monitors after around 1890. The clerestory roofs of railroad cars, introduced during the early 1860s, were sometimes known as "monitors" (see fig. 3.4). George M. Pullman's private car, "The Monitor" (1877), no doubt helped to popularize the term.[30]

Monitors were often framed in an ad hoc manner, and those of light wood framing were considered fire hazards, even though they represented a considerable investment in labor and materials. Before the end of the nineteenth century, monitors usually stopped one bay from the end of the structure where light also entered from windows in the end walls (see figs. 3.12 and 6.10). The side walls of monitors were filled with louvers, sash, or combinations of the two. Wood slats or iron louvers permitted warm air to move out of the building yet kept rain out (see figs. 9.5 and 10.6). Initially, monitor walls held intermittently spaced sash; later, they were completely filled with double-hung, sliding, or pivoting sash (fig. 8.8). The monitors of the Pennsylvania Railroad Shops (1873; West Philadelphia) had center-pivoting sash that could be operated in sections with mechanical devices.[31]

FIGURE 8.8 This small building in the Rogers Locomotive and Machine works in Paterson, New Jersey, must have been a well-lighted workshop with a monitor roof and transom lights above sets of wide doors that could be opened for light. Other structures visible in the photograph also have roof monitors.

Monitors designed primarily to ventilate were narrow structures, only several feet wide, that extended for most of the length of the roof and had side walls fitted with slats or sash (see fig. 6.2). This type of monitor was first called a ventilator or hood. The Brooklyn Navy Yard blacksmith shop (c. 1855) had a 10-foot-wide, 3-foot-high ventilator that extended the length of the L-shaped roof. It was framed with cast-iron members attached by cast-iron brackets to the upper purlins of the main roof. Ventilating monitors were put into service during the 1850s at the foundry of Jackson & Wiley (Detroit) and the Industrial Works of Bement & Dougherty (Philadelphia; see fig. 10.3). The ventilating monitor roofs on several buildings of the Wason Car Manufacturing Co. works (1872–1873; Springfield, Massachusetts; fig. 2.8) were called deck-roofs. The upward movement of air to ventilating monitors of production sheds was sometimes enhanced by fresh air intakes. In the one-story shops erected for the Chicago, Milwaukee and St. Paul Railroad in Milwaukee (c. 1880), there were fresh air registers in the floor, and flues inserted into pilasters 6 feet above the floor level also discharged fresh air. The ventilation system of the Continental Iron Works was based on circular openings under each window and 14-foot-wide monitors.[32]

Monitors intended primarily to light manufacturing space, known as "lanterns" or "clerestories" during the nineteenth century, were wider structures. This form of monitor, however, was not as efficient a ventilator because there was considerable roof area above the window level. Light monitors generally rose above the entire central bay of the structure and were often 16 to 25 feet wide and had side walls 5 to 7 feet tall. Engineers recommended that monitors of this type be at least one-fourth the width of the main roof. The light monitor's ventilating capabilities were improved with top-hung continuous sash and mechanical ventilators placed at the ridge. Standard specifications for production sheds related the net area of monitor openings to the square footage of floor area, depending on whether the building was a machine shop or a forge shop.[33]

The brick end walls of production sheds often echoed the section of the roof monitor. The extension of monitors over the full length of the shop (rather than stopping short of the end bays) accompanied the installation of traveling cranes in central bays under wide monitors. End walls of the structure were then extended upward to enclose the ends of the monitor. Often pierced by several windows at the level of the monitor, they extended above the roofline in the manner of a parapet to protect the roof.

Double monitors were used on some production sheds that housed foundries and other heat-intensive processes. The wider, lower monitor allowed light to enter, while the high, narrow monitor provided efficient ventilation (see foundries in figs. 1.5 and 3.6). By the 1850s the double monitor was in use at the Safe Harbor Iron Works (by 1852; near Harrisburg, Pennsylvania) and the Anchor Iron Works (by 1857; Cincinnati). The double monitor roof of the main building of the Albany Iron Works (c. 1853) was framed with 135-foot-long trusses of cast and wrought iron and covered with pine boards and sheet tin. The lower portion had a "vertical rise of 6 feet over the rows of [interior] pillars and [was] entirely of iron and glass." Near the ridge of the roof was a break of 18 inches for ventilating "latticework." The double monitor of the John Nash & Co. car wheel shop (c. 1875; Cincinnati; see fig. 2.9) had window openings filled with tilting sash. The form of the double monitor changed little throughout its use during the nineteenth century. Perhaps the extreme height of the roof and the improvements in mechanical ventilators contributed to the double monitor's demise.[34]

The freestanding production shed, with its single monitor, dominated the industrial landscape during the nineteenth century. As the spacing of buildings in works became more compact and the size of the sheds, which consisted of adjacent crane-served bays, became significantly larger, the roofline changed as well as monitors were placed side by side. Heralding the change, three monitors extended the full length, and two shorter ones rose above the flat roof, of the machine shop erected by the Lobdell Car Wheel Company (c. 1887; Wilmington, Delaware; fig. 3.1).[35]

The problem of ventilating industrial buildings was also improved by mechanical ventilators. Revolving fans, housed in sheet-metal enclosures, were placed on the roof ridge or on a flat roof to draw warm air out of the structure. These ventilators became more important as the footprints of industrial buildings grew.

Sawtooth Roofs

No one who has ever seen a machine-shop interior lighted by the saw-tooth roof can have any adequate idea of the effect of the abundant overhead illumination which it secures.

ENGINEER HORACE ARNOLD, 1896

A sawtooth roof, a series of parallel one-sided skylights, was placed generally so that only northern light, not direct sunlight and its heat, was admitted into an industrial building (fig. 8.9). As defined by an engineer, the sawtooth was a skylight with a cross section similar to that of a 30-60-90-degree triangle; the hypotenuse was horizontal, and the right angle formed the ridge. Only the short, more vertical leg was glazed; the longer side formed the roof proper. Sawtooth roof sections could be placed across the width or length of the structure, or even diagonally, in order to admit northern light. One engineer considered the introduction of the sawtooth roof one of the most important advances in the design of industrial buildings, though he admitted that appearance, uniformity, and symmetry were sacrificed for practical usefulness.[36]

Americans were hesitant to use the sawtooth roof first known to them as the British "weave shed roof" for their one-story "weave sheds" because of the snow load where most of the industry was located. Before it became common in northern industrial cities, the sawtooth roof was probably used in the South, where the glare of the sun was more of a problem. In 1879 fire insurance executive Edward Atkinson advocated the use of one-story structures covered with sawtooth roofs as buildings housing Fourdrinier machines in paper mills, machine shops for heavy work, and printing plants. Several factors led to the adoption of this roof form for textile industry

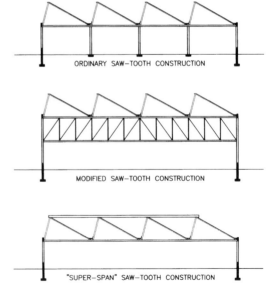

FIGURE 8.9 Americans devised alternative framing methods to support sawtooth roofs in order to reduce the number of interior columns. In tradtional sawtooth roof framing, columns supported each valley of the roof. Long-span trusses allowed the removal of many columns but increased the height of the building and construction costs. In "Super-Span" sawtooth construction, the sawtooth was formed between the top and bottom chords of trusses, and a second system of lightweight trusses (not visible in the drawing) was placed behind the glazed portion of the roof.

ORDINARY SAW–TOOTH CONSTRUCTION

MODIFIED SAW–TOOTH CONSTRUCTION

"SUPER–SPAN" SAW–TOOTH CONSTRUCTION

buildings and machine shops around 1890. The desire to use wider spaces than those traditionally lighted by a combination of windows, skylights, and roof monitors demanded better roof lighting. The availability of faster machinery, coupled with the introduction of electric drive, increased interest in one-story buildings, where vibration was less likely to limit the speed at which machinery could be operated. Improvements in heating, ventilating, and caulking enabled the construction of sawtooth roofs that did not leak or create overheated conditions.[37]

Many early examples of sawtooth roofs were associated with the textile industry, even though monitor roofs were first used on one-story weave sheds and dye houses. The silk dyeing works of Jacob Weidmann (c. 1882; Paterson, New Jersey) had two buildings with sawtooth roofs. During the mid-1880s, sawtooth roofs appeared on one-story silk mills in the New Jersey–Pennsylvania area, including the Otz Silk Mills (West Hoboken, New Jersey). By 1890 a number of sawtooth roofs had been erected in the Philadelphia area, the weave shed of Planet Mills (Brooklyn) had been rebuilt with a sawtooth roof, and a sawtooth roof had also been used on the Farr Alpaca Co. works (Holyoke, Massachusetts).[38]

Soon the roof form appeared on the production sheds of other industries where large floor areas and a comparatively low headroom were needed. The machine shops of the Straight Line Engine Works (1889; John E. Sweet, engineer; Syracuse, New York) and the De La Val Co. (c. 1896; Frederick Hart, designer; Poughkeepsie, New York) were among the noted early examples of large, sawtooth-roofed metalworking shops.[39]

During the 1890s, factory designers often concealed the "unpleasant exterior effect of the sawtooth roof" by extending walls as parapets. One engineer noted that by the 1910s, the possibilities and limitations of the sawtooth roof had been explored and, like other new things, the roof form had been used to excess and there were objections to its higher cost and less effective ventilation. With its complicated framing, considerable flashing, and internal gutters, a sawtooth roof was more expensive than other types—as much as 40 to 60 percent higher than a flat roof without skylights, and also more than a monitor roof.[40]

Double systems of trusses were utilized to eliminate or limit the number of columns in sawtooth-roofed buildings. This method of framing, which became known as the "modified sawtooth roof," added the depth of the second truss system to the height of the building (see fig. 8.9). Around 1920 the Ballinger Co. improved on this type of roof with their "Super-Span" design. Lightweight longitudinal trusses placed directly in back of the glazed portion of the sawtooth were supported by heavier transverse trusses, the top chord of which extended above the roof and tied together the ridges of several sawtooth forms. A Super-Span sawtooth roof could cover a structure 100 feet wide and any length without the use of interior columns, and when supported by columns placed 60 to 88 feet apart, it was suited for even wider buildings. The Super-Span roof of the Atwater Kent Manufacturing Co. plant (c. 1924; Philadelphia) enclosed 11 acres.[41]

More Roof Forms

Attention to the industrial buildings to be seen from the train when entering any large city will almost convince one that no new forms of roof are possible. Everything seems to have been tried at least once.

ENGINEERING NEWS-RECORD, 1936

An era of extensive experimentation in the engineering of roof forms coincided with the construction of much larger open-plan production sheds, a development made possible and practical by lightweight steel roof framing, electric drive, and the elimination of millwork. The availability of steel sash, particularly continuous top-hung sash, also encouraged the adaptation of roof forms. Engineers analyzed the ventilation of relatively tall one-story shop spaces and realized that a building could not function as a chimney when the monitor outlet was too small for the discharge of heat streams. Moreover, a narrow central monitor required most of the heat to travel a long distance and lose velocity. Roofs that were too high caused heat to diffuse rather than rise.

One of the simplest yet most effective methods of improving roof lighting was to angle the top chord of the outer roof truss panels. A relatively flat-pitched trussed roof with its edges angled about 45 degrees and glazed was excellent for admitting light, but the sloping sash did tend to leak. The Rood & Brown Car Wheel Works foundry (c. 1880; Buffalo, New York; fig. 8.10) had a roof of this type (see also figs. 2.14, 8.2, and 10.7). The Truscon Steel Co. offered trusses with sloping end panels as an option for its flat-roofed standard structures during the 1920s and 1930s. Architect Albert Kahn frequently used a wide monitor with sloping sides at the center of each bay of large production sheds during the mid-1930s. He noted that the windows on the new Chevrolet plant in Baltimore were inclined 20 degrees to provide better lighting than that supplied by the vertical monitor windows on the nearby Fisher Body plant.[42]

Willingness to test roof forms was evident in the design of a one-story silk mill building erected by the Klots Throwing Co. (1896; Carbondale, Pennsylvania). The central bay of the roof, half the building's 150-foot width, was covered by a monitor. The side bays had half-monitors, or modified sawtooth roofs, facing outward (see fig. 8.2). The unusual roofline, only partially concealed by the extension of the brick end walls as stepped gables, became known as the "silk mill roof."[43]

Around 1900, a new form of monitor was introduced. Known as the "Aiken roof," after its designer, and also as the "high and low bay" roof (see figs. 7.10 and 8.11), it provided more light without adding roof height. Purlins were positioned alternately on the top and bottom chords of trusses to create monitors that were separated by expanses of lower, flat roof and extended across a structure's width rather than its length. Vertical windows were set in the clerestory walls. The roof (which had about the same amount of surface as a flat roof) was considered an economical alternative

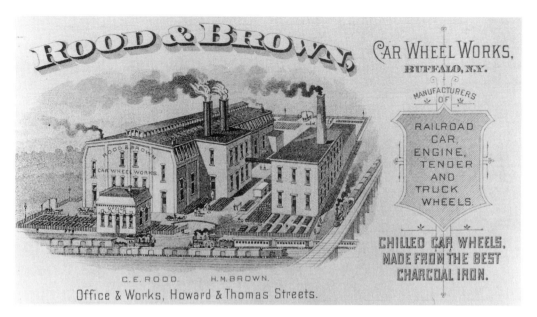

FIGURE 8.10 Inclined sash mirrored the angle of the top chord of the end panels of trusses at the edge of the roof of the Rood & Brown Car Wheel Works foundry in Buffalo.

FIGURE 8.11 Two generations of factory roofs are evident in this view of the main fabricating shop of the Phoenix Iron Company in Phoenixville, Pennsylvania. On the older building (on the left), ventilators rose above the juncture of the intersecting gabled roofs. Additions to the structure were constructed with Aiken, or "high and low bay," roofs.

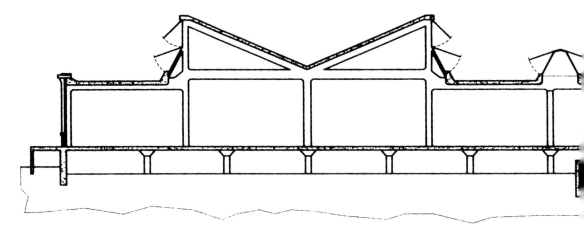

FIGURE 8.12 The "Pond truss," "butterfly," or "M" roof was engineered for maximum performance in ventilating and lighting the factory interior. Small "A-frames" served as air-intake ports; air exited through the larger monitors.

to the sawtooth roof because it was less expensive and required no roof valley gutters. An Aiken roof enclosed the immense steel-framed structure (1,612 feet long, with a minimum width of 240 feet and a height of 50 feet) of the Standard Steel Car Co. (c. 1910; McClintic-Marshall Construction Co.; Butler, Pennsylvania).[44]

The Pond truss and Pond continuous sash (fig. 8.12) were introduced a decade later by David Lupton's Sons Co. to take advantage of natural air currents and foster a slow, uniform movement of air. The signature feature of the Pond truss was the M, or "butterfly," profile of the monitor. The reversal of the shape of the monitor, with the double-pitched roof rising to the sides, created more wall area to be filled with sash. Tall M-shaped monitors, air outlets, were alternated with one or more air inlets, either Pond A-frames (small, low-pitched vents) or low-roofed fresh air bays. Both forms were best enclosed with top-hung Pond continuous sash, which was operated mechanically to control the movement of air.[45]

The Pond truss roof was popular during the 1910s and 1920s, but like the sawtooth roof, it was viewed as "lacking in aesthetic outline." Parapets (see fig. 10.1) were sometimes employed to conceal the unusual outlines of these roofs. One of the most extensive installations of the Pond truss roof was at the Dayton Engineering Laboratories' Domestic Engineering Co. (1917; Morraine, Ohio), where 40 acres were enclosed under one roof.[46]

The profiles of many Pond truss roofs, particularly those of foundries in industrial areas, were left exposed. They distinguish several of the buildings in the Ford Motor Co.'s River Rouge works (Dearborn, Michigan). Albert Kahn's firm modified the Pond truss by angling the outer portion of the M-roof upward to create a slightly taller range of windows and an even more distinctive shape. Pond trusses were dominant elements in some of Kahn's most noted designs, including the De Soto Division Press Shop (1936; Detroit) and the Chrysler Half-Ton Truck Plant (1937; Detroit).[47]

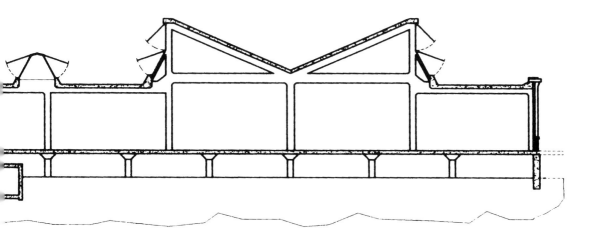

FIGURE 8.13 "Tree-form columns" of welded steel framed wide bays and eliminated small members of sawtooth roof trusses in a 1937 addition to the Lincoln Electric Co. Works.

During the 1920s and 1930s experimentation with roof forms continued. Large-span production sheds erected for the aircraft industry during the late 1930s introduced variations of roof monitors that often incorporated double systems of trusses. The hinged-arch roof spanning the 185-foot-wide final assembly building of the Douglas Aircraft Co. (1936; Taylor & Taylor, architects and engineers; Santa Monica, California) was further distinguished by sheathing applied to create sawtoothlike skylights.[48]

Welded steel connections eliminated trusses, made wider spans possible, and brought an elegant, simplified form to the sawtooth roof. Around 1936 The Austin Co. developed a continuous sawtooth frame formed of welded beams that could economically span bays up to 50 feet in width. Such simple "tree-form columns" supported sawtooth roofs over the 40-foot-wide bays of an addition to the Lincoln Electric Co. plant (1937; Cleveland; fig. 8.13).[49]

From the floor to the roof, the factory was engineered with care. Demands for strength, span, resistance to fire and vibration, good lighting, and adequate ventilation were met in various ways. During the hundred-year period we have examined, progress was made in each of these requirements. But as engineers designed factories to serve industry, they had another matter in mind as well—the appropriate industrial aesthetic.

In the simpler buildings which more nearly approach the loft build-

ing in type, the exterior problem is harder. Here, reliance must be

placed on the direct handling of the materials and the most careful

study of proportion in bay spacing and window arrangement. This

is not a matter of applied architecture.

CRITIC TALBOT HAMLIN, 1940

A RECONCILIATION OF AESETHETIC TRADITIONS 9

The exterior of an industrial building should truthfully express in a simple direct form that it is a factory building.

HENRY T. NOYES, 1919

The rhetoric of engineers and architects and the general literature describing industrial facilities provides a means of recognizing the aesthetic component of industrial architecture—a content that has often been overlooked by casual observers, architects, and critics. The existence of any artistic intent on the part of factory designers has even been questioned because of the bias of commentators trained in the formal arts against the design work of engineers. Critics have looked for familiar architectural ornament at the expense of appreciating the functional aspects of industrial building designs and the competent, sometimes even innovative, engineering. They have admired factories that could be compared favorably to other building types, as if no other means of evaluation could be imagined. As the evidence presented in this chapter suggests, an understanding of the industrial aesthetic lies in a different direction. It must be grounded in the appropriate context— the pragmatic and progressive fields of engineering and industry.

The question of architectural style has often intruded unnecessarily into the consideration of the aesthetics of the industrial architecture. The styles that were used for other types of buildings have not formed the basis of industrial architecture; moreover, no single "industrial style" has dominated factory construction. Instead, an engineering-derived aesthetic engendered a dynamic approach to design that incorporated new materials, building techniques, and forms that could meet the functional demands of engineered factory buildings.

Traditional emphasis on architectural style thus fails to provide a framework for meaningful analysis of industrial architecture. Indeed, a fully developed Renaissance Revival or Gothic factory is like an octagon-shaped dwelling—an intriguing curiosity that reflects personal choice, but should not be a standard by which other designs are judged. Industrial buildings that were neither strictly utilitarian nor high-style designs have always prevailed in the United States. While engineers have considered an emphasis on decoration inappropriate, they have not avoided the use of ornamental architectural elements in industrial architecture. They have often employed a limited number of such elements to stand in for, or evoke, architectural style and thereby relate industrial buildings to the preferred expression of the day. Features associated with distinct architectural styles have been incorporated into factories but have not defined the aesthetic.

Should industrial buildings, then, be considered undistinguished in design, or even amateurish caricatures of high-style idioms? The answer is an emphatic no. The aesthetic basis of American industrial building design was an ideal of beauty based on function, utility, and process held by engineers, not the formality or picturesqueness associated with recognized architectural styles. There was an accepted correct "feel" or tone for industrial architecture that expressed strength, stability, and function and eschewed the use of lavish or extensive decoration (fig. 9.1). In order to understand the aesthetic content of factories, we must be aware of the attitudes toward design of those involved with building for industry. The manufacturer had an interest in the appearance of his works that was driven by self-image. Just as the engineer's design work has dominated factory building, it also provides a basis for understanding the aesthetic

FIGURE 9.1 The building erected in 1871 in Newark, New Jersey, and later acquired by the Johnston & Murphy Co., shoe manufacturers, displays the character considered appropriate for a factory during the nineteenth century.

content of industrial architecture. Though engineers seldom wrote about matters of aesthetics, when they did, they were clear about their aesthetic sensibilities. The rivalry between the engineering and architectural professions during the nineteenth century, a competition that repressed the recognition of the engineer's aesthetic, is also an aspect of this story. Not surprisingly, architects approached the design of the works differently and grafted architectural style onto the factory. Finally, an approach to the design of factory buildings emerged that drew on the strengths of both professions. At that point, asserted engineer Willard Case, functional beauty became linked with a modern industrial spirit.

THE MANUFACTURER'S INTEREST IN FACTORY AESTHETICS

A building of such pleasing architectural quality and dignity as would not only be a source of pride to its directors, stockholders and employees, but would in a measure, express to the public the purpose and ideals of the Company . . .

AMERICAN ARCHITECT, 1912

For most industrial building projects, the manufacturer—whether involved in the building project actively or as the client of an engineer or architect—was interested primarily in the technical and economical aspects of the project. After all, the industrialist needed to make a profit to stay in business and therefore wanted a manufacturing facility in which he could produce goods at a cost that kept his offerings competitive in the marketplace. In fact, historian Richard Candee has documented that the main interest of textile mill owners was the replication of mill designs of proven economic success.

Nevertheless, industrialists also had a real interest in the appearance of their works, which represented considerable financial investment and hopes for continued economic success. Works that appeared substantial and commodious also implied technological and organizational mastery. Interest in an attractive factory was coupled with pride in ownership and the desire for a prominent position in the community. A view of the factory or works—only slightly idealized—often appeared in business letterhead and advertising. The high visibility of a plant in an urban area prompted attention to its appearance, though the prominence of a manufacturing works in a more rural location also led to the blending of architectural effect with economic dominance. An 1872 description of A. Field & Sons (Taunton, Massachusetts) suggested another reason to construct a good-looking works: "In their architectural finish, together with their inside decoration, and the order, neatness, and propriety of their arrangements," the account noted, the Field buildings "are at once models of industrial economy, and a constant school of culture for those engaged there."[1]

Even if they were not particularly interested in architecture, manufacturers must have had some awareness of how Americans had become both fascinated with industrial progress and repelled by certain aspects of it as more of them stood "face to face with the machine." Descriptions of American industry generally focused on the sublime impact of machinery and manufacturing processes rather than the buildings that housed them. For example, a description of an automatic flour mill operating in New York City during the 1840s noted the "gigantic and beautiful spirit" of the mill. Moreover, not an inch of room, an ounce of power, or a moment of time was wasted.[2]

The extent to which the general public saw any similar type of beauty or responded to the aesthetic the engineer was offering in industrial buildings, as opposed to considering them as pragmatic solutions, is difficult to assess. In general, machine technology was associated with the positive attributes of a progressive nation, in contrast to traditional ways linked with Europe and the past. It seems likely that factory buildings also represented such advancement. But a symbol of progress was not necessarily admired as an aesthetic achievement. Perhaps the ability of an observer to respond to functional beauty depended on the extent to which the individual had an affinity for common engineering knowledge or formal art. Civil engineer Henri Haber commented that during the 1870s Americans were receptive to strictly utilitarian engineering design because their country was enjoying a practical and technological age when technical skill was valued, even in art. But he was certain that they would appreciate engineering design with inherently beautiful forms even more.[3]

The descriptions of industrial works in nineteenth-century technical and trade literature—admittedly accompanied by overstatement—nevertheless provide a means of gauging the industrialist's and general public's interests in their appearance. The Wason Car Mfg. Works (1872–1873; George C. Fisk, proprietor and designer; Springfield, Massachusetts; see fig. 2.8), reported the *National Car Builder*, had an office building that was "an architectural gem." Its broken outlines, tasteful colors, and relieving ornament represented the steady, businesslike aspect of the place of business. Visitors to the American Watch Co. works (Waltham, Massachusetts; fig. 9.2) were impressed by the fine aesthetic taste manifested in all its arrangements and surroundings, which included a park and workers' cottages. The company's 1883 report to its stockholders proclaimed that "we shall at last have a factory large enough, substantial, handsome, comfortable, convenient and yet not too fine for our very nice purposes; it is even now a true Palace of Industry of which you may well be proud."[4]

German brewmasters who dominated the American industry took great pride in their buildings and often incorporated their insignia into the elaborate ornamentation of breweries. This detailing reflected their desire to present an architectural presence that corresponded with the magnitude of their businesses, as well as their good taste and wealth. In fact, the breweries' exteriors emphasized these considerations rather than technically advanced aspects of the facilities. The brewmasters' intentions were perhaps quite obvious, but other industrialists no doubt also equated the architectural presence of their works with their prosperity and good taste.[5]

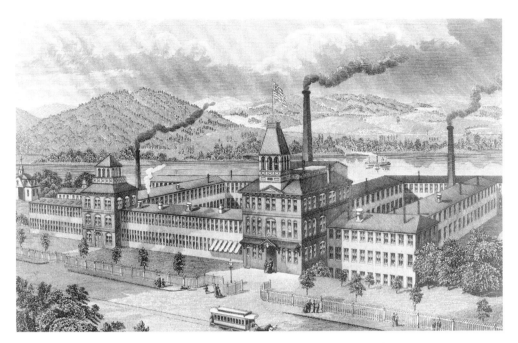

FIGURE 9.2 The management of the American Watch Co. in Waltham, Massachusetts, took great pride in its "Palace of Industry," depicted here during the 1870s.

In 1923 architectural engineer Frank D. Chase attributed a new attentiveness to the ideal of the "handsome factory" to college-trained executives and their wives. He suggested that this group's interests in the development of residential and civic art and architecture had extended to the factory as well. At any rate, executives made sure that their portion of the plant—administration buildings, directors' suites, and executives' offices—were handsomely appointed. Engineer Henry Grattan Tyrrell noted other sources of interest in the appearance of the factory: To him, "aesthetic treatment of modern plants" was often part of an advertising strategy and meant to demonstrate the adoption of employee welfare and model factory programs.[6]

The Model Factory Movement

The grass plots and trees on the site and between the buildings may strike the manufacturing engineer, accustomed to crowded yards and rooms, as a little odd. But order and neatness are as desirable outside as inside, and tidiness throughout is a better testimonial to efficient management and supervision than that appearance of ever-busy activity which leaves no time for clearing up.

ENGINEERING, 1902

The model factory movement that emerged during the last decades of the nineteenth century promoted improvements in industrial hygiene and safety as well as in the appearance of industrial works. Because the manufacturer needed a stable and content workforce of skilled and general laborers that would not interrupt production, he was responsive to the argument that better-looking factories would attract more desirable workers and probably hoped that an attractive environment would help control the workforce. As historian Lindy Biggs notes, engineers and industrialists took what was viewed by reformers as an idealistic, humanitarian idea and turned it into a practical tool for increasing production. This attitude was expressed by engineer D. C. Newman Collins, who asserted that the inside of the factory was important as an earning factor; it was there that "human equipment lives, breathes, and grinds out product." The cost of maintaining one man in service was sufficient to demand some consideration of his mental and physical comfort.[7]

The industrial welfare movement emphasized aspects of industrial buildings that most directly affected the morale, health, and safety of employees—such things as lighting and ventilation, and even the color of interior paint. The configuration, construction, or suitability of factories for the production process were usually not addressed. Although most elements of the model factory ideal were not primarily architectural, they still influenced the design of factory buildings and works layouts. The movement introduced new structures to the works, including "welfare" or "employee" buildings that housed washing and changing facilities, medical clinics, lunchrooms, and other employee services (fig. 9.3). Interest in providing healthy and attractive surroundings also prompted owners to have the works, particularly the entrance, landscaped and perhaps also to construct parks and gardens. The model factory owner often made gestures to welcome the

FIGURE 9.3 The Welfare Hall at the National Cash Register Co.'s works in Cincinnati housed employee lunchrooms and changing rooms, as well as medical and educational programs.

public by providing a visitor's entrance, reception rooms, and areas from which to view the operations.[8]

The building erected for the Cream of Wheat Co. (1903–1904; Harry W. Jones, architect; Minneapolis) demonstrated how even a small operation could be a model factory. A cream-colored brick and terra-cotta building that resembled a "concert hall or conservatory more than it does a factory" was erected on a visible downtown lot. The second floor of the six-story structure was devoted to the comfort of the mostly female operatives and housed a cafe, locker rooms, and rest rooms. Employees could also enjoy an Italian garden beside the structure and a roof garden over the engine room.[9]

THE ENGINEER'S FUNCTIONAL BEAUTY

There is a pleasurable effect produced upon the mind by forms resulting from, or balanced by, the direct action of the mechanical forces of nature.

ENGINEER GEORGE F. DEACON, 1869

Art critics have long acknowledged that there are different types of beauty, the embodiment of perfection in form and appeal. They include standards of beauty based on formal elegance and on the variation of form associated with the picturesque. The beauty of the awe-inspiring sublime has been recognized in both the natural world and man-made features. Engineers would surely add to this list a functional beauty derived from the perfect adaptation of means to an end. It was this latter ideal of beauty that generated an architectural aesthetic for industrial buildings.

The general public, like architects and architectural critics, has remained largely unaware of engineers' allegiance to functional beauty; moreover, observers without the specialized education of engineers have little ability to consider aspects of it. Appreciation for elegance in structural action, for the equilibrium of countervailing forces in cables and columns, and for the calculations that permit the construction of dramatic forms are certainly conditioned responses.

Alan Holgate, a civil engineer working in the late twentieth century, interprets the special perceptions of engineers, particularly those not based entirely on calculations. Just like a well-designed machine, a well-built factory building could be pleasing for an engineer to observe. The education of engineers instills an admiration for efficiency in all undertakings and a "job well done," little patience for clumsy and inefficient design, and the desire to avoid expenditures for "useless" ornamentation and unnecessary features. These attitudes are evident in the simplicity and truthfulness in their designs. Engineers perceive beauty in the form of an object particularly well adapted to a defined set of objectives and constraints. Yet they recognize that the "educated taste" of others has been "revolted by the permanent divorce of the useful and the beautiful" (in the language of the 1860s) and they attempt to reconcile the two. To this end, engineers and mechanics strive to incorporate beautiful forms—rather than ornament or decoration—as well as safety, strength, functionality, and durability into their designs for machinery and structures.[10]

Civil engineer Henri Haber issued a call for such "artistic engineering" during the 1870s and urged engineers to raise the standard of their work by making all necessary parts and forms "tending to ornament"—in other words, intrinsically beautiful. To create more pleasing engineering works, he also recommended avoiding monotony and using correct proportion and symmetry (except when the practical aspects of the project dictated otherwise) to create impressions of dignity, clearness, and boldness. To Haber, neither statics nor aesthetics should dominate. Instead, the union of art with the laws of strength and gravity should be the goal.[11]

According to George F. Deacon, a British civil engineer, members of his profession see and solve structural and architectural design problems in ways that are based on an appreciation of the forms found in nature. He described an aesthetic derived from mechanical principles and asserted that engineers were aware of the need to develop an inherent beauty in scientifically designed structures. To represent the engineer's ideal of beauty, Deacon turned to the curve of a lady-fern, in which the force of gravity was exactly balanced by the resistance of the stalk to flexure. He asserted that evidence of mechanical forces should not be modulated by ornament or partially hidden by other components of engineered structures. The design problem, then, was how to produce forms and curves that had lines of equilibrium that the eye would immediately perceive as natural solutions and that would therefore be pleasing.[12]

Similarly, the twentieth-century engineering aesthetic articulated by Henry Grattan Tyrrell, primarily in relation to bridge design, recommended that engineers look to nature for guidance in the design of forms and the placement of ornament. Perhaps Tyrrell had Deacon's lady-fern in mind. His guidelines for engineering design included conformity with the environment, the economic use of material, and the expression of purpose and construction. Like other engineers, Tyrrell believed that superfluous decoration minimized the effect of the whole and that ornament was not architecture. Beauty existed in every structure that was designed according to principles of economy—the greatest simplicity, the fewest members, and the most pleasing outline consistent with construction—even though the result might consist of forms unfamiliar to the public.[13]

Alan Holgate argues that the training engineers receive leads to their perception of the solidity, bulk, and immobility of structural elements, reactions that differ from those of architectural critics, who often respond to the dynamic qualities of walls and towers. An interest in detail directs engineers' examinations of a design outward from the scrutiny of small elements to an evaluation of the complete form. Those trained in the arts, in contrast, often look first at a work's overall composition. Engineers often transform visual information into abstract models, or diagrams, that represent processes, while architects, having less interest in structural concepts, focus on the formal logic or patterns in visual information. Engineers create and respond to forms that have a robust and forceful quality, particularly if they also incorporate purposefulness and efficiency into beauty. We can assume, then, that to engineers, long expanses of factory walls, stiffened by pilasters, presented a pleasing expression of how the wall was manipulated to provide strength and to permit large window openings. In the same way, a factory roof form dictated by the need for light and ventilation was a perfect union of bold functional beauty and utility.[14]

Engineers have not been the only designers to appreciate this type of functional beauty. During the 1840s the American sculptor Horatio Greenough called for an American architecture that evoked the aesthetic ideals of engineers. The sculptor specifically praised the simplicity in the mechanics' (or engineers') style and recognized a functional aesthetic: "By beauty I mean the promise of function." Stating that "[buildings] may be called machines each individual of which must be formed with reference to the abstract type of its species," Greenough utilized a metaphor for describing factories that engineers would turn to several decades later.[15]

Functional Beauty and Industrial Architecture

In building construction, truth must control, originality must invent, science must construct.

AMERICAN ENGINEER, 1874

Observers have suggested that an engineering-derived aesthetic has an unselfconscious quality. It can have a natural, unforced appearance, but that attribute should not imply a lack of aesthetic intent. Engineers were quite serious about presenting an appropriate utilitarian aesthetic when designing factory buildings. Moreover, they maintained that architectural style—style derived from the beautiful shapes of elements and the use of ornament to relieve monotony and emphasize structure—should be generated by, rather than be adopted for, factories. Engineers made a clear distinction between an overlay of decoration and the straightforward and integrated enhancement of ornament.[16]

The prominent British engineer Sir William Fairbairn recounted how mill engineers made the first "architectural" improvements to early British textile mills and advanced their design beyond square brick boxes. Fairbairn designed a mill in 1827 that he considered to be of this improved type, though a structure without any architectural pretension (fig. 9.4). To Fairbairn, forming the corners of the building into pilasters and adding a slight cornice relieved the monotony of plain walls and represented the engineer's aesthetic notions. He also scornfully related how architects designed factory buildings that vied with institutions and public buildings as works of art but did not necessarily incorporate the best engineering available. The aesthetic that Fairbairn depicted as the engineer's was characteristic of most factory building design in the United States. In fact, the main building of Talbott & Brother's Machine Works (c. 1853; Richmond, Virginia; fig. 9.5), with its corner pilasters and a slight cornice, was quite similar in spirit to Fairbairn's 1827 mill.[17]

G. D. Dempsey, a British engineer who published plans for industrial buildings, noted that by the 1850s engineers had mastered an "undecorated style" considered appropriate for industrial buildings. He asserted that factories should not reflect any useless expenditure for decorative elements that interpreted architectural styles or concealed blank walls. This view was shared by another engineer who considered an industrial building to form a single unit with the equipment it housed and who commented that it did not come under the classification of "architecture" as the term was generally understood.[18]

The manner in which a standardized design for Storehouse A of the Rock Island Arsenal (1867; Rock Island, Illinois; fig. 9.6) was refined by the military engineers in charge of its construction reveals a sensitivity to aesthetic issues but little interest in any specific architectural style. The officers who oversaw the building project were dissatisfied enough with the plans provided by the Chief of Ordnance (which were nearly identical to those drawn for similar facilities in Indianapolis and Columbus) to propose changes. They were responsible for altering the roofline, the cornice design, and the shape of window openings, and also raising the height of the tower and increasing the size of its clock faces. Although the final design incorporated many

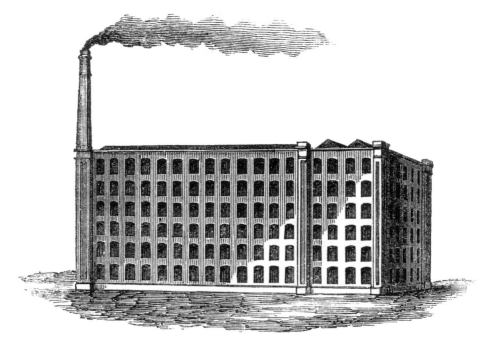

FIGURE 9.4 Sir William Fairbairn provided this illustration to demonstrate how he had used pilasters and a cornice in 1827 to make a textile mill appear less like a brick box.

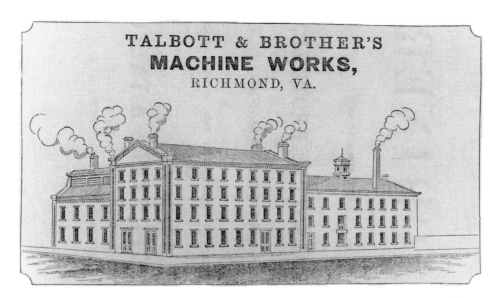

FIGURE 9.5 Talbott & Brother's Machine Works, erected in Richmond, Virginia, exhibited the detailing suggested by Sir William Fairbairn (see fig. 10.2) to be appropriate for industrial buildings.

elements associated with Renaissance architecture, Major D. W. Flagler stated that "no name can be given to the exterior architecture."[19]

As noted in chapter 1, descriptions of manufacturing works routinely commented on the substantial and commodious qualities of factory buildings, their well-engineered construction, and suitability to their purpose, the elements that constituted a functional beauty. Descriptions of a works or new building seldom addressed the question of architectural style; when the term did appear, it seemed to connote a pleasing appearance or good taste rather than any particular manner of ornament. The *Trade Review*'s report on the new works of Wilcox, Treadway & Co. (1880; Cleveland) noted that the magnificent red brick edifice formed "a striking object owing to loftiness, extent, solidity, and general style of architecture—a style, however, without other enrichments than those suitable to a manufactory." A reporter's comments in 1871 on the works of various concerns in Worcester, Massachusetts, noted both extremes of the style spectrum. The Washburn & Moen Manufacturing Co. works (fig. 9.7) was described as "built entirely of brick, in our latest style of modern factory architecture," with "a very fine appearance"—a comment that referred in part to the mansard roof. The brick loft building of Witherby, Rugg & Richardson, in contrast, was considered "plain in design, and evidently built more with an eye to usefulness and strength than for architectural display."[20]

Mill engineers did not hesitate to address the issue of appropriate architectural expression for the textile industry. C. John Hexamer asserted that the first principle in architecture—and foremost in buildings intended for manufacturing purposes—was utility and that all other considerations were

FIGURE 9.6 A standardized design for Storehouse A of the Rock Island Arsenal, though refined by military engineers in charge of its construction, was still considered to have no traditional architectural style.

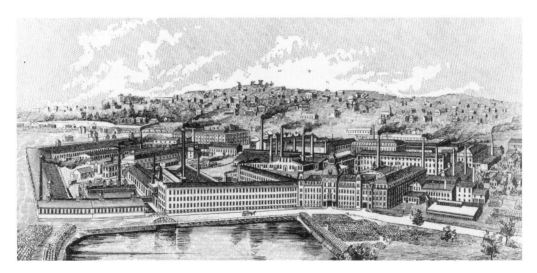

FIGURE 9.7 The north works of the Washburn & Moen Manufacturing Co. was considered to be of the latest "style" of factory architecture.

subservient. The engineer cautioned against erecting a mill in bad proportions, resulting in "a hideous mass of stone, an eyesore to mankind," and suggested that the ideal mill was an evenly proportioned, decent-looking building. In a similar vein, C. J. H. Woodbury suggested that utility, along with stability and convenience, should be especially noticeable in factories. He regretted that some of the mills erected during the second half of the nineteenth century had not been truthful in the matter of design and that architects had attempted to incorporate classical architecture into them. Woodbury considered mills with Romanesque arches copied from churches and mansard roofs "exiled" from their true function of decorating homes to be "dishonest."[21]

The opinions offered by industrial engineers during the early twentieth century tended to emphasize the same points. For psychological reasons, factories should present a pleasing appearance and avoid "monotonous continuity," although any additional elaborations could be justified only when charged to the advertising account. One engineer went so far as to assert that embellishments were useless, frills were superfluous, and all were unwarranted expenses because ornamentation did not earn money. But the growing sentiment that factory buildings should present as good an appearance as possible was acknowledged as well.[22]

The functional aesthetic of American engineers enjoyed the attention of European modernist architects during the 1910s and 1920s. To the French architect Le Corbusier, engineers were inspired by the law of economy, though their work was governed by mathematical calculations. Moreover, they achieved harmony in design. The architect recognized that the engineer "has his own aesthetic, for he must, in making his calculations, qualify some of the terms of his equation." Le Corbusier contrasted the spirit of innovation in engineering with the firm grip of tradition in architecture, stating, "The American engineers overwhelm with their calculations our expiring architecture." Yet historian Terry Smith points out that to Le Corbusier and his peers, American industrial buildings seemed to be products of the "American System of Manufactures," or in some cases spontaneous vernacular structures, so lacking in style that no professional architect would have designed them. Neither the European architects nor their American counterparts considered engineers' factories to be carefully designed buildings that could be regarded as modern architecture.[23]

FUNCTIONALISM VERSUS FORMALISM

Between the two branches of the profession there is a great gulf that as yet no engineer has been found capable of bridging, but . . . the difference should be recognized and clearly understood and the way opened by which the two groups can be made, not only to inspire each other, but to produce something greater and better in the way of construction than either group can possibly hope to obtain alone.

WILLIAM BARCLAY PARSONS, 1911

A widespread philosophical schism between art and science during the nineteenth century affected the relationship between architects and engineers, despite their common interests. Engineers, intimately involved in the process of technological modernization, developed pragmatic and innovative solutions for building projects. Architects, on the other hand, sought to distinguish architecture from building through an emphasis on expressive and formal design. While engineers found artistic satisfaction in functional design and the expression of structure, architects worried about the sacrifice of beauty for such requirements. Both professions insisted that beauty, utility, and structure be given due consideration. Nonetheless, the engineer valued, above all, rational and functional qualities, while the architect demanded "architectural effect."[24] The differences between the two disciplines became readily apparent when architects turned their attention to industrial building design.

The engineer's desire to work without the interference of the architect in an industrial building project was succinctly reported by engineer John E. Sweet: "The architect, unless he be one who has made a special study of it, is liable to do more harm than good." Engineers considered architects incapable of building for utility; one was sure that it was virtually impossible for architects to work out satisfying artistic expressions for steel structures with brick curtain walls. Consequently, the design of industrial buildings ought to be left to the engineer with the proviso that he not be at liberty to perpetrate "an offence to the public eye."[25]

When architects began to write about industrial building design just before the turn of the nineteenth century, they emphasized the need for appropriate aesthetic interpretation and the suitability of various architectural styles, an approach adapted from their other work. They either chose not to acknowledge or were unaware that in factory design there was a prevalent engineering aesthetic that they might want to interpret. An editorial in an 1879 issue of the *American Architect and Building News* suggested that cotton and woolen mills were particular eyesores to architects because they represented the minimum of result and almost the maximum of wasted opportunity. Architects knew unsightliness was not essential to strength or function, and they could not help but wonder how all mill owners could be affected by the same lack of appreciation for "architectural effect."[26]

This editorial initiated an exchange of opinions in the architectural press on the appropriate aesthetic for industrial buildings. It also expressed the critical stance that architects consistently adopted toward the work of nonarchitects who provided industrial building designs. Architects also reciprocated the hostility that they felt from the fire insurance industry. Not only were the insurance companies assuming the work of their profession by providing plans and specifications for structures; they were also doing so with what the architects perceived to be little interest in the appearance of mill buildings. Penurious industrialists who dared to forget that a building could not be made beautiful without some sacrifice of money or convenience were said to be part of the problem. Insurance company executive

Edward Atkinson, representing the opposing camp, responded that mill owners had little use for the industrial buildings architects designed because they were unsafe to insure and not strong enough for the work to be undertaken in them. The situation would continue, Atkinson asserted, as long as professional architects considered engineers and builders to have a separate and distinct function from their own. Atkinson posed a fundamental, if rhetorical, question: "Which is the true architect, he who subordinates architectural effect to the conditions of safety and fitness for intended use, or he who sacrifices either or both of the latter to the former?"[27]

THE ARCHITECT'S SEARCH FOR APPROPRIATE EXPRESSION

When an architect does achieve something worthwhile with the simplest materials and under the most strictly utilitarian limitations, it is a greater monument to his skill, perhaps, than the millionaire's residence.

AMERICAN ARCHITECT, 1909

The architectural profession turned its attention to the design of industrial buildings around the turn of the nineteenth century, although certainly architects had been involved before then in the design of factories. As the national architectural press began to provide technical information about factory buildings, the discussion of industrial building aesthetics shifted to this venue from the engineering press, though the latter continued to report on new structures. Architects who wrote about industrial building design often took the opportunity to make a case for their involvement in such design projects. Hence, they emphasized their superior ability to plan complicated buildings and to use pleasing proportions and did not hesitate to criticize the standard of factory building design established by engineers. Yet neither architects nor critics often articulated—beyond sweeping generalities—what constituted good factory design.

Even as they boasted of their ability to plan, architects did not conceive of the industrial building design project as driven by suitability, utility, and function, as engineers did. They remained primarily interested in the question of style—specifically, the adaptation of recognized architectural styles—for the manufacturing works. To them, it was inconceivable not to evoke or adapt the styles they were using for other types of buildings for factory design projects.

The exchange of opinions about mill buildings in the *American Architect and Building News* (noted earlier) constituted much of the critique of factory design offered by the architectural press during the nineteenth century. Only a handful of industrial building designs, without any explanatory text, were presented. These were artistic renderings that enhanced picturesque buildings with towers, including a machine shop (c. 1876; H. M. Francis, architect) and a paper mill (c. 1881; J. A. Dempwolf, architect; fig. 9.8). The industrial buildings presented during the first decades of the twentieth

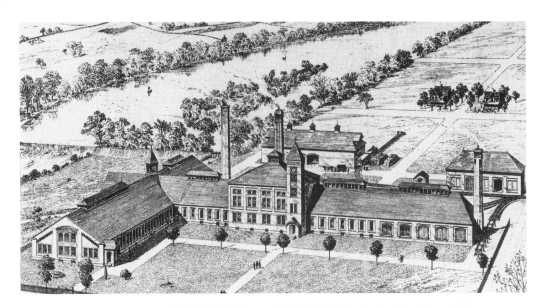

FIGURE 9.8 Architect J. A. Dempwolf's design for the Spring Grove Paper Mills was one of the few industrial works projects presented in the architectural press during the late nineteenth century.

FIGURE 9.9 Architectural critics considered the warehouse at Nos. 173–175 Duane Street, New York City, to be a particularly well designed structure in a utilitarian style.

century were more often accompanied by information on their structural and functional components than by architectural critique. For example, the American Arithmometer Co. factory (c. 1905; Detroit) was featured because architect Albert Kahn used hollow tile and reinforced concrete construction for its floor and roof. Around 1910 reports on industrial buildings became more regular, and some publications offered annual reviews.[28]

During the late nineteenth century, a few architectural critics began to recognize the functional aesthetic espoused by engineers and architecture that had "no style." Although they were drawing attention to aspects of the engineer's functional aesthetic, these critics noted almost exclusively the work of architects.

Maria van Rensselaer, who turned her attention to the subject during the mid-1880s, was among the first critics to appreciate and articulate the aesthetic of functional beauty. She recognized beauty in structural articulation, approved of a more limited use of ornament, and considered architecture an art that ought be judged as a practical solution for the problem at hand. Van Rensselaer singled out one building to represent the ideal utilitarian aesthetic (fig. 9.9). The architectural firm Babb, Cook & Willard, she argued, had made the most of inexpensive materials, a limited amount of ornament, and the narrow site of a modest warehouse at Nos. 173–175 Duane Street, New York City (1879–1880). Great round arches that were its dominant artistic elements both furnished and expressed strength in the facade. Twenty years later, Russell Sturgis seconded van Rensselaer's praise of the Duane Street warehouse for the same reasons.[29]

Indeed, architectural critic Russell Sturgis brought the first regular reporting on industrial building design to the architectural press. His telling critiques (which began in 1904) in the *Architectural Record* demonstrated an appreciation for both a functional engineering aesthetic and "architectural effect"; they were illustrated with buildings erected in New York City and Chicago.

According to Sturgis, around 1880 a new tone and style for urban warehouse design was established in the designs of Babb & Cook, Charles C. Haight, and other architects; this approach emphasized the functional aspects of the design rather than ornament. Sturgis pointed out that this new style ranged from obviously utilitarian structures that had virtually no ornament to those that merely suggested that functional elements were more important than making the exterior "traditionally architectural." In fact, he admired structures that made the leap to incorporate and express modern and functional elements boldly and simply, without disguise. He came to question the appropriateness of nearly all types of historically derived ornament on factory and warehouse buildings.[30]

Although few architects discarded the trappings of architectural style, many did attempt to develop a suitable, utilitarian approach to commercial and industrial building design. Structures of this type erected in Chicago had walls opened to the maximum extent allowable with steel framing and were articulated in a rationalized manner. Architect Peter B. Wight characterized this work as striving to express the axiom "function before precedent." He argued that the public appreciated good utilitarian design that was unornamented yet relieved from monotony by the best disposition of parts to express function.[31]

From the perspective of the architect, factory designs with rationalized stylistic references, traditional materials, and placement of ornament succeeded where those of the engineer failed. Architects who specialized in industrial architecture offered designs that appeared familiarly pleasing and projected a sense of strength and seriousness of purpose. Such was the architect's compromise between the absolute functionalism of the engineer and a devotion to traditional architectural effects. Architect Harvey Wiley Corbett commented in 1918 that not so long ago, the architectural critic fired his last and most bitter shot when he remarked that a building "looks like a factory." But Corbett also reported a new attitude: There was no harm in a factory looking like one; rather, the artistic error occurred when a factory looked like something else.[32]

Architects Adapt Architectural Styles for Industrial Buildings

While such designs are Gothic in character they are more and more exhibiting a freedom and originality that promises in time to develop into a well-defined architectural style for American industrial buildings.

ARCHITECT GEORGE C. NIMMONS, 1919

The attitudes of architects just reviewed are evident in their designs for factory buildings. For many, simplifying and adapting a favorite style for an industrial loft building satisfied the creative impulse and provided sufficient "architectural effect." Architects considered certain elements—such as trabeated Greek forms and Gothic buttresses, with their emphasis on the expression of structure—most appropriate for this type of work.

The fact that many architects turned to Gothic forms in the design of factory buildings is ironic, considering the interest that architectural theorists had in the style. During the mid–nineteenth century the French architect and scholar of Gothic architecture Eugène Emmanuel Viollet-le-Duc had recommended Gothic structure as a source of inspiration for modern architecture because it demonstrated ingenious and practical means of solving difficult structural problems. While he advocated designing buildings in the spirit of those who worked in the Gothic and the use of materials in a manner that reflected their own qualities, Viollet-le-Duc also warned against imitations—the Gothic revival. Some architects who designed factory buildings shared Viollet-le-Duc's admiration of the Gothic and interpreted its spirit by conveying a truthfulness in structural features. But most designers took an easier route and created an "industrial Gothic" style by replicating, to varying degrees, piers, buttresses, and ornament.[33]

George C. Nimmons, the principal of a large architectural firm in Chicago, specialized in industrial building design. Though he thought that many factories had been successfully detailed in the Renaissance style, Nimmons preferred the Gothic (fig. 9.10). To him, a similarity between buttresses and exterior piers—carried only up as far as needed—and the use of wall copings rather than projecting cornices recommended it. Entrances could be emphasized by Gothic tracery and ornament, and the sprinkler system water tank could be enclosed in a tower similar to those of cathedrals. According to architectural critic C. Matlack Price, Nimmons insisted on the use of such massive, buttressed towers to give a "fine dignity and dominant note" to a "free and colloquial sort of brick and stone Tudor-Gothic style structures." The architect justified the expense of such architectural character by noting that it represented only 5 percent of the cost of the structure. To give context to his efforts, Nimmons argued that he had to design without a guiding American industrial style of architecture; he considered himself to be among the designers who were beginning to prefer the honest expression of construction and functions.[34]

The solemnity and grace of classical architecture, however, provided a means of introducing a dignified, and even civic, character into industrial designs. Critic C. Matlack Price was impressed by Willis Polk's work in this idiom, especially his designs for several public utility power plants in California that awakened the sense of civic beauty that such every-day utilitarian

FIGURE 9.10 Architect George C. Nimmons's preference for the industrial Gothic is evident in the C. P. Kimball Co. works (c. 1916; Chicago).

structures could have. Albert Kahn's use of ornament on commercial and industrial buildings was considered "classic in feeling, but modern in design." His design for the office building for the Hudson Motor Car Co. works (c. 1915; Detroit), for example, was detailed with channeled piers supporting friezelike bands enriched with medallions and curved parapets. The firm Wallis & Goodwillie turned to the Georgian style as a suitable idiom for the Nela Park research facility of the National Division of the General Electric Co. (c. 1914; Cleveland). The precedents of the academic quadrangle and the hierarchy of Georgian ornamentation guided the design of this "University of Industry."[35]

Howard Van Doren Shaw combined modern fireproof construction methods with an adaptation of several historic styles for structures erected in Chicago. A three-story attached colonnade, executed in "a rational use of the classical formula," on the Ginn & Co. warehouse struck at least one observer as compatible with the utilitarian purpose of the building. For the Lakeside Press building of R. R. Donnelly (1897), Shaw chose a distinctive medieval idiom. A later building for R. R. Donnelly (1912) had a vigorous Gothic presence and a prominent tower.[36]

Architects were also responsible for a picturesque strain in industrial architecture. The new facility for the Country Life Press (1910–1911; Kirby & Petit, architects; Garden City, New York) was a steel and concrete structure that housed a modernized production line. The exterior of the two-story structure, though, with its machicolated parapet and its ornamental terra-cotta elements at the main entrance, belied the facility's progressive aspects. The same firm also designed a modernized plant for the American Bank Note Company (1909–1911; the Bronx), and in this case, the expressive quality of the design was a better match with the manufacturing process. For this facility, which printed bank securities and foreign currencies, the architects used an arsenal-like appearance and expressed a sense of strength and security through the use of massive brick piers and arches. A Swiss-chalet-style building erected on "Time Hill" for the Gruen Watchmakers' Guild (c. 1922; Cincinnati) was also symbolic of the work that took place within. The style of the structure was suggested by the visibility of the hilltop site and the Swiss type of watches manufactured. Half-timbered stucco, tapestry brickwork, and a roof of green-glazed tile concealed modern fireproof construction.[37]

Expressive industrial architecture extended to promoting cleanliness for food product companies like bakeries, dairies, and ice cream manufacturers. Gleaming facades of glazed white architectural terra-cotta (which offered little foothold for soot and dirt and could be kept clean) represented a sanitary standard that was maintained within. The link was made by the Ward Bread Co.'s slogan for its chain of bakeries: "snow white temples of cleanliness." The light-colored glazed facade of the Loose-Wiles "Sunshine" Biscuit Co. building (c. 1916; William Higginson, architect; Long Island City, New York; see fig. 1.9) was a highly visible symbol of sanitary baking for commuters on the Long Island Railroad by day. Special lighting—an illuminated sign on the

roofline and bulbs outlining each floor level and a crowning arcade—
ensured that the facility was noticed by night-time travelers as well.[38]

A "MODERN INDUSTRIAL SPIRIT"

The controlling elements in the general exterior treatment of a factory building must
necessarily be the mass form [sic] of the building, the disposition of its structural members, and the color and texture of the main masses of material employed.

ENGINEER WILLARD CASE, 1922

Historian Raymond Merritt asserts that architecture and engineering
reunited at the beginning of the twentieth century and that the technical
skills and aesthetic principles of form and function that engineers had developed were embraced by both professions. The collaboration that Merritt
notes was by no means universal, and there remained differences in how
architects and engineers approached the design of industrial buildings.
Architect Eugene Schoen readily admitted his profession's debt to the engineer for practical matters—the development of a standardized approach to
design and construction and the demonstration that one could design but a
single bay, in plan and elevation, to be used throughout a factory. The *Architectural Record* recommended in 1919 that architects consider "the esthetics
of engineering." Designers in both professions were urged to discover the
dignity and beauty in a structure and to insist on the outward expression of
inner construction.[39]

According to engineer Willard Case, writing in the early 1920s, a
demand for better-looking factory buildings was prompted by the construction of unattractive reinforced concrete structures. These unfortunate
examples, more than any other factor, led both plant owners and engineers
to seek the assistance of architects in building projects. The resulting collaboration, asserted Case, formed the basis of a "modern industrial spirit" for
industrial building design, a quality that expressed the contemporary mood
of "simplicity, lack of pretense, and solidity." It also symbolically conveyed
"industrial freedom, joy in work, equality of all labor—brain and manual—
in the rights to the most comfortable of working conditions and surroundings and pride in the business of which we are a part."[40]

On a more pragmatic note, when structural members created an appearance of stability and rigidity, this type of factory looked like what it was—a
strongly fabricated frame, well knit together against lateral distortion. A
successful design exhibited strength, proper proportions, clean lines, and
attractive coloring and finish and avoided ornamentation not associated
with structural elements. Case noted that the design of industrial buildings
had hardly been reduced to any one of the well-defined "orders of architecture," though he acknowledged the popularity of a severe Gothic idiom.

Case offered several examples of industrial buildings that could perform
well and could also represent the owner's character, the engineer's ability,

FIGURE 9.11 Engineer Willard Case praised the machine shop of the Busch-Sulzer Bros. Diesel Engine Co. for looking like what it was, "a strongly fabricated frame, well knit together against lateral distortion."

FIGURE 9.12 The reinforced concrete loft of the Piqua Hosiery Co. was considered by engineer Willard Case to embody a "modern industrial spirit."

and the architect's skill. He admired the Busch-Sulzer Bros. Diesel Engine Co. machine shop (Arnold Co., engineers; St. Louis; fig. 9.11), a "strictly utilitarian design" with dark red brick pilasters and the judicious use of white cement as foundation walls, window sills, and copings. Architect E. W. Russ's somewhat more ornate reinforced concrete loft building for the Piqua Hosiery Co. (Piqua, Ohio; fig. 9.12), detailed in a modernized classic manner, was the example Case chose to epitomize the "modern industrial spirit."

The appearance of a factory or manufacturing works has a theoretical foundation in an engineer's calculations, artistic ideals, and interest in processes. It also reflects the degree to which engineers, who regarded industrial facilities as the master machine, extended the principles of machinery design to the structures that housed manufacturing processes. Yet general aesthetic principles must be translated into practice; the following chapter examines this next step.

FACTORIES AS ARCHITECTURE   10

I envy the architects of purposeful industrial buildings. They have opportunity to work out real buildings spontaneously, without self-consciousness. Of such buildings we have admirable examples in this country.

ARCHITECT FRANK LLOYD WRIGHT, 1931

T he industrial engineering aesthetic that guided factory design work included an architectural language that translated the general aesthetic ideals of engineers into elements of the built environment. Once familiar with these design principles and elements, we can "read" the aesthetic content of industrial buildings and revise our evaluation of them as merely utilitarian facilities.

PRINCIPLES OF INDUSTRIAL BUILDING DESIGN

In 1929 civil engineer Charles Evan Fowler noted four fundamental principles that guided the work of the engineer in designing bridges and other structures: simplicity, symmetry, harmony, and propriety. Simplicity, to the engineer, connoted a "truth-telling" in structural design and the absence of contrivance and of frivolous or inappropriate details—not mere lack of complexity. It also meant basing a design strictly on functional factors. Though symmetry was a fundamental aspect of bridge forms, balance was often substituted in other types of structures designed by engineers. Harmony between the framing and exterior cladding of a structure and among the various components of a design was critical to the engineering aesthetic. Fowler noted that his list was similar to a comparable group of ideas that guided the work of the architect: sincerity, propriety, style, and scale. A major difference between the approaches of the two professions was that engineers could seldom consider style as it was understood in architecture.[1]

Fowler wrote of ideals that had long influenced engineers's work in the design of factories. We can also detect more definitive design criteria at work in industrial architecture:

- a blended dichotomy of organic and standardized plans, forms, and construction, as dictated by actual, rather than implied, functionalism;
- a regularity of form and articulation imposed by programmatic needs for light and ventilation and relieved by the expression of various internal functions;
- a reliance on framed construction—both traditional methods of building and innovative and best-practice techniques—and either the accentuation of structural elements or the concealment of the frame with an engineered curtain wall; and
- an emphasis on rationalized simplicity in design and the inherent qualities of materials that furthers the expression of strongly fabricated structures.

The engineering aesthetic explored in chapter 9 and the functional aspects of industrial buildings, especially those examined in part II, form the basis of this set of flexible design principles. There were many aesthetic decisions to be made in factory design, and the manner in which these principles have been applied warrant our examination.

A Fusion of Organic and Standardized Design

Often both plans for industrial works and for the buildings that comprised the plant exhibited a blending of organic and standardized design. Though engineers approached these design problems from an organic, or functional, approach, the inclusion of similar suboperations in works of many types eliminated the need to begin each works layout or building design as a new problem. As diverse as manufacturing processes were, engineers came to understand that they could be efficiently accommodated in a limited number of plant layouts and building types. Hence, they offered model plans (like those presented in chapter 3) and refined such schemes for specific applications.

To engineers, standardization involved the conscious, rational selection of materials, sizes, products, means, and processes. Standardization represented fitness to industrial conditions and accomplishing tasks in the easiest, quickest, and most successful way. It was related to efficiency, which in turn was used to judge the suitability of a factory building. A building's fitness for profitable manufacture of goods was a quantifiable, as well as a qualitative, factor since it could be calculated from the overhead charge imposed on each unit of production. In short, an efficient industrial plant was one in which materials and finished products would be transported over the shortest distance horizontally, picked up and set down as infrequently as possible, and handled by machinery with a minimum expenditure of cheap power.[2]

The advantages of standardized industrial building design and construction were realized during the mid–nineteenth century. The concept is evident in the plan proposed for the Rock Island Arsenal in 1866 that comprised a group of identical structures, all suitable for use as shops, even though some were used for storage. The construction of the Pullman Palace Car Co. works (1880; Solon S. Beman, architect; Pullman, Illinois) was noted for its economies of scale and standardization of materials and methods. As companies erected large plants of new materials, standardized building methods became widely utilized. For instance, walls consisting of concrete on metal lathe—dubbed the Ambridge wall—enclosed many of the buildings of the American Bridge Co. plant (c. 1902; Ambridge, Pennsylvania).[3]

Standardized construction methods and building forms reduced costs in design and construction, although initial outlay came to be considered secondary in importance to production costs. Engineers were also very conscious of the changing nature of manufacturing operations; the use of standardized designs checked their desires to design special-purpose plants. As engineer H. K. Ferguson noted in 1936, the factory owner was no longer interested in complicated or "trick designs" and often wanted industrial buildings in a hurry. It made sense, then, to refine a standard product rather than attempt one that was radically new and theoretically improved.[4]

Standardized Factory Design

The Austin Method is a square deal way of planning, erecting, equipping and maintaining buildings. It makes you in effect your own architect, engineer, builder.

ADVERTISEMENT OF THE AUSTIN CO., 1907

The best design solutions for factories that emerged during the innovative and experimental decades at the turn of the century became the standardized building types of the twentieth century. Some engineers, without fanfare, modified their successful designs for use elsewhere. At the same time, standardized designs were emphasized as manufacturers marketed lines of industrial buildings. The models of most companies were starting points for building design and were readily adapted to individual requirements; many of the resulting structures did not appear exactly as presented in catalogs. The plant manager was assured by trade literature that he could avoid the choice between the cheapest building and one that would be least expensive in the long run, since he could get both in a carefully chosen and customized standardized structure.[5]

Standardized industrial buildings became widely available as iron- and steel-framed structures during the last decades of the nineteenth century.

FIGURE 10.1 One of the buildings erected by The Austin Co. for the Dayton Metal Products Co. was an expanded version of a standard model. A comparison of this structure with another Austin building, fig. 7.3, indicates how differently these "standardized" buildings were finished on the exterior.

FIGURE 10.2 "The Gibralter," one of the several standardized buildings offered by the Crowell-Lundoff-Little Co., was a reinforced concrete structure of "unlimited utility." Suitable for a factory, warehouse, storage building, or even stores and offices, it could be faced with brick, terra cotta, or stone.

By 1883 the Standard Roof and Bridge Co. was offering manufactured iron buildings and warehouses in addition to its line of iron and fireproof building components. During the 1890s the Milliken Bros. line of products included manufacturing buildings, sheds, and market buildings, along with cast-iron and sheet-metal building components. The firm boasted that it had made a specialty of designing and building machine shops, foundries, and shops.[6]

More types of standardized factory buildings became readily available during the 1910s. The Austin Co. in Cleveland was one of the most prominent firms that supplied standardized designs. The firm's first catalog (1913) offered ten standard buildings, both production sheds and lofts, that could be combined and varied to meet the needs of the customer (fig. 10.1; see also fig. 7.3). The purchase of an Austin building represented savings in the cost of design and also speed in erection, because standard buildings could be shipped almost immediately after a contract was signed; steel-framed structures could be erected in thirty to sixty working days.[7]

By 1916 a dozen companies offered standard factory designs. The Crowell-Lundoff-Little Co. (also headquartered in Cleveland) offered buildings that were distinguished from those of its competitors mainly by their names. This firm's models included "The Miracle" and "The Premier," as well as the more prosaic "Monitor" and "Textile" (fig. 10.2). The Jones and Larson Corp. (Long Island, New York) also offered industrial steel buildings that it designed, fabricated, delivered, and erected. During the 1920s the Truscon Steel Co.'s structures were from one to four bays wide, covered with trussed roofs, and clad in combinations of glazed and solid panels. By 1930, Truscon's products were reconceived as various types of bays, each with its own trussed roof, that could be combined in any configuration. A Pacific Coast concern that used the trade name Coasteel offered five types, and all sizes, of industrial buildings.[8]

Rectangularity of Form and Regularity of Articulation

The standardization of factory design depended on the building blocks of industrial buildings—the bay area between interior columns. Repetition of bays of uniform size resulted in the regular, rectangular forms of industrial buildings, as well as a similarity in the interior space from building to building. The placement of bays to form relatively narrow, but long, structures was based on the need for light. The regularity in the size and placement of window openings was a response to the identical dimensions of the bays within and the need for even illumination.

This standardized interior space determined the placement of service elements. For example, in order to provide access and services to all portions of textile mills or industrial lofts, stair and utility towers were placed in a central location (if only one was needed) or evenly spaced throughout the length of the structure. In a similar way, the exterior facade might be interrupted at regular intervals by hoistways, openings filled with doors rather than with windows.

Production sheds had regular forms for the same reasons, and often were bilaterally symmetrical, with a taller gabled central bay flanked by lower lean-tos. Monitors were centrally placed, and skylights usually were spaced for even lighting and ventilation. An exception to this common practice was the elimination of one side bay in order to permit extensive glazing of one wall of the erecting bay.

Aesthetic Expression Derived from the Framed Structure

Framed structural systems predominate in industrial building construction. American builders developed a preference for the framed structure over the load-bearing mass masonry wall that was dominant in Europe, asserts historian James Marston Fitch, because of its technological and economical advantages. A structural frame was more efficient than load-bearing masonry in meeting the demands of industry. It was economically feasible because America had an abundant supply of the proper materials—wood, iron, and steel. Fitch also notes that Americans appreciated the degree to which both the skeleton and the engineered curtain wall that enclosed it could be rationalized.[9]

Both loft buildings with prominent pilasters and the glazed envelopes of production sheds owe their form and aesthetic character to the framed structure (see fig. 6.12). Factories could be detailed to manifest strength and stability when the framing was expressed and accentuated on the building exterior. On the other hand, framed structures could be entirely hidden from view by engineered curtain walls; in this case, it was obvious that the enclosing wall was carried by the frame.

Brick bearing walls were made skeletal in form, as much like a framed system as possible, through the concentration of loads in thick piers, or pilasters. Brick walls of pilasters and thinner panel walls were articulated in various ways. Arcaded forms, in which two or more stories were linked visually by arched spandrels that joined soaring pilasters, exuded structural strength and had an inherent ornamental quality (see figs. 2.3, 3.10, 4.2, 9.9, and 10.3). Pilasters were sometimes truncated at the floor level of the top story of lofts or a few feet from the roof of a one-story structure (see fig. 10.7). This abrupt termination that made pilasters more like buttresses revealed their functional role; where the strength of pilasters was not needed, they were eliminated.[10]

When both vertical pilasters and horizontal spandrels and stringcourses were emphasized, facades appeared as articulated grids and often featured a lively interplay of elements. The German architect Karl Friedrich Schinkel was a designer of "gridded pilaster screens" who exposed interwoven layers of brick as an expression of the framed structure within. Schinkel's forms were commonly incorporated into American commercial and industrial buildings of pilaster and panel wall construction during the last half of the nineteenth century. The facade grid might be detailed to have a marked vertical or horizontal emphasis or to reveal subtle layers of brickwork. The structural quality of these designs was often reinforced with the placement of ornament at load-bearing locations, such as at the spring points of arches or window lintels and as capitals and bases of pilasters. In these ways, brick could be detailed to provide its own ornamental quality or could be accented by terra-cotta or stone elements.[11]

The gridded articulation of the facades of industrial loft buildings remained a dominant theme even as interior steel framing reduced the structural role of the brick exterior wall to that of an enclosing wall. Gridded facades seemed appropriate because of their structural quality, particularly when steel lintels framed wide window openings. Indeed, architects and engineers found it difficult to move away from facade schemes developed for the brick pilaster-articulated and gridded wall (see fig. 9.10).

Simplicity in Design and the Rationalized Use of Ornament

As engineers explained in chapter 9, the limited use of ornamentation in factory design was a conscious aesthetic choice. Undecorated structures also had an efficient, machinelike, "no-fuss" quality. Simplicity was a design ideal to the engineer and did not represent a default or minimal effort approach to industrial building design.

The austere wall of wood, brick, or stone, long a basic element of American architecture, was initially an expedient choice because of the scarcity of skilled labor and the need for economy in building. It remained a common element in industrial building design for both aesthetic and practical considerations. The vibration generated by machinery and the movement of materials throughout the works, particularly with exterior hoists, argued against adding projecting ornamental elements to plain walls. In a similar way, a parapet or corbelled brick cornice, rather than a projecting cornice, often terminated the upper edge of an exterior wall.

Functional simplicity was also evident in the ways that industrial buildings were designed and detailed for service, more so than for distinctive architectural effect. The materials utilized in industrial buildings offered long-term durability and ease of maintenance. For example, the rounded edges of bullnose brick and granite dressed with a rock face were less likely to become damaged than standard brick and smooth-cut granite. Reinforced concrete elements with beveled edges were, likewise, less liable to chipping.[12]

The ground story of industrial buildings incorporated many service-related elements. Slightly projecting stone foundations protected the lower portions of factories from vehicles moving into position at loading bays. For the same reason, the corners of ground-level openings were edged with metal strips or guarded by projecting bollards. Long ranges of sturdy loading platforms extended along facades to give access to railcars or trucks. They were sheltered by sheet-metal awnings supported by utilitarian brackets of angle iron or ornamental ones of wrought iron. Large openings, placed where needed, were filled with doors that rolled upward or folded back into reveals to be out of the way. Transoms above these doorways helped to light and ventilate the ground story. In urban areas where the basement level of the building extended under the sidewalk, the underground vaults were covered with large slabs of granite forming the sidewalk. A portion of the vault might be covered with vault lights—panels of iron or concrete into which small prisms of glass were set—that were either placed flush with the sidewalk or raised as stepped vault covers.

The engineering aesthetic incorporated a rationalized use of ornament. To the engineer, ornament was appropriate when it emphasized structural elements and provided relief from monotony. J. W. Carpenter, who considered himself both an architect and an engineer, condemned the fancy industrial building as "a horror to look at" unless its structural elements, "far more beautiful in their varied outline than the most gorgeous display," were also visible. Clarence Morse Barber, a civil engineer working in Cleveland, considered ornamentation more beautiful when it appeared to be really of service—for example, a bracket. Engineers recommended the relief of monotony through the use of elements that added character but also had functional roles, such as projecting pilasters that added rigidity to a structure and external projections that enclosed elevator shafts and stairways.[13]

Architects also rationalized the placement of ornament: They thought it was appropriate on prominent features of the factory building, such as entrances and towers that enclosed water supply tanks or stairs. Architect F. M. Gardiner asserted that the entrance established the character of a factory. It could suggest a dignity of purpose, inspire awe, or offer a welcome to workers and visitors, or, by using its trademark or insignia, convey the firm's status. Some entrances incorporated cast stone or tilework that depicted the work within. Such gestures ranged from a simple cast-stone plaque featuring a product or a tool to a pictorial frieze.[14]

The Central Manufacturing District in Chicago demonstrated the architectural profession's rationalized and standardized approach to industrial building design and its detailing (see fig. 5.3). S. Scott Joy, staff architect of the district, cited the origins of the architectural program as the obvious advantage of giving warehouse and manufacturing buildings architectural effect and the desire for unity of expression without monotony. He oversaw the addition of cream-colored terra cotta to dark red "standard district brick" to accentuate the verticality of pylons and piers and to form pier caps, belt courses, cornices, and copings. Economies of scale were realized through the repeated use of a limited number of terra-cotta profiles and moldings, even though the intent was variety in detailing and ornamental features.[15]

The articulation and limited, rationalized ornamentation of factory buildings often accentuated the monumentality inherent in such structures.

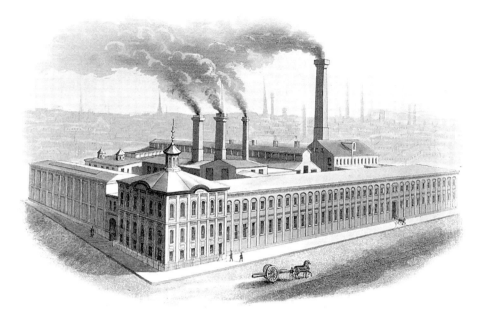

FIGURE 10.3 Pilasters joined at the top to form arcades emphasized the strength of the brick walls of the William Bement & Son works (c. 1870; Philadelphia). The brick buildings also incorporated elements of the American round-arched style.

The visual impact of expanses of factory walls was heightened by corresponding long rows of identical window openings. Facades articulated in a rhythmic manner with the projecting forms of pilasters and pylons or with arcades that united several stories under massive arches achieved a structural monumentalism (fig. 10.3; see also figs. 2.3 and 3.10). Projecting pavilions and pedimented parapets added to the formal and intimidating quality of industrial loft buildings (see figs. 3.7, 8.4, and 9.1). The monumental presence of production sheds, established by their immense sloping roofs and soaring chimneys, might be furthered by long expanses of window walls, framed with borders of brick or metal (see figs. 6.12, 10.16, and 10.18).

The Aesthetic Character of Brickwork

Both engineers and architects recognized that they could capitalize on the intrinsic characteristics of brickwork to create an appropriate utilitarian appearance for industrial buildings. This approach also provided an alternative to the architect's reliance on expensive terra-cotta and stone ornamentation.

Locally made common brick was the material of choice for industrial buildings throughout most of the nineteenth century. During the 1880s, the types of brick available to the builder expanded significantly. Products were introduced in a wider range of natural colors—buffs and darker, richer tones—and sizes, including narrow Roman bricks. Building designers could also choose "paving brick" that was stronger than common brick yet less expensive than face brick, or mottled "iron-spot" face brick, a strong, durable, but expensive material. Brickworks also began to market lines of patterned brick that were similar in appearance to unglazed terra-cotta units.

Some designers of manufacturing buildings sought to create a brick aesthetic based on the expressive use of these new products. Iron-spot and blended shades of brick (sometimes called tapestry brick, for it displayed the natural range of colors produced in a kiln firing) were utilized in lieu of the standard red factory brick. Mortar was colored to blend or contrast with brick. The use of extra-wide mortar joints or narrow "butter" joints also influenced the character of the brickwork and helped provide architectural character with little additional expense. Patterned brick and splayed (angled) and rounded units were incorporated into factory buildings as a relatively economical and rational means of relieving plain brickwork.

Arched door and window openings in brick industrial buildings represented structural elements that added to aesthetic character. All door and window openings were capped by relieving arches that transferred the weight of the wall above the openings to the wall area between them. It was most expedient to extend these arches through the entire thickness of the wall and thereby avoid the use of a wood lintel, a less durable and more flammable element. In some cases, though, the arch was concealed by a stone or cast-iron lintel set into the exterior portion of the wall. Accepted practice limited the span of brick arches and thus determined the size and form of window and door openings in industrial buildings.

The segmentally arched shape for window openings dominated in brick structures because of practical and economical considerations. This shape was most often laid as a "rough arch" of standard brick with wedge-shaped mortar joints. In a gauged arch, bricks, rather than the mortar joints, assumed the wedge form. Because bricks that could be shaped as wedges were softer (and weaker) than other bricks, gauged arches were not as strong as rough ones. Indeed, when gauged arches—often round-headed in shape—framed window openings, interior or unseen rough arches usually formed much of the openings and supported the wall above. Consequently, round-headed windows were often limited to the top story of industrial and commercial lofts, where the strength of the arched opening was not as critical. Segmental and round arches were sometimes laid as rowlock arches, formed of small bricks laid in concentric rings; they were not as strong as bonded arches but were easier to lay and sufficiently strong.[16]

TRANSLATING AESTHETIC THEORY INTO PRACTICE

The work of both engineers and architects provides a means of examining how the engineering aesthetic described in the preceding chapter and the principles just discussed were put to use in the design of industrial buildings. Engineers developed a brick industrial architecture that adapted a recognized architectural style and interpreted their aesthetic sensibilities. Architects' reinforced concrete designs and their struggles with the artistic issues surrounding this type of work generated a discourse that reveals much about their approach to a proper aesthetic for factory buildings.

The American Round-Arched Style in Industrial Buildings

The aesthetic ideals of engineers are quite evident in their designs for brick industrial buildings. As noted earlier, masonry construction in small units offered the perfect way both to express simplicity and harmony in design and to emphasize structural elements, provide relief from monotony, and develop an inherent ornamental language. Some engineers worked within the traditional, simplest forms and methods of brick masonry construction to satisfy the artistic impulse (see figs. 1.7, 4.2, and 9.1). Others—more than is generally acknowledged—were also interpreting the American round-arched architectural style (see fig. 10.3).

The American round-arched style, an interpretation of an idiom developed in Germany by progressive architects during the 1830s and 1840s, forms the artistic basis of much building in brick for industry and commerce. The *Rundbogenstil*, as the style was known in Germany, synthesized classical and medieval architecture—particularly the round-arched elements of those styles—and relied on brick and locally available stone. Characteristic of the style were pilasters and horizontal bands forming grids; elaborate brick corbelling, especially corbel tables; and molded surrounds emphasizing arched door and window openings. During the 1850s and 1860s the vocabulary of this mode was expanded to include windows set off by projecting archivolts enriched with dentils, segmentally arched windows, and polychrome patterned brick.

The *Rundbogenstil* was brought to the United States by German immigrant architects and builders and was pictured in pattern books and architectural periodicals (fig. 10.4). Round arches appeared in American religious architecture by the mid-1840s and soon thereafter in public buildings like the Astor Library (1849–1853; Alexander Saeltzer, architect; New York City) and the Pay Department Building in the Brooklyn Navy Yard (c. 1868). American designers and builders tended to incorporate the style into exterior forms and detailing but rarely used it in their interiors. The term *Rundbogenstil* was seldom used in the United States; instead, the idiom was denoted by the terms *Byzantine, Romanesque, Norman, Lombard, Anglo-Norman, modern Italian,* or *Lombard-Venetian.* Architectural historian Kathleen Curran, an authority on its American adaptation, suggests the term "American round-arched style."[17]

Thomas Alexander Tefft, an American architect considered to be a master of the idiom, was responsible for the admired Union Depot in Providence

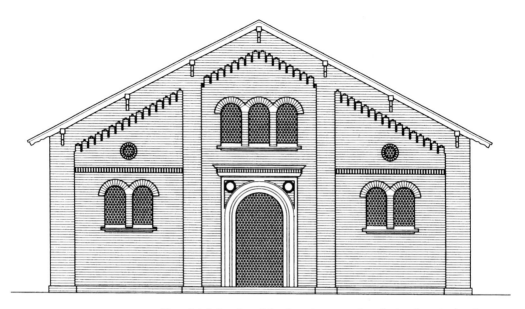

FIGURE 10.4 Many brick facades of the American round-arched style articulated with flat pilasters and corbel tables were similar to this design, which appeared in an 1883 German patternbook.

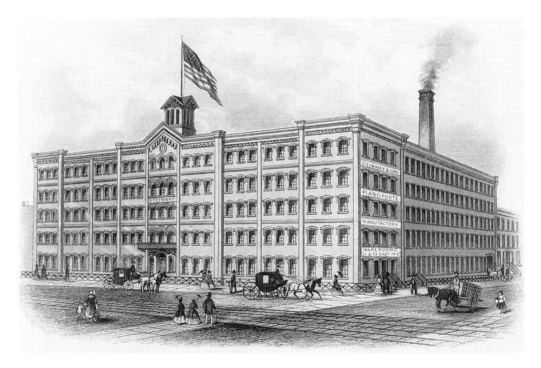

FIGURE 10.5 The main facade of the Steinway & Sons manufactory (1859, 1865 addition) in New York City was described as exhibiting the "modern Italian style," one of the terms used to indicate the *Rundbogenstil*.

(1847). With its bold forms and ranges of arched openings, as well as towers similar to those rising along the sides of textile mills, the Union Depot demonstrated that the round-arched style was appropriate for industrial and commercial projects as did some of the architect's other buildings. Tefft's scheme for a first Howard Building (1847; Providence) featured pilasters and corbel tables that established a facade grid for the three-story masonry structure that echoed its interior framing. This type of organizing grid appeared in many industrial and commercial buildings, both lofts and production sheds. A case in point was Tefft's design for a "merchandise house" (warehouse) that was erected near the Providence Union Depot (1849). The architect's 1853 replacement Howard Building (after the earlier structure burned) was quite different. Instead of a controlling grid, he relied on varied patterns of round-arched window openings that evoked a medieval flavor; this scheme also found application in industrial building design.[18]

The American round-arched style provided an appropriate architectural character for utilitarian commercial and industrial buildings and expressed many of the ideals of the engineering aesthetic. The forms were familiar to masons and were easy and economical to build because no additional materials or trades were necessary for their execution. The practical reasons for using segmentally arched openings meant that round-arched openings did not predominate, even in this style of building. Most important, the round-arched style was generated by—not applied to—a building's structure.

In the hands of builders, engineers, and architects who were adept at combining the familiar elements of the round-arched style, factories readily acquired inherent architectural effect (fig. 10.5). Corbelled brickwork, the incremental increasing in the thickness of the wall, provided a means of modeling the wall while accenting structure and providing patterned relief. Horizontal corbel tables spanned panel walls to join pilasters where additional wall thickness was needed. Ornamental corbel tables distinguished several of the buildings of the Pennsylvania Railroad Shops at West Philadelphia (c. 1873; Joseph M. Wilson, engineer; fig. 10.6) that were detailed in the American round-arched style and even had round-arched windows.[19]

The American round-arched style offered a means of minimizing the box-like nature of a flat-roofed industrial building. Brick cornices were built up from corbel tables and projecting courses and might incorporate panels, geometric forms, or bricks set at angles as "dogs' teeth." They also eliminated the need for cornices of combustible wood or more expensive sheet metal. The extension of a brick cornice as a pedimented parapet above the flat roofline suggested a three-dimensional roof form to observers on the street. These brick pediments were often detailed with a central medallion and surrounding panels rather than with classical forms. Several such pediments rose above the flat roof of the otherwise utilitarian Eberhard Faber Pencil Co. buildings (1861 and later; Brooklyn) and terminated warehouses owned by Henry J. Meyer, erected between 1867 and 1875 in New York City.[20]

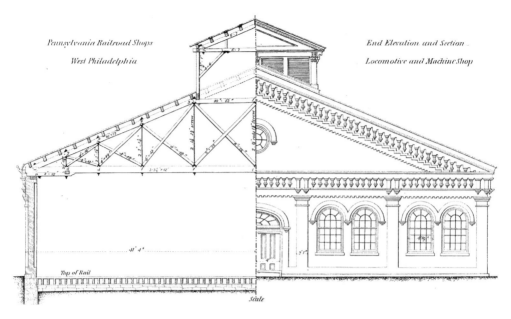

FIGURE 10.6 Engineer Joseph M. Wilson detailed the locomotive and machine shop at the Pennsylvania Railroad Shops at West Philadelphia (c. 1873) with pilasters, corbel tables, and round-arched windows with molded hoods in the manner of the American round-arched style.

FIGURE 10.7 Both the production shed and the water tank tower at the Rensselaer & Saratoga Railroad Green Island Shops indicate the designer's familiarity with the American round-arched style.

The many guises of the round-arched style are evident in its use during the 1860s for various types of industrial buildings in the vicinity of Troy, New York. The facades of the Gurley Building (1862; Troy), an urban loft structure, incorporated a sophisticated double layering of arched openings. In contrast, severe pilasters and corbel tables articulated the end walls of the brick production sheds of the Rensselaer Iron Works Rail Mill (1866; Alexander L. Holley, engineer; Troy) and the Green Island Shops of the Rensselaer & Saratoga Railroad (1872; fig. 10.7). Pilasters terminated with a corbel table stiffened the walls of a polygonal water tower at the Green Island works. The Troy Gas Light Co. gasholder (1873; Frederick A. Sabbaton, engineer; Troy) was a carefully detailed structure with pilaster-framed bays, corbelled horizontal elements, two tiers of round-arched window openings with projecting heads, and a corbelled cornice.[21]

The Architectural Problem of Concrete

Up to the advent of concrete we had depended for so many years on brick, stone, terra cotta, and various decorative materials for architectural effects that we had come to regard a building with an exterior of any other material as unattractive. The human being sets up ideals of beauty based upon what the eye has been accustomed to through long use.

CEMENT AGE, 1910

As they began to design reinforced concrete factory buildings during the first decades of the twentieth century, architects debated the aesthetic problem of the building type. Some designers lauded the plasticity of the new material—the ease with which it could be shaped with formwork—and considered that quality a guide for artistic development. Others argued that the material was no more easily molded that terra cotta and suggested that other design considerations should direct its use. Ironically, this long-term discussion seemed not to matter at all to most engineers and manufacturers. They valued reinforced concrete buildings for other reasons (as outlined in chapter 6).

The intrinsic qualities of concrete were responsible for the aesthetic dilemma. The surface of poured concrete typically exhibited imperfections, as well as the imprint of the grain and joints between the boards of formwork. This raw surface, which had little articulation and a cold texture and color, was considered unattractive. Architects turned to surface treatments, including paint and the application of a thin coat of cement plaster or a thicker coat of parging (which often soon failed). Concrete surfaces were also worked with tools to expose small stones in the aggregate.

The unattractive visual qualities of concrete were coupled with the challenge of detailing the gridded, window-frame-like facades of multistory loft buildings (see figs. 1.8, 1.10, and 10.2). The standardization of the building program of industrial lofts—their bay dimensions, story heights, and building widths—took place before the introduction of reinforced concrete construction. These dimensions and the limited choices in pane size and configurations of steel sash, not the fine sensibilities of the architect, were what determined the proportions of lofts' exterior elements. Consequently, "architectural effect" depended primarily on the articulation of the facade grid.

Soon after reinforced concrete became commonly used, architects turned their full attention to "the architectural problem of concrete." Architect and scholar A. D. F. Hamlin argued that it was harder to alter approaches to decorative design than to incorporate new methods of construction. The monolithic concrete structure represented a difficult and novel challenge in form, texture, and color. It was easiest—if not logical or satisfying—to fall back on the traditions of masonry architecture and to design formwork to replicate familiar elements—columns, arches, modillions, corbels, and pediments. That approach was never completely successful because the familiar forms could be replicated, but the color and texture of worked stone could not. The appropriateness of Mediterranean and Mission-style architecture of the American Southwest as sources of inspiration for concrete buildings was rationalized on the basis of a similar monolithic quality of plastered and stuccoed buildings. The details of these styles were less influential in factory design than was the way they relied on massing, fenestration, and broad shadows for architectural effect. Hamlin hoped that a focus on two fundamental aspects of reinforced concrete—its plastic and monolithic qualities—would produce good designs.[22]

A Range of Architectural Effects in Reinforced Concrete

The debate about aesthetic issues was confined to generalities as architects worked out more specific solutions in building designs. Several strategies pursued are evident more in their design work than in their rhetoric. "All-concrete" structures, in which the concrete structure was exposed, presented the greatest challenge (see fig. 10.2). For some structures of this type, formwork was manipulated to produce molded ornament. Small strips of lath inserted into the forms created rusticated piers; similarly, an entablature could be suggested by attaching a series of moldings to the interior of formwork. Francis S. Onderdonk Jr. christened this attempt to replicate masonry as a "wood-centering style." The appearance of familiar forms of architectural embellishment probably helped all-concrete factories to become accepted, particularly in areas developed as manufacturing centers. This acceptance was suggested by the change in the lofts erected in the Bush Terminal complex from brick-clad to all-concrete exteriors after 1905 (see fig. 3.19).[23]

Nevertheless, brick and terra cotta continued to be applied as veneer to conceal concrete skeletons. Most architects preferred the appearance of brick-sheathed reinforced concrete factory buildings, and it appears that their clients did too. Large design-build firms were responsible for buildings that ranged from all-concrete, to combined brick and concrete, to entirely brick-clad, suggesting that the client and local practice determined which reinforced concrete aesthetic would be employed. In some cities, like Chicago, a very large proportion of reinforced concrete structures were sheathed with brick. The popularity of all-concrete buildings in California was an exception to the national trend. An official of the Turner Construction Company noted that during the 1920s, his firm erected about an equal number of structures with all-concrete exteriors and those with exposed concrete skeletons and brick spandrel walls. In both urban and plant settings, a brick veneer did help new buildings blend in visually with older ones. Construction cost had little to do with the matter; during the 1910s, a brick-clad concrete structure cost about the same as either an all-concrete or steel-framed one.[24]

Regardless of the degree to which the concrete frame was revealed, formed to resemble masonry construction, or hidden by brick, the reinforced concrete loft building had a fairly standardized form and articulation. The uniform programmatic aspects of the building, noted above, led to the use of three types of formulaic facade designs.

As a baseline, starkly plain, generic grids of piers and floor slabs, of both all-concrete structures and those with brick panel walls, remained unrelieved by any articulation of the grid or addition of ornament (see fig. 1.10). Historian Amy Slaton has asked why designers and industrialists accepted these bald, skeletal forms. She concludes that they were not necessarily perceived as lacking in aesthetic quality and that they reflected the artistic and mass-produced nature of the products manufactured in them. Indeed, this type of boldly functional structure was described in a 1916 issue of the *American Architect* as one that "undoubtedly gave an impression of solid worth and not infrequently an impression of what might be called rugged dignity or grim beauty."[25]

Decorated reinforced concrete facades exhibited applied ornament near the top of the wall to draw the eye away from the monotonous grid (see fig. 1.8). Ornament seems to have been added as an afterthought. Emblem-like forms and colored tiles were placed at the top of exterior pilasters as a substitution for the capital and also in the frieze area below a minimal cornice or parapet. Historian Reyner Banham regards these labels as ghosts of decorative devices. Another observer noted the similarity between these ornaments and the medals awarded during World War I.[26]

Articulated grid facades, those manipulated to provide relief from monotony or to emphasize verticality or horizontality, produced some of the most satisfying design solutions. Architect Louis E. Jallade's Thomson Meter Co. building (c. 1909; Brooklyn) was an early attempt at this type of design. An exposed concrete grid was terminated as an arcade at the crowning story and detailed with concrete mullions. Specially colored brick and light-colored terra cotta added to the facade helped to create the effect of a sparkling, well-lighted cage. More typical was the accentuation of the corners of reinforced concrete buildings through the use of pylons formed by exaggerated and grouped pilasters or through pediments over corner bays. The American Chicle Co. Building in Long Island City (c. 1920; Ballinger & Perrot) had corner pylons that balanced the central tower rising through the facade. The pylons marked the location of stairs and elevators and also created the classically derived design terminations that served as resting points for the trained eye. On other lofts, ranges of vaguely classical pilasters, perhaps formed into arcades that united several stories, led the eye upward and minimized the structural grid. Some of the most striking interpretations of this approach featured dark brick-clad piers rising the height of the facade past narrow, light-colored floor slabs positioned as recessed horizontals. Schenck & Williams's deftly articulated Factory Building No. 2 for the Dayton Engineering Laboratories Co. (c. 1916; Dayton, Ohio; fig. 10.8) illustrated the extent to which the grid could be manipulated for architectural effect.[27]

"Industrial Gothic" in reinforced concrete represented another way of making the articulated grid expressive. Many architects who had found a rationale for the Gothic in brick continued to use it for the new material. Cast-in-place decorative forms and piers treated as buttresses evoked the Gothic and emphasized the height of the all-concrete Fletcher Building

FIGURE 10.8 Dark brick-clad piers soared the height of the facade, past narrow, light-colored floor slabs, in the gridded facade of Factory Building No. 2 of the Dayton Engineering Laboratories Co.

(1920–1922; Helmle & Corbett, architects; New York City; fig. 10.9). The industrial Gothic in concrete ranged from the restraint of the A. M. Creighton Building (c. 1923; Harold Field Kellogg, architect; Lynn, Massachusetts) to the exuberance of the Hollywood Terminal Building (c. 1927; Morgan, Walls & Clements, architects; Los Angeles).[28]

Architect Cass Gilbert transformed formulaic design into the inspired and turned the problem of reinforced concrete into triumph. "The simpler the form, the better the design" was Gilbert's guiding maxim for working with reinforced concrete. The architect was the first, but not the last, to see something "very fine in a great gray mass of building, all one color, all one tone, yet modified by the sunlight or shadow to pearly gray of wonderful delicacy," in two industrial buildings of his design erected in Brooklyn.[29] Gilbert's Austin-Nichols Warehouse (1913–1914) had character provided by the proportions of narrow, slitlike window openings and their rhythmical grouping in flat walls that had no surface texture or ornamentation. To the architect, the deep window reveals and the shadows they cast provided an essential sense of strength, solidity, and dignity.[30]

Similar ideas guided Gilbert's next essay in concrete, the United States Army Supply Base (1918; fig. 10.10), whose aesthetic quality was derived from a masterful subdivision of the facades by carefully detailed pylons,

FIGURE 10.9 This interpretation of the industrial Gothic in reinforced concrete came from the drawing board of the architectural firm Helmle & Corbett.

FIGURE IO.IO Cass Gilbert relied on simple forms to convey power and strength in the design of the United States Army Supply Base in Brooklyn.

piers, and mullions. The vast scale of the two main buildings and the fine proportions of the severe design demonstrated again that ornamental detail was unnecessary. To a contemporary observer, the great gray buildings of the Brooklyn facility rose above the streets and waterfront like some vast medieval city's wall. Their scale and strength dominated the landscape, giving an impression of power and strength. Ornament was not only unnecessary but would have seemed flippant in so great and impressive a mass.[31]

INDUSTRIAL MODERNISMS

Architecturally speaking, how impossible it would have been to have clothed a planning scheme of this rational character with the dress of some archaeological style!

ARCHITECT HARVEY WILEY CORBETT, 1930

There are many similarities between the engineering—or industrial—aesthetic and modern architecture. Factories share with other modern buildings an emphasis on volume and regularity in massing, as opposed to symmetry, and a dependence on the intrinsic nature of materials and proportion, rather than applied ornament, for architectural effect. Nevertheless, a lag between the appearance of the European modern aesthetic and the updating of design in the United States was as evident in the field of industrial architecture as it was in other types of buildings. This was so even though, as Albert Kahn commented, "factory construction, being less handicapped by precedent, was the first to take notice."[32]

Scholars recently have begun to explore the concept of an American industrial modernism. This term implies that there was a difference in the modernist aesthetic achieved in industrial building design and the one attained in other, more "high-style" architecture. There has only been limited recognition of the engineering aesthetic I argue has been dominant in industrial architecture. Accordingly, we have only begun to explore the impetus for and means of blending the industrial aesthetic with high modernism.

One type of explanation for the similarity between industrial building design and architectural modernism lies in a link between the modernization of the factory during the late nineteenth century and modernity in expression, a materialist basis for artistic change. This interpretation places the development of industrial modernism in the hands of engineers, who, as they turned to new ways of building with steel and engineered curtain walls, were forced to abandon traditional aesthetic norms. Other accounts privilege the aesthetic sensibilities of architects and suggests that industrial modernism emerged when they adopted, and by implication improved upon, the aesthetic ideals of engineers. There was another plausible route to industrial modernism—the direct adaptation of the new ideals of modern architecture to industrial buildings.

Historian Terry Smith's definition of industrial modernism provides a starting point for the examination of this aesthetic turn of events. To Smith, industrial modernism was based on an actual—rather than symbolic—functionality and on the transposition of the values of engineering into those of architecture. Smith grounds his argument in the work of Albert Kahn's firm for Ford and other automobile manufacturers. He notes the difference between the actual functionalism of the industrial buildings designed by Kahn for Ford's Highland Park plant and the symbolic functionalism of works by European modernists. According to Smith, the industrial modern was typified by the one-story automobile plant of the early twentieth century. Moreover, he asserts that Kahn supervised the birth of a modernity that integrated the values of functionalism with those dominating architecture.[33]

Hence, Smith suggests four criteria for analysis: actual functionality and its expression, the importance of engineering values, the role of the architect, and the influence of European modernist architecture. But uneven development in these factors prevents us from determining any definitive turning point or linking any one individual with the advent of American industrial modernism, and scholars will probably never agree on which advances were most significant. Functionally modernized conceptualization of manufacturing space and the expression of actual functionalism reached a mature level around the turn of the nineteenth century in the work of engineers. The values and aesthetic ideals of engineers guided the aesthetic content of these facilities. Around this same time, architects turned their attention to industrial building design. But their approach, grounded in traditional notions of architectural beauty, worked not to accelerate but to retard the integration of either a functional engineering aesthetic or architectural modernism into industrial building design. It took some time for these designers to blend European architectural modernism and its symbolic funtionalism with their factory designs and to embrace the values and aesthetics of engineers in their factory work.

We can enhance our understanding of an American industrial modernism by examining how architects gradually responded to new currents in European design. We will see that a few factories reflected avant-garde design. At the same time, the modernism evident in production sheds led to a striking and mature articulation of the new aesthetic. This functional modernism, especially when interpreted by architects, produced some of the more noteworthy examples of an American industrial modernism.

Architectural Tradition Prevails

America is far behind many countries in Europe. It has yet to show a plant as beautiful as the Van Nelle plant in Rotterdam or the Austrian Tobacco plant at Linz, or any one of several of the great factories of Sweden or England; but the pioneering work already accomplished has shown the way, and the best of the American work is probably in advance of the European in its efficiency.

CRITIC TALBOT HAMLIN, 1940

The development of an industrial modernism in the United States was affected by the schism between architects and engineers during the nineteenth century. In addition to the differences in aesthetic ideals noted in the preceding chapter, architects and engineers had different relationships with materialistic and technological modernization. For engineers, the last decades of the nineteenth century were a time of rapid changes in technology that affected manufacturing and building construction. Engineers were participants, intimately involved in these technological changes and in the planning and operation of industrial and commercial corporations. They were responsible for modernized conditions in industry and society.

The architectural profession primarily reacted to and interpreted this technological change. Architects remained in the grip of artistic tradition and convention and were interested in the adaptation of historic styles to new uses. Albert Kahn noted the confusion in the profession during the early years of the twentieth century from the vantage point of 1939. He recalled how Peter Behrens and his followers established a new standard for industrial building design that was based on simplification, the avoidance of traditional applied ornament, the intelligent employment of building materials, and a sense of fitness. Kahn asserted that this approach appeared first, if hesitantly, in the United States in industrial architecture, even though "we were still steeped in Eclecticism and hardly beyond the so-called Beaux-Arts period."[34]

Indeed, the rhetoric and design projects of architects during the early twentieth century suggest that industrial building design was rationalized within the traditional conceptualization of architecture before it was modernized. This was so even though architects were relatively free from the precedents of historical styles and prototypes in the design of industrial plants. Particularly after the turn of the century, the larger scale of structures and new building materials brought real novelty to the design problem. Factory design offered a chance to create that elusive, long-called-for, indigenous American style of architecture. But for the most part, the opportunity was forfeited, and no alternative to traditional "architectural effect" was actively pursued.

American Industrial Architecture Responds to European Modernism

European modernism, as interpreted in buildings for industry, was hardly unknown to American architects. They were introduced to such work through their travel and study in Europe and architectural periodicals. In the *American Architect*, for example, views of Peter Behrens's Turbine Erecting Shop of the A.E.G. (1909; Berlin), Hans Poelzig's Water Works (Posen), and several other structures were presented as novel designs by pioneers in a new industrial architecture.[35]

When architect Frank E. Wallis compared European and American factory design in 1915, he regretted that it was his own profession, not the industrialist client, who had failed to advance industrial design in the European manner. After all, he asked, "what did any of us ever bring back from England or from Germany more interesting to a manufacturer than an idea for his own residence?" Emphasizing the economics of factory architecture, Wallis noted that German manufacturers, who operated with a small profit margin, nevertheless managed to erect factory buildings with aesthetic character. Wallis asserted that whether "the architectural styles developed in Germany may or may not appeal to us is beside the question. She has combined the Classic, the Gothic, and good red herring in the designs of her industrial buildings."[36]

American industrial buildings that exhibited the spirit of European design were exceptions to the general state of affairs but suggest how the new ideas were experimented with. For the Thompson Malted Food Co. plant (c. 1915; Waukesha, Wisconsin; fig. 10.11), architect Henry C. Hengels evoked the emphasis of the Secessionist school of architecture on bold forms in a series of interlocking cubes with broad expanses of concrete walls. Window openings were determined by function, not pattern or symmetry. A lanternlike central portion was articulated with a multistory window group outlined by a tile border, while a wing that housed machinery had quite limited fenestration.[37]

The firm Purcell & Elmslie provided a remarkably innovative design for the International Leather and Belting Corporation plant (1917–1918; only partially erected in Chicago; fig. 10.12). The plan for the facility, which included a pair of production sheds, a loft building with attached offices, a small building of undetermined function, and two courtyard areas, may have been as functional as it was formal. The design of the buildings maintained a balanced dichotomy between the strength of massed masonry and the transparent fragility of glazed curtain walls. The side window walls of the loft and the production sheds appeared to be supported and protected by solid masonry end walls, whose structural quality was emphasized by their battered form and their ranks of projecting buttresslike piers. The implied strength of the masonry was furthered by a massed tower rising from the office building.[38]

The glazed box of Walter Gropius's Bauhaus School (1926; Dessau, Germany), one of the icons of the new international style of architecture, did have counterparts across the Atlantic Ocean. The steel frame's tractability was suggested by its contrasted exposure and enclosure by multistory glazed panels in a building for the Worcester Pressed Steel Co. (c. 1931; Joseph D. Leland & Co., architects and engineers; Worcester, Massachusetts; fig. 10.13). According to architectural critic Talbot Hamlin, this project conveyed a new kind of beauty—one dependent on materials—as well as lightness and strength.[39]

Architect Ely Jacques Kahn, responsible for several noted tall loft buildings for industrial use in New York City during the 1920s and 1930s, articulated and practiced an industrial modernism. For Kahn, modernity in design always began with such practical principles as adequate light; if it evolved through the elimination of unnecessary decorative features, something new might develop. He relied on fine proportion, balance of mass, and the agreeable color of materials for architectural effect.[40]

Kahn and his partner, Robert Allan Jacobs, designed one of the most noted and controversial interpretations of industrial modernism, the New York City Municipal Asphalt Plant (1940). Although this admired work was featured in the Museum of Modern Art's review of architectural modernism, "Built in USA, 1932–1944," the general public was not certain the design was a success. After all, it was not obvious that the unusual form of each of the buildings was generated by the manufacturing process that took place within, rather than by aesthetic whim. The sweeping elliptical arch of the plant's most prominent building was, in fact, dictated by the most efficient enclosure of its machinery. The influence of European modernism is evident in the use of ribbonlike strips of windows, which were located, nonetheless, to illuminate production processes.[41]

Critic Henry Russell Hitchcock and architect Philip Johnson, who promoted the international style in the United States, took note of industrial architecture in the early 1930s: "On the whole, American factories, where the client expects no money to be spent on design, are better buildings and at least negatively purer in design than those constructions in which the

FIGURE 10.11 Architect Henry C. Hengels's Secessionist-inspired design for the Thompson Malted Food Co. features bold forms and relates fenestration to function.

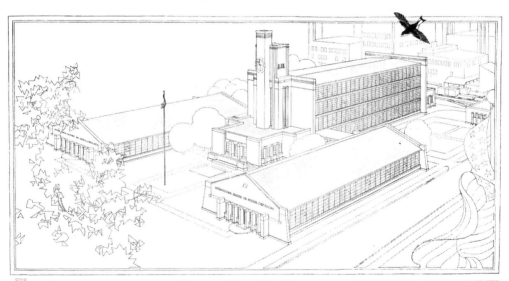

FACTORY FOR THE INTERNATIONAL LEATHER AND BELTING CORPORATION

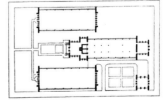

FIGURE 10.12 The contrast between the strength of massed piers and the transparency of window walls distinguishes this design for International Leather and Belting Corporation plants by the architectural firm Purcell & Elmslie.

FIGURE 10.13
The Worcester Pressed Steel
Co. plant, designed by Joseph
D. Leland & Co., was a sophisti-
cated interpretation of the
modern glazed box.

architect is forced by circumstances to be more than an engineer." Gropius's
Bauhaus School and the Van Nelle Tobacco, Tea & Coffee Factory
(1928–1930; Brinkman & Van Der Vlugt, architects) represented European
advances in industrial architecture in Hitchcock and Johnson's "Modern
Architecture: International Exhibition" at the Museum of Modern Art
in 1932.[42]

The other factory design in the exhibit was the Starrett-Lehigh Building
(1930–1931; Cory & Cory; Yasuo Matsui, associate architect; New York City).
This structure, which covered an entire block and rose to nineteen stories,
was both a structurally complex feat of engineering and a blending of the
functionalism of American industrial architecture with the influence of the
horizontal aesthetic of European modernism of the 1920s. The design was
structurally expressive throughout; the role of the steel-framed central service and circulation core (which functioned as a "vertical street") was
acknowledged by soaring pilasters. More dominant in the design, however,
were the two wings of reinforced concrete with walls slightly cantilevered
beyond the exterior columns, which permitted the continuous bands of windows and rounded corners.[43]

A Modernistic Approach in the 1930s

Adding no meretricious "architectural" trappings, the architects achieved their effect by the opposite approach of dramatizing only what was utterly essential and typical.

CRITIC DOUGLAS HASKELL, 1939

As architects searched for appropriate expression for factories, they turned to American modernistic architecture, now usually known as the Art Deco and Moderne styles. The machine-derived aesthetics associated with these idioms had a significant impact on commercial building design of the era and seemed appropriate for factories as well.

The irregular massing of skyscrapers erected during the heyday of the modernistic styles offered a way to free large industrial lofts from the boxlike form that economic and functional considerations traditionally had dictated. The Port of New York Authority Commerce Building (c. 1932; Abbott, Merkt & Company, architects; New York City), which occupied an entire block, was governed by setback provisions of the city building code. Its highly modeled form, with setbacks at the taller end portions and crowning the long midsection, provided both relief in the massing of the structure and a means of avoiding monotonous gridded facades.[44]

The American Moderne idiom and its horizontal banding was evoked in industrial loft buildings, which for functional reasons had as much window area as possible. The tentative detailing of early lofts with continuous glazing, like that of the James Lees & Sons Co. (1922; Ballinger Co.; Bridgeport, Pennsylvania; see fig. 7.8), became more assured during the 1930s. An addition to the American Can Co. plant (c. 1937; Carl G. Preis, architect and engineer; Jersey City, New Jersey), where only horizontal bands interrupted the expanses of steel sash, seemed startlingly light in form compared to the older sections of the complex. The exterior envelope of an eight-story corn mill for General Foods (1937; H. K. Ferguson Co., engineers and builders; Kankakee, Illinois; fig. 10.14) also consisted of continuous concrete spandrels and industrial sash. Setbacks at the ends of the structure added complexity in massing to a building that was intended to have a "clean-cut, pleasing exterior without resort to ornament."[45]

After the hiatus in building during the depression years of the early 1930s, industrial buildings often exhibited a bold Moderne look and featured sleek and smooth exteriors (most likely walls of reinforced concrete or concrete stucco) and modernistic motifs. Plants and office buildings were made to appear efficient and up-to-date through the use of rounded corners, steel canopies, horizontal bands, and strip windows. The Austin Co. promoted this fresh, progressive look for industry through its "Industry Goes Modern" advertising campaign in *Fortune* magazine.[46]

Architectural critic Douglas Haskell characterized larger projects in this mode as having "pseudo-streamlined monumentalism." A limited number of strong motifs dominated this work, such as the central tower that was a counterpoint to the long bands of glass block and terra cotta on the

FIGURE 10.14 Bands of concrete spandrels and continuous glazing formed the exterior envelope of a corn mill designed by the H. K. Ferguson Co.

Campana Sales Company factory (c. 1937; Childs & Smith, Frank D. Chase, associated architects and engineer; Batavia, Illinois). The Church & Dwight plant (c. 1940; The Austin Co.; Syracuse, New York) was another noted design of this type.[47]

The Industrial Modernism of the Production Shed

In buildings for heavy industry, such dominant forms as the high monitor roof or the butterfly truss roof often confer striking interest; or else the simple great scale of walls all of glass gives a surprising dignity.

CRITIC TALBOT HAMLIN, 1940

Another strain of industrial modernism developed from the manner in which engineers designed production sheds. From the 1890s on, this type of factory building was continually modernized and was, quite literally, engineered as a master machine. The bold, organic form and detailing of engineered curtain walls had few ties to established conventions of academic architecture. As engineer Charles Evan Fowler noted, the engineer, as building designer, was forced to abandon all aid and comfort from the Old World and the past (traditional architecture) because of the newness of his material—steel. When presented with a project of this type, architects seemed willing to follow the lead of engineers.

As noted in the first section of this chapter, the steel frames of one-story factories were generally enclosed by a protective and glazed curtain wall that concealed the framing within. When sash and sheathing were placed on the exterior of the steel frame, functional demands for glazing—not the dimensions of the steel-framed bay—governed wall articulation. As the walls of buildings of these types were freed from traditional forms of load-bearing elements, such as window openings with vertical orientation, a functional and modern type of design emerged. The replacement of more and more sheathing with sash occurred at the time that the interior spaces were conceived of as specialized bays. Consequently, in the tradition of architectural modernism, an emphasis on volume and its enclosure characterized the design of such structures.

The freedom offered by the curtain wall and the emphasis on volume began to become more obvious during the 1910s. For instance, the long, unbroken expanses of a glazed monitor served as a parapet for the one-story Houghton Mifflin Press building (c. 1912; Newhall & Blevins, architects; Cambridge, Massachusetts) and emphasized the structure's volume. The Gorham Manufacturing Co. building (c. 1912; designed by the "company's architect"; Providence; fig. 10.15) was detailed to give the impression of intersecting volumes and to stress the main component of the master machine. The central crane-served bay projects slightly in front of flanking lean-tos and is terminated by a minimalist, flattened pediment.[48]

The curtain wall devoted to daylighting the industrial building could be manipulated in various ways. The main machine shop of the Consolidated Press Co., a division of the E. W. Bliss Co. (c. 1919; Hastings, Michigan; fig. 10.16), the work of architectural engineer Frank D. Chase, brings to mind the Fagus Shoe Last factory (1911–1912; Walter Gropius and Adolf Meyer, architects; Alfred-an-der-Leine, Germany). The volume of the structure and

FIGURE 10.15 This Gorham Manufacturing Co. building suggests how an emphasis on volumes and the central crane-bay evoked an industrial architectural modernism.

FIGURE 10.16 Architectural engineer Frank D. Chase used glazed white brick to frame the window walls of the machine shop of the Consolidated Press Co.

FIGURE 10.17 Architect Richard Sundeleaf intended that nothing in his essay in structural character could be characterized as ornamenting the Woodbury & Co. warehouse in Portland, Oregon.

the purpose of the walls were emphasized by narrow bands of glazed white brick that framed the window wall of each facade. Architect Richard Sundeleaf's warehouse for Woodbury & Co. (c. 1940; Portland, Oregon; fig. 10.17) was a stunning essay in structural character. Steel sash was set behind a structural grid of exaggerated, rounded vertical piers and projecting, continuous, horizontal mullions. The architectural firm Cory & Cory updated its interpretation of industrial modernism with the buildings in Johnson & Johnson's industrial complex in New Brunswick, New Jersey (c. 1940). Long expanses of strip windows punctuated sleek exteriors clad with light-colored brick, glazed terra-cotta tile, and marble.[49]

The Production Sheds of Albert Kahn

Industrial architecture must necessarily deal with the practical first, with proper functioning of the plant, with best working conditions, efficiency and flexibility, with economical and safe construction, and only last with external appearance.

ARCHITECT ALBERT KAHN

Albert Kahn, the most prominent American architect to specialize in industrial building design, practiced an industrial modernism based on the direct, frank expression of function. The designs Kahn's firm provided for production sheds blended the sophisticated detailing of an architect with the advances made by the engineering profession. The structures generally made use of the most recently developed and best-practice configurations for industrial buildings and structural engineering, though certainly the firm was responsible for innovations of this type. This complete immersion in the engineering aspects of design problems no doubt generated the firm's industrial modernism. It was this combining of the engineering with the architectural that distinguished many of the firm's designs. Kahn also stressed the need for simplification and the intelligent use of building materials to develop a sense of fitness in the external appearance of factories.[50]

With the Geo. N. Pierce plant (1906; with Lockwood, Greene & Co., associated engineers; Buffalo, New York), Kahn began to master the modernization of building for industry brought about by engineers and to respond to their aesthetic ideals. This project capitalized on the concept of the integrated production plant based on an organic plan and and buildings designed for specific functions (as described, in brief, in chapter 6). The Pierce plant was also a relatively early use of reinforced concrete construction. It would be interesting to know if Kahn allowed, had no alternative for, or insisted upon the unornamented, rationalized engineering aesthetic that prevailed in the project. The careful detailing and the duality of the standardization and restlessness of nonterminated facades present in the Buffalo plant remained visible in the firm's work.[51]

The distinctive form of the Packard Motor Car Company Forge Shop (1910; Detroit) was generated by the decisions to have the shape of the building reveal that a traveling crane was suspended from its roof trusses and to add features to improve lighting and ventilation. The architectural articulation of the production shed seems to have been an attempt to organize wall planes but keep them subordinate to the bold form of the envelope. Bay divisions were minimized with the use of steel columns only slightly wider than the framing elements of industrial sash. The complex grid of the lower walls, filled with paired doors, panels, and industrial sash, was terminated by the sleek, continuous band of louvers enclosing the side of the roof area. This shop was one of the few buildings of its type to receive the attention of the architectural press, though it was considered to be an engineering achievement rather than an aesthetic one. Perhaps the architectural profession was intrigued by the fact that an architect, rather than an engineer, had sanctioned such a frank expression of functional design; but maybe the real significance of this project was not its novelty but the architect's affirmation of an engineering aesthetic.[52]

Themes that would dominate in future schemes for large-scale production sheds were apparent in the design of the Industrial Works (c. 1915; Bay City, Michigan; fig. 10.18). The long expanse of one side wall (without an attached lean-to) was filled with bands of concrete stucco and steel sash that conceal bay framing within. Doors interrupt the lower bands in a configuration presumably based on internal functions. Architectural convention

FIGURE 10.18 Several themes that recur in the factories of Albert Kahn are evident in the Industrial Works in Bay City, Michigan.

appears in the end wall of the structure, where buttressed corner piers and a gabled parapet frame oversize window and door openings. The other end of the structure appears to be abruptly terminated, even sliced off, at a specific length. This dispensation with a compositional terminus reflects the standardized units of interior space and construction, as well as a modernist aesthetic.[53]

The Kahn firm again demonstrated its familiarity with new types of manufacturing space developed by engineers—series of adjoining one-story bays of various heights and widths—in the design of the Ford Motor Co.'s Eagle Plant, B Building (1917; River Rouge complex, Dearborn). This type of building had been erected for two decades, but only infrequently in the scale established at "the Rouge." Wartime materials shortages probably influenced the substitution of wood framing for the low, one-story lean-tos that flanked the immense steel-framed central portion of the structure, an area 51 feet wide and over 1,700 feet long in which materials handling aisles alternated with erecting bays. Though the building had a distinctive silhouette and the long side walls had continuous sash set above lean-tos, the structure lacked both cohesion in articulation and a striking architectural presence. The Eagle Plant was the first to enclose an entire Ford manufacturing operation in a single structure and on one floor; it was also the company's first steel-framed structure, though both of these practices were common in industry by the 1910s. Its importance lies in the milestones it represented for the Ford Motor Company's building program, more so than in the larger narrative of industrial building design.[54]

A more confident, integrated modern aesthetic prevailed in the design of the Ford Glass Plant at River Rouge (1922). Like the B Building, the glass plant consisted of a series of bays with varied roof configurations determined by the bays' different manufacturing and materials handling functions. A monumentalism was established by the uniform continuous glazing of the exterior envelope and arresting roof forms, as well as by the row of sentinel-like chimneys that rose near the end of the structure.

During the early 1920s, the production sheds designed by Kahn's firm exhibited a mature industrial modernism. His buildings of the late 1930s, including the Chevrolet Motor Division Commercial Body Plant (1935; Indianapolis) and the De Soto Press Shop (1936), manifested innovative structural engineering and celebrated various engineered factory roof forms. Kahn's architectural treatment of production shed roofs distinguishes his work from that of many of his contemporaries. Edged with smooth expanses of concrete stucco, Kahn's roofs often floated on top of glazed sheds. Another aspect of his work was the dynamic quality achieved by eliminating the exterior expression of bay framing and by nonterminated facades, which seemed to anticipate future expansion.[55]

Architectural critic Talbot Hamlin found a surprising dignity in the simple great scale and even a "magnificent classical regularity" in Kahn's glass-walled sheds and monitored shop buildings. These forms were always best when simply treated, as typified by the Chrysler Half-Ton Truck Plant of

1937 (Detroit). Indeed, the Chrysler plant was one of only two industrial buildings recognized in the Museum of Modern Art's "Built in USA, 1932–1944" exhibit.[56]

More aesthetic and engineering design work has gone into plans for factory buildings than has generally been acknowledged. Industrial buildings have incorporated both the influences of common, traditional methods of building and the most innovative or best-practice methods of construction. A generic engineering aesthetic has been combined with the most avant-garde architectural styling, and standardized or systematized design has been modified as demanded by functional considerations and paired with various exterior treatments. These dichotomies have been reconciled in many generations of commodious, substantial, and aesthetically pleasing industrial buildings.

GLOSSARY

The Terminology of Industrial Architecture

Note: This glossary draws on definitions in the *Oxford English Dictionary*; Cyril M. Harris, *Dictionary of Architecture and Construction*; Donald Friedman, *Historical Building Construction*; Russell Sturgis, *A Dictionary of Architecture and Building*; Louis C. Hunter, *A History of Industrial Power in the United States, 1780–1930*: vol. 1, *Waterpower*, and vol. 2, *Steam Power*; John R. Connelly, *Technique of Production Processes*; Henry J. Cowan, *Dictionary of Architectural Science*; Henry H. Saylor, *Dictionary of Architecture*; Webster, *An American Dictionary of the English Language (1839)* and *A Dictionary of the English Language (1853)*; *Dictionary of the English Language (1863)*; Stormouth, *A Dictionary of the English Language (1895)*; Worcester, *A Dictionary of the English Language (1896)*; and Whitney, *The Century Dictionary (1911)*.

Aiken roof A roof consisting of alternating high and low bays formed by positioning roof purlins to span the top, and then the bottom, chords of trusses; vertical walls were filled with window sash. The term was also used to mean a roof in which roof monitors extended across the width of the structure. The roof takes its name from Henry Aiken, a consulting engineer with a practice in Pittsburgh during the early twentieth century.

American round-arched style Architectural historian Kathleen Curran's term for the American interpretation of an architectural style that originated in Germany and was there known as the *Rundbogenstil*. The term *Rundbogenstil* was seldom used in the United States during the nineteenth century; instead *Byzantine, Romanesque, Norman, Lombard, Anglo-Norman, modern Italian*, or *Lombard-Venetian* denoted the idiom.

Angle, angle iron In steel-framed construction, an L-shaped structural member of iron or steel.

Arcade A series of arches, including their supporting members.

Architectural effect A term used during the late nineteenth and early twentieth centuries to imply that a structure had been designed to be aesthetically pleasing. For example, in 1888 William Barnet Le Van described a chimney capital as not essential to the working of the chimney but "pleasing to the eye by its architectural effect."

Archivolt An ornamental molding on the face of an arch that follows the curve of the opening.

Bay A regularly repeated interior space defined by beams and their supporting columns.

Beam A structural member whose primary function is to carry transverse loads.

Bearing wall construction Construction in which loads are transmitted to the foundation by walls.

Bent In steel-framed construction, a two-dimensional frame, usually consisting of columns and the truss they support; a bent is positioned transverse to the length of a structure.

Blacksmith or forge shop The building in which iron was heated in forges and beaten, or hammered, into desired shapes; it can be identified by the number of small chimneys that rose through the roof and marked the location of the forges within.

Boiler house A freestanding structure, or half of a boiler and engine house complex in which steam boilers were situated. Boilers not housed in separate buildings were installed in the boiler room.

Boiler shop The portion of the works, often a freestanding structure, where boilers were assembled.

Bollard A post of metal or concrete positioned at a door frame or corner of a building to protect the lower wall and frame.

Bowstring truss A truss in which the lower chord is horizontal and the upper chord is the arc of a parabola, or a similar curve.

Bull-nose brick A brick with a rounded corner.

Butterfly monitor or roof A roof shape with two planes that rise from the center to the eaves with a valley in the center; also known as an "M-shaped roof" and a "Pond truss roof."

Buttress A mass of masonry set at a right angle to a wall, as a pier, but having a greater projection.

Cast iron In building construction, elements of iron cast in a foundry which have high compressive strength and low tensile strength.

Clerestory In industrial buildings, the term referred to a series of window openings in the side walls of a monitor that provided light and ventilation in a manner similar to that of a more typical clerestory, a range of windows set in a wall that rises above the roof of another part of the same structure.

Continuous sash Long sections of steel sash supported from the top and pivoted outward by a mechanical device.

Continuous skylight A long expanse of sash set flush with the surface of a roof.

Corbel A horizontal projection on the face of a brick wall formed by one or more courses of brick, each projecting over the course below.

Corbel table A projecting stringcourse supported by corbels.

Cornice The projecting element at the top of a wall; a decorative development of a utilitarian coping.

Corrugated sheet metal Sheets of metal formed into parallel curved ridges and furrows to provide additional mechanical strength.

Counterbalanced sash Double-hung sash connected by sash cords or chains passing over pulleys in such a way that one automatically lowers when the other is raised; the weight of one sash balances the other.

Crane A hoist with the added capacity of moving the load in a lateral direction; cranes are usually classified by mode of horizontal transfer—rotary or rectilinear. See jib crane and traveling crane.

Craneway A portion of a structure, equal to one or more stories in height, that supports and provides space for the operation of a traveling bridge crane that moves materials both longitudinally and vertically.

Curtain wall A nonbearing wall that encloses a building. In factories, curtain walls of masonry, precast concrete panels, glass, or sheet metal are attached between columns or piers but are not supported by girders or beams of the frame.

Daylight factory A term that came into use during the 1910s to describe a building with wall area filled with windows to the extent possible. The term was often used to describe reinforced concrete loft buildings that had large bays filled with industrial steel sash; these structures had nearly double the amount of sash area as lofts with brick exterior walls. The term was also used to describe production sheds with large expanses of glass. The Ballinger Co. used the term *daylight building* in 1922 to promote loft buildings constructed with cantilevered floors that supported sash uninterrupted by concrete piers.

Dentil One of a series of blocklike projections forming a molding.

Double monitor A roof that incorporates a narrow monitor at the roof ridge (for ventilation) above a wider one (for light) that covers about a third of the building's width.

Double-hung sash Window sash with two vertically sliding units.

Elevator bulkhead A structure on the roof that encloses the upper portion of the elevator shaft.

Enclosure wall An exterior nonbearing wall in skeleton construction anchored to columns, piers, or floors but not necessarily built between columns or piers.

Engine house A freestanding building, or half of a boiler and engine house complex that housed a steam engine. Engines housed in main buildings of the works were installed in the engine room.

Erecting shop The building, or perhaps part of a structure, used for the final assembly of large products; its equipment often included vice benches, timber, blocking, plates and wedges for leveling work, and lifting tackle or cranes.

Factory An abbreviation of *manufactory* that denotes a building used for manufacturing. The term has been used to indicate a type of activity rather than to signify a specific type of building. *Factory* was used throughout the nineteenth century, though it did not thoroughly displace *manufactory* until around the turn of the century, when it acquired the broad meaning of "any place where goods or products are manufactured or repaired, cleaned or sorted, in whole or in part, for sale or for wages."

Fenestration The arrangement, or pattern, of window openings in a building.

Fink truss A truss used to support long spans that is in the form of three isosceles triangles, the outer two of which have their bases along the sloping upper chord.

Fire door A fire-resistant door assembly, usually of metal-sheathed wood, fitted with an automatic closing mechanism.

Fire protection A combination of materials, measures, and practices for preventing fire and for minimizing loss through proper design and construction of buildings, the use of detection and extinguishing systems, the establishment of adequate firefighting services, and the training of occupants in fire safety and evacuation.

Fire resistance Capacity of a material or assembly to withstand combustion characterized by its ability to confine a fire or continue to perform structurally; later meanings emphasized retention of structural integrity for a specified period of time.

Fire-resistive construction The arrangement of a building to limit the spread of fire by isolating hazardous operations and vertical flues, through which fire could quickly travel, by compartmentalizing a large building with fire walls and sealing off each floor from others, and by using fire doors and fire shutters.

Fire shutter A fire-resistant metal shutter, either mounted at the sides of the window opening or rolled down from a housing attached at the lintel.

Fire wall Usually an interior wall 12 inches thick and extended above the roof for 3 feet, all openings fitted with self-closing fire doors or shutters; a wall intended to stop the spread of fire. Modern usage implies construction that meets rating requirements mandated by building codes.

Fireproof construction Building construction in which structural members are of noncombustible materials. Buildings of fireproof construction were defined by the New York City building code of 1892 as "constructed with walls of brick, stone, iron or other hard, noncombustible materials, in which the floors and roofs shall be of materials similar to the walls. The stairs and staircase landings shall be built entirely of brick, stone, iron or other hard, incombustible materials. No woodwork or other inflammable material shall be used in any of the partitions, furrings of ceilings in any such fire-proof buildings, excepting, however, that the doors and windows and their frames, the trims, the casings, and interior finish when filled solid at the back with fire-proof material, and floor boards and sleepers, directly thereunder, may be of wood." The term was also used to refer to aspects of fire-resistive construction.

Fireproof An absolute quality that does not exist; the term is used to denote highly fire-resistant material or construction.

Fitting or fitting-up shop The building, or perhaps a section of a structure, in which "fitters" assembled smaller parts or where parts were brought together for final assembly. Before the widespread use of interchangeable components, the fitter utilized files, grinding wheels, and vice benches to make pieces fit together. Later, this type of work was more subassembly.

Formwork The wood or metal forms into which reinforcement is placed and concrete is poured in monolithic reinforced concrete construction.

Foundry A facility, usually a freestanding building, where pig iron was reheated and cast into molds. Foundries provided space for preparing molds, heating iron in furnaces called cupolas, pouring molten iron (often with the assistance of cranes), and finishing castings.

Floor load capacity The live load safely carried by a floor assembly, expressed in pounds per square foot.

Framed structure A building with a structure composed primarily of an arrangement of beams, girders, and columns, as opposed to masonry bearing walls and floor arches.

Gallery In production sheds, a side aisle, which may consist of a ground floor and one or more upper levels, flanking a central crane-served bay; also referred to as a lean-to.

Girder A large or principal beam employed to support concentrated loads at isolated points along its length.

Guy A supporting rope or wire anchored at one end and attached to a structure (such as a chimney) at the other end to stabilize it.

Head-house A relatively narrow multistory structure at one end of a lower, generally larger, one-story building. Head-houses fronted armory drill sheds, stood at the head of rope walks, and were erected adjacent to one-story productions to provide space for offices and activities that could be housed in a loft structure.

High and low bay roof A type of roof in which roof monitors extended across the width of the structure; also known as an "Aiken roof."

Hoist A pulley and rope or chains used to lift an object. The term also refers to a powered set of pulleys and gears that raise and lower a platform on which goods are moved, a platform elevator.

Hollow tile Structural clay tile; hollow masonry building units of terra cotta or fire clay.

-house Half of a compound noun indicating that a structure was used to keep for future use the material indicated in the first half, i.e. oilhouse, storehouse.

Howe truss A truss consisting of top and bottom chords connected by diagonal compression members and vertical tension members.

I-bar In steel-framed construction, a small structural member with a cross section that resembles the letter I with flanges extending from a central web.

I-beam In steel-framed construction, a major structural member with the same cross section as an I-bar.

Industrial engieer An individual who studies the problems of organization, personnel, equipment, buildings, and all the features of management and control in industrial or commercial organizations. The industrial engineer also analyzes plant conditions, applies remedies where improvements are possible, and establishes standards.

Industrial engineering A profession dealing with the organization, personnel, equipment, buildings, and the features of management and control in industrial and commercial organizations.

Industrial loft A multistory building with relatively large, open floor areas—lofts—in which various types of light manufacturing operations are housed. The program of an industrial loft is to provide adequate light, ventilation, and materials handling devices for production areas as unobstructed as possible by columns and auxiliary functions, such as elevators.

Industrial park An area planned and developed for industrial use and managed to provide utilities and other services to its facilities, which are either leased or owned. Around 1950 *industrial park* replaced *manufacturing district* as the term for such areas.

Industrial rail Rail of a smaller-than-standard gauge that traversed manufacturing works on which cars were either pushed by hand or moved by various types of power in order to transport materials throughout the facility. Spur lines of standard rail that entered works and extending through their yards were also considered industrial rail.

Industrial steel sash Sash formed of rolled steel sections holding relatively small panes of glass usually combined into large expanses with units of operable and fixed sash.

Jib crane A rotary crane from which the load is suspended from a trolley that moves horizontally.

Joist One of a series of parallel beams used to support floor and ceiling loads, supported in turn by larger beams, girders, or bearing walls.

Lantern Any structure rising above the roof of a building with openings in its sides that admits light into the interior. During the nineteenth century, this term was replaced by *monitor*.

Lean-to A side bay of a one-story production shed, lower than the central bay, and with its single-pitched roof it has the typical form of a lean-to addition, even though it was usually included in the original construction; also referred to as a gallery.

Live load The weight of all materials placed in a building; the live load safely carried by a floor assembly is expressed as the floor load capacity in pounds per square foot.

Loading bay An internal loading platform located at the shipping doors of an industrial or commercial building.

Loading dock or platform A platform, either timber-framed or of reinforced concrete construction, at the height of a cart, railroad car, or truck bed. A loading platform generally extends on the outside of a building along a railroad spur or adjacent to a yard area or street for truck access. The term *loading dock* may refer to a platform positioned on the interior of a building adjacent to large door openings.

Loft Originally, any upper floor, especially the one under the roof. In the United States, the term came to mean any upper level without partitions or elaborate finish intended to be used for manufacturing or storage.

Loft building A large multistory building leased to a number of tenants engaged in manufacturing, often in a single industry; a term adopted for the power building during the late nineteenth century.

Machine shop The building, or perhaps a portion of a structure, used for the cold shaping of iron and steel by means of machines.

Manufactory A place where goods are made; in American usage during the nineteenth century, largely interchangeable with *factory* and *workshop*.

Manufactures During the early nineteenth century, the collective term referred to products of art that were made chiefly by machinery.

Manufacturing district A term introduced during the first decades of the twentieth century for an area developed for industrial use by more than one firm; replaced around 1950 by the term *industrial park*.

Materials handling The movement of supplies, components, and products in the process of manufacture throughout the works and warehouses, as well as in mines and at dock facilities.

Mezzanine A partial floor or large balcony area inserted above the ground floor. In industrial buildings, mezzanines were used for tool and supply storage, toilers and locker rooms, and offices.

Mill A building specially designed or fitted with milling machinery used for grinding or reducing to powder. By the time industrial buildings were erected in the United States, *mill* was part of a compound term for a building fitted with machinery for a certain industry, such as a flour mill or textile mill.

Mill building A framed structure, a production shed, consisting of two rows of columns carrying crane runways and supporting a roof and usually flanked by lean-tos at the sides. The structure's walls (of brick, sheet metal, or some other type of fire-resistant material) and roof admitted light into the interior. This term referred to this type of one-story production shed, *not a textile mill building*, in engineering literature during the late nineteenth and early twentieth centuries.

Mill Construction A term used to describe slow-burning construction. In 1928, defined by the National Lumber Manufacturer's Association as a way of building in which the interior framing and floors are of timber, heavy solid masses with smooth flat surfaces, so as to expose the least number of corners and to avoid concealed spaces, which may not be reached readily in case of fire.

Mill engineer According to *Lambs Textile Industry* (1911), the mill engineer determined the general arrangement of a plant, the kind and amount of power, the arrangement of machinery to transmit power, and the design of the building.

Millwork Louis Hunter defined millwork as the machinery of power transmission that distributed power throughout industrial works and subdivided it into parcels of energy as required. It consisted of varied combinations of shafting, pulleys, bands, belts or rope, assorted toothed wheels or gears, and perhaps clutches.

Monitor A term in use by the 1880s in the United States to refer to a section of the roof of an industrial building raised for light and ventilation, the sides of which were fitted with fixed or movable louvers or sash; a linear version of a roof lantern. The term may have been adopted from railroad passenger cars with roofs raised for the insertion of windows; George M. Pullman's well-known private car of this type was named "The Monitor."

Ordinary construction Nonfireproof building construction that made use of floor joists and stud partitions.

Oscillation The swaying of an entire building resulting from the movement of cranes or machinery and unstable building construction.

Panel wall A nonbearing wall in skeletal construction built between columns or piers and entirely supported at each story.

Parapet The portion of a wall that extends above the roofline.

Pavilion A projecting section of a large building; often emphasized by the detailing of the gable face of an intersecting gable roof as a pediment.

Pediment The triangular face of a roof gable, especially in its classical form, framed by moldings.

Phoenix column An iron column of circular or polygonal cross section, composed of a number of arc sections with flanges projecting radially outward; flanges of adjacent sections were bolted together to form the complete shape. This type of column, originally patented by the Phoenix Iron Works, was later produced by other companies as well.

Pilaster A small vertical projection on the face of a wall to increase its rigidity or to provide additional support for a girder or truss; sometimes called a wall pier or engaged pier.

Pivoting sash A unit of sash that rotates about a fixed horizontal (or perhaps vertical) pivot, located near the center of the opening.

Plant A term that at the end of the nineteenth century began to replace *the works* as a name for a large manufacturing facility. One early twentieth century definition of *plant* used the criteria of 500 employees.

Plate In steel-framed construction, a thin, flat sheet of material.

Pond truss A monitor with a double-pitched roof rising to the sides, providing a taller wall where sash could be hung in a vertical plane. Tall M-shaped monitors, which were air outlets, were alternated with one or more air intake bays, either "Pond A-frames" or bays of a similar configuration. The name of the truss is that of its designer, Clarke P. Pond of Philadelphia.

Power building A large structure, often an industrial loft, portions of which were leased to tenants along with the provision of steam or electric power for manufacturing.

Powerhouse A facility in which power is generated and converted for use in industrial works.

Pratt truss A truss consisting of top and bottom chords and regularly spaced vertical compression members and diagonal tension members; used in medium to long spans.

Production shed A one-story industrial building engineered to enclose spaces of considerable height and to have wide bays yet the strength and stability to support overhead traveling cranes. A rectangular structure, often of considerable width and with roof lighting.

Purlin A roof-framing member positioned horizontally between principal rafters or trusses.

Pylon In the context of early-twentieth-century buildings, often of the Art Deco-style, a massed or overscale pilaster that often had a slight batter, or angle.

Radial brick A type of brick with a curved face; a radial brick was larger than a common brick, often 4 inches by 6 inches; the ends of the brick are the radii of a circular structure, such as a chimney.

Reinforced concrete construction Concrete masonry construction in which steel reinforcement, generally either connected rods or ribbed rebar, is so embedded that the materials act together in resisting forces.

Rigid frame A structural framework of welded steel or reinforced concrete in which all columns and beams are rigidly connected and there are no hinged or pinned joints.

Rowlock arch An arch built so that the ends of bricks are visible and two or more concentric rings of brick ends frame the opening.

Rundbogenstil An architectural style originating in Germany that synthesized classical and medieval architecture, particularly round-arched elements, which were executed in brick and locally available stone. Characteristic of the idiom were pilasters and horizontal bands forming grids, elaborate brick corbelling, and molded surrounds emphasizing arched door and window openings.

Sash A framework holding the glazing that fills a window opening; may operate in a variety of ways—for example, sliding, pivoting, and tilting; a collective term for the window sash of a structure.

Sawtooth roof A series of parallel one-sided skylights, or half-monitors, placed so that only north light is admitted into a building; also called a weave shed roof and silk mill roof. The roof projections, triangular in section, are positioned so that the shorter, more vertical slope is glazed and the longer slope forms the roof. Fairbairn used the term in 1865: "The shed principle lighted from the roof, or the 'saw-tooth' system." When this type of roof form became more generally utilized in the United States during the 1880s, the term sawtooth was used to describe it.

Shop A place in which work was done, usually distinguished from a factory by a smaller number of workmen employed or the more limited use of machinery. In 1814 Latrobe used the phrase *shops of the company* to mean the works, which consisted of a smith shop, boiler shop, filer's shop, ship joiner's shop, and carpenter's shop, as well as the office and warehouse. The term *shop* continued to denote the functional divisions of the works, even after they were brought together in open-plan, one-story works.

Silk mill roof A sawtooth roof; the name derives from the early use of the sawtooth roof, in the United States, on silk mill weaving sheds. Also, a combination monitor and sawtooth roof.

Skeletal construction A type of construction in which loads are transmitted to the foundation by a rigidly connected framework of metal or reinforced concrete and the enclosing panel walls and partitions are supported by girders at each story.

Skylight A glazed opening in a roof, either a simple glazed frame set in the plane of a roof or a box skylight, a structure extending from the roof plane with upright or sloping sides and its own roof.

Span The distance between two adjacent supports, such as the columns in a loft building or production shed.

Special purpose plant A facility designed for a particular manufacturing application or engaged in the continuous manufacture of a single product, such as a cement plant; it might have an unusual form generated by the arrangement of the production process or perhaps have built-in equipment like vats or ovens.

Specialized curtain wall A wall enclosing a framed structure with areas of window sash and sheathing determined by functional considerations, not by the traditional proportions and configuration of wall and window openings.

Splayed opening A window or door whose frame is angled with respect to the face of the wall in order to admit more light.

Stack A short steel chimney.

Steel mill building A production shed with a self-supporting steel frame enclosed by a lightweight covering, usually fire-resistant.

Store, storehouse Early-nineteenth-century terms for structures in which stores were placed for safekeeping. By the late nineteenth century, *storehouse* referred to a storage building in a manufacturing works, rather than an independent or general purpose warehouse.

Stringcourse A plain or molded horizontal continuous band on an exterior wall.

Transept In industrial buildings, transepts, often transportation corridors, crossed shop areas at right angles in a manner similar to how a transept intersects the main axis of a cruciform-plan church.

Traveling crane A crane in which a trolley moves across a bridge that spans overhead tracks; the assembly moves longitudinally as well, so that the entire floor area below and between the tracks is served by the crane.

Universal space plant A structure, perhaps of standardized design, that could be adapted easily for a variety of operations.

Vibration The shaking of a building due to the movement of its elastic floors and beams; movement caused by some external source, such as the motion of machinery or water flowing over a dam, not by a lack of structural stability.

Warehouse A house, or building, for the keeping of wares, or goods. In manufacturing works, completed items awaiting shipment were stored in warehouses, while materials and supplies were kept in storerooms and storehouses.

Warren truss A truss consisting of top and bottom chords connected by diagonals (without vertical members), which form a series of approximately equilateral triangles.

Weave shed A one-story structure to house looms. In Great Britain, a weave shed typically had a sawtooth roof, but those erected in the United States during the nineteenth century had monitor roofs prior to the adoption of the sawtooth roof during the 1880s and 1890s.

Web In steel-framed construction, the portion, or member, of a truss between the chords or in a girder between the flanges. Its principal function is to resist shear on the span.

Window wall A term that appeared in Fenestra brand steel sash trade literature for walls in which there are large, continuous expanses of sash instead of individual windows.

Wire glass A shatterproof material in which wire mesh is embedded between two layers of glass; it was reportedly "hardly known until the late 1880s."

Works The term used to denote a manufacturing operation during the nineteenth century. An engineering term of British origin, the works initially referred to civil engineering projects, such as fortifications, docks, and bridges, and then included the buildings and equipment of an industrial establishment. Americans adopted the terms *gasworks* and *brickworks* as well as *the works*, which they applied to compound facilities, such as ironworks, and to mechanized operations, like machine works. Indeed, Americans adopted the term for nearly all types of manufacturing operations.

Workshop A term used interchangeably with *shop* to mean a place for doing a certain type of work.

Wrought iron In building construction, iron shaped by forging—hammering and rolling—that is easily welded, superior to steel in resisting corrosion, yet has less tensile and compressive strength than steel.

NOTES

PREFACE

    1. Pierson, "Notes on Early Industrial Architecture in England," 1–4.

    2. Fitch, *American Building*, 26, 48.

    3. Lindy Biggs has used the terms *engineered factory* and *rational factory* to denote the introduction of predictability and order. See Biggs, "The Engineered Factory," S174, and *The Rational Factory*, 6.

    4. Peters, *Building the Nineteenth Century*, 33.

CHAPTER 1

    1. Descriptions in Barber, *Connecticut Historical Collections*, and Bowen, *Sketchbook of Pennsylvania*, demonstrate the mid-nineteenth-century use of industrial works terminology.

    2. The discussion of the meanings of various terms in this chapter was based on definitions in Webster, *An American Dictionary of the English Language* and *A Dictionary of the English Language*; *Dictionary of the English Language*; Stormouth, *Dictionary of the English Language*; Sturgis, *Dictionary of Architecture and Building*; Worcester, *Dictionary of the English Language*; Whitney, *The Century Dictionary*; and *Oxford English Dictionary*.

    3. Silsby, Race & Holly catalog, cover.

    4. *Worcester: Its Past and Present*, 130; *Age of Steel* (1890), advertising pages; Hess, "Works Design," 499; "New Thinking on Industrial Buildings," 98, 101.

    5. Ure, *The Philosophy of Manufactures*, 13. Cooke-Taylor, *Introduction to a History of the Factory System*, 3, also discusses the use of the term. *Factory* also had an early meaning as the business of "factors," agents who transacted business for nonresident plantation owners. Tann, *The Development of the Factory*, 5, notes the emergence of workshops that were not adjuncts to dwellings, and that contained several forges or looms, as an embryonic type of factory.

6. Webster, *American Dictionary of the English Language*, 1839; George M. Price, The Modern Factory, 66.

7. Stilgoe, "Molding the Industrial Zone Aesthetic" and *Metropolitan Corridor*, and Nye, *American Technological Sublime*, have explored this aspect of American industry. Wosk, *Breaking Frame*, also discusses the artistic interpretation of technology and industry.

8. Works of that type included Bishop, *A History of American Manufacturers*; *Industrial America*; Lossing, *The American Centenary*; Greeley et al., *The Great Industries of the United States*; Bolles, *Industrial History of the United States*; and Van Slycke, *Representatives of New England Manufactures*. Several histories of individual firms appear in the bibliography.

9. Candee, "The 'Great Factory' at Dover, New Hampshire," 49, and "Architecture and Corporate Planning," 17, 40. According to Candee, builders sought permission to measure as well as inspect the Lowell mills. Consequently, the standard four-story mill with monitor roof of the 1830s, and then the five-story mill with plain roof of the 1840s, became templates for other mills.

10. Navin, *The Whitin Machine Works*, 36; Charles Bigelow, cited and attributed to Bigelow in Duncan Hay, "Building 'The New City on the Merrimack,' " 117.

11. "Convenient Foundry Arrangement," 1; C. P. Turner, "The Senior Mechanics' Trip to New England," 112–116; Gifford, "Design of the King Bridge Company's New Riveting Shop," 281; Meakin, *Model Factories and Villages*, 85.

12. "Buffalo Steam Engine Works," 191, was a reprint of a description from the *Buffalo American*, which suggests that local newspapers were a source for such articles prior to their appearance in technical journals. "Industries in America," 17. See Pursell, "Testing a Carriage," for a list of the articles. In "Public Relations or Public Understanding?," 591, David A. Hounshell reports that the description of the McCormick Reaper Works that appeared in the May 14, 1881, issue was prepared by Cyrus McCormick Jr. as an idealized description of his operation.

13. "Visit to the works" articles to be featured in many types of technical periodicals. They continued to appear in publications such as *Iron Age*, *American Machinist*, and *Foundry* into the twentieth century.

14. Webster defines *commodious* in this manner throughout the nineteenth century. Reyner Banham, *A Concrete Atlantis*, notes the effort to provide commodiousness in factory buildings. Shriner, *Paterson, New Jersey*, 187.

15. See Helena Wright, "Insurance Mapping and Industrial Archeology," 1–18.

16. Carpenter, "Shops and Shop Buildings," 240.

17. Corbett, "Facts, Factories and Frills," 233.

18. See Peters, "Architectural and Engineering Design," 28–30, and *Building the Nineteenth Century*, 347–349.

19. Stilgoe, *Common Landscape of America*, 4–5, 300–333. In the phrase *common engineering knowledge*, Stilgoe considers *common* to mean "understood and agreed upon by all."

20. Hubka, "Just Folks Designing: Vernacular Designers and the Generation of Form," in Upton and Vlach, *Common Places*, 426–432.

21. Candee, "Three Architects of Early New Hampshire Mill Towns," 158–159, 161, traces how two builders/architects became involved in mill building. Eggert, *Harrisburg Industrializes*, 63–66.

22. Trelease, *The North Carolina Railroad*, 53.

23. "American Machinery—Mattewan," 253, cited in Pursell, *Early Stationary Steam Engines in America*, 100; Samuel B. Lincoln, *Lockwood, Greene*, 74–75, quoting Gibb and Navin.

24. Van Slycke, *Representatives of New England Manufactures*, 1:193, 2:430; Shriner, *Paterson, New Jersey*, 200.

25. "A Model Pacific Coast Manufacturing Plant," 313–317; "The Main Shops of the American Locomotive Co.," 130–131.

26. Carpenter, "Shops and Shop Buildings," 240; Coes, "The Rehabilitation of Existing Plants," 370, quoted in Nelson, *Managers and Workers*, 12.

27. See Samuel B. Lincoln, *Lockwood, Greene*, 9–48; Eggert, *Harrisburg Industrializes*, 52–55.

28. Lintner, "Mill Architecture in Fall River," 185–196, also reviews the work of several other Fall River mill engineers; Navin, quoted by Samuel B. Lincoln, *Lockwood, Greene*, 73–74; Bahr, "New England Mill Engineering," 207–212; Frank P. Sheldon & Son, *A Half Century of Achievement*; Samuel B. Lincoln, *Lockwood, Greene*, 171–172. D. A. Tompkins, and Stuart W. Cramer were also prominent mill engineers with practices in the southern United States.

29. Bahr, "New England Mill Engineering," 211; Main, *Industrial Plants*.

30. See Biggs, "The Engineered Factory" and *The Rational Factory*, for a review of the industrial engineer's interest in factory design during the early twentieth century.

31. Sargent, "Design and Construction of Metal-Working Shops—1," 1; Wharton, "Planning the Industrial Plant—1," 433.

32. The American Institute of Architects did not allow its members to participate in construction work, though after World War II, the former distinctions between purely architectural and purely engineering services broke down. If the client lost any advantages from competitive bidding and the advice of disinterested professionals, he gained the services of an integrated team of designers, engineers, and construction superintendents with a design-build firm. "Building in One Package," 93; *American Silk Journal* (1897); *Harpers Weekly* (May 1911); *Factory* 14 (January 1915), advertisement; James C. Stewart Co., *Some Stewart Structures*; "The Construction of the Westinghouse Electric Co.'s Plant at Manchester, England," 301.

33. Chase, *The Modern Foundry* and *A Better Way to Build Your New Plant*; Ballinger Co., *"Super-Span" Saw-tooth Buildings* and *Buildings for Commerce and Industry*.

34. Turner and Dixon had worked for Ernest L. Ransome. The early work of the company was presented in the Turner Construction Co., *A Record of War Activities*, *Buildings by Turner*, *To Commemorate the 40th Anniversary*, *50 Years of Buildings by Turner*, and its house organ, *The Turner Constructor*.

35. Aberthaw Construction Co., *Modern Industrial Plants in Connecticut*; Stone, *History of Massachusetts Industries*, 2:1493; Stone & Webster, *Stone & Webster, 1888–1932*, 7.

36. See Grief, *The New Industrial Landscape*, for more on The Austin Co.

37. Navin, *The Whitin Machine Works*, 70.

38. "Aesthetic Consideration in Factory Designs," 243.

39. Perry, "Exteriors of Industrial Buildings," 323.

40. Hildebrand, *Designing for Industry*, 59–60, 153–157. The Austin Co., though based on district offices, also relied on the collaboration of experts, according to "Building in One Package," 93–95.

CHAPTER 2

1. Examples of conversions include a former church that was remodeled and expanded in 1867 into a warehouse at 41–45 Vestry Street, New York City, and a public school building on Staten Island that housed a carriage manufactory; New York City Landmarks Preservation Commission, *Tribeca North Historic District Report*, 114, and Sachs, *Made on Staten Island*, 55. The saddler's shop at the corner of Water and Fletcher Streets, New York City, was advertised in the *New-York Gazette and General Advertiser* (February 21, 1804), quoted in Rock, *New York City Artisan*, 116–118.

2. Dienstag, *In Good Company*, photographs following 46.

3. "Mansfield Machine-Works," 6; "The Manufacture of Agricultural Machinery," 370.

4. Greeley et al., *The Great Industries of the United States*, 513.

5. See Mark Brown, "The Architecture of Steel," chapter 3.

6. McGaw, *The Most Wonderful Machine*, 224.

7. Fleming, *America's Match King*, 16–18, 38–39, 110, relates the development of the match making firm.

8. Sawyer, "Mills and Mill Engineering," 513.

9. The standard module width in New York City was 25 feet, while 20 feet was the norm in Chicago. This width also reflected the strength of wood under tension and the convenience in shipping and handling lumber. C. W. Westfall, "Buildings Serving Commerce," in Zukowsky, *Chicago Architecture*, 80–82; New York City Landmarks Preservation Commission, *Tribeca North Historic District Report*, 22.

10. *Store and loft building* was the term used for multistory structures erected in New York City for commercial and industrial use; it appeared in 1862 in the first building code adopted by the city.

11. Noyes, "Planning for a New Manufacturing Plant," 76.

12. "New York Dock Trade Facilities Building," 329–332; "Starrett-Lehigh Building," 30–35.

13. Wharton, "Planning the Industrial Plant—I," 434; Rabinowitz, "Needs in Lower Broadway Loft Section," 881.

14. Harlan & Hollingsworth Co., *Semi-Centennial Memoir*, 172–177.

15. Wilcox, "Iron Works," 181.

16. Schiffer, *Survey of Chester County, Pennsylvania, Architecture*, 221; Milton Thomas Richardson, *Practical Carriage Building*, 1:12–14; Wicks, "The Manufacture of Pleasure Carriages," 79; "Manufactory of Otis Brothers & Co.," 164.

17. "The New Works of the Wason Car Manufacturing Company," 215–216; Lossing, *The American Centenary*, plate.

18. Garner, *The Model Company Town*, 135; Robert Vogel, *A Report of the Mohawk-Hudson Survey*, 91.

19. "The Manufacture of Standard Scales," 290.

20. Hogan, *Thoughts about the City of St. Louis*, 56; "A Model Establishment," 18; Arnold, "Modern Machine-Shop Economics, II," 281; "Foundry and Pattern Departments of the B. F. Sturtevant Company," 122.

21. In "American Iron and Steel Works," the series of articles by Holley and Smith, published from 1878 to 1880 in the British journal *Engineering*, the authors used the terms *iron works*, *steel works*, *rolling mills*, and *iron mills*. Hutchinson, "Mill Building Construction"; Seaver, "Iron Mill Buildings"; and Tyrrell, *Mill Building Construction* and *A Treatise on the Design and Construction of Mill Buildings*, address this type of one story production shed, not textile mills.

22. Banham, *A Concrete Atlantis*, 61, offered the term *single-story clerestory production shed*, which is shortened here.

23. Because iron founding and brass casting used different types of receptacles for heating metal, they were generally housed in separate buildings, though a small brass-casting operation might be situated in a wing attached to an iron foundry.

24. Wilcox, "Iron Works," 181. According to Wilcox, when the foundry was a wood-framed structure, the interior became covered with the dust of casting sand, which some proprietors considered to serve as a protective, fireproof layer.

25. White, "Cincinnati Locomotive Builders," 117; "Water-Supply Fixtures and Machinery," 148.

26. Simpson, *History of the Metal-Casting Industry*, 211–216; "The Russel Wheel & Foundry Co.," 991–993; Becker and Lees, "Building a Factory," 487;

Chase, *A Continuous Foundry for Automobile Castings*; Tyrrell, *Engineering of Shops and Factories*, 207.

27. "A Modern Steam Specialty Manufacturing Plant," 369–372; Biggs, *The Rational Factory*, 124.

28. Flagler, *A History of the Rock Island Arsenal*, 320, 326, 336. Flagler thought the army would consider this building the finest forging shop in the world. David Bigelow, *History of Prominent Mercantile and Manufacturing Firms*, 305; a portion of the structure was used as a boiler erecting shop. *Asher and Adams' New Columbian Railroad Atlas*, 115.

29. Perrigo, *Modern Machine Shop Construction*, 23; Tyrrell, *Engineering of Shops and Factories*, 206–207.

30. David Bigelow, *History of Prominent Mercantile and Manufacturing Firms*, n.p.; Van Slyke, *Representatives of New England Manufactures*, 2:498.

31. "The Holly Manufacturing Co.," 32–33 and plates.

32. Barker, *The Management of Small Engineering Workshops*, 10, 19; "New Shops of the Grant Tool Co.," 199; Fryer, *Architectural Iron Work*, 4.

33. *Asher & Adams' New Columbian Railroad Atlas*, 50.

34. DuBoff, "Electric Power in American Manufacturing," 38. This section draws on recommendations in Morse, *Power Plant Engineering*; Meyer, *Steam Power Plants*; Murray, *Electric Power Plants*; and Koester, *Steam-Electric Power Plants*; see also Des Granges, "The Designing of Power Stations," 361–369.

35. Wilcox, "Iron Works," 181. In the absence of a separate engine house, the steam boiler and engine plant or waterwheel or turbine were located in a main building of the works. In urban locations, the steam plant was often placed in the basement. For instance, in the William Wrigley Jr. Co. works (c. 1914; Chicago), the power plant occupied nearly half of the basement of the main manufacturing building. The boiler room, which extended up through the first story, was adjacent to a coal pocket positioned under the rail that delivered it, and a radial brick chimney rose from one corner; the engine room adjoined it. "New Home of Spearmint," 11–13.

36. "Boiler House and Stack," 90.

37. This section is based on the description of chimney construction in Le Van, "The Loftiest Chimney in America," 244, 276–277; Christie, "Recent American Chimney Practice," 267–279; Koester, *Steam-Electric Power Plants*; Perrigo, *Modern Machine Shop Construction*, 61–66; and Babcock & Wilcox, *Steam*. See Meyer, *Steam Power Plants*, 131, for recommendations of chimney heights for various types of coal fuel. According to Le Van, the just completed Clark Thread Co. chimney, at 335 feet in height, was considered the tallest chimney in the United States in 1888.

38. Christie, "Recent American Chimney Practice," 267, reported that only three radial chimneys, ordered from Europe, were erected in the United States prior to 1900.

CHAPTER 3

1. Wilcox, "Iron Works," 181, addressed several of these concerns.

2. "Manufacturing Corporations and Manufacturing Villages," 241–243.

3. The literature on company towns includes Garner, *The Model Company Town* and *The Company Town*; Mulrooney, *A Legacy of Coal*, chap. 2 ("The Coal Company Town"), 9–29; and Coolidge, *Mill and Mansion*.

4. Becker and Lees, "Building a Factory," 241–242.

5. Fleming, *America's Match King*, 95.

6. During the 1880s, the machine shop typically comprised about a third of the space of the manufacturing works, according to Hunter, *A History of Industrial Power in the United States*, vol. 2, *Steam Power*, 504, which reported the

findings of the tenth federal census (1880). A similar presence for the machine shop was reported thirty years later, when two British engineers noted that in engineering works the machine shop occupied 35 percent of the floor space, the fitting and erecting shop 20 percent, and the foundry 25 percent of many works. Gibson and Home-Morton, "The Design of Industrial Works," 138.

7. David Bigelow, *History of Prominent Mercantile and Manufacturing Firms*, 277. The Providence Tool Co. was established in 1845 and expanded during the following decade. For example, the Oswego Starch works had over three miles of piping and thirty-three large pumps to move starch suspended in water through the cisterns and vats of the works; *Asher and Adams' New Columbian Railroad Atlas*, 179.

8. Giedion, *Mechanization Takes Command*, 90–92, traces the origins of mechanized production in several industries and documents both the use of these materials handling methods by Johann Georg Bodmer in a machine shop in England and Bodmer's interest in the endless belt for delivering fuel to furnaces. Charles Bigelow, "Memoranda."

9. Edwin Harrington, Son & Co. *Harrington Hoists, Overhead Railway, Travelling Cranes*; "An Overhead Tramrail System," 1; Woodworth, "The Manufacture of Agricultural Machinery," 370.

10. Bolz and Hagemann, *Materials Handling Handbook*, 4.6.

11. "The New Works of the Wason Car Manufacturing Company," 215.

12. When a plant required several tracks, the best layout was considered to be a "ladder turnout," a line that made an acute angle with the main track, from which extended a number of parallel tracks. Becker and Lees, "Building a Factory," 377–380.

13. Glynn, *Rudimentary Treatise*, 23, 39; Towne, *A Treatise on Cranes*, 4; Outerbridge, "Foundry Cranes," 211–223.

14. Du Pont, "Location and Constructions," 206–212 in *Life of Eleuthère Irénée du Pont*. E. I. du Pont had worked in powder manufacture at Essonne and studied with Lavoisier.

15. Lozier, "Taunton & Mason," 345–350, notes that an additional machine shop was erected in 1848 and that more construction took place when the firm began to manufacture locomotives. The Mason Machine Works was featured in *Asher and Adams' New Columbian Railroad Atlas*, 116, and Van Slycke, *Representatives of New England Manufactures*, 2:432. Van Slycke credits William Mason with providing plans for the works.

16. An advertisement in *Scientific American* 42 (November 4, 1848): 55, offering room and power for rent in the "West Street [sic] Foundry, at the corner of Beach and West streets," appears to be for the West Point Foundry and suggests the size of these buildings: three rooms, 40 feet square; one room, 60 feet by 40 feet. A drawing of the facility by David Matthew, a former employee, appeared in "Dawn of the Railroad," 65. Studley, *Connecticut*, 52.

17. "The New Works of the Wason Car Manufacturing Company," 215–216.

18. Arnold, "Modern Machine-Shop Economics, II," 264, considered this works to be especially influential during the mid–nineteenth century.

19. David Bigelow, *History of Prominent Mercantile and Manufacturing Firms*, 474; *Asher and Adams' New Columbian Railroad Atlas*, 88; McCabe, "A Visit to R. Hoe & Co.'s Great New York Plant."

20. Pursell, *Early Stationary Steam Engines in America*, 98–99.

21. Harlan & Hollingsworth Co., *Semi-Centennial Memoir*, 367, and *The Harlan & Hollingsworth Company Ship and Car Builders*.

22. Greeley et al., *The Great Industries of the United States*, 283–284; Kornblith, "From Artisans to Businessmen," 216.

23. Wilcox, "Iron Works," 180–181. The plan was reproduced in Hunter, *A History of Industrial Power in the United States, 1780–1930*, vol. 1, *Waterpower*, 447.

24. Fryer, *Architectural Iron Work*, 2–5. Fryer also emphasized the importance of transportation advantages, good telegraphic and mail connections, and an available skilled labor force.

25. Bridesburg Manufacturing Co., *Descriptive Catalogue*, frontispiece.

26. Enterprise Manufacturing Co., *Catalogue* and *Catalogue and Price List*.

27. J. Estey & Co., *The Estey Organs*; Van Slyke, *Representatives of New England Manufactures*, 1:247.

28. Flagler, *A History of the Rock Island Arsenal*, 118–125.

29. Carver, "Reinforced Concrete Building Work for the United Shoe Machinery Co.," 537–538; Alford and Farrell, "Factory Construction and Arrangement," 1141–1166; Noyes, "Planning for a New Manufacturing Plant," 72–73. Starrett, "Building the Remington Arms Plant," 37–40; Wharton, "Planning the Industrial Plant—1," 433.

30. Becker and Lees, "Building a Factory," 242–244. Jones, *The Administration of Industrial Enterprises*, 85, used the term "Duplicate I" plan; he also illustrated accretionary and quadrilateral plans.

31. "A Large Southern Manufactory," 286; White, "Richmond Locomotive Builders," 68–88. White reports that the facility was updated with larger cranes and new boiler and erecting shops for the Richmond Locomotive and Engine Works and again in 1902 with an erecting shop built by the American Locomotive Company.

32. Arnold, "Modern Machine-Shop Economics, II," 264.

33. "Some Considerations Affecting the Location and Design of Machine Shops," 17–18; Berg, *American Railway Shop Systems*, 24.

34. Arnold, "Modern Machine-Shop Economics, III," 474–477.

35. Ibid., 471–472.

36. "The Ambridge Plant of the American Bridge Co." (January 23, 1904), 102–104; Brill, "Location, Layout and Construction of Manufacturing Plants," 156.

37. Taber, "Tool Plant Reflects New Ideas," 344–345.

38. The facility is depicted as Nathan Haskins' Machinery Depot in David Bigelow, *History of Prominent Mercantile and Manufacturing Firms*, 477, and in "The Works of the Walworth Manufacturing Company," 92. Farmer, *The History of Detroit and Michigan*, 820.

39. Perrigo, "Efficient Departmental Arrangement," 1207–1210.

40. Coes, "The Rehabilitation of Existing Plants," 560–563; Talbot Hamlin, "Factories as Architecture," 480.

41. The Allis-Chalmers works were published many times, including "The New Works of the Edward P. Allis Co.," 382–384, and "The Great West-Allis Plant of the Allis-Chalmers Company," 285–289. The plan of the Allis-Chalmers Co. works was also noted in Sargent, "Design and Construction of Metal-Working Shops—2," 85–86, 89; Becker and Lees, "Building a Factory," 246; Wharton, "Planning the Industrial Plant—1," 436; and Day, *Works Management Library*, 229. See also Peterson, *An Industrial Heritage*, 102–111.

42. Sargent, "Design and Construction of Metal-Working Shops—3," 169. In his series, which began in September 1908 and ran for several months, Sargent presented a sophisticated analysis and rationale for metal-working shop layout. He focused on the planning process, not the design of buildings, and compared and analyzed plant layouts, the space requirements of various departments, and features of manufacturing buildings, as well as cost-effectiveness.

43. A very similar layout, with the shops and erecting bay turned so that the shops were parallel with the foundry rather than the erecting bay, was presented as a "Typical Layout of a Manufacturing Plant" in Turner and Perrigo, *Machine Shop Work and Management*, 13–18.

44. "Destruction by Fire of the Famous Whitely Shops," 224.

45. "Notes of Travel," 331–332.

46. Bush, *Working with the World*, 17–79; "An Apartment Hotel for Factories," 16; Schipper, "Terminal City," 249–255. See also "Bush Tenant Factories," 419–427, and "Erection of a Reinforced Concrete Factory for the Bush Terminal Co.," 282–284, and "The Reinforced Concrete Factories for the Bush Terminal," 36.

47. "A Description of What Has Been Accomplished in Eight Years," 1–9; Joy, "The Central Manufacturing District, Chicago, Ill., Part 1," 123–127, and "The Central Manufacturing District, Chicago, Ill., Part 2," 177–182; Condit, *Chicago, 1910–1929*, 139–141; Lochmoeller et al., *Industrial Development Handbook*, 11–12.

48. Lochmoeller et al., *Industrial Development Handbook*, 12, 14; Condit, *Chicago, 1910–1929*, notes that the Clearing Industrial District was established in 1898 as a classification yard and expanded around the time of World War I as an organized industrial enclave. Dickinson Industrial Development advertisement, *Central Manufacturing District Magazine* 5 (August 1921); Jamme, "Developing an Industrial District," 12.

49. Emerson and Naehring, *Origins of Industrial Engineering*, 95.

50. Samuel B. Lincoln, *Lockwood, Greene*, 134; Kimball, *Principles of Industrial Organization*, 81.

51. Collins, "The Design and Construction of Industrial Buildings," 906–915; Noyes, "Planning for a New Manufacturing Plant," 68, and McConnell, "Industrial Plant Design," 15, 17, warned against designs that were too specialized.

52. Jones, *The Administration of Industrial Enterprises*, 70; Biggs, "The Engineered Factory," S179.

CHAPTER 4

1. Hunter and Bryant, *A History of Industrial Power in the United States, 1780–1930*, vol. 3, *The Transmission of Power*, 115, note that the term *power transmission* applies to the long-range outdoor transport of energy, as in the transmission of power by utilities. *Power distribution* was the process that took place in factories and other shorter distances in applications of hundreds of feet to a mile.

2. Fairbairn, *The Principles of Mechanism*, 175–177; Fitch, *American Building*, 121.

3. The plan for this works is illustrated in Pursell, *Early Stationary Steam Engines in America*, 55–57, and Hunter and Bryant, *A History of Industrial Power in the United States, 1780–1930*, vol. 3, *The Transmission of Power*, 29–30. The works also had a "man wheel" or tread wheel to supplement the horse walk. Latrobe used a 40-foot-square module for the shops and mill area, which was in the center of a 120-foot-long, two-story structure. Broehl, *John Deere's Company*, 32.

4. DuBoff, "Electric Power in American Manufacturing," 69.

5. Woodworth, "The Manufacture of Agricultural Machinery," 374.

6. "New Shops of the Holyoke Machine Co.," 1–3; Wilcox, "Iron Works," 181.

7. Harlan & Hollingsworth Co., *The Harlan & Hollingsworth Company Ship and Car Builders*; Hunter and Bryant, *A History of Industrial Power in the United States, 1780–1930*, vol. 3, *The Transmission of Power*, 136–137.

8. As might be expected, Pursell, *Early Stationary Steam Engines in America*, 88, and Hunter and Bryant, *A History of Industrial Power in the United States, 1780–1930*, vol. 3, *The Transmission of Power*, 61–62, note the existence of the steam power building.

9. Hunter and Bryant, *A History of Industrial Power in the United States, 1780–1930*, vol. 3, *The Transmission of Power*, 59–62; *The Manufactories and Manufacturers of Pennsylvania of the Nineteenth Century*, 12; *Scientific American* 10 (November 11, 1854): 71, as quoted in Pursell, *Early Stationary Steam Engines in America*, 88; "A Locally Famous Old Beam Engine," 171.

10. Hall, *Biographical History*, 129.

11. Thorough discussions of textile mill building form and the use of power are found in Bahr, "New England Mill Engineering," and Duncan Hay, "Building 'The New City on the Merrimack,' " as well as the articles of Richard Candee.

12. "*The Transmission of Power* by Means of Wire Rope," 225; Staunton B. Peck, "Rope Transmission," 301–338, illustrates both interior and exterior drive installations. "The Ohio Falls Car-Works," 5; *National Car Builder* 2 (August 1872): 1 and (October 1872): 5; Lyon, "Shops of the Walter A. Wood Harvester Co.," 314.

13. "Discussion on the Individual Operation of Machine Tools by Electric Motors," 321–352.

14. DuBoff and Nye, *Electrifying America*, provide good overviews of the electrification of industrial power.

15. In *Power as a By-Product*, Charles Meigs Ripley argued that when steam was needed in the manufacturing process, steam-generated power was virtually a by-product.

16. This summary is based on Jackson, "The Equipment of Manufacturing Establishments," 807-820, and Crocker et al., "Electric Power in Factories and Mills," 840–841. Similar advantages of electric drive were noted in "Subject for Discussion," 1–28, and Gillet, "Electricity in the Machine Shop," 862.

17. In 1900 an American Railway Master Mechanics Association committee made recommendations concerning the use of electric power. Electric drive was not considered a paying investment for a small shop of one building equipped only for light work, though an electric lighting dynamo would be a welcome convenience and could possibly run a few labor-saving tools. For an extensive shop, the installation of a central power station and electric drive would always be advisable. Berg, *American Railway Shop Systems*, 80.

18. DuBoff, "Electric Power in American Manufacturing," 17, 140–141; Passer, *The Electric Manufacturers*, 238–241 noted that by the fall of 1884 Sprague motors for industrial use were ready to market.

19. Jackson, "The Equipment of Manufacturing Establishments," 816; James Robert Moore, "Electricity in Modern Industrial Establishments," 225. Aldrich, "Electric Power for Factories," 194–196, recommended that group drive be used for small machines of 2 horsepower or less. According to the Wilkinson Manufacturing Co. catalog, in that shop the two halves of a shaft with a central clutch were both connected to two electric motors. Consequently, the halves could be run independently, or combined as a single shaft. "New Shop of the Heoffer Manufacturing Co.," 171–175.

20. "Shop No. 3 of the Bullock Electric Mfg. Company," 283–284; Ranney and Hemming, "An Up-to-Date Foundry and Electrical Plant," 735–736.

21. Nye, *Electrifying America*, 232–233. Gibson and Home-Morton, "The Design of Industrial Works," 138, emphasized that the introduction of electricity was the most important influence affecting the shape of industrial buildings.

22. Aldrich, "Electric Power for Factories," 194–196; DuBoff, "Electric Power in American Manufacturing," 146; Hess, "Works Design," 502.

23. Glynn as quoted by Fitzgerald, "The Anatomy of a Victorian Crane," 185–186.

24. "Dock-Yards and Iron Works of Great Britain and France," 16, 43; *American Manufacturing* 13 (May 25, 1876): 8.

25. William Sellers & Co., *Illustrated Catalogue*, 302; Arnold, "Modern Machine-Shop Economics, II," 266.

26. William Sellers & Co., *Illustrated Catalogue*, 318, noted that the first traveling cranes were operated by hand and later by steam, and then by rope drive or square shafting. *Appleton's Mechanic's Magazine and Engineering Journal* 1 (Jan. 1, 1851) reprinted a notice from the *London Artisan* that McNicoll & Vernon's patented steam traveling crane had been recently introduced and its use had spread rapidly. "How [the] Electric Traveling Crane Came," 541, suggested that the first [powered] traveling crane in the United States was a square-shaft,

steam-power-driven crane, imported from England. One of the first American cranes of that type was manufactured by the Morgan Engineering Co. (Alliance, Ohio). Arnold, "Modern Machine-Shop Economics, II," 266.

27. William Sellers & Co., *Illustrated Catalogue*, 302; "A Large Southern Manufactory," 286; "New Shops of the Holyoke Machine Co.," 1–3; "A Model Establishment," 18, implied that steam engines powered the cranes.

28. A crane industry executive recounted that in 1881 an electric motor was used to replace the steam engine and long square shaft of early motorized cranes; "How [the] Electric Traveling Crane Came," 541–543. Edwin Harrington, Son & Co. (a Philadelphia firm) announced in its c. 1887 catalog that it had just completed designs for a traveling crane operated by an electric motor. In "First Electric Traveling Crane," 722, H. Harnischfeger recalled that a Mr. Shaw, instrumental in the development of the three-motor electric crane at the Allis Co., soon thereafter established the Shaw Electric Co. to manufacture cranes.

29. William Sellers & Co., *Illustrated Catalogue*, 328; John K. Brown, *The Baldwin Locomotive Works*, 189; Arnold, "Modern Machine-Shop Economics, II," 266; Walker Manufacturing Co., *Hydraulic Cable and General Machinery*, 1893; "The Worthington Hydraulic Works," 290–292.

30. "Enlargement of the Baldwin Locomotive Works," 554–557; Berg, *American Railway Shop Systems*, 24.

31. "An Example of Recent Factory Construction," 1329–1335; "In the Making of a Steam Car," 401; Tom Fisher, "The White Machine-Motor Company," 4, 6; "Unusual Factory Layout Designed to Simplify Operation," 1016.

32. Kurt Ackerman, *Building for Industry*, 24–26; de Maré and Skempton, "The Sheerness Boat Store," 318–324; "The Triumph Company's New Plant," 15; Ripley, *Romance of a Great Factory*, plate; "The Automobile Manufacturing Plant of the Studebaker Corporation," plate 132.

33. Wight, "Utilitarian Architecture at Chicago II," 257. Tyrrell, *Engineering of Shops and Factories*, 124, published a cross section of a building identified as a reinforced concrete warehouse in Chicago that had a crane-bay flanked by second-story balconies with cantilevered sections which may have been the Pfannmueller building. "Industrial Plant with All Structures Built of Reinforced Concrete," 256.

34. The craneways appeared with the construction of the additional six-story loft buildings. Grant Hildebrand, *Designing for Industry*, 52; Terry Smith, *Making the Modern*, 63–67; and Lindy Biggs, "Industry's Master Machine," 108–115, 160–162, imply that the craneways appeared as an addition to the original scheme. See also Arnold and Faurote, *Ford Methods and Ford Shops*, 387–389. Abell, "A New Development in Factory Buildings," 902–904; *Architecture and Building* 52 (February 1920): 26. Correspondence in the Brooklyn Army Supply Base documents, Cass Gilbert Collection, New-York Historical Society, indicates that the army sent a representative to Detroit in May 1918 to investigate overhead cranes and refers to a memorandum received from Mr. Ford in December of that year.

35. Bolz and Hagemann, *Materials Handling Handbook*, 4.6, noted the introduction of the forklift truck, the assembly line, and the mechanization of materials handling in storage and shipping during World War II as the major milestones in materials handling during the first half of the nineteenth century. Love, *Lengthened Shadows*, 27–65.

36. Bahr, "New England Mill Engineering," chapter 6; Snell, "Heating Machine and Other Large Workshops," 269–272; Brickett, *Yarns, Cloth Rooms, and Mill Engineering*, sec. 88, 53–62; "The Lunkenheimer Co.'s Fairmount Works," 185.

37. See Nye, *Electrifying America*, chapter 5, for a description of the impact of electric lighting and electric drive in the factory.

38. General Electric Light Co., *Bulletin*; Nye, *Electrifying America*, 191–192.

39. Kermode, "Factory Lighting," 621–623; Little, "Industrial Gas Lighting," 667–672; *The Isolated Plant* 6 (August 1914). Clothing manufacturers used Nernst lamps with prismatic reflectors for even light and lamps with shades and reflectors. See also E. L. Elliott, "XII—Industrial Lighting," 660–666.

40. Cady, "Industrial Lighting Practice," 56–61.

CHAPTER 5

1. "Hints on Construction and Arrangement," 306–307. Although the materials of the interior framing system were not stated, the text implies that they were cast-iron.

2. Carpenter, "Shops and Shop Buildings," 240.

3. This section draws on Woodbury, *The Fire Protection of Mills*, 121–132, and Tyrrell, *Engineering of Shops and Factories*, 122–136.

4. Wilson, *The Pennsylvania Railroad Shops*, 24.

5. "Shop and Mill Construction," 65; "The Advantages Claimed for Brick and Steel Factory Buildings," 1272.

6. Jenney, "Strength of Buildings," 139.

7. The New York City Building Laws (see note 27) were published in publications such as Fryer, *Laws Relating to Buildings in the City of New York*, and available to engineers and architects as recommended safe building practices. New York City Landmarks Preservation Commission, *Tribeca North Historic District Report*, 47, 100. The former lantern factory is at 429–433 Greenwich Street. Tyrrell, Mill Building Construction, 3.

8. Austin Nichols Warehouse documents, Cass Gilbert Collection, New York Historical Society.

9. Mallick and Grandreau, *Plant Layout-Planning and Practice*, 334.

10. Kidder, *Building Construction and Superintendence*, 440–441, also noted the practice of combining trusses and suspension rods to support floors. "History of the Detroit Dry Dock Company and Dry Dock Engine Works, History of Extant Buildings," 50.

11. "Manufacturing Establishments—Coach Factory of James Goold & Co.," 17.

12. "New Shops of Western Electric Co.," 561–562.

13. Woodbury, *The Fire Protection of Mills*, 50–51, used the records of the mutual insurance companies to rank the most common causes of fire in textile mills between 1850 and 1880. Foreign objects in the picker machines that opened bolls of cotton caused the most fires during that period, followed by the other sources listed in the text. "Recent Fires," 226.

14. Woodbury, *The Fire Protection of Mills*, 137, stated that floors made of brick arches sprung between I-beams were so heavy and expensive as to be rarely feasible. R. J. Walker, "Report of the Secretary of the Treasury on the Warehousing System," 2–7. See fireproof construction entry in glossary for a definition that appeared in the New York City 1892 building code. Fryer, *Laws Relating to Buildings in the City of New York*, 36–37.

15. Rosenberg, "Fire-Proof Buildings," 121–126; Corydon T. Purdy's entries for fireproof and fireproofing in Sturgis, *A Dictionary of Architecture and Building*, vol. 2, cols. 30, 33–41. The confusing aspects of historic terminology are evident in the section on "fireproof construction" in Francis C. Moore, *Fire Insurance and How to Build*.

16. *Asher and Adams' New Columbian Railroad Atlas*, 179.

17. Sprinkler systems are known to have been installed during the early nineteenth century in Zachariah Allen's Allendale Mill and in the textile mills in Lowell in 1845. Parmalee automatic sprinklers were installed in the upper three stories and the opener and picker rooms of the Mechanics Mill (1868–1869; Fall River, Mass.), according to Peck and Earl, *Fall River*, 130. Bahr, "New England

Mill Engineering," 161, notes that in 1884 the mutuals tested 373 types of automatic sprinkler units. Samuel B. Lincoln, *Lockwood, Greene*, 93; Woodbury, *The Fire Protection of Mills*, 37–40. See Cecil D. Elliott, *Technics and Architecture*, 371–374, for more on sprinkler systems.

18. Fryer, *Laws Relating to Buildings in the City of New York*, 56–60.

19. Sara Wermiel, who has extensively studied fireproof construction, described the stock fire insurance companies in "The Role of the Fire Insurance Industry." See also her 1996 dissertation, "Nothing Succeeds Like Failure."

20. *Cyclopedia of Fire Prevention and Insurance*, 1:121, differentiated between fireproof materials, fire-resistant construction, and fireproof construction.

21. See Pierson, *American Buildings and Their Architects*, 42–49, and Sande, "The Textile Factory in Pre–Civil War Rhode Island," 22–28, for arguments of this type. Pierson considers the mill tower to have cultural significance and, when properly proportioned, to be a dynamic climax in many bold and aggressive designs. Sande notes the similarity between the textile mill with a tower and church buildings of the colonial and early republican periods.

22. Robert Vogel, *A Report of the Mohawk-Hudson Survey*, 205–210; "A Large Southern Manufactory," 286.

23. C. Matlack Price, "Architecture" (1917), 49; King, "The Hawthorne Shops of the Western Electric Co.," 413–432; "New Shops of Western Electric Co.," 560; Kohn, "Architecture and Factories," 133; Griffiths, *The Story of the American Bank Note Company*, 69.

24. "A Description of What Has Been Accomplished in Eight Years," 9.

25. "Slow Combustion Construction of Buildings," 223. *Carpentry and Building* and other journals presented materials like the "G & B system of fire-proofing." Edward Atkinson noted the availability of products like "Air cell Asbestos board" and "Sackett wall board" in his entry "Slow-Burning Construction," in Sturgis, *A Dictionary of Architecture and Building*, vol. 3, cols. 530–533.

26. Mattison Co., *Ambler Asbestos Corrugated Sheeting, Asbestos Roofing Slate Shingles and Sheathing*, (1909 and 1913 eds.); Johns Mansville Co., *JM Asbestos Roofing*, Catalog No. 303, *Johns-Manville Asbestoside*, and *Johns-Manville Service to Industry*; Asbestos Protected Metal Co., *Asbestosteel for Roofs and Walls*.

27. Tyrrell, *Mill Building Construction*, 33, included a table of wall thicknesses required by Boston, New York, Chicago, Minneapolis, St. Louis, Denver, San Francisco, and New Orleans. New York City Building Codes, all published in the *Laws of New York*: 1862, chapter 356; 1866, chapter 873; 1871, chapter 625; 1882, chapter 410.

28. Freeman, "Comparison of English and American Types of Factory Construction," 22.

29. Many of the doors and other devices to seal off vertical flues in loft buildings were illustrated in publications such as *Analytic System Handbook on Fire Protection* and *Cyclopedia of Fire Prevention and Insurance*.

30. Fryer, *Laws Relating to Buildings in the City of New York*, 36–37.

31. Abbott, *The Harper Establishment*, 25–27.

32. Ernest Hexamer, *Hexamer General Insurance Surveys*, Map No. 820, Pennsylvania Warehousing Co., 1874.

33. New York City Landmarks Preservation Commission, *The Joseph Loft Silk Mill Designation Report*; New York City Department of Building docket books.

34. Brickett, *Yarns, Cloth Rooms, and Mill Engineering*, sec. 87, 55–65; Sturgis, *A Dictionary of Architecture and Building*, vol. 3, cols. 530–533; Tyrrell, *Engineering of Shops and Factories*, 214.

35. Duncan Hay, "Building 'The New City on the Merrimack,' " 250, 373, notes that vaulted walls were used for the 1852 Pemberton Mill and that this construction method had been tried at Amoskeag and an extension of the Merrimack mill at Lowell. All of the Lowell mills after 1854 had vaulted walls, which provided dead air insulation. The degree to which the inner wall added to the stability of the outer wall depended on the extent to which they were tied

together, probably with iron ties or hoops. Critics of the construction method believed that these ties conveyed moisture from the outside wall to the inner one noted "Slow-Burning Construction," 199. Kidder, *Building Construction and Superintendence*, 228, reported that the hollow or vaulted brick walls were little used in the United States. Duncan Hay, "Building 'The New City on the Merrimack,' " 408, cites the 1864 Central Pacific Mill in Lawrence, Mass., as an example of the shift to pilaster-wall construction practice.

36. Woodbury, *The Fire Protection of Mills*, 134; "Notes and Clippings," 208.

37. Montgomery, *A Practical Detail of the Cotton Manufacture*, 16–17.

38. C. John Hexamer, "Mill Architecture," 1–2.

39. A model plan with vertical elements incorporated into the main block appeared in Brickett, *Yarns, Cloth Rooms, and Mill Engineering*, sec. 89, 26.

40. Early uses of the term *slow-burning construction* include the titles of two letters concerning the subject published in the *American Architect and Building News* 5 (June 21 and July 12, 1879). The term also appeared in Woodbury, *The Fire Protection of Mills*, 3, 57–60, as noted by Candee, "The 1822 Allendale Mill and Slow-Burning Construction," 32; note 1 discusses the etymology of the term.

41. The planks could be joined by sheet-metal "tongues" in a manner similar to tongue-and-groove flooring for the prevention of the passage of dust through the floor. Plank floor construction was also noted to be less expensive and "firmer than those on the old plan." Montgomery, *A Practical Detail of the Cotton Manufacture*, 22–23, described the type of flooring associated with mill construction as providing strength and durability to buildings and did not mention its slow-burning characteristics.

42. Woodbury, "The Evolution of the Modern Mill," 10346; Candee, "The 1822 Allendale Mill and Slow-Burning Construction," 21, 30; Montgomery, *A Practical Detail of the Cotton Manufacture*, 22–23; "Fire-Proof and Plank Floors," 42–43, as cited in Candee, "The 1822 Allendale Mill and Slow-Burning Construction," 30; Sawyer, "Mills and Mill Engineering," 523, suggested that the idea of building roofs like floors occurred to many mill engineers during the early 1860s. Nimmons, "Modern Industrial Plants, Part III," 34–38; Freeman, "Comparison of English and American Types of Factory Construction," 19.

43. Atkinson's pieces included letters to the editor of the *American Architect and Building News* (various issues, 1879); "Slow-Burning Construction," which was included in *The Industrial Progress of the Nation*; and *The Prevention of Loss by Fire*. The *Cyclopedia of Fire Prevention and Insurance*, 170, criticized Atkinson for keeping slow-burning construction in use long after its real usefulness had passed.

44. Woodbury, "Standard Storehouse Construction," 247. Atkinson suggested this application of mill construction in "Slow-Burning Construction"; Perrigo, *Modern Machine Shop Construction*, 50–51.

45. "The Mill Type of Construction," 654; Wermiel, "Nothing Succeeds Like Failure," 260–261; Chapman, "Design of Industrial Buildings," 115; "Cost of Factory Buildings of Timber and of Concrete," 884–886. See Kidder, *Building Construction and Superintendence*, 454, 461, and Hobart, *Millwrighting*, 93, for more on the use of mill construction.

CHAPTER 6

1. Condit, *American Building Art: The Nineteenth Century*, 17.

2. Lyon, "Shops of the Walter A. Wood Harvester Co.," 314–315; Arnold, "Modern Machine-Shop Economics, II," 269.

3. Tyrrell, *Engineering of Shops and Factories*, 62–64.

4. See Pierson, "Industrial Architecture in the Berkshires," and Sande, "The Textile Factory in Pre–Civil War Rhode Island," 13–31.

5. C. John Hexamer, "Mill Architecture," 6, advocated the use of brick arches

over door and window openings rather than stone lintels because of the poor performance of stone during a fire.

6. Fairbairn, *Treatise on Mills and Millwork*, 114, described a structure with pilasters built in 1827 (see fig. 9.4). Munce, *Industrial Architecture*, 6, notes a warehouse with pilasters designed by Telford (1824–1828); G. D. Dempsey, *Engineering Examples*, 63–64; Duncan Hay, "Building 'The New City on the Merrimack,' " 160.

7. Benson, "Incombustible Foundry Buildings," 15; " 'Phoenix' Wall Construction," 315–320. The report on the Phoenix system noted that factory buildings with walls entirely of hollow tile were of recent construction. See also Squires, "The Hollow-Tile Fireproof House," 189–194.

8. De Wolf, "Mill Construction with Steel Frame and Tile Walls," in *Technology and Industrial Efficiency*, 484–486; the General Electric building was pictured in an advertisement in *Building Progress* 1 (1911): 350 and featured in Hollow Building Tile Association, *Handbook of Hollow Building Tile Construction*, 7. "South Philadelphia Works of the Westinghouse Company," 495.

9. Kurt Ackerman, *Building for Industry*, 16, 21–23; Peters, *Building the Nineteenth Century*, 211–218. Peters relates how Althans used materials, such as cannon barrels for columns, and integrated three types of cranes into the structure.

10. Condit, *American Building Art: The Nineteenth Century*, 27–28; Metals in America's Historic Buildings provides more information on the early use of iron in building construction. Kulik, "A Factory System in Wood," in Hindle, *Material Culture of the Wooden Age*, 330; Merritt Roe Smith, *Harpers Ferry Armory and the New Technology*, 277.

11. *Metals in America's Historic Buildings*, 50. Duncan Hay, "Building 'The New City on the Merrimack,' " 373–377, and Bahr, "New England Mill Engineering," 180, document the collapse of the Pemberton and its effects on mill engineering. American engineers also relied on the experimental work on the strength of iron performed in England during the 1830s and 1840s by Eaton Hodgkinson and Sir William Fairbairn.

12. Tyrrell, *Engineering of Shops and Factories*, 71–73; Francis C. Moore, "How to Build Fireproof," 968; "New Foundry for the Semi-Steel Co.," 405.

13. "Corrugated Iron as Building Material," 299.

14. Farley, "The Frankford Arsenal," 142–144; Milliken Bros., *Allowable Working Loads for Phoenix Columns*. Phoenix columns were used in the rebuilding of the Colt Armory after a fire (1867; Hartford, Conn.). Friedman, *Historical Building Construction*, 75, and Misa, 51–53, discuss the Phoenix column.

15. Comments by Grinnel following Sawyer, "Mills and Mill Engineering," 541–543, who asserted that the use of narrow but deep columns, combined with proper bracing, would result in a structure that would be rigid enough to withstand the oscillation of machinery. Grinnel, who presented this scheme as a theoretical design (rather than as a report on a building he had constructed), also emphasized the speed with which such a building could be erected.

16. Flagler, *A History of the Rock Island Arsenal*, 256; this floor construction was part of a fireproof design program described in detail by Flagler. [Scott], *Genius Rewarded*, plates; "The Brown and Sharpe Mfg. Co.'s Works—1," 241; Freeman, "Comparison of English and American Types of Factory Construction," 23, noted that the Manchester Print Works (Manchester, N.H.) and the Colt Armory (Hartford, Conn.) had fireproof floor construction. The Harpers Publishing Co., described in chapter 5, was another well-known example.

17. "The Plant of the Berlin Iron Bridge Co.," 318; Berg, *American Railway Shop Systems*, 90; Case, *The Factory Buildings*, 256.

18. Herbert, *Pioneers of Prefabrication*, 35–40; *Metals in America's Historic Buildings*, 74; Canton Iron Roofing Co., *Illustrated Catalogue*. Standard sheet size was 27 inches by 96 inches; curved corrugated sheets were available in several radii. These materials were manufactured in various thicknesses; sheets of steel

were recommended for roofing, and sheets of iron for interior and exterior wall sheathing.

19. The Watervliet Arsenal storehouse has been recorded by the Historic American Engineering Record (HAER) and is presented in Robert Vogel, *A Report of the Mohawk-Hudson Survey*, 25–43; the structure currently houses a museum. The Watervliet Arsenal storehouse was constructed in a manner similar to that used for the Sheerness Boat Store (1858; G. T. Greene, engineer; Sheerness Naval Dockyard, England). See de Maré and Skempton, "The Sheerness Boat Store," 317–324. Peters, *Building the Nineteenth Century*, 258–261, describes the similar construction of the Kensington Art Museum (1856), known derisively as the "Brompton Boilers."

20. "Corrugated Iron as Building Material," 299; "Corrugated Metal Buildings," 141. The firm of Schweizer & Gruwé of New York City offered a type of all-iron structure, illustrated in "Portable Metallic Sheds," 31; it was promoted as a quickly erected and portable structure (rather than a fireproof one).

21. Two views of the works, by different artists, depicted identical buildings and labeled the materials used; these views appeared in T. C. Snyder & Co., *Illustrated Catalogue*, and Canton Iron Roofing Co., *Illustrated Catalogue*, the successor firm.

22. Milliken Brothers catalog, 156; Berger Manufacturing Co., *Catalogue No. 10*, 28.

23. American Rolling Mill Co., *Catalogue A*; *Alcoa Aluminum Corrugated Sheets for Industrial Uses*.

24. Friedman, *Historical Building Construction*, 49, 69, 74; Seaver, "Iron Mill Buildings," 148–149.

25. Tyrrell, *Mill Building Construction*, 8.

26. Ibid., 9; Ketchum, *The Design of Steel Mill Buildings*, 1st ed., 164, also recommended a similar configuration for side columns where loads were not excessive. Johnson et al., *The Theory and Practice of Modern Framed Structures*, 487, suggested that roof columns and light crane columns might be constructed of Z-bars, channels, or plates and angles, though they preferred channel columns. For heavy crane columns they found it necessary to use plates and angles to provide a column of sufficient width. Dencer, *Detailing and Fabricating Structural Steel*, 159.

27. "New York Fireproof Column Company," *Sweet's Indexed Catalogue of Building Construction*, 290–291.

28. "The Frances Building," 9.

29. "A Modern Factory Building," 315; Sargent, "Design and Construction of Metal-Working Shops—2," 88. Starrett, "Building the Remington Arms Plant," 37–48; no architect or engineer is credited with the design of the plant, though James Stewart & Co. was the builder.

30. "Corrosion of Steel," 343; Frank P. Bennett, *How to Build, Equip, and Operate a Cotton Mill*, 97.

31. The term appeared in Seaver, "Iron Mill Buildings"; Hutchinson, "Mill Building Construction"; Tyrrell, *Mill Building Construction*; and Ketchum, *The Design of Steel Mill Buildings*, 1st ed. The term *mill building* for this type of structure never seems to have been widely used in the building construction field.

32. The early treatises on iron and steel mill building included those listed in the previous note, as well as later editions of Ketchum, *The Design of Steel Mill Buildings*; Tyrrell's expanded works, *A Treatise on the Design and Construction of Mill Buildings* and *Engineering of Shops and Factories*; and Perrigo, *Modern Machine Shop Construction*. Hutchinson, "*Mill Building Construction*," 247; Ketchum, *The Design of Steel Mill Buildings*, 1st ed., 1; and Tyrrell, *Mill Building Construction*, 9, all note the three types of steel mill buildings: steel-framed, masonry-filled walls, load-bearing masonry walls. Perrigo, *Modern Machine Shop Construction*, 27, advocated the use of load-bearing masonry walls. Tyrrell, *Engineering of Shops and Factories*, 98–100, offered cost comparisons.

33. Benson, "Incombustible Foundry Buildings," 14–16; Seaver, "Iron Mill Buildings," 140; Collins, "The Engineering of Industrial Buildings," 31.

34. "The New Lehigh Valley Shops," 302–305; "The Main Shops of the American Locomotive Co.," 130–131.

35. Tyrrell, *Engineering of Shops and Factories*, 193, noted that wood walls were little used in shops and needed to be covered with slate or metal siding.

36. Collins, "The Design and Construction of Industrial Buildings," 923; Nichols, "Choice of Type of Construction," 102.

37. Roth, *Connecticut*, 68–69; Berlin Iron Bridge Co., *Engineers, Architects, and Builders*. Charles M. Jarvis was president and chief engineer of the firm. The influence of the structural iron manufacturers is evident in Johnson et al., *The Theory and Practice of Modern Framed Structures*, which included specifications adopted by the American Bridge Co. in 1900. Bryan was the general manager of the American Bridge Co.

38. This foundry was in the Farrel plant that was north of Bridge Street. Roth, Connecticut, 165–166; The Berlin Iron Bridge Co., *Engineers, Architects, and Builders*, 54–55, 71–73. A building permit was issued for this building in December 1891; "History of the Detroit Dry Dock Company and Dry Dock Engine Works, History of Extant Buildings," 45 .

39. "The Plant of the Berlin Iron Bridge Co.," 317–318; Berlin Iron Bridge Co., *Engineers, Architects, and Builders*, 236–237.

40. Hall, *Biographical History*, 270–271. Kulik and Bonham, *Rhode Island*, notes that the Fuller buildings were still standing in 1978 and that the glass walls were mostly covered.

41. "Shop and Mill Construction," 65–66; "The Advantages Claimed for Brick and Steel Factory Buildings," 1272–1273. The George W. Stafford Manufacturing Co. building (by 1895; Providence) was also of composite construction.

42. "A Factory Building of Steel and Glass," 15; Banham, *A Concrete Atlantis*, 60, notes the innovative design of the Veeder building.

43. "The Plant of the Berlin Iron Bridge Co.," 318. The Berlin Iron Bridge Co. was purchased by the American Bridge Co. in 1900, when J. P. Morgan oversaw the consolidation of nearly thirty companies with Pencoyd Steel; Charles M. Jarvis, president of the Berlin Iron Bridge Co., became a director in the larger firm. "The Ambridge Plant of the American Bridge Co.," 620–623. The plant of the Modern Steel Structural Co. (c. 1901; S. B. Harding of the company, designer; Waukesa, Wis.) was a similar type of design. Massive longitudinal trusses (13 feet deep) were carried on rows of columns, 40 and 80 feet apart, flanking the central bay. "The Modern Steel Structural Co.'s Plant," 7.

44. "Progress in Structural Welding (VII)," 17–19.

45. J. F. Lincoln, "Erection of Buildings by Welding," 72–73; the Electric Welding Co. welded a bridge in Toronto in 1923. Condit, *American Building Art: The Twentieth Century*, 30; Thorpe, "Welded Structural Steelwork," 210; Marsh, "Arc Welding Structural Steel," 29–31. The structure was erected by the American Bridge Co., which did much of the welding in its Ambridge shops. The higher cost was attributed to the fact that shop-welding cost four times as much as riveting.

46. For the development of welded construction see Watson, "Arc Welded Structural Steel Buildings," 151–155; "Progress in Structural Welding (VI)," 16–18; Andrew Vogel, "Welding Trusses for Industrial Buildings," 11–19; and Caldwell, "Automatic Welding of Structural Steel," 30–38.

47. "Welding Builds a Factory," 90–93; "Electro-Motive Corporation Works at La Grange, Illinois," 15–31.

48. Condit, *American Building Art: The Nineteenth Century*, 240, notes that Joseph M. Wilson of Philadelphia began designing reinforced concrete floors around 1890, based on Ransome's early work, and that Niles Poulson's earliest reinforced concrete floors date from c. 1892. *Sweet's Indexed Catalogue of Building Construction*, 290–291.

49. The development of reinforced concrete construction had advanced in Europe, and the early texts on the subject available in the United States and publications like *Cement and Engineering News* (Cleveland) featured many examples of structures erected in France and England. This overview of the subject is limited to the use of the material for industrial buildings in the United States. Turner Construction Company, *Reinforced Concrete*, 3, 33; Humphrey, "The Progress of Two Decades," 22–42; Heidenreich, "Monier Constructions," 208–224; Neher, "Concrete Construction," 377–381.

50. Huxtable, "Progressive Architecture in America," 139–142, and "Concrete Technology in the United States," 141–149; Banham, "Ransome at Bayonne," 383–387, and *A Concrete Atlantis*, 31–37, 70–80.

51. The exterior appearance of the walls conceals their structural complexity. Wall thickness diminished to 15 inches above the third floor. The otherwise cellular wall had 4-foot-wide solid sections where the main floor beams intersected it. Wood window frames were set into the wall as it was poured, and wood blocks were set into the concrete for the attachment of trim pieces (a common method in masonry construction). Expansion joints were provided every 25 feet in the walls and floor slabs. Within the building, there were poured reinforced concrete foundations, tanks, and vaults. For construction details see "A Large Monolithic Factory Building," 188–189; "Reinforced Concrete Construction in a Factory Extension at Bayonne, N.J.," 16. The condition of the Pacific Coast Borax Refinery after the fire was used to validate the fireproof qualities of concrete; see *Reinforced Concrete in Factory Construction*, 1907, 55–58, and later editions.

52. "Reinforced Concrete Construction in a Factory Extension at Bayonne, N.J.," 16–19. The construction of the addition also differed from the original portion in that the corners of square columns were chamfered, making them octagonal in plan. All columns or piers had hollow rectangular sections and faces rebated to form seats for window frames. Special framing at the third-floor level supported two-story-high kettles. According to views included in Mensch, *Architects' and Engineers' Hand-book*, 102–104, Ransome was making use of the skeletal form of loft building construction that had been developed in Europe. "The Kelly and Jones Company's Concrete Steel Factory Building," 153–154.

53. Alford and Farrell, "Factory Construction and Arrangement," 1166, reported that when the United Shoe Machinery Company was established, a committee was appointed to investigate all existing factories and prepare a scheme for a new plant. Architect Frank M. Andrews of Dayton drew plans for steel-framed, brick-faced buildings with wood floors. But before work began, the decision was made to use reinforced concrete construction. Andrews remained as the architect of the project, and Ernest Ransome served as consulting engineer; the Fosburgh Co. was the builder. See also Carver, "Reinforced Concrete Building Work for the United Shoe Machinery Co.," 537–541. The Foster-Armstrong Company Piano Works (by 1905; Despatch, N.Y.), a lesser-known Ransome project that consisted of a row of five three-story buildings, a two-story structure and a foundry, was of a similar scale. "A Fireproof Piano Factory," 32–36; Huxtable, "Concrete Technology in the United States," 147–148.

54. Other firms that constructed reinforced concrete buildings during the first years of the material's use included the Turner Construction Co., the Aberthaw Construction Company, and John W. Ferguson.

According to Draffin, "A Brief History of Lime, Cement, Concrete and Reinforced Concrete," 41–42, and Condit, *American Building Art: The Twentieth Century*, 167–178, C. A. P. Turner should be considered a vocal promoter of flat slab construction that was developed independently by Turner and others. The Swiss engineer Robert Maillart used flat slab construction in 1900. It appears to have first been utilized in the United States by Orlando W. Norcross, a building contractor, who developed the idea as he was erecting a building near Boston. Norcross received a patent for the method of construction in 1902. The Leonard Construction Co. purchased the Norcross patent rights and erected a number of buildings. In 1911 C. A. P. Turner patented a similar girderless system and challenged the Norcross patent that was upheld in court. From 1914 to 1919 (when the Norcross patent expired), all systems of flat slab construction were licensed under the Norcross patents. Turner's work in this field was presented in his book *Concrete Steel Construction. Part I—Buildings*. According to Albert Kahn, "Reinforced Concrete Architecture These Past Twenty Years," 108, the flat slab system of floor construction was initially opposed by architects and engineers because new methods of computation had to be devised; it did become widely used.

Variations in flat slab construction were introduced by two engineers working in Chicago, Theodore L. Condron and F. F. Sinks, by 1909, according to Condron, "A Unique Type of Reinforced Concrete Construction," 824–834. Sinks first modified the conventional beam framing with the use of a broad shallow beam extending between columns. This paneled slab construction later evolved into a "slab-band" system. Condron eliminated the shallow beam and substituted the so-called "drop slab," a square pad or thickening of the slab between the top of a column and the floor slab, and Turner's radial bars were replaced with two-way reinforcement.

55. Larned and Warren, "A New Concrete Wood-Worsted Mill," 218–237; "The Maverick Cotton Mills at East Boston," 527–29; "Mill of Reinforced Concrete Construction," 237; Samuel B. Lincoln, *Lockwood, Greene*, 295; *Reinforced Concrete in Factory Construction*, 1915, 68–74.

56. Early texts on reinforced concrete included reports on structures of this type. A view of the interior of the Sautter-Harle & Co. building, Paris, appeared in *Cement and Engineering News* 9 (October 1900): 51.

57. "The Concrete Erecting Shop of the Ingersoll Milling Machine Co.," 446; *Reinforced Concrete in Factory Construction*, 1907, 89–100.

58. Erwood, "Concrete Construction at Rambler Factory Works," 199–201. The use of "Erwood pipe posts" suggests that the author designed the structures.

59. Foord, *The Factory behind the Great Arrow Car*; *Reinforced Concrete in Factory Construction*, 1915, 143–147; Hildebrand, *Designing for Industry*, 43, and "New Factory for the Geo. N. Pierce Company," 51–55; "A Long Span Concrete Girder Pierce Arrow Motor Car Co.," 529.

60. For example, a reinforced concrete one-story production shed erected in 1917 for the Delco Light Co. (Dayton) was extended around 1927 in steel-framed construction; "Large One-Story Industrial Building," 496.

CHAPTER 7

1. At the Colt Armory during the 1860s, gas lighting was used from seven to eight in the morning and from four to six in the evening. The shift of laborers that worked at night more often broke their tools and spoiled their work; on the whole, they completed no more than half as much as they would by daylight according to Barnard, *Armsmear*, 211.

2. "Enclosed Acreage," 337.

3. Woodbury, "Standard Storehouse Construction," 248.

4. Pittsburgh Plate Glass Co., *Glass, Paints, Varnishes and Brushes*, 125–141; Stimpson, "The Design and Construction of Industrial Buildings—II," 717, discusses the use of ribbed glass.

5. Francis C. Moore, "How to Build Fireproof," 967.

6. Pittsburgh Plate Glass Co., *Glass, Paints, Varnishes and Brushes*, 138, gives this date of introduction for wire glass. The Board of Fire Underwriters and many building and fire departments approved the use of wire glass by the late 1890s, according to George Hayes Co., *The "Hayes" Metal Skylights and Other Glazed Structures*. "A Model Fireproof Factory," 427; Perry, "The Kenyon Factory," 49.

7. Matheson, *Works in Iron*, 226–227, noted that cast-iron windows weathered better than wrought-iron ones. Wilson, *The Pennsylvania Railroad Shops*, 17.

8. "New Foundry for the Semi-Steel Co.," 405; "Steam Engineering Department Shops," 338; " 'Ferroinclave,' a New Fireproofing," 292.

9. C. John Hexamer, "Mill Architecture," 2. The upper sash of the Knisely brand double-hung automatic window closed upon the fusing of links located in the head of the frame, which released counterbalance weights. *Sweet's Indexed Catalogue of Building Construction*, 253; Stewart and Miller, "Reduction of Fire Hazards in Building Construction," 545–569. According to Huntington, *Building Construction*, 439, metal-covered windows were more expensive, more fire-resistant, and more durable than wood windows and more attractive than solid-section steel windows. Hollow metal windows cost more and were more fire-resistant than metal-covered sash.

10. George Hayes Co., *The "Hayes" Metal Skylights and Other Glazed Structures*, 45; Sturgis, *A Dictionary of Architecture and Building*, vol. 2, col. 38; *Sweet's Indexed Catalogue of Building Construction*, 250–261.

11. Reference list of James A. Miller & Bro., *Sweet's Indexed Catalogue of Building Construction*, 257; "Reinforced Concrete Construction in a Factory Extension at Bayonne, N.J.," 19; Mellor, "The Use of Concrete for the Bush Terminal Development," 339; C. A. P. Turner, *Concrete Steel Construction*, 252–253.

12. Alford and Farrell, "Factory Construction and Arrangement," 1149.

13. "Daylight Illumination for Manufacturing Buildings," 238–239. The substitution of American for British sash, presumably iron, represented a savings of $16,000 in the cost of the Austin-Nichols Warehouse (1913–1914; Cass Gilbert, architect; Brooklyn). The figure raises the question of whether the British sash was better or just more expensive than the American products. Austin-Nichols Warehouse documents, Cass Gilbert Collection, New-York Historical Society.

14. "Daylight Illumination for Manufacturing Buildings," 238–239; there was some concern about the heat loss that occurred through the large window areas.

15. Nimmons, "Modern Industrial Plants, Part IV," 148; McMullen, "The Concrete Factory," 9; "A New Steel Sash," 104–105. The announcement noted that the glass was held in place by spring-steel clips, eliminating the older iron pins, and other improvements in design, thereby confirming the existence of earlier types of steel sash.

16. Detroit Steel Products Co., *Pamphlet Y* and *Fenestra Steel Window Walls: The Blue Book of Steel Windows*.

17. David Lupton's Sons Co., *Lupton Specialties* and *Air and Light in Machine Shops*, 23; Hollow Building Tile Association, *Handbook of Hollow Building Tile Construction*, 5th ed.; Detroit Steel Products Co., *Fenestra Steel Window Walls Side Wall Sash*, 4, *Window Walls*, and *Fenestra Steel Window Walls: The Blue Book of Steel Windows*; Mellor, "The Use of Concrete for the Bush Terminal Development," 339; "A New Steel Sash," 104–105; Trussed Concrete Steel Co., *United Steel Sash*. The Patented Specialties Manufacturing Co.'s advertisements appeared in *American Architect* 99 (June 14, 1911).

18. This term was used in Fenestra promotional literature, for instance, Detroit Steel Products Co., *Fenestra Steel Window Walls—Side Wall Sash* and *Fenestra Steel Window Walls: The Blue Book of Steel Windows*.

19. *The Manufactories and Manufacturers of Pennsylvania of the Nineteenth Century*, 32; the double-hung sash had a 12/12 configuration. "Manufacturing Establishments—Coach Factory of James Goold & Co.," 16; *Asher and Adams' New Columbian Railroad Atlas*, 108; Hambourg et al., *Mills and Factories of New England*, plate 47.

20. Hambourg et al., *Mills and Factories of New England*, plate 48; see also plate 50; Hall, *Biographical History*, 177.

21. "A Factory Building of Steel and Glass," 15. Exposing the steel on the exterior required special authorization from the New York City Department of Buildings. Sturgis, "The Fischer Marble Works," 247.

22. "Brown & Sharpe Foundry," 194–196; "Details of a Brass and Iron Foundry," 2–3. The Holyoke Foundry Co. also erected a foundry of this type in 1882; "Convenient Foundry Arrangement," 1–2.

23. Tyrrell, *Mill Building Construction*, 13–14. Ketchum's recommendations were similar in *The Design of Steel Mill Buildings*, 1st ed., 266–270. Perrigo, *Modern Machine Shop Construction*, 53, 100, 101; "A Modern Jobbing Foundry," 247–253.

24. Zink and Hartman, *Spanning the Industrial Age*, 110–111.

25. "Reinforced Concrete for Factory Construction," 119–121; David Lupton's Sons Co., *Air and Light in Machine Shops*, 7, 15. Gerhardt was reported to have patented this type of construction. "Columns Set Back of Walls Give Large Window Area," 809; "A Mammoth Reconstruction Project," 57.

26. Fogg, "New Departure in Building Construction," 26–27; Ballinger Co., *Buildings for Commerce and Industry*, 41–43; David Lupton's Sons Co., *Air and Light in Machine Shops*, 26.

27. Ely Jaques Kahn, "On the Development of Industrial Buildings," in Bollack and Killian, *Ely Jaques Kahn*, [16].

28. The plant was designed in 1929–1930, and by the time construction work was suspended in 1931, its frame had been erected and the walls and roof completed. The structure was completed and put into operation in early 1939. "To Build Windowless Plant," 1114; "No Windows," 887; "Era of All-Metal and Windowless Buildings," 234; "A Windowless Factory," 303–304; Robbins and Folts, *Industrial Management*, 339–348; "Controlled Environment in Windowless Plant," 103, 107.

29. In 1931 the Blandin Paper Co. completed a windowless paper mill in Grand Rapids, Minn., designed by the Jacobson Engineering Co. of St. Paul; the steel and concrete structure with brick walls was detailed with panels of light-colored brick to suggest standard window placement and dark vertical bands to evoke pilasters, according to Boese, *Papermakers*, 188–190. "Rayon Factory for the Industrial Rayon Corporation," 28–29; Talbot Hamlin, "Factories as Architecture," 475; Papadaki, "The Design of Industrial Buildings," 14, 40; "Walls, Roofs, and Floors," 387.

30. Alden D. Walker, "Should Factories Have Windows?" 41; "New Industrial Building Boasts 'Controlled Conditions,' " 106.

CHAPTER 8

1. In *One Hundred Years of Roofing in America*, Vogel and Karamanski trace the history of roofing materials. See also Ketchum, *The Design of Steel Mill Buildings*, 1st ed., 146, 150, 154.

2. G. D. Dempsey, *Engineering Examples*, plate 5; Matheson, *Works in Iron*, 197; Holley and Smith, "American Iron and Steel Works, No. XXXVIII," 103.

3. Duncan Hay, "Building 'The New City on the Merrimack,' " 270; The Factory Mutuals, 226; Samuel B. Lincoln, *Lockwood, Greene*, 91, notes early flat roofs at the 1863 Tremont Co. mill in Lowell and the 1868 Mechanics Mill in Fall River. Vogel and Karamanski, *One Hundred Years of Roofing in America*, 33.

4. Quaker City Dye Works advertisement, *Industrial Review* (December 1882): xvi.

5. Fryer, *Laws Relating to Buildings in the City of New York*, 56–60.

6. *Worcester: Its Past and Present*, 133, 114; Lozier, "Taunton & Mason," 342; *Asher and Adams' New Columbian Railroad Atlas*, 116; the Mason complex also had buildings with single and double monitors and flat skylights in gable roofs. Bolles, *Industrial History of the United States*, 114; *City of Elizabeth, New Jersey Illustrated*, 110.

7. Farmer, *The History of Detroit and Michigan*, 821; *Hartford, Connecticut as a Manufacturing, Business and Commercial Center*, plate.

8. Condit, *American Building Art: The Nineteenth Century*, 21, 125; Tyrrell, *Mill Building Construction*, 9; Johnson et al., *The Theory and Practice of Modern Framed Structures*, 487.

9. *Appleton's Mechanic's Magazine and Engineering Journal* 3 (January 1853): 9. "Iron Roof in the United States Government Navy Yard, Brooklyn," 29–30; this roof was designed by Passavant, Archer, & Co. Berlin Iron Bridge Co. catalog, 58, 78, 64.

10. Birkmire, *Architectural Iron and Steel*, 43, and Kinne, "Roof Trusses," in Hool and Kinne, *Steel and Timber Structures*, 131–132, make similar recommendations. See also Weitzman, *Traces of the Past*, 127–130; Tyrrell, *Mill Building Construction*, 10.

11. Tyrrell, *Mill Building Construction*, 11; Sweet, "Machine Shop Roofs," 299–301; Nisbet, "Machine Shop Roofs," 152–154. In "Roof Trusses," in Hool and Kinne, *Steel and Timber Structures*, 135, Kinne recommended column spacing for various spans.

12. *Asher and Adams' New Columbian Railroad Atlas*, 122; "Extensive Works for the Manufacture of Iron Tubing," 150–151; advertisement in *Ice and Refrigeration* 1 (1891): 106; "New Foundry for the Semi-Steel Co.," 405.

13. These disadvantages were pointed out by Condit in *American Building Materials*, 138.

14. "Corrugated Iron as Building Material," 299; Matheson, *Works in Iron*, 196–197, noted that corrugated sheet iron could be used for roofs of buildings of small span almost without supporting framing. "Iron as a Building Material," 274.

15. David Bigelow, *History of Prominent Mercantile and Manufacturing Firms*, n.p.; Greeley et al., *The Great Industries of the United States*, 195, 609; Karschner, *Industrial Newark*, 137.

16. Candee, "The 'Great Factory' at Dover, New Hampshire," 47; Hambourg et al., *Mills and Factories of New England*, plate 16.

17. Pierson, *American Buildings and Their Architects*, 38–39, 42–43; *The Factory Mutuals*, 222–226; Montgomery, *A Practical Detail of the Cotton Manufacture*, 16–17.

18. Wight, "A Fireproof Addition," 329–330; David Lupton's Sons Co., *Air, Light and Efficiency*, 11–14.

19. Diemer, *Factory Design and Administration*, 93–94.

20. David Bigelow, *History of Prominent Mercantile and Manufacturing Firms*, n.p.; *G. & D. Cook & Co.'s Illustrated Catalogue*, 160.

21. In *Spanning the Industrial Age*, 37, Zink and Hartman make this observation.

22. Candee, "The 'Great Factory' at Dover, New Hampshire," 48–49.

23. Hogan, *Thoughts about the City of St. Louis*, 55.

24. "Progress of Ship-Building—Roof over Building-Slips at St. Peter's Dockyard, Newcastle," 130, plates. Special "rolled rough plate" glass, available in sheets from 12 to 20 inches wide and up to 70 inches long, was developed for this application. Matheson, *Works in Iron*, 216; Wilson, *The Pennsylvania Railroad Shops*, 26; "Rendle's Systems of Glass Roofing," 101; Ketchum, *The Design of Steel Mill Buildings*, 1st ed., 261. Woodbury, *The Fire Protection of Mills*, 135, mentions Rendle skylights.

25. Truscon Steel Co., *Truscon Buildings Standardized*, 13; "The New Detroit Car-Works," 10; "The Ohio Falls Car-Works," 5.

26. Fowler, *General Specifications for Steel Roofs and Buildings*, 4; Papadaki, "The Design of Industrial Buildings," 12; Ketchum, *The Design of Steel Mill Buildings*, 1st ed., 143, 271–272, 337.

27. "A One-Story Workshop," 92.

28. "Dawn of the Railroad," 65, and view from late 1840s or early 1850s,

plates 6 and 7, in Geismar, *Archeological Investigations*. "Dale's Patent Platform and Counter Scale Manufactory," 1; *Gazetteer of the Manufactures and Manufacturing Towns of the United States*, 24.

29. Wood, *Industries of Richmond*, 82–83; *Industrial Review* (December 1882): xvi. Holley and Smith, "American Iron and Steel Works, No. XXXVIII," 103.

30. Keith Reginald Gilbert, *Henry Maudslay, Machine Builder*, 27; Kurt Ackerman, *Building for Industry*, 16, 21–23. G. D. Dempsey, *Engineering Examples*, plates 1, 2; this portfolio of drawings and limited text does not name or comment on the monitors. Seaver, "Iron Mill Buildings," 141, uses the term *monitor*. White, *The American Railroad Passenger Car*, 26–27. The railroad car form was also called a lantern roof, raised roof, deck roof, elevated roof, and steamboat roof. According to Barger, *A Century of Pullman Cars*, 202, Pullman's extravagantly decorated car was used to promote interest in owning such private cars. The *Oxford English Dictionary* dates the American usage of the word meaning the raised portion of a roof to the 1870s.

31. Sweet, "Machine Shop Roofs," 300; Wilson, *The Pennsylvania Railroad Shops*, 20.

32. Ketchum, *The Design of Steel Mill Buildings*, 3d ed., 316; "Iron Roof in the United States Government Navy Yard, Brooklyn," 29–30; David Bigelow, *History of Prominent Mercantile and Manufacturing Firms*, 264 and n.p.; "The New Works of the Wason Car Manufacturing Company," 215. "New Shops of the Chicago, Milwaukee and St. Paul Railroad," 116–117; "The Continental Works, Greenpoint, Long Island," 105.

33. Seaver, "Iron Mill Buildings," 141; Tyrrell, *Engineering of Shops and Factories*, 57; Fowler, *General Specifications for Steel Roofs and Buildings*, 4.

34. Seaver, "Iron Mill Buildings," 142, describes the purpose of a double monitor. Bowen, *Sketchbook of Pennsylvania*, part 1, 65, and part 2, 51; David Bigelow, *History of Prominent Mercantile and Manufacturing Firms*, 94. "Albany Iron Works," 9; Mr. Winslow was credited with the design of the building. Kenny, *Illustrated Cincinnati*, 291.

35. Composite view of the Lobdell Car Wheel Company Works, Hagley Museum and Library pictorial collections.

36. Richmond, "Saw-Tooth Roofs for Factories," 287.

37. "The Construction of Mill Roofs," 44, plate 189, presents a one-story mill with two transverse monitors. "Design for a Slow-Burning Cotton-Mill," 132, plate 200, features a mill complex with a one-story weave shed with four transverse monitors and one over the picker house. Atkinson illustrated his "Slow-Burning Construction" with Wm. H. H. Whiting's one-story mill, which has three transverse monitors. Freeman, "Comparison of English and American Types of Factory Construction," 51, noted the American preference for the monitor roof. The earliest uses of the sawtooth roof in the United States have not been documented. The foundry of the Mitchell, Vance & Co., manufacturers of light fixtures and clocks (c. 1870; New York City), as depicted in the mid-1870s, appears to have three sawtooth skylights; *Asher and Adams' New Columbian Railroad Atlas*, 133.

38. Brockett, *Silk Industry in America*, opp. 117; George Hayes Co., *The "Hayes" Metal Skylights and Other Glazed Structures*; Richmond, "Saw-Tooth Roofs for Factories," 287, pushed the date for the use of sawtooth roofs in the Philadelphia area back to the 1870s. Freeman, "Comparison of English and American Types of Factory Construction," 51; Samuel B. Lincoln, *Lockwood, Greene*, 141. The Milliken Bros. catalog of 1899 featured the sawtooth roof as a special form of roof particularly adapted for the manufacture of textile goods.

39. Arnold, "Modern Machine-Shop Economics, II," 267, and "Modern Machine-Shop Economics, III," 473–474; Tyrrell, *A Treatise on the Design and Construction of Mill Buildings*, 77; Sweet, "Machine Shop Construction,"

224–227; Sweet asserted in "Sawtooth Skylight in Factory Roof Construction," 465, that the Straight Line Engine Co. Works was the first to use the roof.

40. Arnold, "Modern Machine-Shop Economics, III," 477; Tyrrell, *Engineering of Shops and Factories*, 59; Case, *The Factory Buildings*, 279.

41. Ketchum, *The Design of Steel Mill Buildings*, 5th ed., 384–385; Hool and Kinne, *Steel and Timber Structures*, 51–52; Ballinger Co., *"Super-Span" Saw-tooth Buildings*, 3–15; the design was patented in 1920. Anderson, *Industrial Engineering and Factory Management*, 116.

42. Hart, *The Industries of Buffalo*, 255; Tyrrell, *Engineering of Shops and Factories*, 56-57; Truscon Steel Co., *Truscon Buildings Standardized*, 13. "Walls, Roofs, and Floors," 389, reported that Albert Kahn considered the Pond truss costly to maintain.

43. The design for the steel-framed roof was submitted by the Phoenix Iron Company to architect L. C. Holden of New York City. "Novel Design of Roof for a One-Story Factory," 231–232; Ketchum, *The Design of Steel Mill Buildings*, 1st ed., 152, and 5th ed., 385, illustrates this roof form as the "silk mill roof."

44. Nisbet describes the Aiken roof in "Machine Shop Roofs," 152–154. Henry Aiken was a consulting engineer with a practice in Pittsburgh during the early twentieth century. Ballinger Co., *Buildings for Commerce and Industry*, 39; "The Foundry of the Standard Steel Car Co.," 405; Tyrrell, *Engineering of Shops and Factories*, 56–57.

45. Clarke P. Pond of Philadelphia was responsible for the Pond roof design. David Lupton's Sons Co., *Air, Light and Efficiency*, 19–22, and *Air and Light in Machine Shops*, 20–23; Tyrrell, *Engineering of Shops and Factories*, 58; Case, *The Factory Buildings*, 284–85. According to Ketchum, *The Design of Steel Mill Buildings*, 5th ed., 336, the M-profile roof was a modification of the "silk mill roof," which was better for ventilation.

46. Tyrrell, *Engineering of Shops and Factories*, 58; Case, *The Factory Buildings*, 299, 301. David Lupton's Sons Co., *Air and Light in Machine Shops*, 23, states that the first installations of the Pond truss, as well as counterbalanced Lupton steel sash, were at the General Electric's Erie works.

47. Hildebrand, *Designing for Industry*, 164–183.

48. Condit, *American Building Art: The Twentieth Century*, 47; "Long Span Steel Arches Incorporate Sawtooth Roof," 542–44.

49. Talbot Hamlin, "Factories as Architecture," 477–478, 480; Papadaki, "The Design of Industrial Buildings," 12; The Austin Co. press release, December 3, 1937.

CHAPTER 9

1. Candee, "Architecture and Corporate Planning," 40; Greeley et al., *The Great Industries of the United States*, 965.

2. *New York in Slices*, 125.

3. Fitch, *American Building*, 126; Kasson, *Civilizing the Machine*, 145–146; Haber, "Artistic Engineering," 134–136; see also Marvin Fisher, "The Iconology of Industrialism," 360–364.

4. "The New Works of the Wason Car Manufacturing Company," 216; Charles W. Moore, *Timing a Century*, 56.

5. *One-Hundred Years of Brewing*, 137–138. See Appel, "Brewery Architecture in America from the Civil War to Prohibition" and "Artificial Refrigeration and the Architecture of 19th Century American Breweries," for more information on the architecture of breweries.

6. Chase, "The Modern Factory Must Fit Its Job," 14; Tyrrell, *Engineering of Shops and Factories*, 44.

7. Collins, "The Engineering of Industrial Buildings," 30.

8. Tyrrell, *Engineering of Shops and Factories*, 357–363.

9. Knowlton, "The New Building for the Cream of Wheat Co.," 513–514.

10. Holgate, *Aesthetics of Built Form*, especially 9, 43–44, 191, 243–246, informed these comments on the engineer's response to structural form. "Artists and Artisans," 135; see also "Architects and Engineers," 1–5.

11. Haber, "Artistic Engineering," 134–36.

12. Deacon, "The Aesthetics of Construction," 642–644.

13. Tyrrell, *Artistic Bridge Design*, 19–22.

14. Holgate, *Aesthetics of Built Form*, 243–246; Peters, "Architectural Engineering and Design," 25. Billington writes about an engineering aesthetic that governed the design of structures primarily bridges, towers, and office buildings guided by the ideals of efficiency, economy, and elegance; see *The Tower and the Bridge*, chapters 1 and 7. He credits Thomas Telford with recognizing the difference between architecture and engineering and with articulating an engineering aesthetic at the turn of the nineteenth century.

15. "American Architecture," in Small, *Form and Function*, 64–65. Giedion, *Space, Time and Architecture*, 216; Kasson, *Civilizing the Machine*, 144; Fitch, *Architecture and the Esthetics of Plenty*, 46–64, and 131–139, and *American Building*, Wosk, *Breaking Frame*, 204–205, also discuss Greenough.

16. Peters, *Building the Nineteenth Century*, 209, relates how the British architect and theorist, Agustus Pugin, also made this distinction.

17. Fairbairn, *Treatise on Mills and Millwork*, 113–114, considered the Saltaire mill buildings representative of the architect-designed factory building of stature. Talbott & Bro., *An Illustrated Catalog*, 2.

18. G. D. Dempsey, *Engineering Examples*, 15; Collins, "The Design and Construction of Industrial Buildings," 908.

19. Tweet, *The Rock Island Clock Tower*, 2–12, 17; Flagler, *A History of the Rock Island Arsenal*, 109. Major Charles P. Kingsbury was initially in charge of the construction project that was completed by General Thomas J. Rodman. The plan of the building, which had a large rectangular loft area flanked by a projecting tower that housed a hoist opposite a pavilion that enclosed stairways, was dictated by functional and fire-resistant construction considerations. Two rows of iron columns at the lower two floors comprised the interior framing; the roof was supported by a system of trusses.

20. "Wilcox, Treadway & Co. Cleveland Hardware Manufactory," 6; "Worcester," 47.

21. C. John Hexamer, "Mill Architecture," 1; Woodbury, "The Evolution of the Modern Mill," 10329; Frank P. Bennett, *How to Build, Equip, and Operate a Cotton Mill*, 9, noted that beauty in mill architecture resulted from the adaptation of means to an end and the combination of each part into the whole structure, as well as a sense of fitness.

22. Diemer, "The Planning of Factory Buildings," 293; Collins, "The Design and Construction of Industrial Buildings," 908; Kimball, *Principles of Industrial Organization*, 83. Similar sentiments were noted by Berg, *American Railway Shop Systems*, 13, who recommended a neat and substantial appearance and noted that architectural embellishments purely for the sake of an assumed aesthetic effect were out of place in a manufacturing plant.

23. Le Corbusier, *Towards a New Architecture*, 15, 19, translated by Frederick Etchells and quoted in Cheney, *The New World Architecture*, 90; Le Corbusier also stated that only the architect could provide a sense of beauty. Terry Smith, *Making the Modern*, 60.

24. This phrase often appeared in the architectural press and appears to have referred to design elements and schemes driven by aesthetic consideration, rather than functional matters, that usually incorporated traditional architectural ornament.

25. Sweet, "Machine Shop Construction," 223; "Extracts from Chordal's Letters," 1–2; Gibson and Home-Morton, "The Design of Industrial Works," 137.

26. Editorial note, *American Architect and Building News* 5 (April 26, 1879): 129.

27. See *American Architect and Building News* 6: Atkinson, "The Architecture of Mill Buildings," 151–152, and "Slow-Burning Construction," 14; "Slow-Burning Construction" (June 21, 1879), 199; "Slow-Burning Construction" (August 23, 1879), 54–56; and "Design for a Slow-Burning Cotton-Mill," 132 and plates.

28. "Machine Shop at Winchedon," plate; "Spring Grove Paper Mills," 296, plate; no text accompanied the machine shop illustration, though a technical, rather than architectural description, accompanied the plate of the paper mill. See also "Standard Underground Cage Co.'s Works." "Factory of the American Arithmometer Co.," 107–108.

29. Van Rensselaer, "Recent Architecture in America, III," 511–523. Sturgis noted the Duane Street Warehouse in "The Warehouse and the Factory in Architecture—I," 2, fig. 1.

30. Sturgis, "Factories and Warehouses," 369. Sturgis's appreciation of the utilitarian aesthetic was also related in "The Warehouse and the Factory in Architecture—I," 1–17; "The Warehouse and the Factory in Architecture—II," 122–133; and "Some Recent Warehouses," 373–386. Quinan, *Frank Lloyd Wright's Larkin Building*, 113, notes Sturgis's grounding in academic architectural styles and his failure to appreciate the design of Frank Lloyd Wright's Larkin Administration Building; nevertheless, late in life Sturgis seems to have developed an appreciation for utilitarian design.

31. Wight, "Utilitarian Architecture at Chicago I," 189–198, and "Utilitarian Architecture at Chicago II," 249–257. Wight reported favorably on the work of several architects who specialized in industrial work, including Pond & Pond, Hill & Woltersdorf, and Schmidt, Garden & Martin. Woltersdorf's views on aesthetic issues appeared in "An Expression on the Design of Factory and Warehouse Buildings," 237–238.

32. Corbett, "Facts, Factories and Frills," 233.

33. Hearn, *Architectural Theory of Viollet-Le-Duc*, is a good guide to the theorist's writings.

34. C. Matlack Price, "Architecture" (1917), 49; see Nimmons, "Modern Industrial Plants" series, especially part 4, 163–168, for his comments on factory aesthetics. Nimmons illustrated his articles with the work of his contemporaries who shared his approach to industrial design, including Chicago architects Alfred S. Alschuler and S. Scott Joy, as well as the work of Albert Kahn and architectural engineer Frank D. Chase.

35. C. Matlack Price, "Architecture" (1917), 49, and "Ideals in Every-day Architecture and a Passing Tribute to Mr. Willis Polk," 53–55; Edgell, *The American Architecture of To-Day*, 291, 294; Florence Dempsey, "Nela Park," 474–476.

36. Wight, "Utilitarian Architecture at Chicago II," 250–251; C. Matlack Price, "Architecture" (1917), 49.

37. Doubleday, Page & Co., *The Country Life Press*; "The Country Life Press," *American Architect* 99 (June 14, 1911): frontispiece; "Factory of the American Bank Note Company," 490; "An Unusual Design for a Factory," 37.

38. Putnam, "The Modern Industrial Building," 177–180.

39. Merritt, *Engineering in American Society*, 15; Schoen, "Factory of Simms Magneto Co.," 232–233; Weitenkamf, "The Esthetics of Engineering," 366, 368.

40. Case, *The Factory Buildings*, 262; the following summary of Case's argument is taken from pages 257–264.

CHAPTER 10

1. Fowler, *The Ideals of Engineering Aesthetic*, 39–49.
2. Farnham, *Scientific Industrial Efficiency*, 9–10, 91.

3. Flagler, *A History of the Rock Island Arsenal*, 118; Buder, *Pullman*, 52; "The Ambridge Plant of the American Bridge Co.," 620–623.

4. "Enclosed Acreage," 339.

5. Wharton, "Planning the Industrial Plant—2," 47, notes the difference between standardized designs that could be adapted and then fabricated, and prefabricated standard buildings that were kept in stock, ready to ship, and hence not easily altered.

6. Research for this study did not reveal whether there was a steady market for manufactured iron buildings between the iron-framed and corrugated sheet-metal-clad buildings shipped to California during the Gold Rush of 1848 and those offered during the 1880s. Herbert, *Pioneers of Prefabrication*, 46, note 35; Standard Roof and Bridge Co., *L. Sykes & Son*; Milliken Bros. catalog.

7. The Austin Co., *Austin Standard Factory-Buildings*; Grief, *The New Industrial Landscape*, 57–59.

8. Crowell-Lundoff-Little Co., *The Blue Book of Industrial Construction*; Jones and Larson Corp., *Industrial Steel Buildings*; Truscon Steel Co., *Truscon Standard Buildings* and *Truscon Buildings Standardized*; "To Produce Standardized Galvanized Steel Industrial Buildings," 462.

9. Fitch, *American Building*, 9; see also Eaton, *Gateway Cities*, 11–12.

10. The truncation of pilasters appears to have been a late-nineteenth-century practice that was by no means standard. This configuration has been noted on buildings in Buffalo, N.Y.; New York City; Erie, Pa.; Worcester, Mass.; and Chicago.

11. Bergdoll, *Karl Friedrich Schinkel*, 172–208, discusses this aspect of Schinkel's work. There is a marked similarity between his Bauakedemie, 1831–1836, and many brick commercial building facades erected throughout the last third of the nineteenth century in the United States. Schinkel's exposure of interwoven layers was used by European-trained architects; an example is the Nave-McCord Mercantile Company building (1882–1883; Eckel & Mann, architects; St. Joseph, Mo.) featured in Eaton, *Gateway Cities*, 23–25.

12. Banham, *A Concrete Atlantis*, notes the functional detailing of industrial design and the tendency to use traditional elements that provided a level of comfort for both the industrialist and the architect.

13. Carpenter, "Shops and Shop Buildings," 240; Barber's comments appeared in the discussion of J. N. Richardson, "Architectural Engineering," 174; "The Arrangement and Construction of Railway Shop Plants," 57; Diemer, "The Planning of Factory Buildings," 293; Collins, "The Design and Construction of Industrial Buildings," 908, Klaber, "Building the Factory," 367.

14. Gardiner, "Factory Entrances," 119, 123.

15. Joy, "The Central Manufacturing District, Chicago, Ill., Part 2," 177–178.

16. Jennings, "Brick-Work and Brick-Laying—V," 157–158, and "Brick-Work and Brick-Laying—VI," 3–4; Fidler, *Notes on Building Construction*, 27; Brickett, *Yarns, Cloth Rooms, and Mill Engineering*, sec. 87, 47–48.

17. In *Ziegelrohban Taschenbuch für Baukandwerk*, Liebold illustrates many elements of the *Rundbogenstil* that appeared in American commercial and industrial buildings. Curran, "The German *Rundbogenstil* and Reflections on the American Round-Arched Style," 351–373. My interpretation of the *Rundbugenstil* draws on New York City Landmarks Restoration Commission, *130–132 West 18th Street Stables Building Designation Report* and *175 West Broadway Building Designation Report*. William Pierson, "Industrial Architecture in the Berkshires," 226, used the term *Lombard Romanesque* to describe the type of brick textile mills erected between the 1840s and 1890s throughout New England. He noted that the White Rock Factory in Westerly, R.I. (1849), was of this type. See also Pierson, "Richard Upjohn and the American Rundbogenstil."

18. *Thomas Alexander Tefft*, 256–257; and Meeks, "Some Early Depot Drawings," 36, plate 6.

19. Wilson, *The Pennsylvania Railroad Shops*, 2, states that structures at the

Pennsylvania Railroad Shops at West Philadelphia (1865–1873) were built with walls thickened in their upper portions to "provide against any injury to the cornice or roof, in the event of accident to the wall below." Designs for corbelled brick cornices appeared in Cummings, *Architecture*, plate 4, and *Architectural Details*, plate 5. Sloan, *City and Suburban Architecture*, 58, wrote about the use of pilaster strips in facades of "Lombardic" style.

20. The paneled pediments with rondels of the Meyer warehouse at 54–56 Laight Street (1870; George DaCunha, builder/architect) and the main facade of the one at 437–441 Greenwich Street (1875; George DaCunha, builder/architect) are similar to a design illustrated in Liebold, *Ziegelrohban Taschenbuch für Baukandwerk*. York City Landmarks Preservation Commission, *Tribeca North Historic Designation Report*, 28, 96.

21. These buildings, and others in the area, are pictured in Robert Vogel, *A Report of the Mohawk-Hudson Survey*.

22. A. D. F. Hamlin, "The Architectural Problem of Concrete," 163.

23. Onderdonk, "Is a Specific Ferro-Concrete Style Evolving?," 192; see also Frederick L. Ackerman, "The Architectural Theory of Concrete Design," 257–262.

24. The full range of the Ballinger Co.'s work is depicted in their *Buildings for Commerce and Industry*. Perry, "Exteriors of Industrial Buildings," 323. The Turner Construction Co.'s experience in constructing over a thousand industrial buildings from 1902 to 1929 revealed a long-term and increasing preference for brick facing over the all-concrete exterior.

25. Slaton, "What 'Modern' Meant"; see also Slaton, "Origins of a Modern Form," chapter 5. Putnam, "The Modern Industrial Building," 180.

26. Banham, *A Concrete Atlantis*, 26; Norman Weiss offered the alternative interpretation in a class at Columbia University.

27. Groben, "Modern Industrial Plant of the American Chicle Co.," 102–103; "Improved Concrete Construction," 995. Though Jallade was described as one of the first architects to introduce reinforced concrete in this country, as a consulting engineer for the New York branch of the Contancein Reinforced Concrete Co., little is known about his work. "Dayton Engineering Laboratories Co.," plate.

28. Helmle, "The Fletcher Building," 291–293, and "Architectural Expression in Concrete," 11–14; the building was known also as the Varick Street Building. Kellogg, "Co-operation between Architect and Builder," 96–98; T.P. Bennett, *Architectural Design in Concrete*, plate 40.

29. Cass Gilbert, "Industrial Architecture in Concrete," 83–86. Gilbert did not share the view that concrete was a plastic material.

30. Austin-Nichols Warehouse documents, Cass Gilbert Collection, New-York Historical Society; the warehouse was pictured in "Mercantile and Industrial Buildings of Concrete," 87. Gilbert was unable to utilize reveals as deep as he would have liked due to the higher cost of thicker exterior walls.

31. Typescript dated December 30, 1919, Brooklyn Army Supply Base documents, Cass Gilbert Collection, New-York Historical Society. Albert Kahn admired this project for its fine massing and straightforward presence without any overt ornamentation; see "Reinforced Concrete Architecture These Past Twenty Years," 112–113.

32. Kahn, "Industrial Architecture," 5.

33. Terry Smith, *Making the Modern*, 71–75. Kahn has come to loom as large as Henry Ford in industrial history and has yet to receive an impartial evaluation by architectural historians. Perhaps historians will compare automobile plants to their predecessors, such as buggy and wagon manufacturing operations and railroad car works. Smith's analysis of Kahn's work calls for a differentiation between the Kahn-designed functionality and that evident in the utilitarian industrial buildings of the previous fifty years.

34. Kahn, "Industrial Architecture," 5.

35. Koester, "Industrial Architecture," 17–21.

36. Wallis, "Is American Architecture a Live Art?," 85.

37. "Thompson Malted Food Co. Plant," plates.

38. Condit, *The Chicago School of Architecture*, 184–85, 194, fig. 146, reports that only one of the one-story production sheds proposed for the Purcell & Elmslie project was erected at the Chicago and New Haven plants of the firm. Gebhard, "William Gray Purcell and George Grant Elmslie," 231.

39. Talbot Hamlin, "Architecture," 53–54; "Worcester Pressed Steel Co.," 320; *Industrial Architecture*, 35.

40. Ely Jacques Kahn, "On the Development of Industrial Buildings," in Bollack and Killian, *Ely Jacques Kahn*, [15–19].

41. Esperdy, " 'Horrible Modernistic Stuff' "; Mock, *Built in USA, 1932–1944*, 98–99.

42. Hitchcock and Johnson, *The International Style*, 53. A standardized design for Standard Oil Co. filling stations (1931; Clauss & Daub, architects) was also exhibited; see Museum of Modern Art, *Modern Architecture*.

43. New York City Landmarks Preservation Commission, *Starrett-Lehigh Building Designation Report*.

44. Though a zoning resolution of 1916 mandated the setback form for the tall building in New York City, the limited amount of building that took place during World War I and the depression that followed led to the coupling of the exploration of the new forms with the Art Deco idiom of the mid-1920s. "The Port Authority Commerce Building," 274–280.

45. "Factory for American Can Co.," 519–520; Maag, "General Foods' Corn Mill," 8–9.

46. Grief, *The New Industrial Landscape*, 103–104.

47. Haskell, "Architecture" (1938), 49, and "Architecture" (1941), 35.

48. Plates, *American Architect* 101 (June 19, 1912): 366, 268.

49. Nimmons, "Modern Industrial Plants, Part IV," 156–157; "Industrial Buildings Planned for Light and Efficiency," 208–209; Sundeleaf, "Industrial Design for Portland," 26–27; "A Trio of Modern Plants," 331–334.

50. Hildebrand, *Designing for Industry*, 182; Banham, *A Concrete Atlantis*, 87.

51. Hildebrand, *Designing for Industry*, 34–43. Another early example of Kahn's nonterminated facade design was the Packard Motor Car Company Plant Building No. 10 (1906).

52. Two views of the Packard Forge Shop appeared in *American Architect* 99 (June 14, 1911): 240, although there was no accompanying text; "The Forge Shop of the Packard Motor Car Company," 30–33. See also Hildebrand, *Designing for Industry*, 54–55, figs. 17–19.

53. *American Architect* 107 (February 24, 1915): plate; Briggs, "Modern American Factories," 232.

54. Hildebrand, *Designing for Industry*, 93–99.

55. Kahn was by no means the only designer to experiment with a variety of monitor sizes and shapes; he did consciously abandon the sawtooth roof because of the limitations on layout related to the availability of only north light.

56. Talbot Hamlin, "Factories as Architecture," 473–474; Mock, *Built in USA, 1932–1944*, 94–95.

BIBLIOGRAPHY

UNPUBLISHED MATERIAL AND GOVERNMENT REPORTS

Bahr, Betsy W. "New England Mill Engineering: Rationalization and Reform in Textile Mill Design, 1790–1920." Ph.D. diss., University of Delaware, 1987.

Bigelow, Charles. "Memoranda by ? [Charles Bigelow] made during a tour of inspection among various Machine Shops (Probably preparatory to designing Essex Co.'s Machine shop 1847?) From March 16 to March 22." Cataloged as Essex Company Collection, Accession 0022.69, Item #325–326, "Lawrence Machine Shop, 1847–56 Miscellany," Museum of American Textile History, Lowell, Massachusetts.

Biggs, Lindy. "Industry's Master Machine: Factory Planning and Design in the Age of Mass Production, 1900–1930." Ph.D. diss., Massachusetts Institute of Technology, 1987.

Bluestone, Daniel M. *Cleveland: An Inventory of Historic Engineering & Industrial Sites.* United States Department of Interior, Historic American Engineering Record, 1978.

Brown, Mark M. "The Architecture of Steel: Site Planning and Building Type in the Nineteenth-Century American Bessemer Steel Industry." Ph.D. diss., University of Pittsburgh, 1995.

Brown, Sharon. *Historic Resource Study, Cambria Iron Company.* Washington: United States Department of the Interior, National Park Service, 1989.

"Dock-Yards and Iron Works of Great Britain and France." House of Representatives Executive Document No. 14, 38th Cong., 2d sess. 1864.

DuBoff, Richard B. "Electric Power in American Manufacturing." Ph.D. diss., University of Pennsylvania, 1964.

Esperdy, Gabrielle. " 'Horrible Modernistic Stuff': New York City's Controversial Municipal Asphalt Plant." Paper presented at conference titled "Industrial Modernism: Architecture & Ideology," April 21, 1995, Hagley Museum and Library.

Farley, James J. "The Frankford Arsenal, 1816–1870: Industrial and Technological Change." Ph.D. diss., Temple University, 1991.

Fisher, Tom. "The White Machine-Motor Company, The White Co., the White Motor Company." Historic American Engineering Survey, OH-11C.

Gebhard, David. "william Gray Purcell and George Grant Elmslie and the Early Progressive Movement in American Architecture from 1900 to 1920." Ph.D. diss., University of Minnesota, 1957.

Geismar, Joan H. *Archeological Investigations of Site 1 of the Washington Street Urban Renewal Area, New York City*. New York: Cultural Resources Group, Louis Berger & Associates, 1984.

Cass Gilbert Collection, New-York Historical Society.

Hay, Duncan Erroll. "Building 'The New City on the Merrimack': The Essex Company and Its Role in the Creation of Lawrence, Massachusetts." Ph.D. diss., University of Delaware, 1986.

"History of the Detroit Dry Dock Company and Dry Dock Engine Works, History of Extant Buildings." Typescript. Society of Architectural Historians Study tour, 1994.

Kornblith, Gary John. "From Artisans to Businessmen: Master Mechanics in New England, 1789–1850." Ph.D. diss., Princeton University, 1983.

Lozier, John. "Taunton & Mason: Cotton Machinery and Locomotive Manufacture in Taunton, Massachusetts, 1811–1861." Ph.D. diss., Ohio State University, 1978.

New York City Landmarks Preservation Commission. *130–132 West 18th Street Stables Building Designation Report*. Report prepared by Gale Harris, 1990.

———. *175 West Broadway Building Designation Report*. Report prepared by Gale Harris, 1991.

———. *Starrett-Lehigh Building Designation Report*. Report prepared by Jay Shockley, 1986.

———. *The Joseph Loft Silk Mill Designation Report*. Report prepared by Betsy Bradley, 1993.

———. *Tribeca North Historic District Report*. Report prepared by Betsy Bradley, 1992.

———. *Tribeca West Historic District Designation Report*. Report prepared by Betsy Bradley, 1991.

Pierson, William Harvey, Jr. "Industrial Architecture in the Berkshires." Ph.D. diss., Yale University, 1949.

Rutsch, Edward S. *Salvage Archaeology Project, Paterson, N.J., 1973–76*. Paterson: SOPA for Great Falls Development and State of New Jersey Department of Transportation, 1978.

Slaton, Amy. "Origins of a Modern Form: The Reinforced Concrete Factory Building in America, 1900–1930." Ph.D. diss., University of Pennsylvania, 1995.

———. "What 'Modern' Meant: The Construction and Status of the Early Twentieth-Century Reinforced-Concrete Factory Building." Paper presented at conference titled "Industrial Modernism: Architecture & Ideology," April 21, 1995, Hagley Museum and Library.

Slattery, Thomas J. *An Illustrated History of the Rock Island Arsenal and Arsenal Island*. Rock Island, Ill.: Historical Office, U.S. Army Armament, Munitions and Chemical Command, 1990.

Tweet, Roald. *The Rock Island Clock Tower, from Ordnance to Engineers*. Rock Island District, U.S. Army Corps of Engineers, 1977.

Walker, R. J. "Report of the Secretary of the Treasury on the Warehousing System." Senate Executive Document no. 32, 30th Cong., 2d sess., 1849.

Wermiel, Sara. "Nothing Succeeds Like Failure: The Development of the Fireproof Building in the United States, 1790–1911." Ph.D. diss., Massachusetts Institute of Technology, 1996.

———. "The Role of the Fire Insurance Industry in Advancing Structural Fire Protection in Nineteenth-Century America," Research Seminar Paper no. 35, presented May 9, 1996, at the Hagley Museum and Library, Wilmington, Del.

BOOKS

Abbott, Jacob. *The Harper Establishment*. Harper's Story Books No. 10, 1855.

Ackerman, Kurt. *Building for Industry*. London: Watermark Publications, 1991.

The American Advertising Directory and Manufacturers and Dealers in American Goods for 1831. New York: Jocelyn, Darling & Co., 1831.

Analytic System Handbook on Fire Protection. Chicago: Western Actuarial Bureau, 1924.

Anderson, Arthur G. *Industrial Engineering and Factory Management*. New York: Ronald Press Co., 1928.

Anderson, W. J., and Julius Bleyer. *Milwaukee's Great Industries*. Milwaukee: Association for the Advancement of Milwaukee, 1892.

Architecture by Albert Kahn Associated Architects and Engineers, Inc. New York: Architectural Catalog Co., 1948.

Arnold, Horace L., and Fay Leone Faurote. *Ford Methods and Ford Shops*. New York: Engineering Magazine Co., 1919.

Asher and Adams' New Columbian Railroad Atlas and Pictorial Album of American Industry. 1876. Reprint, New York: Rutledge Books, 1976.

Atkins, Paul M. *Factory Management*. New York: Prentice-Hall, Inc., 1926.

Atkinson, Edward. *The Industrial Progress of the Nation*. New York: G. P. Putnam's Sons, 1890.

———. *The Prevention of Loss by Fire, Fifty Years' Record of Factory Mutual Insurance*. Boston: Damrell & Upham, 1900.

Banham, Reyner. *A Concrete Atlantis*. Cambridge: MIT Press, 1989.

Barber, John W. *Connecticut Historical Collections*. New Haven, Conn.: Durrie & Peck and J. W. Barber, 1846.

Barger, Ralph L. *A Century of Pullman Cars. Vol. II. The Palace Cars*. Sykesville, Md.: Greenberg Publishing Co., Inc., 1990.

Barker, Arthur H. *The Management of Small Engineering Workshops*. Manchester: Technical Publishing Co., Ltd., 1903.

Barnard, Henry. *Armsmear: The Home, the Arm and the Armory of Samuel Colt. A Memorial*. New York: Alvord, 1866.

Bennett, Frank P. *How to Build, Equip, and Operate a Cotton Mill in the United States*. New York: Frank P. Bennett Co., 1913.

Bennett, T.P. *Architectural Design in Concrete*. New York: Oxford University Press, 1927.

Berg, Walter G. *American Railway Shop Systems*. New York: Railroad Gazette, 1904.

Bergdoll, Barry. *Karl Friedrich Schinkel: An Architecture for Prussia*. New York: Rizzoli, 1994.

Bigelow, David. *History of Prominent Mercantile and Manufacturing Firms in the United States*. Boston: David Bigelow, 1857.

Biggs, Lindy. *The Rational Factory: Architecture, Technology, and Work in America's Age of Mass Production*. Baltimore: Johns Hopkins University Press, 1996.

Billington, David P. *The Tower and the Bridge: The New Art of Structural Engineering*. New York: Basic Books, 1983.

Birkmire, William A. *Architectural Iron and Steel, and Its Application in the Construction of Buildings*. New York: John Wiley & Sons, 1901.

———. *Skeleton Construction in Buildings*. New York: John Wiley & Sons, 1894.

Bishop, Leander J. *A History of American Manufacturers from 1608 to 1860*. Philadelphia: Young, 1868.

Bland, J. C. *Handbook for Engineers, Architects and Other Workers in Iron and Steel.* Pottsville Iron and Steel Co., 1887.

Boese, Donald L. *Papermakers.* Grand Rapids, Minn.: Charles K. Blandin Foundation, 1984.

Bollack, Françoise, and Tom Killian. *Ely Jacques Kahn: New York Architect.* New York: Acanthus Press, 1995.

Bolles, Albert S. *Industrial History of the United States.* Norwich, Conn.: Henry Bill Publishing Company, 1879.

Bolz, Harold, and George E. Hagemann, eds. *Materials Handling Handbook.* New York: Ronald Press Co., 1948.

Bowen, Eli. *Sketchbook of Pennsylvania.* Philadelphia: Willis P. Hazard, 1852.

Brickett, C. J. *Yarns, Cloth Rooms, and Mill Engineering.* Scranton, Pa., 1924.

Brockett, Linus Pierpont. *Silk Industry in America—A History.* New York: Silk Association of America, 1876.

Broehl, Wayne G. *John Deere's Company: A History of Deere & Company and Its Time.* New York: Doubleday, 1984.

Brown, John K. *The Baldwin Locomotive Works, 1831–1915.* Baltimore: Johns Hopkins University Press, 1995.

Buder, Stanley. *Pullman.* New York: Oxford University Press, 1967.

Buildings and Upkeep. Vol. 1 of *The Library of Factory Management.* Chicago: A. S. Shaw Co., 1915.

Bush, Irving T. *Working with the World.* Garden City, N.Y.: Doubleday, Dorian & Co., 1928.

Campin, Francis. *On the Construction of Iron Roofs.* New York: D. Van Nostrand, 1868.

Case, Willard L. *The Factory Buildings.* Vol. 7 of *Factory Management Course.* New York: Industrial Extension Institute, 1922.

Chandler, Alfred D., Jr. *The Visible Hand: The Managerial Revolution in American Business.* Cambridge: Harvard University Press, 1977.

Chase, Frank D. *A Better Way to Build Your New Plant.* Chicago: Poole Bros., 1919.

———. *A Continuous Foundry for Automobile Castings.* Chicago, 1919.

———. *The Modern Foundry.* Chicago: Clafin-Hill, 1918.

Cheney, Sheldon. *The New World Architecture.* New York: Tudor Publishing Co., 1935.

City of Elizabeth, New Jersey Illustrated. Elizabeth, N.J.: Elizabeth Daily Journal, 1889.

Colby, Frank Moore, ed. *New International Yearbook.* New York: Dodd, Mead & Co., 1914–1942.

Condit, Carl. *American Building Art: The Nineteenth Century.* New York: Oxford University Press, 1960.

———. *American Building Art: The Twentieth Century.* New York: Oxford University Press, 1961.

———. *American Building Materials and Techniques from the First Colonial Settlements to the Present.* Chicago: University of Chicago Press, 1968.

———. *Chicago, 1910–1929.* Chicago: University of Chicago Press, 1973.

———. *The Chicago School of Architecture: A History of Commercial and Public Buildings in the Chicago Area, 1875–1925.* Chicago: University of Chicago Press, 1952.

Conley, Patrick T., and Paul R. Campbell. *Providence—A Pictorial History.* Norfolk, Va.: Donning Co., 1982.

Cooke-Taylor, R. Whately. *Introduction to a History of the Factory System.* London: Richard Bently & Son, 1886.

Coolidge, John. *Mill and Mansion.* New York: Russell and Russell, 1967.

Cowan, Henry J. *Dictionary of Architectural Science.* New York: John Wiley & Sons, 1973.

Cox, Arthur J., and Thomas Malin. *Ferracute—The History of an American Enterprise.* Bridgeton, N.J.: A. J. Cox, 1985.

Cox, Jacob Dolson, Sr. *Building an American Industry: The Story of the Cleveland Twist Drill Co. and Its Founder. An Autobiography*. Cleveland: Cleveland Twist Drill Co., 1951.

Crowther, Samuel. *John H. Patterson: Pioneer in Industrial Welfare*. Garden City, N.Y.: Doubleday, Page & Co., 1923.

Cummings, M. F. *Cummings' Architectural Details*. New York: Orange, Judd & Co., 1873.

———. *Architecture*. Troy, N.Y.: Young & Benson, 1865.

Cyclopedia of Fire Prevention and Insurance, vol. 1. Chicago: American Technical Society, 1912.

Day, Charles. *Works Management Library: Industrial Plants, Their Arrangement and Construction*. New York: Engineering Magazine, 1911.

Dempsey, G. D. *Engineering Examples: Working Drawings of Stations, Engine-Houses, Manufactories, Warehouses, Workshops, etc*. London: Atchley & Co., 1856.

Dencer, F. W. *Detailing and Fabricating Structural Steel*. New York: McGraw-Hill, 1924.

Dictionary of the English Language. London, 1863.

Diemer, Hugo. *Factory Design and Administration*. New York: McGraw-Hill, 1914.

Dienstag, Eleanor Foa. *In Good Company*. New York: Warner Books, 1994.

Dunham, Clarence W. *Planning Industrial Structures*. New York: McGraw-Hill, 1948.

Eaton, Leonard K. *Gateway Cities and Other Essays*. Ames: Iowa State University Press, 1989.

Edgell, G. H. *The American Architecture of To-Day*. New York: Charles Scribner's Sons, 1928.

Edwards, Richard, ed. *Industries of New Jersey*. New York: Historical Publishing Co., 1883.

Eggert, Gerald G. *Harrisburg Industrializes: The Coming of Factories to an American Community*. University Park: Pennsylvania State University Press, 1993.

Elliott, Cecil D. *Technics and Architecture*. Cambridge: MIT Press, 1992.

Emerson, Harrington. *The Twelve Principles of Efficiency*. New York: Engineering Magazine Co., 1919.

Emerson, Howard, and Douglas C. E. Naehring. *Origins of Industrial Engineering: The Early Years of the Profession*. Norcross, Ga.: Industrial Engineering & Management Press, 1988.

Ennis, William Duane. *Works Management*. New York: McGraw-Hill, 1911.

The Factory Mutuals, 1835–1935. Providence: Manufacturers Mutual Fire Insurance Company, 1935.

Fairbairn, William. *The Principles of Mechanism and Machinery of Transmission*. Philadelphia: Henry Carey Baird, 1867.

———. *Treatise on Mills and Millwork. Part II, On Machinery of Transmission and Construction and Arrangement of Mills*. London: Longmans, Green, & Co., 1865.

Farmer, Silas. *The History of Detroit and Michigan, or The Metropolis Illustrated*. Detroit: Silas Farmer & Co., 1884.

Farnham, Dwight T. *Scientific Industrial Efficiency*. 1917. Reprint, Easton, Pa.: Hive Publishing Co., 1974.

Ferry, W. Hankins. *The Legacy of Albert Kahn*. Detroit: Wayne State University Press, 1970.

Fidler, Henry. *Notes on Building Construction*. London: Rivingtons, 1879.

Fitch, James Marston. *American Building—The Historical Forces That Shaped It*. New York: Schocken Books, 1973.

———. *Architecture and the Esthetics of Plenty*. New York: Columbia University Press, 1961.

Flagler, Major D. W. *A History of the Rock Island Arsenal*. Washington: Government Printing Office, 1877.

Fleming, William Franklin. *America's Match King: Ohio Columbus Barber*. Barberton, Ohio: Press of Barberton Historical Society, 1981.

Foord, John. *The Factory behind the Great Arrow Car*. Buffalo, N.Y.: Geo. N. Pierce Co., c. 1908.

Ford, William F. *The Industrial Interests of Newark, New Jersey*. New York: Van Arsdale & Co., 1874.

Fowler, Charles Evan. *General Specifications for Steel Roofs and Buildings*, 3d ed. New York: Engineering News Pub. Co., 1897.

———. *The Ideals of Engineering Aesthetic*. New York: Gillette Publishing Co., 1929.

French, J. H. *Historical and Statistical Gazeteer of New York State*. Syracuse: R. P. Smith, 1860.

Friedman, Donald. *Historical Building Construction*. New York: W. W. Norton & Co., 1995.

Fryer, William J. *Architectural Iron Work*. New York: John Wiley & Sons, 1876.

———. *Laws Relating to Buildings in the City of New York*. New York: Record and Guide, 1892.

Garner, John. *The Model Company Town*. Amherst: University of Massachusetts Press, 1984.

———, ed. *The Company Town*. New York: Oxford University Press, 1992.

Gazeteer of the Manufactures and Manufacturing Towns of the United States. New York: J. M. Bradstreet & Son, 1866.

Giedion, Sigfried. *Mechanization Takes Command*. New York: W. W. Norton & Co., 1948.

———. *Space, Time and Architecture*. Cambridge: Harvard University Press, 1967.

Gilbert, Keith Reginald. *Henry Maudslay, Machine Builder*. A Science Museum Booklet. London: Her Majesty's Stationery Office, 1971.

Glynn, Joseph. *Rudimentary Treatise on the Construction of Cranes and Machinery*. London: John Weale, 1849.

———. *A Treatise on the Construction of Cranes and Other Hoisting Machinery*. London: John Weale, 1873.

Gordon, Robert B., and Patrick M. Malone. *The Texture of Industry*. New York: Oxford University Press, 1994.

Greeley, Horace, et al. *The Great Industries of the United States*. Hartford, Chicago, and Cincinnati: J. B. Burr & Hyde, 1872.

Grief, Martin. *The New Industrial Landscape: The Story of The Austin Co*. Clinton, N.J.: Main Street Press, 1978.

Griffiths, William H. *The Story of the American Bank Note Company*. New York, 1959.

Hall, Joseph D. *Biographical History of the Manufacturers and Business Men of Rhode Island at the Opening of the Twentieth Century*. Providence: J. D. Hall & Co., 1901.

Halper, Albert. *The Foundry*. New York: Viking Press, 1934.

Hambourg, Serge, Noel Perrin, and Kenneth Breisch. *Mills and Factories of New England*. New York: Harry N. Abrams, 1988.

Harris, Cyril M. *Dictionary of Architecture and Construction*. New York: McGraw-Hill, 1975.

Hart, John F. *The Industries of Buffalo: A Resume of the Mercantile and Manufacturing Progress of the Queen City of the Lakes*. Buffalo: Elstner Publishing Co., 1887.

Hartford, Connecticut as a Manufacturing, Business and Commercial Center. Hartford: Hartford Board of Trade, 1889.

Harvey, T. Edgar, ed. *Commercial History of the State of Kentucky*. Post D, Kentucky Division of the Travelers' Protective Association of America, 1899.

Haven, Charles T., and Frank A. Belden. *A History of the Colt Revolver*. New York: Bonanza Books, 1940.

Hay, Geoffrey D., and Geoffrey P. Stell. *Monuments of Industry, an Illustrated Historical Record*. Edinborough: Royal Commission on the Ancient and Historical Monuments of Scotland, 1986.

Hearn, M. F., ed. *The Architectural Theory of Viollet-Le-Duc: Readings and Commentary*. Cambridge: MIT Press, 1990.

Hendrick's Commercial Register of the United States. 1905.

Henley's Encyclopaedia of Practical Engineering and Allied Trades. New York: Norman W. Henley Publishing Co., 1906.

Herbert, Gilbert. *Pioneers of Prefabrication—The British Contribution in the Nineteenth Century*. Baltimore: Johns Hopkins University Press, 1978.

Hexamer, Ernest. *Hexamer General Insurance Surveys, 1867–1897*. Philadelphia.

Hildebrand, Grant. *Designing for Industry: The Architecture of Albert Kahn*. Cambridge: MIT Press, 1974.

Hindle, Brooke, ed. *Material Culture of the Wooden Age*. Tarrytown, N.Y.: Sleepy Hollow Press, 1981.

Hitchcock, Henry-Russell, and Philip Johnson. *The International Style*. 1932. Reprint, New York: W. W. Norton & Co., 1995.

Hittell, John S. *The Commerce and Industry of the Pacific Coast of North America*. San Francisco: A. L. Bancroft & Co., 1882.

Hobart, James F. *Millwrighting*. New York: Hill Publishing Co., 1909.

Hogan, John. *Thoughts about the City of St. Louis, Her Commerce and Manufacturers, Railways, etc.* St. Louis: Republican Steam Press Printers, 1854.

Holgate, Alan. *Aesthetics of Built Form*. Oxford: Oxford University Press, 1992.

Holme, C. G., ed. *Industrial Architecture*. London: The Studio, Ltd., 1935.

Hool, George A., and William S. Kinne, eds. *Steel and Timber Structures*. New York: McGraw-Hill, 1924.

Horner, Joseph G. *The Modern Iron Foundry*. London: Henry Frowde and Hodder & Stoughton, 1923.

Hunter, Louis C. *A History of Industrial Power in the United States, 1780–1930*. Vol. 1, *Waterpower*. Charlottesville: University Press of Virginia, 1979.

———. *A History of Industrial Power in the United States*. Vol. 2, *Steam Power*. Charlottesville: University Press of Virginia, 1985.

Hunter, Louis C., and Lynwood Bryant. *A History of Industrial Power in the United States, 1780–1930*. Vol. 3, *The Transmission of Power*. Cambridge: MIT Press, 1991.

Huntington, Whitney Clark. *Building Construction*. New York: John Wiley & Sons, 1929.

Industrial America or *Manufacturers and Inventors of the United States: A Biographical and Descriptive Exposition of National Progress*. New York: Atlantic Publishing & Engraving Co., 1876.

International Library of Technology. *Mill Engineering. Part 1*. Scranton, Pa.: International Textbook Co., 1902.

Ireson, William Grant. *Factory Planning and Plant Layout*. New York: Prentice-Hall, 1952.

Johnson, J. B., C. W. Bryan, and F. E. Turneaure. *The Theory and Practice of Modern Framed Structures*. New York: John Wiley & Sons, 1909.

Jones, Edward D. *The Administration of Industrial Enterprises*. New York: Longmans, Green & Co., 1926.

Jones, Franklin D., and Edward K. Hammond. *Shop Management and Systems*. New York: Industrial Press, 1918.

Karschner, Terry. *Industrial Newark*. Newark: Society for Industrial Archaeology, 1985.

Kasson, John F. *Civilizing the Machine: Technology and Republican Values in America, 1776–1900*. New York: Grossman Publishers, 1976.

Kenny, D. J. *Illustrated Cincinnati*. Cincinnati: George E. Stevens, 1875.

Ketchum, Milo S. *The Design of Steel Mill Buildings and the Calculation of Stresses in Framed Structures*. New York: Engineering News Publishing Co., 1903 (1st ed.), 1914 (3d ed.), 1932 (5th ed.).

Kidder, Frank E. *Building Construction and Superintendence*. New York: William T. Comstock, 1900.

Kimball, Dexter S. *Principles of Industrial Organization*. New York: McGraw-Hill, 1925.

Koester, Frank. *Steam-Electric Power Plants*. New York: D. Van Nostrand Co., 1910.

Kouwenhoven, John. *Made in America: The Arts in Modern Civilization*. Garden City, N.Y.: Doubleday, 1948.

Kulik, Gary, and Julia C. Bonham. *Rhode Island: An Inventory of Historic and Engineering Sites*. Washington: Government Printing Office, 1978.

Lansburgh, Richard H., and William R. Spriegel. *Industrial Management*. New York: John Wiley & Sons, 1940.

Le Corbusier. *Towards a New Architecture*. Trans. Frederick Etchells. London: John Rodker, 1931; reprint, New York: Dover Publications, 1986.

Liebold, B. *Ziegelrohban Taschenbuch für Baukandwerk*, vol. 1. Holzminden: C. C. Mullersche Buchhandling, 1883.

Lief, Alfred. *The Firestone Story*. New York: McGraw-Hill, 1951.

Life of Eleuthère Irénée du Pont. Trans. Bessie G. du Pont. Newark: University of Delaware Press, 1924.

Lincoln, Samuel B. *Lockwood, Greene: The History of an Engineering Business, 1832–1958*. Brattleboro, Vt.: Stephen Greene Press, 1960.

Lochmoeller, Donald C., Dorothy A. Muncy, Oakleigh J. Thorne, and Mark A. Viets. *Industrial Development Handbook*. Washington: Urban Land Institute, 1975.

Lossing, Benson J. *The American Centenary: History of the Progress of the Republic of the United States during the First One Hundred Years of Its Existence*. Philadelphia: Porter & Coates, 1876.

———. *History of American Industries and Arts*. Philadelphia: Porter & Coates, 1878.

Love, John W. *Lengthened Shadows*. Cleveland: Ellwell-Parker Co., 1943.

Macfarlane, John J. *Manufacturing in Philadelphia, 1683–1912*. Philadelphia: Philadelphia Commercial Museum, 1912.

Main, Charles T. *Dyehouses*. 1924.

———. *Industrial Plants*. 1911, 1915, 1923.

———. *Notes on Mill Construction*. 1886.

The Making of America. Vol. 3, *Industry and Finance*. Chicago: Making of America Co., 1905.

Mallick, Randolph W., and Armand T. Grandreau. *Plant Layout-Planning and Practice*. New York: John Wiley & Sons and London: Chapman & Hall, 1951.

The Manufactories and Manufacturers of Pennsylvania of the Nineteenth Century. Philadelphia: Galaxy Publishing Co., 1875.

Matheson, Ewing. *Works in Iron: Bridge and Roof Structures*. London: E. & F. N. Spon, 1873.

McGaw, Judith. *The Most Wonderful Machine*. Chapel Hill: University of North Carolina Press for the Institute of Early American History and Culture, 1994.

McGrain, John W. *From Pig Iron to Cotton Duck—A History of Manufacturing Villages in Baltimore County*, vol. 1. Baltimore: Baltimore County Public Library, 1985.

Meakin, Budgett. *Model Factories and Villages*. London: T. Fisher, 1905; reprint, New York: Garland, 1985.

Meeker, Ellis R. *New Jersey: Historical, Commercial and Industrial Review*. Elizabeth, N.J.: Ellis R. Meeker, 1906.

Mensch, L. J. *Architects' and Engineers' Hand-book of Re-Inforced Concrete Constructions.* Chicago: Cement and Engineering News, 1904.

Merritt, Raymond H. *Engineering in American Society, 1850–1875.* Lexington: University Press of Kentucky, 1969.

Metals in America's Historic Buildings. Washington: Government Printing Office, 1980.

Meyer, Henry C., Jr. *Steam Power Plants—Their Design and Construction.* New York: McGraw Publishing Co., 1904.

Misa, Thomas J. *A Nation of Steel.* Baltimore: Johns Hopkins University Press, 1995.

Mock, Elizabeth, ed. *Built in USA, 1932–1944.* New York: Museum of Modern Art, 1944.

Montgomery, James. *A Practical Detail of the Cotton Manufacture in the United States.* Glasgow: John Niven Jr., 1840.

Moore, Charles W. *Timing a Century: History of the Waltham Watch Company.* Cambridge: Harvard University Press, 1945.

Moore, Francis C. *Fire Insurance and How to Build.* New York: Baker & Taylor Co., 1903.

Moore, James D. *Plant Layout and Design.* New York: Macmillan, 1962.

Morse, Frederick T. *Power Plant Engineering.* New York: D. Van Nostrand, 1953.

Morton, Hawley Winchester. *Details of Mill Construction.* Boston: Bales & Guild Co., 1907.

Mulrooney, Margaret M. *A Legacy of Coal: The Coal Company Towns of Southwestern Pennsylvania.* Washington: Government Printing Office, 1989.

Munce, James. *Industrial Architecture.* New York: F. W. Dodge Corp., 1960.

Murray, Thomas Edward. *Electric Power Plants, A Description of a Number of Power Stations.* New York, 1910.

Museum of Modern Art. *Modern Architecture: International Exhibition. 1932.* Reprint, New York: Arno Press, 1969.

Navin, Thomas R. *The Whitin Machine Works since 1831—A Textile Machinery Company in an Industrial Village.* Cambridge: Harvard University Press, 1950.

Nelson, Daniel. *Managers and Workers: Origins of the New Factory System in the United States, 1880–1920.* Madison: University of Wisconsin Press, 1975.

Newark, N.J., Illustrated. Newark: Progress Publishing Co., 1901.

New York in Slices. New York: William H. Graham, 1849.

New York State Business Directory. Boston: Adams, Sampson & Co., 1864.

Nye, David E. *American Technological Sublime.* Cambridge: MIT Press, 1994.

———. *Electrifying America: Social Meanings of a New Technology, 1880–1940.* Cambridge: MIT Press, 1990.

Oliver Evans Chapter of the Society for Industrial Archeology. *Workshop of the World.* Philadelphia: Oliver Evans Press, 1990.

One-Hundred Years of Brewing. Chicago: H. S. Rich & Co., 1903; reprint, New York: Arno Press, 1974.

Orear, George W. *Commercial and Architectural St. Louis.* St. Louis: Jones & Orear, 1888.

Passer, Harold C. *The Electric Manufacturers.* Cambridge: Harvard University Press, 1953.

Payne, William. *Cleveland Illustrated: A Pictorial Hand-Book.* Cleveland: Fairbanks, Benedict & Co., 1876.

Peck, E. C. *Modern Factory Management—Buildings and Manufacturing Equipment.* Cleveland: Lincoln Extension University, 1932.

Peck, Frederick W., and Henry H. Earl. *Fall River and Its Industries.* New York: Atlantic Publishing and Engraving Co.; Fall River, Mass.: Benjamin Earle & Son, 1877.

Perrigo, Oscar E. *Modern Machine Shop Construction, Equipment, and Management.* New York: Norman W. Henley Publishing Co., 1906.

Peters, Tom F. *Building the Nineteenth Century.* Cambridge: MIT Press, 1996.

Peterson, Walter F. *An Industrial Heritage: Allis-Chalmers Corporation.* Milwaukee: Milwaukee County Historical Society, 1976.

Phelan, Thomas. *The Hudson Mohawk Gateway: An Illustrated History.* Northridge, Calif.: Windsor Publications, 1985.

Pierson, William Harvey, Jr. *American Buildings and Their Architects: Technology and the Picturesque, The Corporate and the Early Gothic Styles.* Garden City, N.Y.: Anchor Books, Anchor Press/Doubleday, 1980.

Price, George M. *The Modern Factory: Safety, Sanitation and Welfare.* New York: John Wiley & Sons, 1914.

Pursell, Carroll W., Jr. *Early Stationary Steam Engines in America.* Washington: Smithsonian Institution Press, 1969.

———. *The Machine in America.* Baltimore: Johns Hopkins University Press, 1995.

Quinan, Jack. *Frank Lloyd Wright's Larkin Building—Myth and Fact.* Cambridge: MIT Press and the Architectural History Foundation, 1987.

Richards, J. *On the Arrangement, Care, and Operation of Wood-Working Factories and Machinery: Forming a Complete Operator's Handbook.* London and New York: E. & F. N. Spon, 1885.

———. *A Treatise on the Construction and Operation of Wood-Working Machines . . . .* London and New York: E. & F. N. Spon, 1872.

Richards, J. W. *The Functional Tradition in Early Industrial Buildings.* London: Architectural Press, 1958.

Richardson, Milton Thomas. *Practical Carriage Building,* vol. 1. New York: M. T. Richardson Co., 1903.

Ricker, N. Clifford. *A Treatise on the Design and Construction of Roofs.* New York: John Wiley & Sons, 1912.

Ripley, Charles Meigs. *Power as a By-Product.* c. 1916.

———. *Romance of a Great Factory.* Schenectady, N.Y.: Gazette Press, 1919.

Robbins, E. C., and F. E. Folts. *Industrial Management: A Case Book.* New York: McGraw-Hill, 1932.

Rock, Howard B. *New York City Artisan, 1789–1825.* Albany: State University of New York Press, 1989.

Roth, Matthew. *Connecticut—An Inventory of Historic Engineering and Industrial Sites.* Washington: Society for Industrial Archaeology, 1981.

Sachs, Charles. *Made on Staten Island: Agriculture, Industry, and Suburban Living in the City.* New York: Staten Island Historical Society, 1988.

Sanderson, Edmund L. *Waltham Industries: A Collection of Sketches of Early Firms and Founders.* Waltham, Mass.: Waltham Historical Society, 1958.

Schiffer, Margaret Berwind. *Survey of Chester County, Pennsylvania, Architecture, 17th, 18th and 19th Centuries.* Exton, Pa.: Schiffer Publishing Ltd., 1976.

[Scott, John]. *Genius Rewarded, or The Story of the Sewing Machine.* 1880.

Shriner, Charles A. *Paterson, New Jersey, Its Advantages for Manufacturing and Residence: Its Industries, Prominent Men, Banks, Schools, Churches . . . .* Paterson, N.J.: Press Printing and Publishing Co., 1890.

Shubin, John A., and Huxley Madeheim. *Plant Layout.* New York: Prentice-Hall, 1951.

Simpson, Bruce L. *History of the Metal-Casting Industry.* Des Plaines, Ill.: American Foundrymen's Society Publication, 1946.

Sloan, Samuel. *City and Suburban Architecture.* Philadelphia: J. B. Lippincott & Co., 1859.

Small, Harold A., ed. *Form and Function—Remarks on Art by Horatio Greenough.* Berkeley and Los Angeles: University of California Press, 1947.

Smith, Merritt Roe. *Harpers Ferry Armory and the New Technology: The Challenge of Change.* Ithaca, N.Y.: Cornell University Press, 1977.

Smith, Terry. *Making the Modern: Industry, Art, and Design in America*. Chicago: University of Chicago Press, 1993.

Souster, Ernest G. W. *The Design of Factory and Industrial Buildings*. London: Scott, Greenwood & Son, 1919.

Spretson, N. E. *A Practical Treatise on Casting and Founding*. London: E. & F. N. Spon, 1878.

Stilgoe, John R. *Common Landscape of America, 1580–1845*. New Haven, Conn.: Yale University Press, 1982.

———. *Metropolitan Corridor: Railroads and the American Scene*. New Haven, Conn.: Yale University Press, 1983.

Stocker, Harry E. *Materials Handling*. New York: Prentice-Hall, 1943.

Stone, Orra. *History of Massachusetts Industries—Their Inception, Growth and Success*. vols. 1, 2. Boston: S. J. Clarke Publishing Co., 1930.

Stormouth, James. *A Dictionary of the English Language*. New York: Harper & Bros., 1895.

Studley, Gerard L. *Connecticut—The Industrial Incubator*. Hartford: American Society of Mechanical Engineers, 1982.

Sturgis, Russell. *A Dictionary of Architecture and Building*. 1902. Reprint, Detroit: Gale Research Co., 1966.

Swingle, Calvin F. *Practical Hand Book for Millwrights*. Chicago: Frederick J. Drake & Co., 1910.

Tann, Jennifer. *The Development of the Factory*. London: Cornmarket, 1980.

Taylor, Frederick Winslow. *Shop Management*. New York: American Society of Mechanical Engineers, 1903.

Technology and Industrial Efficiency. New York: McGraw-Hill, 1911.

Thomas Alexander Tefft: *American Architecture in Transition, 1845–1860*. Exhibition catalog. Providence, R.I.: Brown University Department of Art, 1987.

Towne, Henry R. *A Treatise on Cranes*. Stamford, Conn., 1883.

Trelease, Allen W. *The North Carolina Railroad, 1849–1871*. Chapel Hill: University of North Carolina Press, 1991.

Trendall, E. W. *Examples for Roofs, Etc.* London: Henry G. Bohn, 1851.

Trumbull, L. R. *A History of Industrial Paterson*. Paterson, N.J.: Carleton M. Herrick, 1882.

Turner, C. A. P. *Concrete Steel Construction. Part I—Buildings*. Minneapolis: Farnham Printing and Stationery Co., 1909.

Turner, Frederick W., and Oscar E. Perrigo. *Machine Shop Work and Management*. Chicago: American Technical Society, 1914.

Twelvetrees, W. Noble. *Concrete-Steel Buildings*. London: Whittaker & Co., 1907.

Tyrrell, Henry Grattan. *Artistic Bridge Design*. Chicago: Myron C. Clark Publishing Co., 1912.

———. *Engineering of Shops and Factories*. New York: McGraw-Hill, 1912.

———. *Mill Building Construction*. New York: Engineering News Publishing Co., 1901.

———. *A Treatise on the Design and Construction of Mill Buildings*. Chicago: Myron C. Clark Publishing Co., 1911.

Upton, Dell, and John Michael Vlach, eds. *Common Places: Readings in American Vernacular Architecture*. Athens: University of Georgia Press, 1986.

Ure, Andrew. *The Philosophy of Manufactures, or, An Exposition of the Scientific, Moral, and Commercial Economy of the Factory System of Great Britain*. London: Charles Knight, 1835.

Van Slycke, J. D. *Representatives of New England Manufactures*. 2 vols. Boston: Van Slycke & Co., 1879.

Vogel, John N., and Theodore J. Karamanski with William A. Irvine. *One Hundred Years of Roofing in America*. Rosement, Ill.: National Roofing Contractors Assoc., 1986.

Vogel, Robert M., ed. *A Report of the Mohawk-Hudson Area Survey*. Washington: Smithsonian Institution Press, 1973.

Warshaw, H. T., ed. *Representative Industries in the United States*. New York: Henry Holt & Co., 1928.

Webster, Noah. *An American Dictionary of the English Language*. New York: White & Sheffield, 1839.

———. *A Dictionary of the English Language*. New York: F. J. Huntington, 1853.

Weitzman, David. *Traces of the Past*. New York: Charles Scribner's Sons, 1980.

West, Thomas D. *American Foundry Practice*. New York: John Wiley & Sons, 1882.

Western Actuarial Bureau. *Analytic System Handbook on Fire Protection*. Chicago, 1924.

White, John H., Jr. *The American Railroad Passenger Car*. Baltimore: Johns Hopkins University Press, 1978.

Whitney, William Dwight. *The Century Dictionary*. New York, 1911.

Wilentz, Sean. *Chants Democratic—New York City and the Rise of the American Working Class, 1788–1850*. New York: Oxford University Press, 1984.

Wilkinson, Chris. *Supersheds*. London: Butterworth Architecture. 1991.

Wilson, Joseph Miller. *The Pennsylvania Railroad Shops at West Philadelphia*. Offprint from *Journal of the Franklin Institute*. Philadelphia: Merrihew & Son, 1873.

Wolf, George A. *Industrial Trenton*. Wilmington, Del.: George A. Wolf, 1900.

———. *Industrial Wilmington*. Wilmington, Del.: George A. Wolf, 1898.

Wood, James P. *Industries of Richmond, Her Trade Commerce, Manufactures and Representative Establishments*. Richmond: Metropolitan Publishing Co., 1886.

Woodbury, C. J. H. *The Fire Protection of Mills and Construction of Mill Floors; Containing Tests of Full Size Wood Mill Columns*. New York: John Wiley & Sons, 1882.

Worcester, Joseph E. *A Dictionary of the English Language*. Philadelphia: J. B. Lippincott Co., 1896.

Worcester: Its Past and Present . . . Illustrated . . . . Worcester, Mass.: Oliver B. Wood, 1888.

Wosk, Julie. *Breaking Frame: Technology and the Visual Arts in the Nineteenth Century*. New Brunswick, N.J.: Rutgers University Press, 1992.

Zink, Clifford W., and Dorothy White Hartman. *Spanning the Industrial Age*. Trenton, N.J.: Trenton Roebling Community Development Corp., 1992.

Zukowsky, John, ed. *Chicago Architecture, 1872–1922: Birth of a Metropolis*. Munich: Prestel-Verlage, 1987.

TRADE LITERATURE

Aberthaw Construction Co. *Modern Industrial Plants in Connecticut*. 1920.

Alcoa Aluminum Corrugated Sheets for Industrial Uses. 1930.

Alfred Box & Co. *Cranes*. Philadelphia, c. 1896.

———. *Northern Liberty Works*. Philadelphia, c. 1880.

Allis-Chalmers Co. *Bulletin No. 1519*. July 1909.

American Cement Tile Manufacturing Co. *Bonanza Cement Tile Roofing*. 1909.

American Rolling Mill Co. *Catalogue A, Roofing Department*. 1902.

Asbestos Protected Metal Co. *Asbestosteel for Roofs and Walls, Bulletin 53*. Beaver Falls, Pa., 1913.

The Austin Co. *The Austin Book of Buildings*, 8th ed. Catalog no. 20, c. 1925.

———. *Austin Standard Factory-Buildings* ("The Austin Method"). Cleveland, 1913.

Babcock & Wilcox. *Steam: Its Generation and Use with Catalogue of the Manufactures of the Babcock & Wilcox Co.*, 20th ed. 1889.

Ballinger Co. *Buildings for Commerce and Industry*. Philadelphia, 1924.

———. *"Super-Span" Saw-tooth Buildings*. Philadelphia, 1924.

Berger Manufacturing Co. *Berger's Ferro-Lithic Plates*. 1910.

———. *Catalogue No. 10*. c. 1915.

Berlin Iron Bridge Co. [Catalog.] East Berlin, Conn., c. 1888.

————. *Engineers, Architects, and Builders in Iron and Steel*. Hartford: Case, Lockwood & Brainard, c. 1892.

Bridesburg Manufacturing Co. *Descriptive Catalogue of Machines Built by the Bridesburg Manufacturing Company*. 1867.

Brown Hoisting and Conveying Machine Co. *"Brownhoist" Cranes*. Cleveland, 1903.

————. *"Brownhoist" Patent Automatic Hoisting and Conveying Appliances*. Cleveland, 1900.

Builders' Iron and Fire-proof Work, Bridges, Roofs, Girders. Philadelphia, 1883.

Canton Iron Roofing Co. *Illustrated Catalogue of Canton Iron Roofing Co.* Canton, Ohio, 1888.

Chalmers-Spence Co. *Manufacture of Non-conducting Coverings, Asbestos Products, Fire-proof Materials*. Philadelphia, 1885.

Clark Thread Co. *A Thread Mill Illustrated*. Newark, c. 1882.

Crowell-Lundoff-Little Co. *The Blue Book of Industrial Construction. Economy Factory Buildings*. Cleveland, Ohio, c. 1918.

David Lupton's Sons Co. *Air, Light and Efficiency*. 1917.

————. *Air and Light in Machine Shops*. 1920.

————. *Lupton Products Service* (no. 7). c. 1925.

————. *Lupton's Architectural Sheet Metal Works Catalog*. c. 1910.

————. *Lupton Service Products* (no. 11). 1922.

————. *Lupton Specialties*. 1910.

Detroit Steel Products Co. *Fenestra Solid Steel Windows*. c. 1920.

————. *Fenestra Steel Window Walls—Side Wall Sash*. c. 1920.

————. *Fenestra Steel Window Walls: The Blue Book of Steel Windows*. 1924.

————. *Pamphlet Y, Detroit Fenestra Window Sash*. c. 1915.

————. *Window Walls, Their Cost and Their Advantage*. 1920.

Doubleday, Page & Co. *The Country Life Press, Garden City, New York—Its Garden, Its Home, Its Sun Dial*. New York: Friends of Doubleday, Page & Co., 1913.

Duplex Hanger Co. *Duplex Malleable Iron, Joist Hangers, Wall Hangers, Concrete Block Hangers*. Cleveland, 1930.

Edwin Harrington, Son & Co. *Harrington Hoists, Overhead Railway, Travelling Cranes*. Philadelphia, c. 1887.

Emery & Co. *Annual Circular of Emery & Co., Prop. of the Albany Agricultural Works*. Albany, 1853.

Enterprise Manufacturing Co. *Catalogue, Enterprise Mfg. Co. of Pennsylvania*. Philadelphia, 1874.

————. *Catalogue and Price List of the Enterprise Manufacturing Company of Pennsylvania*. 1883.

Frank P. Sheldon & Son. *A Half Century of Achievement*. Providence, R.I.: F. P. Sheldon & Son, 1921.

G. & D. Cook & Co.'s *Illustrated Catalogue of Carriages and Special Business Directory*. New Haven, Conn., 1860.

General Electric Light Co. *Bulletin*. Nos. 4–18, 1882–1883.

George Hayes Co. *The "Hayes" Metal Skylights and Other Glazed Structures, Fire-Proof Wireglass Windows, etc., Lathing and Fireproof Construction*. New York, 1898.

————. *Treatise on Metal Lathing as a Most Important Factor in the Construction of Buildings: Embracing a System of Fire-Proof Construction*. New York, 1898.

Harlan & Hollingsworth Co. *The Harlan & Hollingsworth Company Ship and Car Builders—Their Plant and Operations*. Wilmington, 1898.

————. *Semi-Centennial Memoir of the Harlan & Hollingsworth Co., Wilmington, Del., 1836–1886*. Wilmington, c. 1886.

Hollow Building Tile Association. *Handbook of Hollow Building Tile Construction*, 5th ed. 1924.

J. Estey & Co. *The Estey Organs*. c. 1876.

James C. Stewart Co. *Some Stewart Structures.* 1909.

Johns Manufacturing Co. *Descriptive Price List . . . Asbestos.* Chicago: Johns Manufacturing Co., 1889.

Johns Manville Co. *JM Asbestos Roofing, Catalog No. 303.* 1909.

———. *Johns-Manville Asbestoside.* 1924.

———. *Johns-Manville Service to Industry.* 1924.

Jones and Larson Corp. *Industrial Steel Buildings.* Maspeth, N.Y., c. 1930.

Lincoln Electric Co. *Arc Welding: The New Age in Iron and Steel.* Cleveland, c. 1926.

Mattison Co. *Ambler Asbestos Corrugated Sheeting.* Ambler, Pa., 1909.

———. *Asbestos Roofing Slate Shingles and Sheathing.* Ambler, Pa., 1906.

Milliken Bros. *Allowable Working Loads for Phoenix Columns of Iron and Steel, for
Buildings.* New York, 1890.

———. [Catalog.] New York, 1899.

National Fire Proofing Company. *Long Span Fireproof Construction in Reinforced
Terra Cotta Hollow Tile.* 1908.

Niles Tool Works. *Catalog of the Niles Tool Works.* Hamilton, Ohio, 1891.

O. Meeker & Co. *Newark Foundry.* c. 1835.

Phoenix Iron Co. *Useful Information for Architects, Engineers, and Workers in
Wrought Iron and Steel of the Phoenix Iron Co.* 1890.

Pittsburgh Plate Glass Co., *Glass, Paints, Varnishes and Brushes, Their History,
Manufacture and Use.* Pittsburgh, 1923.

Power Transmission Council. *Principles of Mechanical Power Transmission.* New
York, c. 1947.

Pusey & Jones Corporation. *A Trip through the Puseyjones [sic] Plant.* Wilmington,
1948.

Reeves, Buck & Co. *Phoenix Iron.* c. 1854.

Reinforced Concrete in Factory Construction. New York: Atlas Portland Cement Co.,
1907, 1915.

Rogers Locomotive Works. *Locomotives and Locomotive Building.* New York, 1876.

Silsby, Race & Holly. [Catalog.] 1852.

Simonds Saw & Steel Co. *Saws—Knives—Files.* Catalog no. 39.

Standard Roof and Bridge Co. *L. Sykes & Son, Engineers and Manufacturers of Iron
Buildings, Warehouses, Builders' Iron and Fire-proof Work, Bridges, Roofs,
Girders.* Philadelphia, 1883.

Stone & Webster. *Industrial Buildings.* Boston, 1918.

———. *Stone & Webster, 1888–1932.* New York and Boston, c. 1932.

Sweet's Indexed Catalogue of Building Construction for the Year 1906. New York:
Architectural Record.

T. C. Snyder & Co. *Illustrated Catalogue: Iron Roofing, Siding and Ceiling, Fire-proof
Doors and Shutters, Eave Troughs and Conductors, Iron Ore Paint.* Canton,
Ohio, 1886.

Talbott & Bro. *An Illustrated Catalog of Machinery.* Richmond, c. 1860.

Truscon Co. *Truscon Steel Hy-Rib and Metal Lath.* 1909.

Truscon Steel Co. *Truscon Buildings Standardized for All Industrial Requirements,
Catalog No. 220.* Youngstown, Ohio, 1930.

———. *Truscon Standard Buildings Built with Standard Stock Units.* Youngstown,
Ohio, 1922.

Trussed Concrete Steel Co. *United Steel Sash.* Detroit, 1913.

Turner Construction Co. *Buildings by Turner.* New York, 1939.

———. *To Commemorate the 40th Anniversary of the Founding of the Turner Construction Co., May 6, 1902.* New York, 1942.

———. *50 Years of Buildings by Turner.* New York, 1952.

———. *A Record of War Activities.* New York, 1918.

———. *Reinforced Concrete.* New York, 1905.

Walker Manufacturing Co. *Hydraulic Cable and General Machinery.* Cleveland,
1893.

Wilkinson Manufacturing Co. [Catalog.] Bridgeport, Pa., c. 1900.

William Sellers & Co., Inc. *Illustrated Catalogue and General Description of Improved Machine Tools for Working Metal.* Philadelphia, 1895.

Worthington Pump and Machinery Corporation, *100 Years, 1840–1940: Worthington.* Harrison, N.J., 1940.

JOURNAL ARTICLES

Abell, O. J. "A New Development in Factory Buildings." *Iron Age* 93 (April 9, 1914): 902–904.

Ackerman, Frederick L. "The Architectural Theory of Concrete Design." *American Concrete Institute Proceedings* 23 (1927): 257–262.

"The Advantages Claimed for Brick and Steel Factory Buildings." *Iron Age* 56 (December 19, 1895): 1272–1273.

"Aesthetic Consideration in Factory Designs." *American Architect* 99 (June 14, 1911): 243.

"Albany Iron Works." *Appleton's Mechanic's Magazine* 3 (January 1853): 9.

Aldrich, William S. "Electric Power for Factories." *Cassier's Magazine* 18 (July 1900): 194–196.

Alford, L. P., and H. C. Farrell. "Factory Construction and Arrangement." *American Society of Mechanical Engineers Journal* 33 (July–December 1911): 1141–1166.

"The Ambridge Plant of the American Bridge Co." *Engineering Record* 48 (November 21, 1903): 620–623; (November 28, 1903): 648–652; (December 5, 1903): 684–686; (December 12, 1903): 720–723; (December 19, 1903): 722–724; (December 26, 1903): 816–818; 49 (January 2, 1904): 23–26; (January 9, 1904): 50–53; (January 16, 1904): 77–79; (January 23, 1904): 102–104.

"American Bridge Shop Practice." *Engineering News* 39 (April 21, 1898): 256–258.

"American Industries—No. 59. The Manufacture of Standard Scales." *Scientific American* 43 (November 6, 1880): 285, 290.

"American Machinery—Mattewan." *Scientific American* 5 (April 27, 1850): 253.

"An Apartment Hotel for Factories." *Bush Magazine* 3 (October 15, 1916): 16.

Appel, Susan K. "Artificial Refrigeration and the Architecture of 19th Century American Breweries." *Journal of the Society for Industrial Archaeology* 16 (1990): 21–38.

———. "Brewery Architecture in America from the Civil War to Prohibition." In *The Midwest in American Architecture*, ed. John Garner. Urbana and Chicago: University of Illinois Press, 1991.

"Architects and Engineers." *Van Nostrand's Engineering Magazine* 13 (January 1870): 1–5.

"The Architectural Utility of Iron." *Iron Age* 11 (January 9, 1873): 1.

Arnold, Horace L. "Modern Machine-Shop Economics, I—The Location of the Shop." *Engineering Magazine* 11 (April 1896): 59–66; "Modern Machine-Shop Economics, II—Prime Requisites of Shop Construction." (May 1896): 263–298; "Modern Machine Shop Economics, III—A Modern Plan for a Modern Shop." (June 1896): 469–477.

"The Arrangement and Construction of Railway Shop Plants." *Engineering News* 36 (July 23, 1896): 56–57.

"Artists and Artisans." *Scientific American* 15 (August 25, 1866): 135.

Atkinson, Edward. "The Architecture of Mill Buildings." *American Architect and Building News* 5 (May 10, 1879): 152.

———. "Slow-Burning Construction." *American Architect and Building News* 6 (July 12, 1879): 14.

———. "Slow-Burning Construction." *Century Magazine* 37 (February 1889): 566–579.

"The Automobile Manufacturing Plant of the Studebaker Corporation at South

Bend, Indiana." *Architecture and Building* 52 (November 1920): 96–98, plates.

Banham, Reyner. "Ransome at Bayonne." *Journal of the Society of Architectural Historians* 42 (December 1983): 383–387.

Becker, O. M., and William J. Lees. "Building a Factory." *System* 10 (September 1906): 239–250; (October 1906): 377–386; (November 1906): 484–489; (December 1906): 583–591; 11 (January 1907): 28–35; (February 1907): 163–168; (March 1907): 279–283; (April 1907): 387–392.

Benson, O. "Incombustible Foundry Buildings." *Iron Trade Review* 31 (June 23, 1898): 14–16.

Biggs, Lindy. "The Engineered Factory." *Technology and Culture* 36 (April 1995): supplement 174–188.

"Boiler House and Stack." *Carpentry and Building* 4 (May 1882): 90.

"The Bridge and Structural Shops of the American Bridge Co. at Gary." *Engineering News-Record* 65 (June 29, 1912): 704–708.

Briggs, Warren R. "Modern American Factories." *Architecture* 38 (September 1918): 231–233.

Brill, George M. "Location, Layout and Construction of Manufacturing Plants." *Western Society of Engineers Journal* 13 (April 1908): 149–172.

"Brown & Sharpe Foundry." *American Engineer* 2 (October 1881): 194–196.

"The Brown and Sharpe Mfg. Co.'s Works—1. Description of the Buildings and Views of Several Departments." *Machinery* 7 (April 1901): 239–243.

"The Buffalo Car-Works." *National Car Builder* 4 (January 1873): 11.

"Buffalo Steam Engine Works." *New York State Mechanic* 1 (May 1842): 191.

"Building in One Package." *Architectural Forum* 82 (January 1945): 93–109.

"Bush Tenant Factories." *Insurance Engineering* 10 (October 1905): 419–427.

Cady, Cecil I. "Industrial Lighting Practice." *Pencil Points* 25 (March 1944): 56–61.

Caldwell, George A. "Automatic Welding of Structural Steel." *Journal of the American Welding Society* 7 (January 1928): 30–38.

Candee, Richard M. "Architecture and Corporate Planning in the Early Waltham System." In *Essays from the Lowell Conference on Industrial History 1982 and 1983*, ed. Robert Weible. North Andover, Mass.: Museum of American Textile History, 1985.

———. "The 1822 Allendale Mill and Slow-Burning Construction: A Case Study in the Transmission of an Architectural Technology." *Journal of the Society for Industrial Archaeology* 15 (1989): 21–34.

———. "The 'Great Factory' at Dover, New Hampshire: The Dover Manufacturing Co. Print Works, 1825." *Old-Time New England* 66 (Summer–Fall 1975): 39–51.

———. "Three Architects of Early New Hampshire Mill Towns." *Journal of the Society of Architectural Historians* 30 (May 1971): 155–163.

Carpenter, J. W. "Shops and Shop Buildings." *Engineering News* 6 (July 22, 1876): 240.

Carver, George P. "Reinforced Concrete Building Work for the United Shoe Machinery Co., Beverly, Mass." *Engineering News* 53 (May 25, 1905): 537–541.

Chapman, Howard. "Design of Industrial Buildings." *American Architect* 107 (February 24, 1915): 113–115.

Chase, Frank D. "The Modern Factory Must Fit Its Job." *Central Manufacturing District Magazine* 7 (March 1923): 14–17, 54–57.

Christie, William. "Recent American Chimney Practice." *Cassier's Magazine* 29 (February 1906): 267–279.

"Chronology of the Nineteenth Century." *Machinery* 7 (December 1900): 115–125.

Clarke, C. W. E. "The Generation and Utilization of Power in Industries." *American Architect* 99 (June 14, 1911): 240–241.

Coes, Harold V. "The Rehabilitation of Existing Plants as a Factor in Production Costs." *Engineering Magazine* 59 (June 1915): 357–371 and (July 1915): 560–573.

Collins, D. C. Newman. "The Design and Construction of Industrial Buildings." *Engineering Magazine* 33 (September 1907): 906–930.

———. "The Engineering of Industrial Buildings." *Iron Age* 74 (December 1, 1904): 30–31.

"Columns Set Back of Walls Give Large Window Area." *Engineering News-Record* 80 (April 25, 1918): 809.

"The Concrete Erecting Shop of the Ingersoll Milling Machine Co." *Machinery* 12 (May 1906): 446–449.

"A Concrete-Steel Factory Building with 52-Foot Roof Girders." *Architectural Record* 49 (January 15, 1904): 67–71.

Condron, Theodore L. "A Unique Type of Reinforced Concrete Construction." *Western Society of Engineers Journal* 14 (November–December 1909): 824–834.

"The Construction of Mill Roofs—A View of a One-Story Weaving Mill." *American Architect and Building News* 6 (August 9, 1879): 44, plate 189.

"The Construction of the Westinghouse Electric Co.'s Plant at Manchester, England." *Journal of Worcester Polytechnic Institute* 5 (1901–1902): 301.

"The Continental Works, Greenpoint, Long Island, A Model Foundry." *Manufacturer and Builder* 2 (April 1870): 105–106.

"Controlled Environment in Windowless Plant for Simonds Saw & Steel Co." *Architectural Record* 85 (June 1939): 103–109.

"Convenient Foundry Arrangement." *American Machinist* 6 (January 27, 1883): 1–2.

Corbett, Harvey Wiley. "Facts, Factories and Frills." *American Architect* 113 (February 27, 1918): 233–238.

"Corrosion of Steel." *Insurance Engineering* 4 (October 1902): 343.

"Corrugated Iron as Building Material." *Industrial Monthly* 3 (1872): 299.

"Corrugated Metal Buildings." *Industrial America* 1 (June 5, 1885): 141.

Cory, R. G., and W. M. Cory. "Planning for Laundry Efficiency." *Architectural Record* 72 (October 1932): 253.

"Cost of Factory Buildings of Timber and of Concrete." *Engineering News* 76 (November 9, 1916): 884–886.

"The Country Life Press." *American Architect* 99 (June 14, 1911): plate.

Crain, G. D., Jr. "The Logic of the One Story Factory." *Iron Trade Review* 57 (July 15, 1915): 138.

Crocker, F. B., V. M. Benedict, and A. F. Ormsbee. "Electric Power in Factories and Mills." *Western Society of Engineers Journal* 1 (1896): 840–841.

Curran, Kathleen. "The German Rundbogenstil and Reflections on the American Round-Arched Style." *Journal of the Society of Architectural Historians* 47 (December 1988): 351–373.

"Dale's Patent Platform and Counter Scale Manufactory, Lansingburgh, N.Y." *Mechanic's Advocate* 1 (February 25, 1847): 1.

"Dawn of the Railroad." *American Heritage* 35 (August–September 1984): 65.

"Daylight Illumination for Manufacturing Buildings." *American Architect* 99 (June 14, 1911): 238–239.

"Dayton Engineering Laboratories Co." *American Architect* 109 (March 22, 1916): plate.

Deacon, George F. "The Aesthetics of Construction." *Van Nostrand's Engineering Magazine* 1 (July 1869): 641–644.

Dean, F. W. "What Is Mill Building Construction?" *Engineering News-Record* 79 (December 27, 1917): 1184.

De Maré, Eric, and A. W. Skempton. "The Sheerness Boat Store (1858–1860)." *Royal Institute of British Architects Journal*, 3d ser., 68 (June 1961): 317–324.

Dempsey, Florence. "Nela Park." *Architectural Record* 35 (June 1914): 467–503.

"A Description of What Has Been Accomplished in Eight Years." *Central Manufacturing District Magazine* 1 (November 1917): 1–9.

Des Granges, Donald. "The Designing of Power Stations." *Architectural Forum* 51 (September 1929): 361–369.

"Design for a Slow-Burning Cotton-Mill. By Mr. Richard S. Atkinson, Boston." *American Architect and Building News* 6 (October 25, 1879): 132, plate 200.

"Destruction by Fire of the Famous Whitely Shops at Springfield, O." *Machinery* 8 (March 1902): 224.

"Details of a Brass and Iron Foundry." *American Machinist* 5 (April 15, 1882): 2–3.

Diemer, Hugo. "The Planning of Factory Buildings and the Influence of Design on Their Productive Capacity." *Engineering News* 50 (March 24, 1904): 292–294.

"Discussion—Monumental Buildings." *American Concrete Institute Proceedings* 24 (1928): 121.

"Discussion on the Individual Operation of Machine Tools by Electric Motors; Opening Remarks by Charles Day." *Journal of the Franklin Institute* 158 (November 1904): 321–352.

Dolke, W. Fred, Jr. "Some Essentials in the Construction of an Industrial Building." *American Architect* 111 (February 21, 1917): 112–116.

Draffin, Jasper O. "A Brief History of Lime, Cement, Concrete and Reinforced Concrete." *Journal of the Western Society of Engineers* 48 (March 1943): 41–42.

DuBoff, Richard B. "The Introduction of Electric Power in American Manufacturing." *Economic History Review* 30 (1967): 509–518.

Durfee, W. F. "A Power Crane." *American Society of Mechanical Engineers* 5 (1883): 131–137.

Dwyer, Pat. "Getting Ready for Huge Production." *Foundry* 47 (October 1, 1919): 697–702.

"The Egan Company—Their New Buildings at Cincinnati, O." *Age of Steel* 67 (April 12, 1890): 1.

"Electro-Motive Corporation Works at La Grange, Illinois." *Architectural Record* 81 (February 1937): 15–31.

Elliott, E. L. "XII—Industrial Lighting." *Illuminating Engineer* 2 (1907–1908): 660–666.

"Enclosed Acreage." *Engineering News-Record* 116 (March 5, 1936): 337–342.

"Enlargement of the Baldwin Locomotive Works." *Railway Age* 34 (November 21, 1902): 553–559.

"Era of All-Metal and Windowless Buildings Is Close at Hand." *Iron Age* 127 (January 15, 1931): 234–235, 291.

"Erection of a Reinforced Concrete Factory for the Bush Terminal Co." *Engineering Record* 53 (March 3, 1906): 282–284.

Erwood, John. "Concrete Construction at Rambler Factory Works." *American Machinist* 29 (August 16, 1906): 199–201.

"An Example of Recent Factory Construction: The Automobile Works of the White Company, Cleveland, Ohio." *Iron Age* 79 (May 2, 1907): 1329–1335.

"An Example of Western 'Shopitecture.' " *American Machinist* 5 (October 7, 1882): 5.

"Extensive Works for the Manufacture of Iron Tubing." *Industrial Monthly* 5 (July 1874): 150–151.

"Extracts from Chordal's Letters." *American Machinist* 4 (April 9, 1881): 1–2.

"A Factory Building of Steel and Glass." *Engineering News* 40 (July 7, 1898): 15.

"Factory Buildings." *Architectural Record* 85 (June 1939): 97–102.

"Factory for American Can Co., Jersey City, N.J." *Architectural Forum* 61 (December 1937): 519–520.

"Factory of the American Arithmometer Co., Detroit, Mich." *American Architect and Building News* 87 (April 1, 1905): 107–108.

"Factory of the American Bank Note Company." *Architecture and Building* 43 (August 1911): 490–494.

Fairbairn, William. "Report on Fire Proof Warehouses." *Practical Mechanic and Engineer's Magazine* (Glasgow) 4 (January 1845): 105–108.

Fairbrother, F. A. "Processes Affect Design of Automobile Factories." *Engineering News-Record* 93 (November 20, 1924): 834–836.

Ferguson, J. E. "Welding of Structural Steel." *Journal of the American Welding Society* 10 (July 1931): 39–43.

' "Ferroinclave,' a New Fireproofing." *Insurance Engineering* 5 (April 1, 1903): 291–303.

"Fire-Proof and Plank Floors." *American Mechanics Magazine* 2 (August 30, 1825): 42–43.

"A Fireproof Piano Factory." *Insurance Engineering* 9 (January 1905): 32–36.

"Fire-Resistant Roofs." *Insurance Engineering* 6 (September 1903): 215.

Fisher, Marvin. "The Iconology of Industrialism, 1830–60." *American Quarterly* 13 (Fall 1961): 347–364.

Fitzgerald, R. S. "The Anatomy of a Victorian Crane: The Coburg Boiler Shop Crane and Its Technological Context." *Industrial Archaeology* Review 12 (Spring 1990): 185–193.

Fogg, William R. "New Departure in Building Construction—The Glass Front Factory." *Building Age* 44 (November 1922): 26–27.

"The Forge Shop of the Packard Motor Car Company, Detroit." *American Architect* 114 (July 3, 1918): 30–33.

"Foundry and Pattern Departments of the B. F. Sturtevant Company." *Machinery* 9 (November 1903): 121–124.

"The Foundry of the Standard Steel Car Co." *Engineering Record* 62 (November 26, 1910): 405.

"The Frances Building." *Inland Architect* 13–14 (February 1889): 9.

Freeman, John R. "Comparison of English and American Types of Factory Construction." *Association of Engineering Societies Journal* 10 (January 1891): 19–51.

"Fulton Boiler Works." *Age of Steel* 67 (May 3, 1890): 12.

"The Fulton Foundry and Machine Works." *Iron Age* 79 (January 10, 1907): 133–135.

Gardiner, F. M. "Factory Entrances." *American Architect* 111 (February 21, 1917): 117–123.

"General Principles of Industrial Building Planning." *Architectural Forum* 39 (September 1923): 89–94.

"Geo. J. Fritz's Foundry and Machine Works." *Age of Steel* (September 15, 1888): 15.

"The German Niles Tool Works, Berlin." *Engineering* 79 (May 30, 1902): 701–704.

Gibson, George H., and A. Home-Morton. "The Design of Industrial Works." *Mechanical Engineer* 24 (July 30, 1909): 137–140; (December 20, 1909): 845–848.

Gifford, George E. "Design of the King Bridge Company's New Riveting Shop." *Association of Engineering Societies Journal* 8 (June 1894): 281–294.

Gilbert, Cass. "Industrial Architecture in Concrete." *Architectural Forum* 39 (September 1923): 83–86.

Gillet, Louis A. "Electricity in the Machine Shop." *The Engineer* 40 (November 2, 1903): 811; (November 16, 1903): 862–864.

"The Great West-Allis Plant of the Allis-Chalmers Company, Milwaukee, Wis." *Machinery* 8 (February 1903): 285–289.

Greene, Stephen. "Modification in Mill Design Resulting from Changes in Motive

Power." *New England Cotton Manufactures Association Proceedings* 63 (October 1897): 128–136.

Groben, William E. "Modern Industrial Plant of the American Chicle Company." *Architecture and Building* 52 (December 1920): 102–104, plates.

Haber, Henri J. "Artistic Engineering." *Engineering News* 7 (May 26, 1877): 134–136.

Hamlin, A. D. F. "The Architectural Problem of Concrete." *American Architect and Building News* 91 (May 4, 1907): 163.

Hamlin, Talbot. "Architecture." In *New International Yearbook for the Year 1931*, ed. Frank Moore Colby, 53–54. New York: Dodd, Mead & Co., 1932.

———. "Factories as Architecture." *Pencil Points* 21 (August 1940): 469–482.

Harnischfeger, H. "First Electric Traveling Crane Built in the United States." *Iron Age* 118 (September 9, 1926): 722.

Haskell, Douglas. "Architecture." In *New International Yearbook for the Year 1938*, ed. Frank Moore Colby, 49. New York: Dodd, Mead & Co., 1939.

———. "Architecture." *New International Yearbook for the Year 1940*, ed. Frank Moore Colby, 35. New York: Dodd, Mead & Co., 1941.

Heidenreich, E. Lee. "Monier Constructions." *Western Society of Engineers Journal* 5 (1900): 208–224.

Helmle, Frank J. "Architectural Expression in Concrete." *Architectural Forum* 34 (January 1921): 11–16.

———. "The Fletcher Building." *Architecture* 42 (October 1920): 291–293.

Hess, Henry. "Works Design as a Factor in Manufacturing Economy." *Engineering Magazine* 27 (July 1904): 498–520.

Hexamer, C. John. "Mill Architecture." *Journal of the Franklin Institute* 120 (July 1885): 1–17.

Hildebrand, Grant. "New Factory for the Geo. N. Pierce Company, Buffalo, New York, 1906." *Journal of the Society of Architectural Historians* 29 (March 1970): 51–55.

"Hints on Construction and Arrangement of a Wood Working Establishment." *Manufacturer and Builder* 1 (October 1869): 306–307.

"The Holly Manufacturing Co." *Manufacturer and Builder* 20 (February 1888): 32–33, plates.

Holley, A. E., and Lenox Smith. "American Iron and Steel Works, No. XXXVIII— The Works of the Phoenix Iron Company." *Engineering* (February 5, 1880): 103–104.

Hounshell, David A. "Public Relations or Public Understanding?: The American Industries Series in *Scientific American*." *Technology and Culture* 21 (October 1980): 589–593.

"How [the] Electric Traveling Crane Came." *Iron Age* 118 (August 26, 1926): 541–543.

Humphrey, Richard L. "The Progress of Two Decades." *American Concrete Institute Proceedings* 20 (1924): 22–42.

Humphreys, J. H. "The Design and Construction of Modern Engineering Workshops." *Mechanical Engineer* 10 (December 13, 1902): 798–800.

Hunting, E. N. "Reinforced Concrete Applied to Modern Shop Construction." *Engineering* 81 (March 16, 1906): 357–359.

Hutchinson, George H. "*Mill Building Construction* with Details from Actual Practice." *Engineer's Society of Western Pennsylvania Transactions* (1892): 247–263; *Engineering News* 48 (November 10, 1892): 446–451.

Huxtable, Ada Louise. "Concrete Technology in the United States, Historical Survey." *Progressive Architecture* 41 (October 1960): 141–149.

———. "Progressive Architecture in America—Reinforced-Concrete Construction. The Work of Ernest L. Ransome, Engineer, 1884–1911." *Progressive Architecture* 38 (September 1957): 139–142.

"Improved Concrete Construction." *Real Estate Record and Guide* 74 (December 4, 1909): 995.

"Industrial Buildings." *Architectural Forum* 99 (August 1953): 98–100.

"Industrial Buildings Planned for Light and Efficiency." *American Builder* 38 (June 1925): 208–209.

"Industrial Plant with All Structures Built of Reinforced Concrete." *Engineering Record* 67 (March 8, 1913): 256–258.

"Industries in America." *Scientific American* 40 (January 11, 1879): 17.

"In the Making of a Steam Car." *The Automobile* 17 (September 19, 1907): 401–402.

"Iron as a Building Material." *Practical Mechanic's Journal* 5 (1852–53): 273–274.

"Iron Roof in the United States Government Navy Yard, Brooklyn." *Practical Mechanic's Journal* 8 (1855–56): 29–30.

Jackson, Dugald C. "The Equipment of Manufacturing Establishments with Electric Motors and Electric Power Distribution." *Western Society of Engineers Journal* 1 (1896): 807–820.

Jamme, Louis T. "Developing an Industrial District." *Central Manufacturing District Magazine* 7 (August 1923): 12–16, 83.

Jenney, William Le Baron. "Strength of Buildings." *Engineering News* 7 (May 26, 1877): 139.

Jennings, Arthur Seymour. "Brick-Work and Brick-Laying—V." *Carpentry and Building* 11 (August 1889): 157–158; "Brick-Work and Brick-Laying—VI." 12 (January 1890): 3–4.

Joy, S. Scott. "The Central Manufacturing District, Chicago, Ill., Part 1." *Architectural Forum* 34 (April 1921): 123–127; "The Central Manufacturing District, Chicago, Ill., Part 2." *Architectural Forum* 34 (May 1921): 177–182.

Kahn, Albert. "Industrial Architecture." *Michigan Society of Architects Weekly Bulletin* 13 (November 7, 1939): 5–9.

———. "Reinforced Concrete Architecture These Past Twenty Years." *Proceedings of the American Concrete Institute* 20 (1924): 106–121.

Kahn, Felix. "Comments on Industrial Engineering." *The Architect* 16 (September 1918): 123–127.

Kellogg, Harold Field. "Co-operation between Architect and Builder." *Architectural Forum* 39 (September 1923): 96–98.

"The Kelly and Jones Company's Concrete Steel Factory Building." *Engineering Record* 49 (February 6, 1904): 153–154.

Kermode, J. T. "Factory Lighting." *Illuminating Engineer* 2 (1907–1908): 621–623.

King, H. R. "The Hawthorne Shops of the Western Electric Co." *Western Society of Engineers Journal* 11 (1906): 413–432.

Klaber, John J. "Building the Factory." *Engineering Magazine* 51 (June 1916): 355–367.

Knowlton, Howard S. "The New Building for the Cream of Wheat Co." *Engineering Record* 50 (October 29, 1904): 513–514.

Koester, Frank. "Industrial Architecture." *American Architect* 106 (July 8, 1914): 17–21.

Kohn, Robert D. "Architecture and Factories." *Architectural Record* 25 (February 1909): 131–136.

"A Large Monolithic Factory Building." *Engineering Record* 38 (July 30, 1898): 188–189.

"Large One-Story Industrial Building." *Engineering News-Record* 99 (September 29, 1927): 496–499.

"A Large Southern Manufactory." *Industrial Review* 2 (1883): 286.

Larned, E. S., and Frank E. Warren. "A New Concrete Wood-Worsted Mill." *Cement Age* 4 (April 1907): 218–237.

Le Van, William Barnet. "The Loftiest Chimney in America." *Manufacturer and Builder* 20 (November 1888): 244; (December 1888): 276–277.

"Lidgerwood Manufacturing Co." *Scientific American* 58 (June 2, 1888): 341.

Lincoln, J. F. "Erection of Buildings by Welding." *Journal of the American Welding Society* 7 (September 1928): 72–83.

Lintner, Sylvia Chace. "Mill Architecture in Fall River: 1865–1880." *New England Quarterly* 22 (June 1948): 185–196.

Little, T. J. "Industrial Gas Lighting." *Illuminating Engineer* 2 (1907–1908): 667–672.

"A Locally Famous Old Beam Engine." *Steam Engineering* 3 (February 1902): 171.

Lockhardt, William F. "Largest Concrete Loft Building on Manhattan Island." *Concrete* 18 (April 1921): 165–168.

"A Long Span Concrete Girder Pierce Arrow Motor Car Co." *Engineering Record* 62 (November 5, 1910): 529.

"Long Span Steel Arches Incorporate Sawtooth Roof." *Engineering News-Record* 117 (October 15, 1936): 542–544.

"The Lunkenheimer Co.'s Fairmount Works." *Steam Engineering* 4 (December 10, 1902): 185.

Lyon, Tracy. "Shops of the Walter A. Wood Harvester Co., at St. Paul, Minn." *Engineering News* 31 (April 19, 1894): 314–315.

Maag, J. Henry. "General Foods' Corn Mill." *Architectural Concrete* 4 (1938): 8–9.

"Machine Shop at Winchedon." *American Architect and Building News* 1 (March 4, 1876): plate.

Main, Charles T. "Industrial Building since 1874." *Engineering News-Record* 92 (April 17, 1924): 658–660.

"The Main Shops of the American Locomotive Co., Schenectady." *Engineering Record* 48 (August 3, 1903): 130–131.

"A Mammoth Reconstruction Project." *Central Manufacturing District Magazine* 4 (April 1920): 57.

"Mansfield Machine-Works." *National Car Builder* 3 (December 1872): 6.

"Manufactory of Otis Brothers & Co., at Yonkers, N.Y." *The Technologist* 2 (June 1871): 164.

"The Manufacture of Agricultural Machinery." *Machinery* 8 (August 1902): 369–375.

"The Manufacture of Engines, Saw Mills and Grain Separators." *Scientific American* 43 (March 17, 1883): 157–163.

"The Manufacture of Leather Belting." *Industrial Monthly* 2 (September 1873): 1.

"The Manufacture of Standard Scales." *Scientific American* 43 (November 6, 1880): 290.

"Manufacturing Corporations and Manufacturing Villages." *New Englander* 7 (May 1849): 240–253.

"Manufacturing Establishments—Coach Factory of James Goold & Co." *New York State Mechanic* 1 (December 11, 1841): 17.

"Manufacturing Plant of the Continental Can Company, Clearing, Ill." *American Architect* 58 (February 27, 1918): 253–258.

Marsh, F. A. "Arc Welding Structural Steel." *Welding Engineer* 12 (May 1927): 29–31.

Matte, J. "Structural Welding." *Journal of the American Welding Society* 77 (July 1928): 37–47.

"The Maverick Cotton Mills at East Boston." *Engineering Record* 62 (November 5, 1910): 527–529.

Mayer, William E. "A Modern Industrial Plant." *Architectural Concrete* 5 (1939): 32–33.

Maynicke, Robert. "The Mercantile Building." *Real Estate Record and Guide* 73 (June 11, 1904): 1429–1437.

McCabe, John F. "A Visit to R. Hoe & Co.'s Great New York Plant." *Printing Trade News* (February 1910).

McConnell, J. M. "Industrial Plant Design." *Journal of the Western Society of Engineers* 28 (January 1923): 1–17.

McKibben, Frank P. "Present Status of Welding Steel Buildings by Electricity."
  Journal of the American Welding Society 7 (September 1928): 97–113.

McMullen, Ernest W. "The Concrete Factory." *Architectural Forum* (July 1919):
  7–12.

Meeks, Carroll L. V. "Some Early Depot Drawings." *Journal of the Society of Architectural Historians* 8 (January–June 1949): 33–42.

Melcher, Charles W. "The Plant and Product of the Ingersoll-Sergeant Drill Co."
  Western Society of Engineers Journal 2 (1897): 571–583.

Mellor, A. D. "The Use of Concrete for the Bush Terminal Development." *Cement
  Age* 11 (December 1910): 336–342.

"Mercantile and Industrial Buildings of Concrete." *Architect and Engineer* 62
  (July 1920): 81–89.

"Mill of Reinforced Concrete Construction." *Building Age* 33 (April 1911): 237.

"The Mill Type of Construction." *Machinery* 10 (August 1904): 654.

"A Model Establishment." *Age of Steel* (July 20, 1889): 18.

"A Model Fireproof Factory." *Insurance Engineering* 11 (May 1906): 427.

"A Model Pacific Coast Manufacturing Plant." *Iron Trade Review* 48 (February 9,
  1911): 313–317.

"Model Plant of the New Britain Machine Co." *Machinery* 10 (August 1904):
  639–645.

"Model Works for the Manufacture of Machinists' and Boiler-Makers' Tools for
  Railway Repair Shops." *Manufacturer and Builder* 6 (September 1874):
  198–200.

"A Modern Factory Building." *Engineering News* 35 (May 14, 1896): 315.

"A Modern Jobbing Foundry." *Foundry* 23 (February 1904): 247–253.

"A Modern Steam Specialty Manufacturing Plant." *Iron Trade Review* 48 (February 16, 1911): 369–372.

"The Modern Steel Structural Co.'s Plant, Waukesa, Wis." *Engineering News* 43
  (January 5, 1901): 7.

Moore, Francis C. "How to Build Fireproof." *Western Society of Engineer's Journal*
  4 (1899): 967–972.

Moore, James Robert. "Electricity in Modern Industrial Establishments." *American Architect* 99 (June 14, 1911): 225.

Neher, C. R. "Concrete Construction." *Architects' and Builders' Magazine* 2
  (August 1901): 377–381.

"The New Detroit Car-Works." *National Car Builder* 3 (September 1872): 10.

"New Foundry for the Semi-Steel Co." *Engineering News* 39 (June 23, 1898): 405.

"New Gisholt Foundry." *Machinery* 11 (October 1905): 68.

"New Home of Spearmint." *Isolated Plant* 6 (February 1914): 11–13.

"New Industrial Building Boasts 'Controlled Conditions.'" *Architectural Record*
  88 (November 1940): 105–107.

"The New Lehigh Valley Shops." *Iron Age* 75 (January 26, 1905): 302–305.

"New Power Plant of the Warrenton Woolen Co." *Isolated Plant* 2 (October
  1910): 24–27.

"The New Shop Ball Engine Co. Erie, Pa." *Machinery* 12 (March 1906): 351–353.

"New Shop of the Heoffer Manufacturing Co." *Machinery* 11 (December 1905):
  171–175.

"New Shops of the Chicago, Milwaukee and St. Paul Railroad, Milwaukee."
  National Car Builder 12 (October 1881): 116–117.

"New Shops of the Grant Tool Co." *Machinery* 8 (March 1902): 197–201.

"New Shops of the Holyoke Machine Co. at Worcester, Mass." *American Machinist* 6 (March 10, 1883): 1–3.

"New Shops of Western Electric Co." *Machinery* 12 (July 1906): 560–562.

"A New Steel Sash." *Concrete Engineering* 3 (April 1910): 104–105.

"New Thinking on Industrial Buildings." *Architectural Forum* 99 (August 1953):
  91–109.

"The New Works of the Edward P. Allis Co., at Milwaukee, Wis." *Engineering News* 45 (May 23, 1907): 382–384.

"New Works of the Ingersoll-Sergeant Drill Co." *Machinery* 11 (May 1905): 461–467.

"The New Works of the Wason Car Manufacturing Company." *National Car Builder* 4 (September 1873): 215–216.

"The New Worthington Hydraulic Works at Harrison, N.J." *Engineering News* 50 (December 31, 1903): 584–587.

"New York Dock Trade Facilities Building." *American Architect* 135 (March 5, 1919): 329–332.

Nichols, John R. "Choice of Type of Construction." *Architectural Forum* 39 (September 1923): 99–104.

Nimmons, George. "Modern Industrial Plants, Part I." *Architectural Record* 44 (November 1918): 414–421; "Modern Industrial Plants, Part II." (December 1918): 533–549; "Modern Industrial Plants, Part III—Plans and Designs." 45 (January 1919): 27–43; "Modern Industrial Plants, Part IV—Discussion of the Various Types of Windows for Industrial Buildings." (February 1919): 148–168.

———. "Some Industrial Buildings." *Architectural Record* 38 (August 1915): 228–245.

Nisbet, D. F. "Machine Shop Roofs." *Cassier's Magazine* 29 (December 1905): 152–154.

"Notes and Clippings, New England Cotton Mills." *American Architect and Building News* 5 (June 28, 1879): 208.

"Notes of Travel: Chicago to New Orleans via St. Louis." *Engineering News* 34 (November 14, 1895): 331–332.

"Novel Design of Roof for a One-Story Factory." *Engineering News* 35 (April 2, 1896): 231–232.

"No Windows." *American Machinist* 73 (December 4, 1930): 887.

Noyes, Henry T. "Planning for a New Manufacturing Plant." *Modern Manufacturing, The Annals* 85 (September 1919): 66–89.

"The Ohio Falls Car-Works." *National Car Builder* 2 (February 1872): 5.

Onderdonk, Francis S., Jr. "Is a Specific Ferro-Concrete Style Evolving?" *American Concrete Institute Proceedings* 25 (1929): 192–207.

"A One-Story Workshop." *Carpentry and Building* 5 (May 1883): 92–93.

Outerbridge, A. E., Jr. "Foundry Cranes." *Cassier's Magazine* 10 (July 1896): 211–223.

"An Overhead Tramrail System." *American Machinist* 7 (May 10, 1884): 1.

Papadaki, Stamo. "The Design of Industrial Buildings." *Architectural Record* 81 (February 1937): 3–14, 40.

Partridge, W. E. "Fire-Proof Construction." *National Car Builder* 11 (June 1880): 94.

Peck, Staunton B. "Rope Transmission." *Western Society of Engineers Journal* 2 (1897): 301–338.

"The Pennsylvania Steel Company's Model Bridge Plant." *Engineering Record* 48 (September 26, 1903): 360–363; (October 10, 1903): 423–426; (October 17, 1903): 455–458.

Perrigo, Oscar E. "Efficient Departmental Arrangement." *Iron Trade Review* 47 (December 29, 1910): 1207–1211.

———. "Shop Construction—1." *Machinery* 8 (October 1902): 41–43.

Perry, J. P. H. "Exteriors of Industrial Buildings." *Architectural Forum* 51 (September 1929): 313, 323–327.

———. "The Kenyon Factory." *Concrete Engineering* 2 (February 1909): 47–49.

Peters, Tom F. "Architectural and Engineering Design: Two Forms of Technological Thought on the Borderline between Empiricism and Science." In *Bridging the Gap: Rethinking the Relationship of Architect and Engineer*. New York: Reinhold Van Nostrand, 1991.

' "Phoenix' Wall Construction." *Insurance Engineering* 6 (October 1903): 315–320.

Pierson, William Harvey, Jr. "Notes on Early Industrial Architecture in England." *Journal of the Society of Architectural Historians* 9 (January–June 1949): 1–32.

———. "Richard Upjohn and the American Rundbogenstil." *Winterthur Portfolio* 21 (1986): 223–242.

"The Plant of the Berlin Iron Bridge Co." *Engineering News* 26 (October 3, 1891): 316–318.

"Portable Metallic Sheds." *Manufacturer and Builder* 8 (February 1876): 31–32.

"The Port Authority Commerce Building—New York." *Architectural Record* 73 (April 1933): 274–280.

"Power and Transmission Plant of the Cleveland Twist Drill Co." *Machinery* 8 (June 1902): 310–311.

Price, C. Matlack. "Architecture." In the *New International Yearbook for Year 1916*, ed. Frank Moore Colby, 49. New York: Dodd, Mead & Co., 1917.

———. "Architecture." In the *New International Yearbook for Year 1917*, ed. Frank Moore Colby, 42–43. New York: Dodd, Mead & Co., 1918.

———. "Ideals in Every-day Architecture and a Passing Tribute to Mr. Willis Polk." *Architect and Engineer* 51 (October 1917): 53–55.

"Progress in Structural Welding (VI)." *American Contractor* 51 (April 26, 1930): 16–18.

"Progress in Structural Welding (VII)." *American Contractor* 51 (May 3, 1930): 17–19.

"Progress of Ship-Building—Roof over Building-Slips at St. Peter's Dockyard, Newcastle." *Practical Mechanic's Journal* 4 (1851–1852): 130.

Pursell, Carroll W., Jr. "Testing a Carriage." *Technology and Culture* 17 (January 1976): 82–92.

Putnam, Edward H. "The Modern Industrial Building." *American Architect* 109 (March 22, 1916): 177–182.

Rabinowitz, Aaron. "Needs in Lower Broadway Loft Section." *Real Estate Record and Guide* (May 16, 1914): 881.

Ranney, William D., and Robert N. Hemming. "An Up-to-Date Foundry and Electrical Plant." *Engineering/Steam Engineering* 4 (November 1, 1904): 735–736.

"Rayon Factory for the Industrial Rayon Corporation." *Architectural Forum* 70 (January 1939): 28–32.

"Recent Fires." *Scientific American* 3 (April 8, 1848): 226.

"Reinforced Concrete Building Containing One Hundred Thousand Square Feet, Completed in Three Months." *Concrete Engineering* 3 (July 1910): 174.

"Reinforced Concrete Construction in a Factory Extension at Bayonne, N.J." *Engineering Record* 50 (July 2, 1904): 16–19.

"The Reinforced Concrete Factories for the Bush Terminal." *Engineering Record* 53 (January 13, 1906): 36.

"Reinforced Concrete for Factory Construction." *Building Age* 32 (March 1910): 119–121.

"Rendle's Systems of Glass Roofing." *Manufacturer and Builder* 13 (May 1881): 101.

"Repair and Construction Shops of the New-York Central and Hudson River Railroad, at West-Albany." *National Car Builder* 3 (August 1872): 7–8.

Richardson, J. N. "Architectural Engineering." *Association of Engineering Societies Journal* 6 (May 1887): 173–179.

Richmond, Knight C. "Saw-Tooth Roofs for Factories." *American Society of Mechanical Engineers Proceedings* 28 (November 1906): 287–300.

Rohrer, Albert L. "A Modern Foundry." *Cassier's Magazine* 21 (February 1902): 292–305.

Rosenberg, Theodore. "Fire-Proof Buildings." *Association of Engineering Societies Journal* 5 (February 1886): 121–126.

"The Russel Wheel & Foundry Co., Detroit." *Iron Trade Review* 40 (June 29, 1907): 991–993.

"Samuel T. Tatum Company's New Plant." *Cincinnati Industrial Magazine* 1 (July 1901): 17.

Sanborn, Edward H. "A Decade of Machine Shop Progress from 1890 to 1900." *Cassier's Magazine* 23 (March 1903): 667–669.

Sande, Theodore A. "American Industrial Architecture from the Late Eighteenth to the Mid-Twentieth Century." *Journal of the Society of Architectural Historians* 35 (1976): 265–271.

———. "The Textile Factory in Pre–Civil War Rhode Island." *Old Time New England* 66 (1975): 13–31.

Sargent, William P. "Design and Construction of Metal-Working Shops—1." *Machinery* 15 (September 1908): 1–3; "Design and Construction of Metal-Working Shops—2." (October 1908): 85–90; "Design and Construction of Metal-Working Shops—3." (November 1908): 169–173.

"Sawtooth Skylight in Factory Roof Construction [discussion]." *American Society of Mechanical Engineers Proceedings* 28 (November 1906): 465.

Sawyer, Edward. "Mills and Mill Engineering." *Journal of the Association of Engineering Societies* 8 (November 1889): 513–552.

Schipper, J. Edward. "Terminal City—A Triangle of Efficiency." *The Automobile* 30 (August 5, 1914): 249–255.

Schoen, Eugene. "Factory of Simms Magneto Co., Watsessing, N.J." *American Architect* 99 (June 14, 1911): 232–233.

Seaver, John W. "Iron Mill Buildings." *Proceedings of the Engineering Society of Western Pennsylvania* 8 (1892): 129–155.

"Shop and Mill Construction." *Engineering News* 31 (January 25, 1894): 65–66.

"Shop No. 3 of the Bullock Electric Mfg. Company." *Machinery* 9 (February 1904): 283–284.

"The Shops of the Westinghouse Electric and Manufacturing Company." *Engineering Record* 32 (June 1, 1895): 6–9.

"Slow-Burning Construction [letter]." *American Architect and Building News* 5 (June 21, 1879): 199.

"Slow-Burning Construction [letter]." *American Architect and Building News* 5 (August 23, 1879): 54–56.

"Slow Combustion Construction of Buildings." *Carpentry and Building* 13 (September 1891): 223–226.

Snell, Henry I. "Heating Machine and Other Large Workshops." *Cassier's Magazine* 23 (November 1902): 269–272.

"Some Considerations Affecting the Location and Design of Machine Shops." *American Machinist* 22 (September 28, 1899): 17–18.

"South Philadelphia Works of the Westinghouse Company." *Industrial Management* 65 (June 1918): 494–497.

"The South's Development—50 Years of Southern Progress." *Manufacturer's Record* 8 (December 11, 1924): part II.

"Special-Purpose Plant." *Architectural Forum* 99 (August 1953): 98–99.

"Spring Grove Paper Mills." *American Architect and Building News* 9 (1881): 296, plate.

Squires, Frederick. "The Hollow-Tile Fireproof House." *Architecture and Building* 44 (May 1912): 189–194.

"Standard Underground Cage Co.'s Works." *American Architect and Building News* 31 (January 9, 1891): plate.

Starrett, Theodore. "Building the Remington Arms Plant." *Architecture and Building* 48 (March 1916): 37–48.

"Starrett-Lehigh Building." *Architectural Record* 71 (January 1932): 30–35.

"Steam Engineering Department Shops, N.Y. Navy Yard." *Machinery* 8 (July 1902): 337–343.

"Steam Plant Plans." *Engineers' Review* 16 (May 1905): 8–16.

Stewart, Perez M., and Rudolph P. Miller. "Reduction of Fire Hazards in Building Construction." *Insurance Engineering* 4 (1902): 545–569.

Stilgoe, John R. "Molding the Industrial Zone Aesthetic: 1880–1929." *Journal of American Studies* 16 (1982): 5–24.

Stimpson, Herbert F. "The Design and Construction of Industrial Buildings—I." *Engineering Record* 59 (May 29, 1909): 693–695; "The Design and Construction of Industrial Buildings—II." (June 5, 1909): 716–743.

Sturgis, Russell. "Factories and Warehouses." *Architectural Record* 19 (May 1906): 368–375.

———. "The Fischer Marble Works." *Architectural Record* 17 (March 1905): 246–248.

———. "Some Recent Warehouses." *Architectural Record* 23 (May 1908): 373–386.

———. "The Warehouse and the Factory in Architecture—I." *Architectural Record* 15 (January 1904): 1–17; "The Warehouse and the Factory In Architecture—II." (February 1904): 122–133.

"Subject for Discussion: The Electrical Distribution of Power in Workshops, Nov. 15, 1900." *Journal of the Franklin Institute* 151 (January 1901): 1–28.

Sundeleaf, Richard. "Industrial Design for Portland." *Architectural Concrete* 6 (1940): 26–27.

Sweet, John E. "Machine Shop Construction." *Cassier's Magazine* 3 (January 1893): 223–228.

———. "Machine Shop Roofs." *Cassier's Magazine* 28 (August 1905): 299–301.

Taber, Dann O. "Tool Plant Reflects New Ideas." *Iron Trade Review* 68 (February 3, 1921): 344–349.

"Thompson Malted Food Co. Plant." *Western Architect* 21 (March 1915): plates.

Thorpe, W. H. "Welded Structural Steelwork." *Engineering* 124 (August 12, 1927): 210–211.

"Timber Framing Multi-Story Industrial Buildings." *Engineering News-Record* 99 (July 7, 1927): 20–22.

Titley, Arthur. "Works Engine Houses." *Cassier's Magazine* 34 (July 1908): 195–201.

"To Build Windowless Plant." *Iron Age* 126 (October 16, 1930): 1114.

Tolles, Bryant F. "Textile Mill Architecture in East Central New England: An Analysis of Pre–Civil War Design." *Essex Institute Historical Collections* 107 (July 1971): 223–253.

"To Produce Standardized Galvanized Steel Industrial Buildings." *Iron Age* 118 (August 12, 1926): 462.

Totten, A. I. "The Evolution of the Railroad Shop." *Railway Review* 55 (October 3, 1914): 408–411.

"The Transmission of Power by Means of Wire Rope." *Manufacturer and Builder* 1 (August 1869): 225.

"A Trio of Modern Plants." *Architectural Forum* 75 (November 1941): 331–334.

"The Triumph Company's New Plant." *Cincinnati Industrial Magazine* 1 (June 1909): 15.

Turner, C. P. "The Senior Mechanics' Trip to New England." *Journal of the Engineering Society of Lehigh University* 4 (June 1889): 112–116.

Tweedy, R. L. "The Aesthetic Consideration of the Modern Manufacturing Plant." *American Architect* 99 (June 14, 1911): 216–218.

"The Union Special Machine Company's Plant, Chicago, Illinois." *Architectural Record* 44 (August 1918): 159–163.

"Universal Space Plant." *Architectural Forum* 99 (August 1953): 100–101.

"An Unusual Design for a Factory." *Building Age* 44 (February 1922): 37.

"Unusual Factory Layout Designed to Simplify Operation." *Engineering News-Record* 79 (November 29, 1917): 1016–1017.

"Utilitarian Structures and Their Architectural Treatment." *American Architect* 96 (November 19, 1909): 183–185.

Van Rensselaer, Maria G. "Recent Architecture in America, III—Commercial Buildings." *Century Magazine* 28 (n.s. 6) (August 1884): 511–523.

Vogel, Andrew. "Welding Trusses for Industrial Buildings." *Journal of the American Welding Society* 7 (January 1928): 11–19.

Walker, Alden D. "Should Factories Have Windows?" *Michigan Society of Architects Weekly Bulletin* 16 (March 31, 1942): 41, 45.

Wallis, Frank E. "Is American Architecture a Live Art? Does It Stand the Factory Test?" *Architectural Review*, n.s. 3 (October 1915): 81–88.

"Walls, Roofs, and Floors." *Engineering News-Record* 116 (March 12, 1936): 384–390.

Wason, Leonard C. "Reinforced-Concrete Structures for Manufacturing Purposes." *Engineering Magazine* 33 (June 1907): 395–407.

"Water-Supply Fixtures and Machinery." *Manufacturer and Builder* 13 (July 1881): 148.

Watson, C. G. "Arc Welded Structural Steel Buildings." *Iron and Steel Engineer* 4 (March 1927): 151–155.

Weitenkamf, F. "The Esthetics of Engineering." *Architectural Record* 45 (April 1919): 366–369.

"Welding Builds a Factory." *Engineering News-Record* 117 (July 16, 1936): 90–93.

"West Albany Locomotive Works." *Scientific American* 15 (October 20, 1866): 264–265.

Wharton, Hugh M. "Planning the Industrial Plant—1." *Industrial Management* 57 (June 1919): 433–437; "Planning the Industrial Plant—2." 58 (July 1919): 47–50.

White, John H., Jr. "Cincinnati Locomotive Builders, 1845–1868." *Smithsonian Institute United States National Museum Bulletin* 245 (1965).

———. "Richmond Locomotive Builders." *Railroad History* 130 (Spring 1974): 68–88.

Wicks, Hamilton S. "The Manufacture of Pleasure Carriages." *Scientific American* 40 (February 8, 1879): 79–80.

Wight, Peter B. "A Fireproof Addition to the Works of the Northwestern Terra Cotta Company, Chicago." *Building Progress* 1 (November 1911): 325–330.

———. "Utilitarian Architecture at Chicago I." *Architectural Record* 27 (February 1910): 189–198; "Utilitarian Architecture at Chicago II." (March 1910): 249–257.

Wilcox, Charles G. "Iron Works—Their Location, Arrangement and Construction." *Scientific American* 3 (September 15, 1860): 180–181.

"Wilcox, Treadway & Co. Cleveland Hardware Manufactory." *Trade Review* 13 (January 31, 1880): 6.

Willey, Day Allen. "Engineering Works in Concrete." *Cassier's Magazine* 38 (June 1910): 149–150.

Wilmoth, W. F. "The Buildings of the National Biscuit Company." *American Architect* 101 (June 19, 1912): 270–272.

"Windowed vs. Windowless Buildings." *Architectural Forum* 74 (May 1914): 333–337.

"A Windowless Factory." *Architecture* 63 (May 1931): 303–304.

Woltersdorf, Arthur. "An Expression on the Design of Factory and Warehouse Buildings." *American Architect* 99 (June 14, 1911): 237–238.

Woodbury, C. J. H. "The Evolution of the Modern Mill." *Scientific American Supplement* (May 26, 1888): 10329–10331; (June 2, 1888): 10346–10347.

———. "Standard Storehouse Construction." *Engineering Record* 24 (September 19, 1891): 246–248.

Woodworth, Joseph V. "The Manufacture of Agricultural Machinery." *Machinery* 8 (August 1902): 369–375.

"Worcester." *Manufacturer and Builder* 3 (February 1871): 47.

"Worcester Pressed Steel Co." *Architectural Record* 69 (April 1931): 320.

"The Works of the Walworth Manufacturing Company." *The Technologist* 1 (April 1870): 92.

"The Worthington Hydraulic Works." *Engineering News* 29 (March 23, 1893): supplement 290–292.

Wright, Frank Lloyd. "Unmodern Building." *New York Times*, October 4, 1931, sec. 9, p. 2.

Wright, Helena. "Insurance Mapping and Industrial Archeology." *Journal of the Society for Industrial Archaeology* 9 (1983): 1–18.

CREDITS

Figure 1.1 O. Meeker & Co., *Newark Foundry*. Courtesy of Hagley Museum and Library.

Figure 1.2 Lossing, *The American Centenary*. Courtesy of Hagley Museum and Library.

Figure 1.3 *Mechanic's Advocate* 1 (February 25, 1847): 1. Courtesy of the General Research Division, New York Public Library, Astor, Lenox and Tilden Foundations.

Figure 1.4 *Manufacturer and Builder* 6 (September 1874): 198. Courtesy of Hagley Museum and Library.

Figure 1.5 *Industrial Review* 2 (1883): 286. Courtesy of Hagley Museum and Library.

Figure 1.6 From the collections of the Virginia Historical Society.

Figure 1.7 Peck and Earl, *Fall River and Its Industries*, 129. Courtesy of Hagley Museum and Library.

Figure 1.8 Courtesy of Lockwood, Greene.

Figure 1.9 Turner Construction Co., *A Record of War Time*. Courtesy of the Cleveland Public Library.

Figure 1.10 Stone & Webster, *Industrial Buildings*. Courtesy of Hagley Museum and Library.

Figure 2.1 *Scientific American* 40 (February 22, 1879): 110. Courtesy of Hagley Museum and Library.

Figure 2.2 Wolf, *Industrial Wilmington*. Courtesy of Hagley Museum and Library.

Figure 2.3 Orear, *Commercial and Architectural St. Louis*. Courtesy of Hagley Museum and Library.

Figure 2.4 Hagley Museum and Library, Pictorial Collections, 72.244.100.

Figure 2.5 *Manufacturer and Builder* 7 (1875): 150. Courtesy of Hagley Museum and Library.

Figure 2.6 Hagley Museum and Library, Pictorial Collections, 75.425.1.

Figure 2.7 *American Machinist* 5 (October 7, 1882): 5. Courtesy of Hagley Museum and Library.

Figure 2.8 Lossing, *The American Centenary*. Courtesy of Hagley Museum and Library.

Figure 2.9 Kenny, *Illustrated Cincinnati*, 291. Courtesy of Hagley Museum and Library.

Figure 2.10 Niles Tool Works, *Catalog of the Niles Tool Works*. Courtesy of Hagley Museum and Library.

Figure 2.11 Courtesy of Department of the Army, Rock Island Arsenal Museum, Rock Island, Illinois.

Figure 2.12 Courtesy of Department of the Army, Rock Island Arsenal Museum, Rock Island, Illinois.

Figure 2.13 *Scientific American* 42 (February 29, 1880): 127. Courtesy of Hagley Museum and Library.

Figure 2.14 Hagley Museum and Library, Pictorial Collections, 74.362.73.

Figure 2.15 *Manufacturer and Builder* 20 (February 1888): plate. Courtesy of Hagley Museum and Library.

Figure 2.16 *Manufacturer and Builder* 20 (February 1888): plate. Courtesy of Hagley Museum and Library.

Figure 2.17 Kenny, *Illustrated Cincinnati*. Courtesy of Hagley Museum and Library.

Figure 2.18 Redrawn by Ellyn Goldkind from *Carpentry and Building* 4 (May 1882): 90.

Figure 2.19 Chase, *A Better Way to Build Your New Plant*, 29. Courtesy of the Science, Industry and Business Library, New York Public Library, Astor, Lenox and Tilden Foundations.

Figure 2.20 Hagley Museum and Library, Pictorial Collections, 87.244.21.

Figure 3.1 Wolf, *Industrial Wilmington*. Courtesy of Hagley Museum and Library.

Figure 3.2 *Industrial Monthly* 2 (September 1873): 1. Courtesy of Hagley Museum and Library.

Figure 3.3 *American Machinist* 7 (May 10, 1884): 1. Courtesy of Hagley Museum and Library.

Figure 3.4 *National Car Builder* 7 (January 1872): cover. Courtesy of Hagley Museum and Library.

Figure 3.5 Towne, *A Treatise on Cranes*, fig. 51. Courtesy of Hagley Museum and Library.

Figure 3.6 Van Slycke, *Representatives of New England Manufactures*. Courtesy of Hagley Museum and Library.

Figure 3.7 *Industrial America*. Courtesy of Hagley Museum and Library.

Figure 3.8 *Asher & Adams' New Columbian Railroad Atlas and Pictorial Album of American Industry*, 88. Courtesy of Hagley Museum and Library.

Figure 3.9 Rogers Locomotive Co., *Locomotives and Locomotive Building*, 14. Courtesy of Hagley Museum and Library.

Figure 3.10 Lossing, *The American Centenary*. Courtesy of Hagley Museum and Library.

Figure 3.11 Redrawn by Ellyn Goldkind from *Scientific American* 3 (September 15, 1860): 180.

Figure 3.12 Fryer, *Architectural Iron Works*. Courtesy of Hagley Museum and Library.

Figure 3.13 Bridesburg Manufacturing Co., *Descriptive Catalogue of Machines Built by the Bridesburg Manufacturing Company*. Courtesy of Hagley Museum and Library.

Figure 3.14 Enterprise Manufacturing Co., *Catalogue and Price List of the Enterprise Manufacturing Company of Pennsylvania*. Courtesy of Hagley Museum and Library.

Figure 3.15 J. Estey & Co., *The Estey Organs*. Courtesy of Museum and Library.

Figure 3.16 *Engineering Magazine* 11 (June 1896): 476. Courtesy of Hagley Museum and Library.

Figure 3.17 Bigelow, *History of Prominent Mercantile and Manufacturing Firms in the United States*, 477. Courtesy of Hagley Museum and Library.

Figure 3.18 Allis-Chalmers Co., *Bulletin No. 1519*, 8. Courtesy of Hagley Museum and Library.

Figure 3.19 Trussed Concrete Steel Co., *United Steel Sash*. Courtesy of Hagley Museum and Library.

Figure 4.1 *American Machinist* 6 (March 10, 1883): 1. Courtesy of Hagley Museum and Library.

Figure 4.2 Hall, *Biographical History of the Manufacturers and Business Men of Rhode Island at the Opening of the Twentieth Century*, 129. Courtesy of Hagley Museum and Library.

Figure 4.3 Clark Thread Co., *A Thread Mill Illustrated*, 24. Courtesy of Hagley Museum and Library.

Figure 4.4 Berlin Iron Bridge Co. catalog. Courtesy of the Smithsonian Institution.

Figure 4.5 *Western Society of Engineers Journal* 2 (1897): 314. Courtesy of the Cleveland Public Library.

Figure 4.6 Power Transmission Council. *Principles of Mechanical Power Transmission*. Courtesy of Hagley Museum and Library.

Figure 4.7 Towne, *A Treatise on Cranes*, fig. 60. Courtesy of Hagley Museum and Library.

Figure 4.8 *Engineering Magazine* 11 (May 1896): 282. Courtesy of Hagley Museum and Library.

Figure 4.9 Redrawn by Ellyn Goldkind from *Engineering News-Record* 79 (November 29, 1917): 1016.

Figure 4.10 *Architecture and Building* 52 (November 1920): plate. Courtesy of the Cleveland Public Library.

Figure 5.1 Woodbury, *The Fire Protection of Mills and Construction of Mill Floors*, 41. Courtesy of Hagley Museum and Library.

Figure 5.2 Woodbury, *The Fire Protection of Mills and Construction of Mill Floors*, 59. Courtesy of Hagley Museum and Library.

Figure 5.3 *Architectural Forum* 34 (May 1921): 179. Courtesy of the Cleveland Public Library.

Figure 5.4 Berlin Iron Bridge Co., *Engineers, Architects, and Builders in Iron and Steel*, 269. Hagley Museum and Library.

Figure 5.5 Redrawn by Ellyn Goldkind from a Hexamer General Survey No. 820.

Figure 5.6 Woodbury, *The Fire Protection of Mills and Construction of Mill Floors*, 108. Courtesy of Hagley Museum and Library.

Figure 5.7 *Architectural Record* 27 (March 1910): 221. Courtesy of Hagley Museum and Library.

Figure 5.8 Duplex Hanger Co., *Duplex Malleable Iron, Joist Hangers, Wall Hangers, Concrete Block Hangers*, 10. Courtesy of Hagley Museum and Library.

Figure 6.1 Hagley Museum and Library, Pictorial Collections, 80.300.

Figure 6.2 Hagley Museum and Library, Pictorial Collections, 68.13.1.

Figure 6.3 Lossing, *The American Centenary*. Courtesy of Hagley Museum and Library.

Figure 6.4 Hagley Museum and Library, Pictorial Collections, 69.170.19074.

Figure 6.5 *Association of Engineering Societies Journal* 8 (November 1889): 542. Courtesy of Hagley Museum and Library.

Figure 6.6 [John Scott], *Genius Rewarded, or The Story of the Sewing Machine*, 1880. Courtesy of Hagley Museum and Library.

Figure 6.7 *Illustrated Catalogue of Canton Iron Roofing Co.* Courtesy of Hagley Museum and Library.

Figure 6.8 Berlin Iron Bridge Co., *Engineers, Architects, and Builders in Iron and Steel*, 31. Courtesy of Hagley Museum and Library.

Figure 6.9 Hagley Museum and Library, Pictorial Collections, 69.170.12252.

Figure 6.10 Berlin Iron Bridge Company, *Engineers, Architects, and Builders in Iron and Steel*. Courtesy of Hagley Museum and Library.

Figure 6.11 Berlin Iron Bridge Company. *Engineers, Architects, and Builders in Iron and Steel*. Courtesy of Hagley Museum and Library.

Figure 6.12 Hall, *Biographical History of the Manufacturers and Business Men of Rhode Island at the Opening of the Twentieth Century*, 270. Courtesy of Hagley Museum and Library.

Figure 6.13 *Engineering News* 40 (July 7, 1898): 15. Courtesy of Hagley Museum and Library.

Figure 6.14 Courtesy of the Lincoln Electric Company.

Figure 6.15 George Hayes Co., *Treatise on Metal Lathing as a Most Important Factor in the Construction of Buildings: Embracing a System of Fire-Proof Construction*, 16. Courtesy of Hagley Museum and Library.

Figure 6.16 *Reinforced Concrete in Factory Construction* (1907), 59. Courtesy of Hagley Museum and Library.

Figure 6.17 Stone & Webster, *Industrial Buildings*. Courtesy of Hagley Museum and Library.

Figure 7.1 George Hayes Co., *The "Hayes" Metal Skylights and Other Glazed Structures*, 43. Courtesy of Hagley Museum and Library.

Figure 7.2 Trussed Concrete Steel Co., *United Steel Sash*. Courtesy of Hagley Museum and Library.

Figure 7.3 *Austin Standard Factory-Buildings*, 14. Courtesy of Hagley Museum and Library.

Figure 7.4 *The Manufactories and Manufacturers of Pennsylvania of the Nineteenth Century*, 32. Courtesy of Hagley Museum and Library.

Figure 7.5 *Architectural Record* 17 (March 1905): 247. Courtesy of Hagley Museum and Library.

Figure 7.6 *American Engineer* 2 (October 1881): 194. Courtesy of Hagley Museum and Library.

Figure 7.7 Courtesy of the Buffalo and Erie County Historical Society.

Figure 7.8 Ballinger Co., *Buildings for Commerce and Industry*, 41. Courtesy of the Cleveland Public Library.

Figure 7.9 Simonds Saw & Steel Co., *Saws—Knives—Files*, 5. Courtesy of the Smithsonian Institution.

Figure 7.10 *Architectural Forum* 70 (January 1939): 28. Courtesy of the Cleveland Public Library.

Figure 8.1 *Industrial Review* (December 1882): xvi. Courtesy of Hagley Museum and Library.

Figure 8.2 Redrawn by Ellyn Goldkind after Ketchum, *The Design of Steel Mill Buildings* (1903), fig. 86.

Figure 8.3 *Ice and Refrigeration* 6 (1891): 106. Courtesy of Hagley Museum and Library.

Figure 8.4 Postcard, author's collection.

Figure 8.5 *Building Progress* (1911): 329. Courtesy of Hagley Museum and Library.

Figure 8.6 *G.& D. Cook & Co.'s Illustrated Catalogue of Carriages and Special Business Directory*, 160. Courtesy of Hagley Museum and Library.

Figure 8.7 Hagley Museum and Library, Pictorial Collections, 87.244.40.

Figure 8.8 Passaic County Historical Society Photograph Collection, 0.02078.

Figure 8.9 Redrawn by Ellyn Goldkind from Ballinger Co., *"Super-Span" Saw-tooth Buildings*, 9.

Figure 8.10 Hart, *The Industries of Buffalo*. Courtesy of the Buffalo and Erie County Historical Society.

Figure 8.11 Hagley Museum and Library, Pictorial Collections, 71.MSS. 916.3535.

Figure 8.12 Redrawn by Ellyn Goldkind from David Lupton's Sons Co., *Air, Light and Efficiency.*

Figure 8.13 Courtesy of The Austin Co.

Figure 9.1 *Newark, N.J., Illustrated,* 106. Courtesy of Hagley Museum and Library.

Figure 9.2 Lossing, *The American Centenary.* Courtesy of Hagley Museum and Library.

Figure 9.3 Crowther, *John H. Paterson: Pioneer in Industrial Welfare,* opp. 231. Courtesy of Hagley Museum and Library.

Figure 9.4 Fairbairn, *Treatise on Mills and Millwork. Part II, on Machinery of Transmission and Construction and Arrangement of Mills,* 114. Courtesy of Hagley Museum and Library.

Figure 9.5 Talbott & Bro., *An Illustrated Catalog of Machinery,* 2. Courtesy of the Virginia Historical Society.

Figure 9.6 Courtesy of Department of the Army, Rock Island Arsenal Museum, Rock Island, Illinois.

Figure 9.7 *Worcester: Its Past and Present,* 107. Courtesy of Hagley Museum and Library.

Figure 9.8 *American Architect and Building News* 9 (1881): plate. Courtesy of the Cleveland Public Library.

Figure 9.9 *Architectural Record* 15 (January 1904): fig. 1. Courtesy of Hagley Museum and Library.

Figure 9.10 *Architectural Record* 45 (February 1919): 167. Courtesy of Hagley Museum and Library.

Figure 9.11 Trussed Concrete Steel Co., *United Steel Sash,* 110. Courtesy of Hagley Museum and Library.

Figure 9.12 Trussed Concrete Steel Co., *United Steel Sash,* 85. Courtesy of Hagley Museum and Library.

Figure 10.1 *Austin Standard Factory-Buildings,* 51. Courtesy of Hagley Museum and Library.

Figure 10.2 Crowell-Lundoff-Little Co., *The Blue Book of Industrial Construction.* Courtesy of the Cleveland Public Library.

Figure 10.3 *The Manufactories and Manufacturers of Pennsylvania of the Nineteenth Century.* Courtesy of Hagley Museum and Library.

Figure 10.4 Redrawn by Ellyn Goldkind from Liebold, *Ziegelrohban Taschenbuch für Baukandwerk,* vol. 1.

Figure 10.5 *Industrial America.* Courtesy of Hagley Museum and Library.

Figure 10.6 Wilson, *The Pennsylvania Railroad Shops at West Philadelphia.* Courtesy of Hagley Museum and Library.

Figure 10.7 Jack E. Boucher, Photographer, Historic American Engineering Record, Library of Congress. HAER NY, 1-GreenI 1-3.

Figure 10.8 *American Architect* 109 (March 22, 1916): plate. Courtesy of the Cleveland Public Library.

Figure 10.9 *Architecture* 42 (October 1920): 293. Courtesy of the Cleveland Public Library.

Figure 10.10 *Architectural Forum* 39 (September 1923): 85. Courtesy of the Cleveland Public Library.

Figure 10.11 *Western Architect* 21 (March 1915): plate. Courtesy of the Cleveland Public Library.

Figure 10.12 William Gray Purcell Papers, Northwest Architectural Archives, University of Minnesota Libraries, St. Paul, Minnesota.

Figure 10.13 *Architectural Record* 69 (April 1931): 320. Courtesy of Hagley Museum and Library.

Figure 10.14 *Architectural Concrete* 4 (1938): 8. Courtesy of Avery Architectural and Fine Arts Library, Columbia University.

Figure 10.15 Trussed Concrete Steel Co., *United Steel Sash,* 92. Courtesy of Hagley Museum and Library.

Figure 10.16 *Architectural Record* 45 (February 1919): 156. Courtesy of Hagley Museum and Library.

Figure 10.17 *Architectural Concrete* 6 (1940): 26. Courtesy of Avery Architectural and Fine Arts Library, Columbia University.

Figure 10.18 *American Architect* 107 (February 24, 1915): plate. Courtesy of the Cleveland Public Library.

INDEX

Page numbers in italics indicate illustrations.

Boilers, 49

Boston, Massachusetts, 24, 69. *See also* East Boston and South Boston

Boulton and Watt, 138

Brattleboro, Vermont, 72

Brewster & Co. blacksmith shop, 34

Brewery architecture, 204

Brick construction,
    aesthetic character of, 232–234
    arched openings in, 162, 213, 217, 234
    as brick veneer on concrete, 240–241
    and pilaster wall construction, 110, 122, 136, *137*, 162, 209, 230, 233
    self-supporting type of, 140, 147, 152
    vaulted walls of, 126, 139
    See also American round-arched style; Facades as grids

Bridesburg Manufacturing Co. works, 71, 72

Bridgeport, Connecticut, 21, 73, 146

Bridgeport, New Jersey, 53, *188*

Bridgeport, Pennsylvania, 97, 173, 251

Brill, George M., 76

Brinkerman & Van Der Vlugt, 250

Bristol, Rhode Island, 170

The Bronx, New York, 120, 170, 220

Brooklyn, New York, 22, 79, 100, 101, 103, 111, 135, 153, 164, 166, 168, 181, 188, 190, 235, 237, 241, 243, 244

Brooklyn Army Supply Base, 22, 103, 243, *244*

Brooklyn Clay Retort and Fire Brick Works, 135

Brooklyn Navy Yard:
    blacksmith shop, 181, 190
    pay department building, 235
    shops, 100, 164, 188

Brown, E. D. B., 147

Brown, John Rhodes, 19

Brown, Mark, 27

Brown Hoisting Machinery Co. works, 164

Brown & Sharpe Works, 11, 141, 146, 170–171, *171*

Brush Electric Co. works, 61, *62*

Buchman & Kahn, 24

Buckeye Steel Casting Co. works, 97

Buffalo, New York, 22, 160, 172, 187, 194, 255

Buffalo Foundry Co. works, 172, *172*

Buffalo Steam Engine Works, 11

Building Codes, 134, 180. *See also* New York City Building Codes

Bullock Electric Mfg. Co. works, 97, 160

Bundy Tubing Co. plant, 176

Burden Iron Co. works, 36, 64

Burlington, North Carolina, 17

Busch-Sulzer Bros. Diesel Engine Co. machine shop, *222*, 223

Bush, Irving T., 79

Bush Terminal, 22, 79–80, *80*, 166, 168, 240

Butler, Pennsylvania, 196

Caldwell, Charles H., *169*, 170

California, 24, 241

Cambridge, Massachusetts, 253

Cambridgeport, Massachusetts, *27*, 76

Campana Sales Co. factory, 251–252

Candee, Richard, 9, 186, 203

Canton Iron Roofing Co. works, 143, *143*

Carbondale, Pennsylvania, 194

Carpenter, J. W., 14–15, 18, 232

Carr & Wright, 24

Case, Willard, 60, 203, 221–223

Casting process, 40–42

Cast iron, 122, 138–142
    window sash, 164

Central Manufacturing District (Chicago), 79–80, 103, *120*, 120–121, 232

Charlestown Navy Yard, 186

Chase, Frank D., 21–22, 51, 205, 252–253, *254*

Chester County, Pennsylvania, 34

Chevrolet Motor Division Commercial Body Plant (Indianapolis), 257

Chevrolet plant (Baltimore), 194

Chicago, Illinois, 24, 79–81, 103, 113, 120, 130, 145, 172, 184, 217, 219, 220, 232, 241, 248. *See also* Chicago Heights and Pullman

Chicago Heights, Illinois, 164, 182

Chicago, Milwaukee & St. Paul Railroad shops, 190

Chickering & Sons works, 69, 69

Chicopee, Massachusetts, 146

Chicopee Mfg. Co. weave shed, 146

Childs & Smith, 252

Chimneys, 40, 42, 50, 51, 51–53, 53

Christie, James, 75, 152